A BRIEF HISTORY OF HUMAN BEHAVIOUR

AND HOW TO BECOME AN ENLIGHTENED GLOBAL CITIZEN

*To George
with kindest regards,,
John*

JOHN PREECE

ISBN 978-0-9575908-0-9

Printed by Witley Press Ltd, Hunstanton, Norfolk, PE36 6AD

ACKNOWLEDGEMENTS

All meta analysis involves reference to a wide range of source material, and my debt in this regard is gratefully acknowledged in the form of a comprehensive bibliography. Especial thanks are due to Desmond Morris, author of "The Naked Ape" and many other seminal books, for his expert guidance in the compilation of this text.

For my family

INTRODUCTION

A great many books have been published on the subject of citizenship, but almost all have so far confined themselves to a scrutiny of the rights and responsibilities of living within the enclave of a specified nation state and of conforming with its values and culture. But globalisation has created a new dimension in the way peoples of the world need to relate to each other. Whilst it has been relatively easy to categorise the rights all humans have in common, it has proved more difficult to define the responsibilities of global citizenship, particularly when these conflict with narrower partisan and doctrinal interests. The clash of competing cultures can only be overcome by informed compromise based on historical knowledge. All social progress involves a reappraisal of past failures and a rationalisation of the way in which these can be put right. For this reason, legacy precepts and practises have to be relinquished if their practical utility has expired.

Retrospective studies of the human species show that nearly all personal behavioural dysfunction arises as a direct result of idiosyncratically, and usually unwittingly, flawed parental nurture. By contrast, most communal behavioural dysfunction has proven to be the product of compulsive prejudices engendered by polarised tenets and edicts, and in particular those disseminated through racial discrimination, religious intolerance, pseudo religions such as communism and fascism, or by nationalistic xenophobia.

Whichever way it manifests, remedial measures for all forms of societal malaise depend upon the propagation of a more profound and generally assimilated knowledge of human behavioural mechanisms. An educational initiative which can catalyse this level of communal enlightenment will always require state planning and funding. Nurtural expertise is not instinctive, and parents-to-be have to be primed with the hard evidence upon which it can be optimised. The expunction of chauvinisms, those prejudiced attitudes of mind with which most of us have already been indoctrinated as children, requires a broad mind and the courage to be iconoclastically rational, two attributes for which there is no substitute if we are to attain full maturity as global citizens. During human development, compulsive ideologies were conceived as a way of regulating our various animal appetites, but the conditioned behaviour they induce may be as counter productive as it is unthinking. The ethical dilemma we have thus created for ourselves can only be resolved by the use of pure reason.

Increasing international interdependence has forced us to expand the compass of responsible citizenship worldwide, and to prioritise its application. Our behaviour and that of our children has, in future, to be motivated by the exercise of a visionary logic which combines utility with humanitarianism, and which balances self interests with those of the species as a whole - a dualistic ethos epitomised by the old sailor's aphorism of "one hand for the boat and the other for oneself". But logic cannot exist without knowledge, which in this context necessarily means a basic knowledge of human behaviour derived from its history.

CONTENTS

iii

OVERALL CONCLUSIONS. THE OPTIMISATION OF BEHAVIOUR

TABLES

CHAPTER 1

"KNOW THYSELF....THE PROPER STUDY OF MANKIND IS MAN"
(Alexander Pope 1688-1744 from an Essay on Man)

Some years ago I had the opportunity to be present at a court case and observe the English criminal justice system in action. Sharing the public gallery with me were some twenty young trainee journalists, devotedly preparing for a lifetime spent sifting through the garbage of human misconduct so as to recycle it to their tabloid readership. The man in the dock was one of those unlucky ten per cent of offenders against whom the evidence of crime was so compelling that the police were able to identify and prosecute its perpetrator. But the defending barrister was, as is often the case, so well versed in pleas of mitigation that the soft hearted jury found for acquittal. The ineffectuality of the whole proceedings seemed to be compounded by the consideration that even if the culprit had been convicted, as undoubtedly he should have been, his sentence would subsequently have been halved by the prison governor, and there would have been an eighty per cent chance of him re-offending after release.

Man's behavioural repertoire is rife with imperfections whose stubborn persistence results from his inability to understand his inner self. In the western world reports of substance abuse, crimes against property, sexual and other violent crimes, sexual perversion, juvenile delinquency, corruption, fraud, excessive greed, terrorism and riot confront us daily in the media, whilst prisons overflow and the family unit is in decline. Most of these manifestations of societal pathology are also present in the developing world, often in more florid forms, but here tyranny, turf warfare, torture, mutilatory punishment and slavery are added to the corrosive list of human malfunction. Nor must we overlook the corporate blunders and bunglings such as those which lead to environmental abuse, overpopulation, the inequitable distribution of resources, and dissent over the control of nuclear fission for which the global community as a whole must be held to account.

Why has humanity, alone of all the species, been saddled with this Beelzebub of an evil streak which appears to serve no purpose whatsoever? Not merely futile in its manifestations, it is actively deleterious, and its enigmatic, paradoxical and bizarre nature militates against it being either understood or contained. The zoologist sees humanity's delinquencies and depravities as being anomalous and unique in the animal world, to the evolutionist they represent a contradictory and counterproductive maldevelopment, for the religious adherent they pose an irreconcilable doctrinal dilemma, and for the rationalist they are the final frontier which has to be broached in the quest for universal sociological maturity. Philosophical writings are littered with attempts to come to terms with the deviant conduct of humanity. Plato observed that there are relatively few ways of doing good, but countless ways of doing harm, with the result that the latter have a far greater impact on human life. Likewise, the metaphysisist Bernard Gert was able to demonstrate that a society's morality could be improved more effectively by preventing evil than by doing good. Formal religions employ symbolism to explain the origins of sin and sinning. In the Jewish legend of Adam, a snake is blamed for planting ill advice in humanity's ear, and in the teachings of Islam a mythical "whisperer" is similarly indicted. The Christians conceptualised the antigod Satan as the root cause of all evil, and embellished his anthropomorphised image with horns, tail and a trident. As belief in his potency burgeoned over time, he was not only feared and reviled, but he acquired his own cult following. Some sages have believed evil to be necessary, the political economist T.R.Malthus viewing it as a spur to human creativity and productivity, and the Taoist movement pointing out that compassion can only exist if there is suffering. The ancient Greek philosopher Epicurus confronted us with the paradox that either God wants to abolish evil and cannot, or he can but does not want to, and so must therefore be either impotent or wicked.

The wayward and degenerate trends found in human beings are also paradoxical on several other counts. For instance, primatology shows them to be biologically abnormal in primate terms. Such adverse and antisocial traits are never found in monkeys and prosimians, amongst whom behavioural conformity within the social group is critical to survival in the wild. It is also overtly paradoxical, given the pre-eminent intelligence with which evolution has endowed him, that man has so signally failed to eradicate his underlying deviant tendencies. Modern man can smash the atom, walk on the moon, fly round the earth in a day, and cure most diseases, yet the fundamentally toxic nature and wide diversity of the antisocial acts he commits have changed very little since the stone age. The catalogue of prevailing sins so reviled by biblical pedagogues would serve as well today, notwithstanding several thousand years of intervening admonition.

The most paradoxical aspect of man's perennial misconduct is, of course, the stunting effect it has on human progress and development. Broadly speaking, humanity achieves progress in three cardinal ways: by biological evolution which, arguably, has already reached its end point, by technological progression in which an end point is never likely to be reached, and by sociological progression that has an end point which is attainable, but one which cannot be reached until attitudes change and much more enlightened nurtural and educational policies have been implemented. Man's conduct cannot be shaped any further by human evolution since he has already terminated this process by his own actions - Darwinism operates on the principle that only the fittest survive, but modern medicine enables most of the unfittest also to mature and procreate. The corollary of this must be that in future we shall have to make do with the number and overall arrangement of brain cells we already have as a species, but that we must train ourselves to use them to their maximal advantage. The most important application for the greater cognitive efficiency so achieved will be the elimination of residual dysfunction in human behaviour.

Because the majority of people in a civilised and democratic society find misconduct, and especially habitual misconduct, to be repugnant, they would take concerted action to eliminate it from their midst if they believed that such a proposition was feasible. But the social reforms which would be needed to do so could not be successfully introduced in the absence of a far more profound and generally assimilated understanding of human behavioural mechanisms and how these may be manipulated to achieve social harmony. By default, we have all become inured to societal malaise in all its forms, regarding it as an inevitable concomitant of human existence. Our corporate naiveté is not due either to a lack of interest in human conduct, nor to a dearth of available information - in the space of a few seconds our laptop computers are able to track down around 38 million published articles on the subject, often accompanied by impressive hit rates - but the fundamental underlying conclusions of behavioural science never feed through into the overall public consciousness in a readily comprehensible, succinctly defined or balanced manner. There are a number of contributory causes for this impasse. Ever since its early years, behavioural science has been hampered by the extensive use of theories and counter theories, a strategy which inevitably leads to an element of uncertainty. The extrapolation of postulates from observations of day-to-day conduct can no longer be regarded as adequate for our requirements. The precedent for such methodology was set by Sigmund Freud whose seminal deductions laid the foundations of psychoanalysis, but any research procedure which relies upon an element of intuition has its generally acknowledged limitations. Few would now dispute that the basic tenets so strongly held by Benjamin Spock and J.B.Watson in the field of child

4

development proved grossly misleading, and it seems highly unlikely that such an implausible concept as Freud's "castration complex" would ever have seen the light of day if that pioneer had had access to the findings of modern primatology. Equally distractive has been the subdivision and fragmentation of the study of human behaviour, principally between the academic faculties of psychology, sociology and anthropology, which came about following the massive increase in the size of its remit during the twentieth century, and which caused loss of balance, breadth of vision and focus. Moreover, the field of enquiry from which behavioural data are garnered needs to expand beyont the bounds of these three primary subsets, and span at least a dozen more tangential disciplines. A multidimentional approach not only increases a target subject's knowledge base, but deepens the way it can be understood, allows correlative problem solving, and stimulates ideation. All these shortcomings continue to be reflected in faculty textbooks and in books written for the mass market. To overcome them our analytical methodology must undergo a profound change, and innovate the use of history, prehistory and human behavioural inadequacy as its bedrock sources of evidence. Just as those who set out to study health begin with research into diseases, so students of human behaviour must first investigate human misconduct. But it is only by retracing our simian, ape and human roots that we can view ourselves in true perspective, and, when we do so, our adverse functionality at last becomes intelligible.

Why is knowledge of our retrospect of such fundamental importance to our understanding of our inner selves? Our motivation, which is the engine of our behaviour, is at the very centre of human nature and development, and we must dig deep into our prehistory if we are to understand its mechanisms and distortions. Although these basic mechanisms were laid down at the earliest stages of our evolution as animals, their distortions only appeared during the stages of our final ape-like and primitive human development. Evidence for both these factors has to be obtained from archaeology and a study of our primate cousins in whom our developmental pathways are accurately reflected. On the other hand, the pre-eminent evidence for linking nurtural or genetic causes with their effects on human conduct is derived from human behavioural history, and knowledge of the rudiments of this subject is therefore not only critical to an understanding of the way we behave, but it enables us to avoid replicating the mistakes of our predecessors. There can never be a substitute for real life, real time, retrospective evidence. Unsubstantiated opinionation, speculative theories and numerically inadequate surveys all look shallow by comparison.

What overall conclusions can be drawn from the deeper understanding of human behavioural patterns which retrospective developmental analysis provides? In the first place, it can be seen that, with the exception of disease and natural disaster, all man's unresolved problems are the product of his own misconduct, which, in turn, results either from faulty immature nurture, genetic errors, or overt ineptitude, acting separately or in conjunction. Faulty nurture occurring during early and mid childhood deforms any of the seven fundamental traits ingrained in us as primates. Faulty nurture during adolescence distorts our interpretation of our surround and engenders compulsive prejudice. Sporadic genetic errors cause mental illnesses, including a personality derangement known as chronic malice, but an invidious genetic defect, endemic for the species, makes some of us prone to display risk taking and unprovoked aggression, a propensity which can only be counteracted by a policy of aversion conditioning during childhood. Irrationality causes us to act against our better judgement, and its prevention is a seminal responsibility of impartial education.

Our analysis can now be seen to have furnished us with a potent catalyst for societal maturation, but what practical measures can we adopt and depend upon to convert vision into tangible reality? For many centuries philosophy and organised religion, and more recently academic departments of psychology and sociology, have formulated behavioural models which aspire to pre-empt such obviously adverse functionality and its consequences, but their efforts have not so far led us to utopia, nor do they seem ever likely to do so. Since the ways we have monitored our behaviour in the past have failed us, we must be prepared to change them. Humanity hungers for a new approach to the sociological management of its affairs, based on rock hard evidence, rationality, humanitarianism, and a global concordat, As we have seen, the incontrovertible evidence we need must come from our own history and prehistory, and our own behavioural defects as a species, but rationality and global concordat depend upon the provision of uprated and strictly impartial global educational policies, and humanitarianism basically derives from enlightened and affectionate nurture during childhood.

A more profound and generally assimilated knowledge of human behaviour requires the construction and dissemination of a customised educational module, underwritten, as with other human rights and educational initiatives, by the nation state. Appropriate venues for its tutelage are secondary schools, universities, antenatal clinics, adult evening classes and the internet. It is arguably as important to prepare young people for parenthood and global citizenship as it is to prepare them for their vocation. But the tools of the behavioural scientist's trade now have to be brought into line with the stringent requirements of the scientific method.

For some, behavioural analysis is an irrelevance, unable or unwilling as they are to see themselves objectively. For others, a deeper understanding of human behaviour and misbehaviour comes too late - by the time it has been acquired over a lifetime of experience the opportunity to apply it to the upbringing of children has long since passed. But a grounding in the science of human behaviour, delivered at an appropriate stage of intellectual development, should be regarded as a mandatory birthright and a human right in keeping with its potential. By showing us how our minds work, this scintillating nub of worldly wisdom is the key to the solution of the majority of outstanding human problems, to the banishment of racial, national, religious and other compulsive prejudices which obstruct our sociological maturation, to the deeper understanding of what brings fulfilment and happiness in life, and to the optimisation of the nurtural process which will improve our children's prospects. Its study leads us to set new standards of co-operative integrity and rationality in interpersonal and international relationships. It is, moreover, a subject which has an enduring fascination for us, not only because it teaches us salutary home truths about ourselves, but for the light it helps to shed on the phenomenon of life itself.

CHAPTER 2

OUR QUINTESSENTIAL ASSET

THE HUMAN BRAIN

The bedrock upon which accurate knowledge of human behaviour is founded is an amalgam of human history and of human prehistory as mirrored in the lives of our primate cousins. By taking stock of our past we are able to see how our behavioural traits were derived, and whether they have proved beneficial or detrimental. There has never been a more appropriate or necessary time for humanity to reassess itself in the light of its own behavioural development. An increasing awareness that a wide variety of personal delinquencies remain stubbornly resistant to change, and that narrow partisan interests and globally divisive ideologies are no longer fit for purpose, challenges us to look for new and better ways of ordering our personal lives and of integrating societies world wide. A sociological reorientation of this magnitude can only be realised by those who are prepared to acquire a more profound understanding of how they are motivated. A thirst for enlightened practicality is born of such knowledge.

Audit of human behavioural development must necessarily begin with a brief review of the basic equipment with which evolution has provided us. Whilst the present chapter investigates the function of the human brain, the one which follows examines the seven fundamental traits common to all primates. The book's remaining chapters explore the ways in which man's behaviour has been either refined or degraded since his chimpanzee like ancestor first colonised the African savannah.

All behaviour is an outward expression of brain function. Those who have survived catastrophic brain damage are inert and vegetative. Most of us would agree that such victims have suffered a fate worse than death. The brain is the be all and end all of our existence.

With an appearance and texture reminiscent of blancmange, the brain's functionality, and even its overall purpose, remained a mystery until relatively late in human history. Ancient Egypt, which went to extraordinary lengths to preserve a cadaver's other anatomical assets for use in the next life, discarded the brain as being of no importance after extracting it piecemeal through the back of the nose, the better to pickle the face and head. In mediaeval times the seat of the emotions was variously ascribed to the heart, the solar plexus or the genitalia, and theories as to where the soul was situated were equally extravagant. With the development of the microscope in the 16th century, the extreme complexity of the brain's cellular structure began to be recognised, but it was not until the 20th century that anatomical, surgical and electro-encephalographic studies, animal experimentation, and a variety of scanning techniques using radioactive isotopes began to give more precise details of the way the brain really works.

Brain activity always involves a variable combination of its many anatomical modules. From the behavioural standpoint it is therefore important to categorise the brain's activity according to its functionality and not, as so many books do, in terms of topography. Six major functions have evolved over the aeons in a fixed succession which is replicated during embryonic development as a cadence, beginning with the most basic and ending with the most sophisticated. Anaesthesia suppresses them in the reverse order, as ageing often does.

The Housekeeping Brain controls pulse, blood pressure, respiration, temperature, swallowing, vomiting, sneezing, involuntary coughing, salivation, the sleep and sexual cycles, and the responses of thirst, hunger and fatigue.

The Sensory Brain processes incoming signals dealing with sight, hearing, taste, smell, touch, pain, heat, cold and posture.

The Motor Brain activates all muscles of the body which are under voluntary control. The left and right sides of the brain connect with nerve tracts which cross over to motivate the right and left side of the body respectively and a "stroke" usually paralyses either one side or the other.

The Emotional Brain initiates feelings of anger, fear, sadness, joy or disgust in response to incoming sensory signals.

The Conditionable Brain records long term memory, bonding and fixed behavioural response patterns conditioned by training.

The Unconditionable Brain houses consciousness, cognition, short term memory, rationality, introspection, and the ability to organise and innovate.

The brain's evolutionary pathway, which is mimicked in each human individual during early embryonic development, passed through preliminary worm, fish, reptile, early mammalian and ape-like stages. The first primitive worms were built from a chain of segments which were co-ordinated by a longitudinal nerve. When the need to prospect for food called for forward movement, investigatory organs of smell, sight and hearing were developed at what now became the head end, together with localised neural specialisation to handle incoming sensation. Hardwired housekeeping functionality was steadily increased during the fish, reptile and early mammalian stages, and emotional and conditionable brain development burgeoned during the early mammalian and ape-like stages. Unconditioned brain functionality, which distinguished us from our robot-like predecessors, has been developed progressively since the early mammals evolved.

Despite some writers' assertions to the contrary, the human brain's analogy with computers is too compelling to be dismissed. There are, however, important differences between the two. The brain is a thousand times more powerful in terms of processing than most computers and, because it is capable of using signals of variable strength, it bears more resemblance to an analogue than to a digital machine. Consciousness may be compared with boot-up, the unconditionable brain with computer processing memory, the hardwired housekeeping brain with computer read-only memory, the conditionable brain with the computer's hard disk, and human behaviour and speech with computer output. The computer even has eyes (scanner), and ears (voice recognition) to provide input, The methodology of computing has helped us to understand brain function.

The human brain is by far the most complex known object in the universe. It is three times bigger than that of our nearest developmental rival, the chimpanzee, a difference mostly accounted for by expansion in the area of the unconditionable brain. The new larger brain developed in response to proto-man's descent from tree life to a harsher, bipedal, savannah existence where he had to compete for prey with other, more agile predators. He now needed to hunt, fashion tools, and co-operate, co-ordinate and communicate within a tribal community. The size of an animal's unconditionable brain correlates with the size of its social group, the length of time it spends in play as a juvenile, the range of use of its hands, and its cognitive capacity.

The disproportionately large head required to house a brain of this size posed problems for our ancestral mother during delivery, since the maximally attainable diameter of her pelvic birth canal was limited by the mechanical requirements of her upright bipedal posture. Even today, small mothers may need Caesarean section because of this disproportion, but evolution solved the problem for most women by providing that most of the increase in infantile head size occurs after birth. The brain of a new born human infant is 23% of its adult size, whereas that of the typical new born monkey has already attained 70% of its ultimate growth.

The more primitive a module of brain is in terms of evolution, the more genetically determined, hardwired and immutable its function will be. The more phylogenetically recent a brain module is, the more it can be, and will depend upon being, moulded by environmental experience. The housekeeping brain has to be hardwired, because it maintains the integrity of physiological processes upon which our very existence depends - regulation of the cardiovascular, respiratory, alimentary, thermal, biochemical and biorhythmic mechanisms. These regulatory mechanisms are necessarily automatic and independent of consciousness. The sensory and motor brain modules which respectively receive incoming signals and co-ordinate outgoing skeletal movements are also predominantly hardwired, though capable of limited degrees of modification following prolonged use, injury or illness. The earlier in life that the sensory or motor brains are damaged, the greater the possibility of regeneration or adaptation.

The Emotional Brain and Encounter Signs

When we meet another person our reaction is registered by a series of five encounter signs. These are usually reciprocated and commonly occur in the following order :- facial recognition, facial expression, body language, vocalisation and tactility. If the encounter is with a new situation which does not involve other people, reactivity is limited to facial expression, body language and vocalisation. The basis for these encounter signs is genetic and hardwired, and though many are shared with other primates, and indeed sometimes by other animal species, a few, such as the human smile, are species specific. The ability to memorise faces is present from birth, and the human infant quickly learns to take its emotional cue from its mother's expressions. Discriminatory recognition is much more acute for faces than it is for other objects, since survival has depended upon it, and it is more accurate between members of the same race. Many brain areas are involved in the process, which compares and matches the patterns for three dimensional shape, size, relative position, colour and texture of all features. Age, gender and attractiveness are also taken into account.

There are five basic emotions - anger, fear, joy, sorrow and disgust, and the function of the emotional brain is to brand each new encounter or experience with the sentiment most likely to promote the survival of the individual or "herd". (the term "herd" is used throughout this book to describe a societal group of any species). Emotional branding is rapid and automatic because it is hardwired, and it initiates the appropriate encounter signs, together with involuntary responses and voluntary actions relevant to whichever emotion is called into play (see table 2.1). The whole episode is then stored in long term memory as a learnt experience to guide behaviour in future comparable situations. The emotional brain helps to supply adjectives to the written or spoken noun, the spin in tabloid newsprint, and dichotomy in parliament.

Anger bares the teeth, makes the face redden and glower, makes the body tense and erect, the hair bristle, the fists clench, the pulse race, the blood pressure rise, the pupils dilate, the body sweat and the mouth dry up. Blood flow is increased to the brain and muscles, and diminished to the gut. Growling, roaring or verbal aggression may be followed by physical combat.

Faced with imminent danger, an animal makes a split second reflexive choice between standing its ground and fighting, or turning tail and fleeing. If fear is more likely to favour survival, this emotion blanches the face and produces a terrorised expression, but cardio-vascular, pupillary and sweat responses are similar to those for anger, being triggered through the same autonomic and hormonal pathways (the "fight or flight" reflex). Fear vocalisation is the scream. When the confrontation is a dominance challenge responses may be attenuated, and, if it does not panic, the fearful animal may cower to signify submission.

Joy leads to smiling, laughing, relaxation, hand shaking and hugging. Sorrow manifests as a frown and a dejected facial expression, a bowed head, sagging shoulders, moaning and crying. Disgust leads to pouting, nose wrinkling, an involuntary shiver, aversion of the face, vocalisations of revulsion, a measured retreat, and, occasionally, vomiting.

As well as initiating appropriate physiological and physical reactions, the emotional brain determines mood, and if there is a persistent overplay of one particular emotion, bias is created which distorts judgement. All told, the emotional brain is an important determinant of personality and behaviour. A person who registers too much joy is overoptimistic (or, in extreme cases, manic); one who registers too much sadness is depressive; one who registers too much disgust is phobic and obsessive ; one who registers too much anger is antisocial, and one who registers too much fear suffers from an anxiety state. Taken together, these five over-reactions account for most mental illness, and as most mental illnesses are hereditary, many of the genetic defects involved must clearly be those which determine the integrity of the emotional brain.

The Conditionable Brain and the Reward Centre
The conditionable brain is the archival area where data are stored for prolonged periods of time. These data may be sensory (long term memory), motor (conditioned behaviour), or emotional (bonding and addiction). The more often a sensory impression is received, the behavioural pattern is exercised, or a bond emotion is experienced, the more deeply ingrained and permanent the conditionable brain's retention of it will be. Similarly, if the conditioning process is incentivised, it will prove more compelling. One gets a "tune on the brain" if one hears it too often, children fix their tables in memory by rote and learn better when their efforts are rewarded, army drills and musicians' rehearsals perfect performance (the French for rehearsal is

"repetition"), and the baby quickly bonds with the mother who suckles it.

Eating, slaking one's thirst, and sexual intercourse all induce a feeling of well being and satiety by stimulating a brain area known as the reward centre which is intimately connected with both the emotional and conditionable brain modules. A record of the stimulation of the reward centre by these and other pleasurable sensory, motor or emotional activities is lodged in the conditionable brain and prompts a desire to recreate the pleasurable experience once the feeling of satiety has worn off. The reward centre can be stimulated artificially by chemicals such as nicotine, ritalin, marijuana, narcotics and amphetamines, or by activities such as gambling, all of which may thereby become cyclically addictive. The genetic defect present in 20-30% of Americans predisposes towards dysfunction of the reward centre with resulting recourse to addictive substances and alcohol. This predisposition also occurs in Attention Deficit Hyperactivity Disorder (ADHD) families. An indolent lifestyle, involving overeating and too little exercise, depresses the reward centre, creating a desire for compensatory overindulgence, whereas physical activity increases the blood flow to the brain and reduces stress and depression. Children who take regular exercise do better academically.

The Unconditionable Brain
There has been a threefold increase in human brain size since Homo Sapiens Sapiens evolved from his simple ape-like progenitor. This increase is almost entirely attributable to enhanced development of the brain's unconditionable module, a feature which provides us with intellectual powers of which only rudiments are found in the chimpanzee, and which has enabled us to dominate the planet. 80% of human brain mass is given over to data processing, and 25% of the heart's total output of blood is used to feed the brain with glucose and oxygen, essential nutrients upon whose constant supply nervous tissue

critically depends. Humans have the largest brain in relation to body weight of any animal.

The unconditionable brain module is the seat of consciousness, subjectivity and objectivity, and it continuously monitors the surround, providing awareness, with a faculty for introspection and self critical adjustments to behaviour. It houses short term memory, and dovetails with the conditionable brain in storing and retrieving long term memorisable data upon which it will base future decisions. It provides rationality and a thirst for rational enlightenment, it provides an organisational faculty, and it provides a faculty for innovation, tool use and language. Overly aggressive, chronically malicious and antisocially disordered individuals have dysfunctional frontal lobes - a component of the unconditionable brain. Those whose frontal lobes have been seriously injured display uncontrollable emotional and aggressive outbursts.

Because the electrical impulses used by the unconditionable brain are transient, they have to be constantly refreshed with sensory, motor, or emotional impulses, and when data processing reaches an end point, conclusions have to be transferred to long term memory for retention in the conditionable brain. A person who is distracted from a particular line of thought often finds it difficult to pick up the thread again until reminded. Transfer of sequential memorable experiences to long term memory also takes place during the 15-20 minute long episodes of brain refreshment which occur every 90 minutes during normal sleep, and which are characterised by general muscular relaxation and rapid eye movement (REM). Those deprived of REM sleep fail to memorize.

What do we mean by intelligence and how do we measure it? Suffice it to say that clarity is best served by sticking to dictionary definitions for a term in such common use. Individuals are deemed to be intelligent if they accept, understand, memorize and rationalize the use of data. The terms cognitive, perceptive and sagacious have a somewhat similar meaning (COD64). The closer a blood relationship between two people, the more they share levels of intelligence - a finding born out in studies of adoptees, and identical twins raised apart. Intelligence is also elastic in as much as it is significantly influenced by culture, and can vary in the same individual with time and circumstance. Interestingly, the gap which formerly differentiated the intelligence quotients (IQ) of white and black Americans has now shrunk so significantly that we can discount race as a determinant. Socio-economic class and occupation play a part only in so far as they mould a person's immediate environment. Professionals have higher IQ's than artisans, whilst dysfunctional families score worst.

People differ so markedly in the type and degree of their talents that tests which focus on only one parameter are misleading, because they may not be comparing like with like. Moreover, it has proved possible to identify eight discrete subsets of human intellectual activity by studying victims of trauma in order to locate the particular area of brain with which each of these subsets is associated. That these subsets act independently has also been confirmed by the finding in large scale population surveys that there is no correlation between their distribution. The subsets respectively support skills in linguistics, logic and mathematics, spatial awareness, music, interpersonal relationships, introspection, musculo-skeletal use, and environmental pattern matching (GH83). In genius, prodigy and virtuosity an additional discrete subset is particularly well developed. IQ tests, originally developed for use in French schools, were intended to assess potential, but can only ever measure performance in which cultural influences, and skills already assimilated, necessarily play a part. The difficulty of measuring some subsets has meant that only three of them are regularly tested (linguistic, abstract-visual, and quantitative) together with short term memory. Different grades of test are used for different age groups, With all their shortcomings, an IQ test remains the single most effective predictor of scholastic and occupational attainment, matrimonial stability and parental integrity (GR05).

Life only has value to us if we are able to perceive it, understand it, partake of it, and preferably also to enjoy it. We refer to the mental state which enables us to do these things as consciousness, a state which we readily recognise subjectively in ourselves, but whose existence may be difficult to prove in others suffering from disease, trauma, toxins or other forms of physical insult. What assessable physical differences exist between the conscious and unconscious patient?

Radio signals piggy-back as modulations on a carrier wave, and electrical activity in the brain behaves similarly. An electrical carrier wave oscillating at 40 Hz is present in all areas of the unconditionable brain when in its waking state, and also during REM sleep, but is absent during non-REM sleep, or in coma. Wakeful mental activity and REM sleep both cause the superimposition of heightened bursts of electrical discharge on the carrier wave. Because it also occurs in REM sleep, the carrier wave does not equate with consciousness, but it must be an essential requisite for it.

Consciousness has been defined as a state in which the subject is aware of, and reacts to, a stimulus, but as it stands this definition is unsatisfactory. Reactions to deep stimuli can occur in anaesthetised persons whose state of unconsciousness is not deep, but who are nevertheless unaware of them. Moribund patients may be unable to signal that they are aware, and in the artificial environment of the operating theatre muscle relaxants can deprive the aware patient of the ability to react to pain. Although awareness is the most important criterion of consciousness, inference that it is present may call for the combined objective evidence of both physical reactivity and electrical monitoring. A sophisticated test which can identify the so called "locked in" syndrome uses sensory stimuli to activate brain areas which are still responsive, and which can then be identified from their uptake of radioactive isotopes.

(Sources Reviewed:BDM04, COD64, CR98, DCR72, EHM89, GH93 GR05, GSA00, MD94(a), NGMZ:03:05, RJJ01, SJSI67, SMZ06, WR02).

CHAPTER 3

THE SEVEN PRIME MOTIVATORS

THE BASIS OF ALL PRIMATE BEHAVIOUR

Women have a special rapport with animals, a bond fostered by female maternalism which other creatures instinctively recognise. The science of modern primatology as it now stands would not have been assembled without the dedicated and inspired field work of Jane Goodall on chimpanzees, Diane Fossey on gorillas, Birute Galdikai on orangutans and Thelma Rowell on baboons. Through their eyes, and those of others who have made germane contributions, we are able to build a virtual image of our own prehistoric ancestors, whilst palaeontologists, such as the Leakey family who were closely associated with the first three of these exceptional women, sift through the dust of Africa for skeletal evidence. This corpus of knowledge has not been obtained without risk or sacrifice. Apart from the many hardships which must necessarily be endured throughout such lengthy and arduous investigations, Diane paid with her life at the hands of poachers.

The biological order of primates comprises humans, apes, monkeys and prosimians, and all share seven fundamental behaviour patterns which have been inherited, either hardwired, or in the form of predispositions, from a common evolutionary ancestor. Stripped of human elaboration and sophistication, these common fundamental traits are particularly accurately identifiable in the chimpanzee (with whom we share nearly 99% of our genetic material - GJ90p173), and to a lesser extent in the other great apes - the gorilla, the orang-utan and the gibbon. Human nature cannot be fully understood without a working knowledge of these traits, since they constitute its bedrock. This chapter looks at them briefly in the context of primates in general, (see also Table 3.1), and later text examines their application and misapplication to humanity. .

Reaction to Danger

Common to all animals, and phylogenetically the oldest of the seven fundamental behavioural traits, is the reaction to danger, with its critical importance to survival. Alerted by the senses to imminent peril, the emotional brain makes a split second decision between ferocity and timidity, and initiates the appropriate encounter signs, physiological changes, behavioural actions and mood which have been described in chapter 2. Alertness, preparedness and reactivity are all increased.

If the emotion felt during this state of automatic physiological arousal is one of fear, the animal takes immediate flight. If, on the other hand, the situation engenders anger, then the aggressive response will either be one of self defensive martial combat or, if the attacker is a member of the animal's own "herd", a sparring contest for social or sexual dominance. In the latter case both the threat of danger and reaction to it are attenuated by the fact that familiarisation and herd bonding already exist between the combatants and, as a result, the confrontation employs less lethal weaponry, with tactics which were learned during juvenile play. A bite from an ape or male baboon can easily kill, but within membership of the "herd" serious injury during dominance sparring is rare.

Two other forms of aggression exist in primates - the offensive assault of the hunting carnivore and the chronic malice occasionally exhibited by a genetically dysfunctional animal. These are not reactions to danger and will be discussed in later sections.

Bonding

Bonding is the force of attraction between "herd" members which binds the social unit together. The death and regeneration cycle is fundamental to all but the most primitive life forms and involves genes which are reshuffled between generations to produce variants, some of which will prove more adaptive. This process evolved as a species survival mechanism which was vastly superior to the random spontaneous genetic mutations upon which bacteria relied. Genetic reshuffling requires the initial disassembly of paired chromosomes, so that alternative pairings can be formulated by sexual congress. The corollary of all this is that vulnerable immature organisms are constantly produced, with either a high mortality rate which has to be compensated for by prolific fecundity, or else with an onus on parents to nurture their young if their chances of survival are to be optimised.

Bonding originally evolved as a way of giving the immature organism parental protection. This is, of course, absent in plants and most fish, but present in birds, and is most highly developed in mammals. The earliest and most important bond an animal forms is the two way emotional linkage forged at birth with its mother (Maternal-Infant Bondage). Even when paternity can be established, the fathers of many species take no interest in their genetic offspring, though most will defend the young of the "herd" against attack.

The propensity for bonding is genetically hardwired in the conditionable brain but its focus is defined, conditioned and reinforced by environmental contact. A greylag gosling will, for the rest of its life, follow the first moving object it sees following hatching, whether this be its mother or the drover. (LK66). A human infant is able to recognise its mother's face at the age of two days and its bond is reinforced by the tactile stimuli of her handling and suckling. A non-human primate infant automatically runs to its mother and clutches her fur when danger threatens, and she responds to its cry by gathering it up. A strong infant to mother bond is crucial for the normal development of a primate infant. Isolated infant monkeys raised exclusively with dummy mothers subsequently fail to interact with peers, cannot bond with other "herd" members, the males cannot copulate, and if the females become mothers themselves they fail to bond with their own infants. (HHF69). Orphaned chimpanzees are often adopted by other mothers, failing which they pine and die. (GJ90p14). The mother's attraction towards the infant is equally strong, and her maternal instinct may extend to the infants of other mothers. In the rhesus or baboon this may even prompt "cradle snatching", a phenomenon occasionally seen amongst humans. The maternal bond is felt more strongly towards a daughter than a son, and daughters of more dominant mothers are themselves more dominant.

Whilst she is nurturing it, a breach of acceptable conduct leads a primate mother to rebuff her infant and, because its complete dependence upon her is recognised by both parties, the rebuff strengthens the maternal-infant bond and conditions further behaviour. Once a female non-human primate becomes sexually mature, she is continuously either pregnant or suckling, but rarely conceives more than one foetus at a time, and cannot provide either milk or adequate protection for more than one infant at a time, so that when a successive delivery takes place the older sibling is rejected. (DP72p152). Maternal rejection is emotionally traumatic to the infant and makes it temporarily depressed, jealous, and prone to tantrums, whilst at the same time forcing it to become an independent agent in the wider world. Thereafter, a secondary phase of nurture begins in which sibling and peer bonds will be its emotional lifeline and will condition new patterns of conduct. Humans are the only primates in whom this rejection does not occur, a vital distinction in view of the prolonged state of immature dependence required for the maturation of the human brain. Juvenile dependence is twice as long in humans as in apes, and twice as long in apes as it is in monkeys.

Sibling and Peer Group Bondings strengthen progressively after maternal detachment in non-human primates. Bonding between a new infant and its maternal siblings is particularly strong in baboons, vervets, macaques and chimpanzees. Older sisters bond more noticeably with female infants and older brothers with male infants. As the sexes diverge and link with their equivalent age groups in other maternocentric clusters, peer groups are formed, within which affectionate interactive relationships and the principle of reciprocation foster the development of play, grooming, communication, co-operation and group feeding. Monkeys raised with a mother but no peer group cannot socialise and are aggressive, but have no taste for either play or sex.

Play is a trait limited to young birds and mammals. (DP72p313). Non-human primates derive obvious pleasure from play and young monkeys will indulge in it at every opportunity, whether or not they have adult approval. Occurring most frequently at the "herd" resting times of early morning, midday and evening, it occupies several hours, but ceases at once if an alarm call sounds, or if rumbustuousness spills over into aggression. Invitation to play is by challenge, and is accompanied by a facial expression of pleasurable expectancy which is still sometimes displayed by human children and comedians. This is followed by chuckling, laughing, a jauntiness of gait, tickling, squeezing of toes and fingers, teasing, chasing, and wrestling.

So much time is given over to play that it must clearly have a selective advantage for the species. It is a determinant phase for the development of knowledge, social and technical skills, independence, responsibility, co-operation, dominance ranking, self preservation, hunting skills and later adult bonding. In the experimental rearing of isolated monkeys with a dummy mother, normal development of later sexual behaviour could only be achieved by placing the animal very early in life within a playgroup. Human play additionally incorporates language, fantasy, symbolism and structure, and often invokes simulation as a rehearsal for adult behavioural patterns, as in the use of dolls, toy guns and fancy dress. The human child expends 15% of its energy on play. (BLGGW64p47).

Because the Herd Bond endorses allegiances between "herd" members it has a clear survival value. Non-human primates almost invariably spend their lives in the "herd" into which they were born. The affinity for attachment, at first built up with mother, then with siblings and peers, becomes modified and refocused as the adolescent animal now enters the third phase of its nurture by taking its place as a novice within a dominance ranked hierarchy, where affiliation is tempered by deference towards superiors and vantage is exercised over inferiors.

Socialisation with other herd members is not the only reason for bond formation with them. The feeling of antagonism, which an animal experiences towards members of other "herds" during border disputes, reinforces the need to be accepted as a confederate rather than as an alien, and to profit from the collective security which the closed community offers. Even sick and injured animals make strenuous efforts to keep up with the "herd" on its daily foraging trek. The herd bond is further cultivated by kissing, embracing, grooming, and co-operative behaviour such as food sharing, group nest formation, and corporate defensive deployment on trek, where nursing mothers and juveniles occupy a central position, guarded by male outriders.

Humans intuitively accept that breeding between disparate human races is as feasible as it is between members of their own race, and also that altruism will be more readily displayed towards a conspecific than to a member of another species. This empathic relationship, which is referred to as a species bond, is much weaker than the herd bond, and is thereby always at risk of being obscured by the latter.

Sexual Pair Bonding, other than that engendered by a transitory, albeit impelling, sexual appetite, is conspicuously absent in most primate species. Only 3% of all mammals are monogamous, and the chimpanzee, the most phylogenetically advanced animal other than the human, is flagrantly promiscuous. Whist humans aspire to the ideal of the nuclear family and do possess a pair bonding mechanism, this is frequently overridden. In 2004, for the first time ever, Welsh registrations of births outside wedlock exceeded those within it, a departure which reflects the decreasing emphasis placed upon marriage within the developed world.

Possessiveness

Possessiveness, like reaction to danger and bonding, has a clear survival value. When applied to territory it equates with available food and water supply, and choice of nesting site, all of which relate to the inner rewards of eating, drinking or sleeping. Possessiveness also applies to mate selection, which relates to the inner reward of coitus. Possessiveness is therefore appetite driven and in non-human primates is satiable - when there is a plentiful food supply they live in peace. In humans, possessiveness is often insatiable and compulsive, and hence it is that the miser, hoarder, kleptomaniac, billionaire, harem owner, potentate and imperialist all accumulate with an avidity which knows no bounds and exceeds all reasonable needs.

Many birds and some fish have well defined territories which they demarcate and defend, but foragers such as the non-human primates, have to keep moving forwards in their search for fresh vegetation, and spread themselves out to make the best use of what is available. Each animal therefore defends the ground to the front and on each side of it which offers what it can immediately consume, and repels those who intrude. Other than this, the position within the trek, and the right to commandeer a particular bivouac or sexual partner, is decided preferentially by an animal's position in the dominance hierarchy.

Because the chimpanzee "herd" moves en masse, its forage trek will often impinge on that of other "herds". If food is plentiful, the males search out the territory ahead, and if no other "herds" are present communal feeding ensues. If other "herds" are present, threats and skirmishes follow with adrenergic arousal, after which each "herd" retires to a safe distance. The most aggressive "herd" retains most territory. (DP72p253). Within its defended territory an animal is confident and aggressive, but beyond its borders it is timid and defensive towards strangers. At water holes where supply is unrestricted, rival "herds" usually meet peacefully. (RT72p166).

In non-human primates other than the chimpanzee outright warfare is exceptional, and only occurs in situations which put the food supply of the whole "herd" at risk, such as when snows force high mountain living monkeys to descend to foothills occupied by another conspecific "herd". Human "herd" territorialism is clearly seen in tribalism, nationalism, imperialism and, in its proselytising form, in cult religions.

Vervets and gibbons occupy exclusive "herd" territory which they mark with scent glands. Several other primate species mark territorial claims with scent, urine and faeces, particularly if food is in short supply. Lemurs have scent glands situated on the wrist and beside the anus, and are very territorial, the female of the species being the main protagonist.

Human deaf-blind children identify other individuals by their smell, and some human races find the bodily odour of other races objectionable. The Icelandic aphorism that a man enjoys the smell of his own flatus, and is repelled by that of others, identifies vestigial anal scenting in humans.

Dominance Ranking

Top down command and control within the non-human primate communal unit is maintained by dominance rank interrelationships. In order to counteract the anarchy which would result from unbridled possessiveness for food, water, females and the pick of other desirables, primate societies have evolved a rigid societal mechanism for allocating resources and privileges. All members of the "herd" occupy a fixed position within a hierarchy. This position is determined by aggressive challenges between paired contestants throughout the pecking order from which either dominance or submission ensue. The result determines in which order of preference each animal has access to the choicest leaf, fruit or nut bearing plants, cosy nesting trees or available females.

The dominance mechanism confers two other benefits - it furthers evolutionary principles by enhancing the survival of the fittest and ensuring that the genes of the strongest are most likely to fertilise. It also produces "herd" cohesion and co-operation by top-down behavioural discipline through which each individual knows his place and keeps it on pain of a drubbing.

Adult primate males are more dominant than adult females, and adult females are more dominant than juveniles, but other than this, each animal has to prove itself by confronting the next highest individual in the hierarchy - an analogy with human squash or tennis "ladders". The challenge is aggressive with threats and bombastic displays, which may in themselves suffice to secure submission. Otherwise, a trial of strength follows in which a form of sparring deliberately avoids serious injury.

Both the tactics and the deployment of weaponry of dominance sparring animals differ markedly from those brought to bear in unattenuated aggression. A cat attacking a mouse employs methods which contrast altogether with the way it fights other cats, and the differing reaction patterns correspond with electrical stimulation of different parts of the brain (EEI96p63). The stag uses antlers to spar with conspecifics, but kicks out with its forefeet to ward off predators. Black mamba snakes each carry enough poison to kill eight men, but males of the species contesting breeding dominance never kill each other, merely wrestling to the point of submission. Most primates have large, potentially deadly canine teeth, but fatalities from dominance scuffles seldom occur. Just as play in primate juveniles ceases when it becomes too aggressive, so the herd bond between "herd" members ameliorates aggression during dominance contests. Were it not so, all young males would perish, and the "herd" would wipe itself out. If an animal is wounded, it ceases further challenge for dominance. As "herd" elders start to lose strength and their teeth wear or fall out, challenges from younger males dislodge them from their supremacy.

The threat which presages a primate dominance contest entails the physiological changes which have already been described for anger. Arousal, with facial expressions, body language and vocalisations all imparting ferocity, and hair erection to increase apparent body bulk, may be accompanied by the thrashing of foliage, stamping, charging, and the employment of generally over-exuberant behaviour intended to intimidate. Just as the threatening animal tries to enlarge its appearance, the submitting animal tries to diminish itself by crouching low on the ground, and accompanies this with an appeasing facial expression. During a dog or wolf fight the submissive crouch often causes the dominant animal's aggression to abate. The low submissive crouch is, of course, still seen in human societies as the kow-tow or the Islamic prayer position and, in a less extreme form, as the deep bow of western ritualism or the headbow in Japan.

Supremacy carries responsibilities which the most dominant animals automatically assume. Having emerged as leaders by virtue of their strength, ability and experience, they are respected and obeyed by their inferiors. The "herd" derives overall benefit from the fact that the strongest and most experienced animals rise to positions of authority, and preferentially pass on their genes to the next generation.

Ranking is a feature of all human societies, and the more structured the society, the more rank matters. As with dominion amongst other primates, the antique world required its tribal leaders to be decision makers, protectors, policemen and sages, a combination of responsibilities later segregated by differentiation of labour. During history, human leadership succession has been determined either by inheritance, revolution, the deliberation of a consortium of elders, or by the plebiscite. In adopting the latter, we are reverting to the general primate principle of displacing a leader when he is no longer fit for high office, rather than killing him or waiting for his death.

Socialisation

So far, we have discussed bonding and dominance ranking which are, respectively, the forces of attraction and repulsion between "herd" individuals that form the framework upon which social intercourse takes place. Although all members of a species are by definition capable of interbreeding, the species is always composed of societal subunits (which we may for convenience refer to as "herds"), which originally derived from extended families but whose subsequent size was determined by its ability to co-ordinate and defend itself. Such subunits proved to have better chances of survival than scattered individuals. Predators need to focus on single individuals when they prey, and are distracted by multiplicity. Non-human primate individuals under attack join forces and mob their predators if they cannot escape them. On the trek, non-human primates move forwards in protective formation with mothers and infants in the centre, and male outriders acting as sentinels at the periphery, able to emit the critical alarm signal to which the whole "herd" responds by taking to the trees (LK66p123).

The societal unit of non-human primates is not an amorphous mass like a fish shoal, but a structured unit with leadership, co-operation, co-ordination and mutuality embedded within it. Senior dominant males are the most redoubtable supervisors, defenders and policemen. They take all the important decisions, they control the "herd's" movements on trek, they act as protectors to the vulnerable, the pregnant and suckling mothers, the infants and the juveniles, and they round up stragglers and break up fights between "herd" members. Their greater experience commands respect, their authority imposes discipline, they set examples which others emulate, and if their dealings with the rank and file are seen to be evenhanded, they attract greater support.

Within the "herd" each member is instantly able to recognise all other members, their vocalisations, dominance ranking and behaviour patterns. Non-human primates are diurnal, waking and sleeping with dawn and dusk, active in the morning and late afternoon but, like human Africans and Mediterraneans, resting at midday when the sun is hottest. They live their lives within or in the vicinity of trees, and sleep in clusters - usually in nests fashioned from foliage - which are placed in the forks of tree branches.

Non-human primates cannot speak, but communicate by facial expression, gesture and body language, vocalisation, tactile and olfactory signals. Communication may be one to one, one to all, intraherd or interherd. It is both subjective, expressing the five basic emotions of anger, fear, joy, sorrow and repugnance, plus frustration, and also is objective, signifying the intentions of dominance challenge, predation, friendship, play, sex, begging, appeasement or reassurance. Signals can only refer to the present and evident - future, past and symbolic concepts cannot be exchanged by animals in the wild.

The non-erotic face to face hug with which socialising humans of either sex greet each other has its equivalent in most non-human primates as a non-erotic ventro-dorsal embrace in which one animal mounts another. After a dominance confrontation both animals revert to socialisation patterns of behaviour and the crouch of the submissive animal will sometimes provoke non-erotic mounting in the dominant as an expression of solace. Although the physical positions adopted in both the human and non-primate socialisation embraces are similar to those which preface coitus, the impetus initiating them does not lead to sexual arousal. It is interesting that goal scoring footballers are now subjected to non-erotic mounting by their colleagues.

Actively enjoying each others' company, some non-human primates, especially the chimpanzees, greet, as humans do, by kissing, embracing, patting, handholding and bowing. They have fur which has to be kept free from burrs, ticks and leeches - a necessarily mutual activity called "grooming" which takes up a considerable amount of time and attention, reinforces the herd bond, and is used to promote friendly relations. Chimpanzees have concern for each others' needs and feelings, begging for and sharing food, seeking and giving reassurance and consolation, or pleading for and exhibiting affection.

31

They care for the sick and wounded, and are ready to help companions in distress, even at their own peril. They squeeze pus from each others' wounds, remove splinters, and remove grit from eyes. They use leaves to wipe faeces from each others' fur or to clean runny noses (GJ90p77).

The non-human primate societal unit is a corporate reservoir for the accumulation of survival, social, technical, dominance, sexual and hunting skills. Transmission of these skills is by example. The normal development of infants and juveniles depends heavily upon the social intercourse which occurs within the family, playgroup and "herd".

Whereas tool use by gorillas and orang-utans is rudimentary, chimpanzees use a blade of grass to fish for termites through holes in their tumuli, and teach themselves to stack boxes or join two sections of a pole in order to reach fruit (GJ90p46). Reared in a human household, they can be taught up to 58 American Sign Language signals (EHM89), conjugating some of them (e.g. green-banana for cucumber, rock-berry for brazil nut - GJ90p17) - and give their own name sign when looking in a mirror. Chimpanzees are assessed as having the grammatical skills of a human child of two and a half years of age (NGMZ92:03). They can learn to go to the refrigerator to pour a gin and tonic, turn on the television, or look at a magazine and identify objects within it.

Sexuality
Man's destruction of their forest habitats threatens all four species of great ape - chimpanzee, gorilla, orang-utan and gibbon - with extinction. The demise of these enigmatic creatures, who are our nearest evolutionary relations, would not only deprive us of further knowledge of their own behaviour patterns, but of a deeper understanding of our own. Sexuality is a case in point. Sociosexuality in non-human primates takes the form of four differing and quite distinct mating patterns, all of which are species specific.

- Nuclear family of father, mother and offspring (gibbon, callicebus monkey)
- Harem, with single dominant male, two or more females, and their young. Dominant male aggressivity marginalises non-dominant males. Some harems associate with each other to form larger subgroups (gorilla, most baboons, and macaques)
- Free-for-all promiscuity within the "herd" (chimpanzee, langur, bonnet macaque)
- Sporadic opportunism : Isolationist males fertilise receptive females when they encounter them, but take no interest in offspring who remain the mothers' sole responsibility (orang-utan).

(The fact that man has inherited all four of these behavioural proclivities together as a job lot brands him as a sociosexual mongrel).

Childbirth is seasonal for rhesus monkeys and many baboons, timed to coincide with optimal food supply, but in chimpanzees and gorillas it may occur at any time. With variation between species, pregnancy lasts from five to nine and a half months, and single births are the rule. During childbirth the non-human primate mother segregates herself and labour is rapid. Infant and juvenile mortality exceeds 50% for which only the never ending cycle of pregnancy and lactation in adult females can compensate.

Either sex of non-human primate may solicit coitus, which occurs at the time of maximum female receptivity, as indicated by colour changes in the area around the vaginal entrance and by changes in vaginal odour. Female foreplay in chimpanzees and baboons may begin with her adoption of a crouching position ("presenting"), or with provocation (the female chimpanzee may tug the male's hair or tweak his penis, and is as promiscuous as her partner). New-world female monkeys mark with urine to attract males. The male chacma and alpha hamadryas seduces the female with gentle neck bites (as with the human love bite). Elaborate male courtship displays include swaggering, leaping, thrashing branches, beckoning and producing erections. Grooming by both parties usually preceeds coitus.

There is considerable variation in the frequency and duration of coitus between species. It takes place up to 5 times a day in the male chimpanzee, and as many as 50 times a day in the female chimpanzee during her receptivity, but is much less frequent in the gorilla and orang-utan. Copulation involves repeated pelvic thrusts, and lasts from 10 seconds to 15 minutes depending on the species. Coitus is face to face in the gorilla and bonobo, but face to back in other non-human primates. Most humans adopt face to face copulation, although the quest for novelty prompts experimentation with many other postures. Menstruation is a general characteristic of primates (RT72p112).

Partner bonding only occurs with nuclear family species and, to a much less extent, with harem structured "herds". All primates are hardwired to resist incest, and the chimpanzee mother repels the occasional advance of her son. There is no convincing evidence of coital substitution of the rectum for the vagina in non-human primates and, as has already been described, when mounting occurs between two males or between two females, it is a token of socialisation and is non-orgasmic. Masturbation has been observed in some monkeys, gibbons, and both male and female gorillas.

Predation and Carnivorousness
Animal protein has always been a constituent of primate diet, although in many species the source of this has been restricted to insects and invertebrates. The most primitive primates were insectivores. Prosimians, most monkeys and most apes are predominantly herbivo-insectivorous. Even the awesome looking gorilla is an almost exclusively vegetarian and peaceful creature in its natural habitat. On the other hand, baboons and chimpanzees are herbivo-carnivorous, and hunt for prey - baboons as individual predators, and chimpanzees surrounding their quarry in packs of up to four or more. Although there

is some cross predation between these latter two species, chimpanzees enjoy greater dominance. Baboons eat vervet monkeys and small mammals. Chimpanzees eat monkeys and small mammals, and have been known to steal and consume human infants. The chimpanzee is also cannibalistic, both males and females lynching stragglers from other "herds", and even, occasionally, infants from within their own "herd". Preparing to hunt, chimpanzees become excited and embrace each other to demonstrate alliance. The kill is attended with considerable savagery, during which dismemberment, flaying and blood drinking occur, whilst the flesh is shared out - all parallels of the tribal warfare practised by primitive man. Larger forays also occur in which premeditated belligerence of hunter carnivore brutality, precipitated by a zest for adrenalised risk taking, is vested wholesale upon a rival group.

Man's carnivorousness is of great antiquity. It not only provides him with an energy rich source of food but with essential minerals and vitamins, in relation to some of which vegan diets prove inadequate. Evolving Homo Sapiens Sapiens has been a hunter gatherer throughout his archaeological record.

(Sources Reviewed: AGP06, BJJHLA99, BLDRLJ02, BLGGW64, BV79, CME44, CWR96, DCR72, DP72, EEI96, EHM89, GJ90, HHF69, HKRC63, LK66, LR94, MD94(a), MD94(b), MGS31, RRM71, RT72, VLGJ68).

CHAPTER 4

"I'LL NEVER BE SUCH A GOSLING AS TO OBEY INSTINCT"

INSTINCTS, CONDITIONING AND LEARNING

"I'll never be such a gosling as to obey instinct", so says Coriolanus, and adds "but stand, as if a man were author of himself, and know no other kin". The warrior hero of Shakespeare's play was well used to coping with the instinctive fear that all soldiers feel on the eve of battle. He knew that when he engaged with the enemy he would be able to put into practice the martial skills which his military training had developed in him, but that strategic decisions in the heat of conflict could only be made on the hoof in the light of accumulated experience. Behaviour always requires that we juggle stored information from these three brain archives - instinct, conditioning and long term memory - and a soldier's life will often depend on getting the balance just right.

Human behaviour is either instinctive, conditioned or entrepreneurial. Instinctive behaviour is genetically hardwired during embryonic development, and its data bank and data processing put it beyond voluntary control. The conditionable area of the brain has a data bank which houses both motor and sensory information, the motor protocols expressing themselves as conditioned behaviour, and the sensory data being available as long term memories, precedents which can be imitated, varied or dismissed in the decision making process which provides the basis for entrepreneurial action. The distinction we make between these three forms of behaviour has practical significance. Instinctually pre-set routines cannot be altered, whereas the conditioning process and entrepreneurial behaviour are amenable to educational reform, at least in succeeding generations.

Instinctive Behaviour

Research into instinctive reactivity shows that only the most primitive behavioural patterns are truly immutable in humans. Relevant data have been derived by examining those traits which humans share with other primates, from the investigation of human traits which appear too early in life to have allowed conditioning to take place, and from the study of deaf-blind children, social isolates, and monozygotic twins separately reared from birth. Results show that the housekeeping brain, the emotional brain and species specific encounter signs are all genetically hardwired. The human baby smiles and recognises its mother's voice whilst still in the womb; at birth it cries, it urinates, it grasps with its hand and retracts its foot in response to touch. At two days it recognises its mother's face, turns towards her and suckles (WR02). Deaf-blind children smile, laugh, scratch, cough, sneeze, hiccup, vomit, clench their hands and stamp their feet if annoyed, and nod their head in assertion (EEI96p12).

Conditioning

Of the 30-40 thousand genes which jointly carry all the information needed to construct the human body (IHGSC01p860), and which are replicated in each nucleus of each body cell, half encode information for the brain's structure (CAM10). Even so, this amount of information falls very far short of that required to detail the nature, position and relationships of the many billions of active nerve cells (neurones) in the human brain, each of which may have a thousand or more connections. Estimates of the total number of neurones vary between 10Bn and 100Bn with most authorities favouring the higher figure, which would allow up to 40 Quadrillion potential permutations of brain circuitry (JS96, RJJ01, WR02).

Proliferation of neurones is maximal during the infant's first year, but continues throughout life and is, to some extent, counter-balanced by cell death, the eventual configurational outcome being determined very largely as a response to use. Indeed, environmental, social and cultural influences have a greater impact upon the individual's mental attributes, such as behaviour, and even IQ, than the genes themselves (RJJ01p340). As we know from the domestication of pets, an animal can be trained to behave in a specific and compulsive manner in response to a specific stimulus. Although the propensity for responding in this way is genetically coded, it is only an appropriate environmental stimulus which can trigger the trait's internal imprinting and outward expression. In some cases a single exposure to the stimulus will suffice, but more often reinforcement by repetition and incentivisation are required. Once the reflexive reaction has been established, the animal will always respond in the same way, but only to an identical stimulus. This process is called conditioning.

Conditioned behaviour evolved as a survival mechanism which is particularly important in animals which aggregate in "herds", because it helps to balance out interpersonal relationships. Non-human primates, for instance, have their seven fundamental behavioural traits moulded during juvenility by the conditioning they receive successively from their mother, their peer group and the "herd" at large. The cohesive forces of "herd" bonding and socialisation balance out the distractive forces of possessiveness and dominance challenge, whilst the latter's top-down discipline attenuates egocentrism and aggression, and determines sexual and nesting privilege. As a result, the whole "herd" acts as an integrated unit providing mutual security.

Conditioning is a primitive form of learning in which both the assimilation and, at least in all lower animals, the expression of the trait are compulsively automated. As with all forms of learning, it is reinforced every time the stimulus is repeated, and also if incentivisation is added. In humans, conditioning can sometimes be overridden by an effort of will involving the brain's higher centres, such as when a person with a phobia for heights is desensitised by the use of gradually incremental exposures, which begin, say, with the subject standing a few feet above the ground. Conversely, an asthmatic who is allergic to roses can, in time, develop asthmatic attacks if presented with an artificial flower.

The use of biologically abnormal substitutes throws the conditioning process off track. We have seen that the seven fundamental behavioural traits of primates have to be environmentally moulded in the conditionable brain during the animal's juvenility and maturation, and that malconditioning of these traits during immaturity is the cause of most personal human misbehaviour. All seven traits involve interactions with other individuals, and one way in which malconditioning occurs is for the normal biological expression of a trait to be dislocated and refocused by the use of a substitute. When this happens, not only is the trait's natural biological target replaced, but the charged emotions which should have attended the normal relationship are inappropriately redirected to the substitute. This process is called substitutive reconditioning.

The pioneer investigator of reconditioning was the Russian physiologist Pavlov who induced false salivation in dogs in response to a rung bell by repeatedly associating this with the presence of food. Eventually the bell became a substitute for food in initiating salivation. Although a few other species than man may spontaneously use substitutes (such as a male dog's use of a table leg to induce orgasm), the strategy is almost uniquely human, and has led to the development of widely diverse, bizarre and frequently inappropriate habituation. The development of habitual substitution is particularly likely to occur if the trait's natural biological target and expression are not available.

The substitutes of early childhood are dummies and thumb sucking in place of nipples, and cuddly toys in place of the maternal embrace.

In adults, an unfulfilled bonding trait leads to the use of pets as child substitutes and deities as parent substitutes (the Christian scripture refers to God as the Heavenly Father). Addictive chemicals stimulate the reward centre and create a particularly compelling form of bond synthesis. Socialisation substitutes are activities such as diary keeping, televised "soaps" viewing, prayer and meditation. Examples of dominance substitutes are whipping posts, "aunt sallys" and punchbags.

Heterosexual substitutes include vibrators, dildos and inflatable dolls. Male homosexuals substitute the human rectum for the vagina. Man, the hunter-carnivore turned sportsman, now preys on fox and fish he has no intention of eating, and goes drag hunting, clay pigeon shooting and paint balling. The plethora of consumer goods on offer in the developed world means that human possessiveness no longer has to focus on the survival value of commodities, and in consequence becomes retargeted onto fashion driven accessories. The resultant skew in market pricing can be absurd. When two artists put identical daubs of paint on canvas, the first to do so can be paid millions of dollars and the second may be sent to prison for plagiarism.

One of the most prevalent forms of substitution is, of course, that which replaces a sense of reality with a state of mental abstraction. This can be achieved by chemicals such as alcohol and narcotics or the smoking laurel leaves of the Delphic Oracle, hyperventilation, the extreme vertigo of the Dancing Dervishes, or sublimation - a form of mental abstraction produced by intense religious meditation or autosuggestion. All produce a sense of unreality which cossets the brain's reward centre and relieves stress, but in the final analysis must be likened to the ostrich's act of burying its head in the sand at the advent of danger.

There is often a price to pay for using behavioural substitution. Smoking, recreational drugs and excessive alcohol all have adverse effects on health, the AIDS pandemic was ushered in by male homosexuality, and religious cult wars have ravaged many areas of the globe. There may also be a conflict of interest between users of different substitutes - between smokers and alcohol drinkers in public places, or between the pet substitution of the animal rights activist and the ritual hunter-carnivore substitutes of the hunting, shooting and fishing fraternity.

The environmental role in stimulating the mature expression of brain function is never more obvious than when the opportunity for doing so is limited to a window in time. Failure to effect conditioning before the window of opportunity closes then leads to permanent sacrifice of the potential attribute. For example, if congenital cataracts in humans are not corrected by the age of six months, blindness is irredeemable. If a squint is not corrected by eight years of age, vision is lost in the lazy eye. Language must be developed in early childhood - social isolates (feral children), or deaf children who are not taught sign language, never catch up in later life and have no sense of question and answer, nor of abstract or future concepts. Particulate speech (there are 600 known distinct speech sounds or phonemes, although only 40-50 of these are employed by any particular language) must be listened to by the age of six months, and regional accents by three years, or they will not be accurately reproducible by most subjects. Language and thought skills are largely determined by the age of three years. Research in 1997 demonstrated that spoken language from an attentive engaged human being had an astonishingly favourable impact on an infant's brain development. The number of different words to which the infant was exposed was the single most important predictor of later intelligence, school success and social competence (HBRT97).

The younger the subject exposed to conditioning, the more permanent the retained imagery, belief or behaviourism is likely to be. The Jesuits claim that an indoctrinated child will remain so for life. The Ottoman Turks in the 17th century extorted a "blood tax" of youths aged 12-14 from noble Christian families in the occupied Balkans. Subjected to the most exacting discipline as Janissaries, these youths were trained to show the Sultan unswerving loyalty, and to exhibit the utmost ferocity in battles waged against their own former co-religionists.

Throughout history, saturation indoctrination has been used for the political and religious purposes of producing unquestioning fanaticism in acolytes. The principles of repetition and incentivisation are stringently applied to suborning the conditionable brain of underlings who are thus motivated to undertake actions involving their own death in return for a promise of immortality or other ephemeral rewards such as heavenly harems, or wealth. The Assassins, Japanese Kamikaze pilots, the Tamil Tigers and Islamic fundamentalists are familiar examples.

Learning in Primates

Behaviour which is not purely instinctive has to be learnt in response to the surround. The more complex social and environmental circumstances in which most primates, and especially humans, live require a larger brain, a longer period of juvenile protected learning and a structured framework for that learning. Primates learn by using three different conduits - imitation, instruction and personal experience (GJ90p214).

Primate young imitate maternal, sibling and peer behaviour, reading and following the encounter signs which others use in response to different situations. One-to-one instruction must play a part, because orphaned chimpanzees cannot learn to use tools or build nests even though they watch others doing so. The acquisition of technical and social skills at all ages is always dependent upon membership of sibling, peer, dominance ranking and "herd" groupings. Chimpanzees, gorillas and orang-utans raised in isolation are not afraid of snakes, but in the wild they learn fear of them from their mothers. The full imitative capacity of the chimpanzee is realised when the animal enters an artificial environment. It can be trained to use basic American Sign

Language and adopts some of man's simpler habits when raised in a human household.

In humans, the ability to learn from personal experience varies with the individual. Some never learn from their mistakes, some have to make a mistake once before they learn, some avoid mistakes by learning from those made by others, and the most astute can avoid errors by deduction, even in situations for which there has been no precedent.

The aptitude for learning logical, mathematical, linguistic, kinetic and social skills also varies with the individual (GH93), and just as each of these faculties can be independently degraded by local brain damage, so the acquisition of new skills increases the processing ability of the area of brain which the skill involves. The representative motor area for the left hand is expanded in fiddle players, the visuospatial area of the right cerebral hemisphere is enlarged in jugglers, and the hippocampus of the conditionable brain is enhanced in taxi drivers because they have to memorize street plans (NGMZ:05:03).

Repetition and incentivisation enhance and accelerate all forms of learning. Mental fatigue, which is more pronounced if data content is boring, decelerates and eventually arrests assimilation. Memories fade over time if they are not refreshed. If an experience is associated with a powerful emotion, memory of it will be etched more forcibly. Recall is always assisted if memorization was organised with the use of devices such as chains of association - mnemonics, jingles or crib lists.

Learning becomes more difficult with age, and this applies particularly to the acquisition of new skills. Japanese macaque monkeys cannot learn to wash potatoes after the age of 12 years, and chimpanzees cannot learn to use sticks to fish termites out of their holes after the age of 5 years. Humans find it increasingly difficult to learn new complex skills such as playing the violin and piano as they approach old age.

The Six Submodules Of The Conditionable Brain And Their Role In Learning

In terms of their functionality, the archives for sensory and motor data which are housed in the conditionable brain may be categorised as six submodules. *Learning By Rote* is required for the retention of data such as multiplication tables, the Morse code and the key positions on a "qwerty" keyboard. Since rote data do not have to be intellectually understood before they are stored in the conditionable brain, the emotional and unconditionable brains play little part in processing them. Repetition, particularly if it is incentivised, is the only requisite for rote memorisation, and though assimilation takes a long time, data retention may be lifelong.

Prior to their transfer to *Sensory Memory*, incoming auditory, visual, tactile and olfactory /gustatory signals are stamped with temporal and spatial references, and also with interpretive input from the unconditionable and emotional brains. Either repetition of the signal or recourse to the associated data will then trigger recall of the bundled data package. The complexity of *Motor Skills* will determine how much repetition, and what degree of understanding by the unconditionable brain, will be needed in their acquisition. Learning to tie shoelaces may take half an hour, to drive a car 30 hours and to play the piano 5 years.

Societal Skills are derived from the seven fundamental primate traits and are assimilated throughout immaturity. *Language* is also assimilated throughout immaturity. *Induced Social Behaviour Patterns* are those acquired from others by a process of involuntary imitation - in humans these traits include gestures, postures, gait, dialect, accent, prejudice, religion, ritual, dress code, mannerisms, diet, lifestyle, and the rites of calendar and passage.

Many data are stored as language and used as such in thought. Heard, spoken, read and written data are all memorisable, but of these written data are best retained, which is why students who practice writing out old exam papers are often more successful.

Entrepreneurial Behaviour

Entrepreneurial behaviour marks the acme and end point of man's evolutionary development, and it has enabled him to rise above his animal origins and dominate the planet. Equally significantly, it confers on him options to broaden his mind, to make balanced judgements, and to shape his own destiny pragmatically, although these options are not regularly exercised. Entrepreneurial behaviour is a function of the unconditionable brain which draws upon the sensory archives of the conditionable brain, comparing and contrasting the latter's contents with each new situation as it presents. An acute awareness of self, the employment of abstract concepts, and projections of future events, all of which are defining attributes of the human species, are incorporated into the thought processes which then prompt fresh actions. Appropriate motor skills and language will be co-opted into the process of execution.

Progressive development in entrepreneurial behaviour has led to the emergence of three crucial new faculties - enhanced organisational expertise, innovation, and a thirst for rational enlightenment - all of which have become increasingly elaborate, refined and trenchant throughout man's post evolutionary phase. A few examples will serve to show the importance of their functionality to the present status and future of the species.

Organisational expertise became a highly effective tool in the hands of such successful militarists as Alexander the Great, Julius Caesar and Napoleon, but it has also enabled man to walk on the moon, to synchronise world wide health campaigns and to assemble global jamborees such as the Olympic Games. Inquisitiveness is a trait exhibited by all carnivores (referred to in the aphorism that "curiosity killed the cat"), but its most potent human application is that of disciplined scientific enquiry, a process which rewarded Portugal's King Henry the Navigator, Leonardo da Vinci and Charles Darwin with far reaching discoveries within the ambit of the natural world. Investigation and innovation often went hand in hand, and a chance everyday event sometimes activated the necessary pertinent train of thought. An overflowing bath was the stimulus for Archimedes' study of specific gravity, a swaying cathedral lamp set Galileo Galilei thinking about isochronism, and when an apple fell on Isaac Newton's head it lead him to formulate the laws of gravity.

Francis Bacon (1561-1626) was the father of scientific methodology, and during the latter half of the second millennium CE inventions followed in profusion. To mention only a few, Galilei invented the thermometer, the telescope and an improved microscope, John Dalton discovered Atomic Theory, Robert Boyle unearthed many of the principles of chemistry and physics as did Michael Faraday those of electricity and magnetism, Thomas Edison had no fewer than 500 inventions to his credit, Albert Einstein revealed his theories of quantum and relativity, and Watson and Crick elicited the structure of the gene. It is, above all, to scientific investigators and inventors that the developed world owes its enlightenment and its rapidly rising living standards. Equally importantly, these pioneers have spearheaded the revolution which will eventually free us all from the slavery of obsessional thought, and enable behaviour to be a consistent and rational function of the unconditional brain.

(Sources reviewed: BA73, CAM10, DDHAAC44, EEI96, EHM89, GA06, GH93, GJ90, GR05, HBRT97, HHF58, IHGSC01, JA72, JS96, MS94, MSBK89, MMG98, NGMZ:05:03, PJ50, RJJ01, SABB99, SHR96, SJR85, SW65, TMSLA87, VL62, WKP08, WMLMA78, WR02)

CHAPTER 5

WHY IS BETTER NURTURE NOT IN OUR NATURE?

Man is a deviant animal. Alone of all the species, he plays the sadistic tyrant, enslaves, engages in torture and fraud, commits sexually motivated atrocity, abuses juveniles both physically and sexually, substitutes unnatural practices for natural processes and becomes addicted to chemicals. When it comes to massacring considerable numbers of his own kind he's in the sinbin with the rat and the chimpanzee, but as regards wholesale genocide he's in a league by himself. As none of these invidious traits has survival value, how did evolution ever make them part of the human behavioural repertoire?

In order to answer this question, we must understand that human development occurred in three very broad stages. The first was shared with the other higher primates and brought man to an equivalent level of evolution. Following this there was a stage, unique to humans, which resulted in considerable enlargement of the brain, greater complexity and sophistication of the societal unit and a protracted period of parental nurture for the human juvenile. The third stage was characterised by man taking charge of his own post evolutionary development, since he now had the intellectual capacity to do so. Traits acquired during all three stages find their expression in modern man, and the fact that not all of these are beneficial, and some are overtly malign, is a measure of the chequered development to which the human species has always been subject.

How can we get to grips with human behavioural dysfunction which manifests in so many different ways and which is so obviously counter-productive? In terms of its causes and outcomes it falls into five main categories - mental illness and the proclivity for waging inter-"herd" warfare which we now know are both genetically transmitted, malconditioning of the seven fundamental primate traits and the genesis of compulsive prejudice which are each the result of faulty nurture of the juvenile, and human ineptitude caused by irrationality. In terms of prevention, mental illnesses pose the most intractable problems. Although, for the most part, these are contained by medical measures, they can only be eliminated at source by eugenic policies. Failure to behave logically has to be counteracted in the long term by raising educational standards. The remaining three categories of human dysfunction account for most of man's problems and can all be prevented, but only if parents and parents-to-be are adequately trained in the art and science of nurture. Assumptions made by previous generations that child upbringing, like coitus, can safely be left to mother nature could not be further from the truth. Nor should we overlook the fact that the impetuosity to procreate frequently overtakes young couples before they have reached the twenty five year milestone of intellectual maturity, leaving them neither the time nor the opportunity to assimilate the evidence based know-how which is so vital to the optimisation of child development.

Why have humans been saddled with a nurtural process which has serious flaws, when evolution has provided the non-human primate with one whose close knit stereotyping secures the "herd" cohesion so critical to survival in the wild? Basically the primate nurtural process falls into three successive phases, moulding infancy, mid childhood and adolescence respectively. Although this plan was retained in essence when human development diverged from that of the apes, a degree of modification became inevitable with the evolution of sexual pair bonding, the subdivision of the "herd" into "households" of nuclear families, and expansion of the period required for protected learning. Whereas nurture from toddlerhood onwards in the non human primate is mediated by peer and "herd" consensus, in humans it has become an extension of parental responsibility - a change of influence whose results are sometimes markedly adverse. A comparison between the two nurtural procedures makes this clear.

During her mature years, the simian or ape mother is continuously either pregnant or suckling, cannot feed nor protect any other than the latest infant to which she has given birth, and therefore rejects it when a subsequent younger sibling is born. This abruption brings to an end the infant's first phase of nurture, which has been exclusively materno-centric, and which has imbued it with principles of conduct suited to a diurnal life style involving trekking, foraging, nesting and responding to alarms. The "carrot and stick" moulding its "moral compass" have been its mother's signalled approval or disapproval. Non-human primate studies show us that the absence of maternal affectionate nurture in the first phase proves disastrous. In captivity, monkey babies isolated from birth are asocial, they react aggressively if put together, some "freezing" in bizarre postures, some making purposeless repetitive movements or staring into space for hours on end. Later in life neither gender can respond sexually, and isolate mothers who conceive ignore their offspring or physically abuse them, sometimes mutilating or killing them (EHM89p150). Female chimpanzees from stable backgrounds become attentive, tolerant and protective mothers, but those chimpanzee mothers who fail to play with, caress and groom their young, engender a lack of confidence which affects later hunting, mating and socialising (GJ90p127).

The non-human primate's second phase of nurture is almost entirely conditioned by its peer group and its siblings. The rough and tumble of play teaches it reciprocity, and thus lays the foundation of its "social contract" which now fosters grooming, food sharing, altruism and alliance. Experimental deprivation of reciprocal socialisation during this phase is critically detrimental. Monkeys raised with a mother but no peer group subsequently showed aggression and little inclination to play, they were reluctant to engage with other "herd" members, and they exhibited no sexual behaviour as adults (HHFZRR58p421).

During its third nurtural phase, the non-human primate juvenile learns to cope with the influences of the "herd" at large, where the incentive for good behaviour will be acceptance as a fully fledged "herd" member, and the punishment for bad behaviour a drubbing meted out by a more dominant member in the ranking hierarchy. With its emphasis on co-operation, discipline, conformity, protocol and mutual security, the third phase makes the young animal intuitively aware of the requirements and value of corporate membership.

In humans, the first phase of nurture is predominantly, though not necessarily exclusively, materno-centric, and it extends from birth to the age of three or four years. Quick to recognise the difference between maternal approval and disapproval, the young child learns to discriminate between right and wrong - the first step in the orientation of its "moral compass". As language is acquired, encouragement, rationality and humour also begin to exert their influence. It is under the auspices of the first phase that the cornerstones of character are laid down - maternal affection which determines infant loyalty and trustworthiness, reasoned and reasonable maternal rebuff which forms the basis of the infant's later self discipline, encouragement which founds self confidence, and the unwavering security which generates later emotional stability.

Evidence of the need for human maternal affection in very early life is as compelling in humans as it is in the non-human primate. Babies who are confined to their cots and not cosseted or held by their mothers or nurses fail to thrive and may actually die. Children who are not embraced and treated with obvious affection when young grow up to be disturbed, scared or dangerous (RJJ01p335). Romanian orphans with an age range of 8 months-5.5 years who were adopted from institutions by Canadian families proved able to form attachments with their adoptive parents, but exhibited ambivalent reactions to them, both wanting yet resisting contact, and rejecting sympathy when they felt upset (CK95).In a Milwaukee study, orphan children who received a lot of attention developed a markedly higher IQ. In one institutional study of two year olds, those allocated individual nurses showed better development within six months (WMLMAE78p437). The average IQ of first borns is superior to that of other siblings. The so-called "Behaviourist" movement of child upbringing, spearheaded by the psychologist J B Watson in the early 20th century, propounded the theory that the demonstration of emotion towards a child such as kissing or cuddling it made it too dependent, and a rigidly structured, impersonal regime was recommended instead. The movement's failure was epitomised by the fact that one of Watson's sons committed suicide and the other became a psychoanalyst (EHM89p305).

The force of attraction provided by parental affection has to be counterbalanced by the use of reasonable rebuff and reproof. When combined with affectionate nurture, a consistently and demonstrably just set of behavioural rules imposed in early childhood translates into self discipline and harmonious co-existence in later life. In monkeys a mother's rebuff of an infant which kicks over the traces not only curbs antisocial behaviour, but also reinforces the infant-maternal bond. An American method of education based on Dr Benjamin Spock's principles of indulgence and the avoidance of frustration produced a generation of unloving, unbearably rude, aggressive and manipulative children (LK66p61). The third and fourth years of human life are the most critical in terms of early disciplinary conditioning. In 1979 the behaviour of two US pre-school groups in this age bracket were compared, one of which had been exposed to strict rules of acceptable behaviour, and the other which was allowed to be permissive, receiving little supervision. The permissive group boys showed 83 instances and the permissive group girls 42 instances of aggression, usually leading to exchanges of blows, verbal abuse and threats. Permissive children were less happy than those disciplined, and their social subgroupings were usually limited to pairs. The disciplined boys, by contrast, showed 5 instances of aggression, none of which were violent, and there was no aggression amongst the disciplined girls. Disciplined children were happier and formed larger subgroups of three or four. (GM79p350).

The correction of bad behaviour is brought about more effectively and permanently when reasoned, mild reproof, rather than a more severe measure, is used (EHM99p294). Excessive or unreasonable forms of discipline have markedly adverse consequences. Parents who overdiscipline their children undermine their self esteem and cause them to overcompensate for this in later life by denigrating others. The life histories of many dictators demonstrate this effect on dominance particularly well. As children, both Hitler and Stalin were habitually and mercilessly beaten by their fathers and their consequential paranoid desire for retribution towards humanity was the main reason for the loss of 50 million lives during the second world war. The English King George the Sixth stammered almost uncontrollably as the result of the overbearing discipline of his father. Overdisciplined children tend to lack confidence and to become anxious, depressed, or obsessive in later life.

The second nurtural phase in humans which spans the years between 3-4 and 8 of the child's life differs markedly from its equivalent in non-human primates. The toddler does not have to cope with maternal rejection on the birth of a younger sibling, which would prove disastrous in the human setting, and derives continuing emotional and physical support from its mother and, in typical circumstances, also from its father. With considerable variation between cultures, peer and sibling group influence forges the youngster's "social contract" on the basis of reciprocity, albeit that this process is monitored by parents and junior school authority. Some human singletons find social integration difficult as adults and adopt overtly defensive attitudes in their dealings with others.

It is during the second phase that encouragement and security in the home environment become maximally important to future development, with the child taking its cue from its parents as role models, with particular reference to the quality of the interparental relationship and the way in which each partner copes with life's stresses. Correspondingly, the trauma of parental divorce and school bullying make their greatest emotional impact at this sensitive time (ER10). Screen violence also engenders aggression and fear below the age of eleven years, particularly in boys, and the younger the child is the more it will be provoked. In the Minnesota Longitudinal Study, ongoing child development was examined in relation to home background. Those children with "secure parental attachment" ranked highest in social competence, were least socially isolated, most popular, most likely to respond empathically to another's distress, least likely to bully or be bullied, twice as likely to form friendships or to spend time with a special friend, more likely to become involved in group activities, were better at forming paired or group relationships, and exhibited more self confidence and better qualities of leadership (TMSLA87).

The third nurtural phase in humans begins around the age of eight years, typically lasting a few years beyond puberty. It exposes adolescents to a maelstrom of productive and counter-productive influences, meted out both by their peers and by society at large, from which their parents are only able to offer diminishing protection. They feel vulnerable, and experience the strong instinctual needs to be accepted as accredited "herd" or "herd" subgroup members, and to climb the dominance ranking ladder as far as others will permit.

Anxious to be seen as confederates and not as aliens, both the male and the female human tenderfoot demonstrate allegiance to the "herd" by behaving submissively towards its members, and by openly discriminating in its favour. They have thereby paid their membership fees, but by the same token the seed of prejudice has been sown within them. Whether this grows into a trait which influences their behaviour compulsively will depend both upon the degree to which they have already been malconditioned by their parents, and upon whether or not they already possess an obsessional gene. Compulsive prejudice is humanity's mischief maker extraordinary. In its less belligerent form it is the basis for our "personal equation", the way we filter our observations and outlook to make them tally with what we would prefer to believe. In its more vociferous form compulsive prejudice fuels and is fuelled by racial, class and gender discrimination, religious intolerance and nationalistic xenophobia. When acted upon by the inherited proclivity for interherd warfare, compulsive prejudice becomes aggressively dynamized, often with grievous consequences.

How do we find ways to rescind the three categories of developmental error which our latest evolutionary stages have bequeathed to us - the idiosyncratic malconditioning of the seven fundamental primate traits, compulsive prejudice engendered and orchestrated by the third nurtural phase, and the invidious taste for interherd warfare passed down from an ape-like ancestor? It is, of course, necessary for society as a whole to understand the nature of these problems, but the sovereign remedy for them can only be administered by parents. Although in later chapters we shall need to elaborate the way in which fundamental primate traits are affected by human malconditioning, let us first summarise them. If security and sensitive maternal affection are lacking in the first and second nurtural phases, an individual will subsequently overreact to danger, and/or bonding mechanisms may be permanently thwarted. There will then be a tendency to overcompensate by retreating from reality and indulging in chemical addiction or fetishism. Possessiveness, compulsively aggravated by lack of early security or discipline, may result in reciditive theft, gambling or hoarding. Malconditioning at any time of nurture, but especially if it occurs during the second phase, may cause a dislocation of socialisation which results in delinquency and other forms of antisocial behaviour. Unhinged sexuality may lead to the manifestation of a wide variety of perversions and sexual atrocities. Distortion of the dominance or the hunter-carnivore traits disinhibits offensive aggression. These pitfalls can only be avoided if parents offer their children unstinting and demonstrable affection, encouragement, and a stable, disciplined family background, if they set unwavering behavioural standards, and if they are prepared to act as positive but impartial role models themselves. The need for these provisions far outweighs any socio-economic considerations, and their implementation produces consistently better outcomes in terms of the educational and vocational attainments of the child, and of its social and marital relationships.

Whilst avoidance of malconditioning of the seven primate traits is a reasonably straightforward exercise in parental common sense, the prevention of compulsive prejudice poses a much more difficult problem, because this is incurred during the third phase of nurture for which the human parent is only partly accountable. This is a time when a responsible parent will examine his or her own prejudices in order to ensure that they are not unwittingly and intuitively transferred. Of equal importance is the need to avoid the "see-saw" effect between generations through which a bigoted viewpoint in the parent engenders its diametrically opposite stance in the teenage offspring. Further than that, prophylaxis is very much a matter of creating a milieu through which a sufficient knowledge of the mistakes of behavioural history is imparted to ensure that these are not repeated. This is most effectively done not only by quoting actual examples taken from reputable publications and broadcasts, but also by openly discussing the misdemeanours of local community members. A balanced database of wisdom garnered in this way is infinitely more effective than a set of rules which tempts the youngster to kick over the traces.

The trait which drives man to wage interherd warfare is in a category of its own, because evidence from studies of chimpanzees in the wild strongly suggests that we share with them an inherited tendency to be gratuitously aggressive - a trait passed down from a common ancestor in the form of an endemic genetic error (see also chapter 21). The problem is compounded if an individual already has a gene-born obsessional persona, or if third phase malconditioning has occurred. Such malign genes cannot be expunged from humanity but they can be culturally suppressed. Once again, the prophylactic use of soundly based historical examples such as those reviewed in later chapters, allows an impartial parent to exert influence - in this context by cultivating an aversion to aggression. By voting and lobbying for higher educational standards, parents can, of course, help to ensure that the next generation is provided with the necessary rationality to be able to keep the peace.

We have so far investigated nurture from the stereotypical viewpoint of parents who strive to do the best for their children, no matter how far they stray from experience based rationality. This approach does not take into consideration those cases where parents exploit the vulnerability of their offspring by giving vent to their own depraved and predatory nature. This most ignominious form of human parental failure, known as child abuse, is a phenomenon which is unknown throughout the rest of the primate world. Reports of recent surveys have shown us that 16% of UK children experience serious maltreatment at the hands of their parents (CP02), and that in western countries as a whole 5% of underage boys and 10% of underage girls suffer some form of sexual abuse, most of which goes unreported (BP08). Nurture of the succeeding generation is so essential to the perpetuation of the species that it is at first difficult to understand how human evolution can have produced a behavioural feature which not only traumatises the child but leads to the deformation of its personality. Abused children frequently become delinquent teenagers and adult miscreants. Two thirds of school truants in a US study reported emotional, physical, sexual or negligent abuse occasioned by their parents, and this was associated with subsequent depression, suicidal tendencies, hostility, delinquency, promiscuity and substance abuse. Since 3% of families are responsible for 25% of criminal offences, it is all too commonly the dysfunctional family which abuses or malconditions, in whom the same scourge is passed on from one generation to another, and by whom child mismanagement is but one of several forms of dysfunction which are manifested. Child abuse is a carbuncle on the face of society which has to be tackled by all the means available to local and legal authority. Measures include preventive education as a component of parenting classes at school, antenatal clinic and adult evening class, and mentoring of young parents by health visitors. Remedial education of perpetrators can be legally enforced, but more serious cases may require removal of the child to foster care, if necessary as soon as it has been born.

As a discrete socio-economic unit, a household must have a resource provider, but does childhood development necessarily require the presence of a second parent? A plethora of studies in the western world, many based in the USA, have attempted to answer this question. During the last three decades of the 20th century the number of unmarried, widowed, divorced and separated mothers trebled to reach a level of 22% of all households with dependent children (GA06p237). Children of single parent households suffer more short and long term economic and psychological disadvantages, have higher school truancy and drop out rates, achieve lower educational levels, exhibit more delinquent activity including drug and alcohol addiction, and have higher suicide rates than their peers. However, whilst the immediate effects of parental divorce or separation are inevitably traumatic, many of the other disadvantages experienced can be attributed to the low economic status of a lone parent, to discord which preceded partner disruption, or to the economic crisis or step parenting problems which followed it. Given adequate supervision and income, and continuity of social networking, the majority of children adjust and recover in the long term.

(Sources reviewed: BA73, CK95, CP02, DEA91, EHM89, ER10, GA06, GH93, GHDR97, GJ90, GR05, HBRT97, HHF58, McLS94, McLB89, McLB97, MHL09, NGMZ:05:03, PJ50, PR97, RJJ01, SHR96, SJR85, TMSLA87, VL62, WKP08, WMLMAE78)

CHAPTER 6

THE TEAM SPIRIT

SOCIALISATION IN PRIMATES

The decibel level to which the hubbub and chatter of a wedding reception, a Women's Institute bun fight or a crowded bar rises can sometimes reach heights which exceed auditory safety, as participants speak progressively louder in order to rise above the general clamour. Most of those present are busily engaged in an interactive process which builds bridges by inducing a sense of camaraderie in others, by massaging egos and by exploring common interests. It is usual for humour and alcohol to oil the wheels. By analogy, we can trace the instinctive motivation for this exercise in ritualised socialisation back to the grooming procedure of non-human primates in which "herd" members dedicate time to plucking parasites from each other's fur. Homo Sapiens Sapiens now has very little fur left to be groomed, and no longer regards nit picking as a social grace.

Darwin's seminal work showed us how a species originated and continues to evolve in accordance with its own unique pattern of development. But each species consists of socially self contained subgroups whose size and location are basically tied to the availability of resources. There are usually, but not invariably, close blood relationships between subgroup members. In this book, societal subgroups are referred to as "herds", regardless of the species to which they belong, in order to avoid the confusion which arises when a different collective term is applied to each separate category of animal. It is also common usage to refer to the bonds which exist between subgroup members as herd bonds.

Evolution is never channelled through the lineage of a single individual nor a single set of genes, but is the outcome of the admixture and interdependence of many, blended for the most part at "herd" level. Whilst fertile sexual relationships are possible between all male and female members of a species, fertile social relationships are normally limited to the "herd". We have already noted in chapter 3 that assemblage of individuals into well integrated "herds", together with the evolution of a larger brain to cope with "herd" logistics, gave primates enhanced survival value.

Before the advent of carnivores, and provided that vegetation was plentiful, herbivores had no competitors nor predators, and no need for either offensive or defensive aggression. When carnivores appeared, herbivores formed themselves into circumscribed protective assemblies, and carnivores found that they needed to group in packs in order to hunt effectively. If vegetation was limited, herbivore "herds" became territorial using defensive aggression, and if prey was in short supply carnivores had to use both offensive and defensive aggression in order to hunt and foil their competitors.

At this juncture, further evolution took place at "herd" level so as to provide societal frameworks which could support these policies. Although there are exceptions, the herbivores, such as the zebra, elk and gorilla, structured their "herds" as social units based on the harem of the alpha male, whose superior strength and build contrasted markedly with the physique of "herd" females (sexual dimorphism) and enabled him to secure exclusive breeding rights over them through exaggerative dominance contests which marginalised other males. His prominent position also cast him in the role of prime defender. The carnivore "herd", on the other hand, put little or no emphasis on alpha sexual monopoly, and its adult males banded together under a leader as a team of near equals when it came to implementing co-ordinated strategies for either predation or interherd competition. Thus both herbivore and carnivore "herd" evolution promoted the survival of the fittest gene, but each used a different methodology for doing so.

The linear relationship which exists between the ratio of a species' brain-to-body size and its social group size suggests that man evolved to live in a social grouping of 125-150 individuals. Circumscribed interactive groupings of this size are still found in present day hunter-gatherer societies and many modern rural communities, and their closer knit social integration and mutuality enable them to eat better, live longer and have more children than their urban co-nationals (WR02p265). Protohumans developed as ground living omnivorous predators 5 million years ago, with rapid bipedal mobility and an upright posture. Evolution of Homo Sapiens Sapiens as a definitive species was reached 195 thousand years ago (SC:BBCR4:12:02:14). The hunter-gathering existence of these early ancestors of ours involved them in co-operative hunting with weapons; in food sharing and storage, in the use of language, tools, clothing, shelter and fire, and in the need to live in self contained, circumscribed groups. With the introduction of crop cultivation, a horticultural "swidden" lifestyle (which necessitated the periodical relocation of smallholding as soil became impoverished), and subsequently sustainable agriculture which emerged eleven thousand years ago, led to the formation of land owning units passed down through the family line. In 1957 the World Ethnographic Sample showed that 60% of all communities still had unilineal systems, of which 85% were patrilineal and most of the others inherited maternally. These unilineal communities were characterised by having a collective residency, security and hospitality, a shared economy, and a religious cult incorporating initiation, weddings, and funerals, beliefs, totems, customs, taboos, restrictions and aversions. At this developmental stage many communities still engaged in blood feuds with neighbouring clans (BV79p247).

Further technical, cultural and intellectual development has produced industrialisation and urbanisation with resulting human conglomerations of enormous magnitude - (Mexico City 8.6 million, Tokyo 12 million, Greater Chunking 30 million, London 7.5 million, New York 18.9 million) - within which the social architecture that man's behaviour patterns were originally evolved to cope with can no longer find expression. By the year 2008, one half of the entire world's population already resided in towns and cities. Only one in four Americans now knows his next door neighbour, impersonality, anonymity and isolationism are used to satisfy the need for personal space, the herd bond atrophies, and the oppressive density of cluttered humanity triggers aggression (see chapter 8). Depravity, delinquency, crime, riot and prostitution are predominantly urban problems.

How Is "Herd" Unity Achieved?
The behavioural mechanisms which integrate and coordinate primate "herds" are bonding, which produces cohesion, dominance ranking which enforces discipline, and socialisation which lubricates and harmonises relationships between members. These three instinctually based traits exert a moderating influence over those other three fundamental traits of possessiveness, competitive sexuality and hunter carnivore offensive aggression which would otherwise prove unbridled and anarchic within the confines of the "herd".

Primates of the same "herd" enjoy each others' company and are riled by the disruptive behaviour of an individual which breaks the common code. Rewards for conformity will be food sharing, playing and teasing, grooming, hugging and kissing, mutual altruism and shared warnings of danger. Rebuffs will be scolding, hitting, chasing and missile throwing. Top-down discipline within the "herd" will be maintained through hierarchical dominance ranking. All this is the socialisation process, a package of behavioural traits predisposed to by instinct, and moulded by conditioning within, and on behalf of, the "herd"

Herd bonding and socialisation are mutually reinforcing, and herd bonding is actually stimulated by the dominance ranking procedure.

Bonding between herd members is the end product of a series of bonding steps in an individual's life history. Infant-maternal, sibling, and peer/ play group bonds condition the primate to be prepared for adult relationships which come to fruition when they are moulded by "herd" socialisation, dominance confrontation and the fear of rejection by other "herd" members. Even the sick or injured primate makes the utmost effort to keep up with the "herd" on forage, knowing that if it fails it will be easy meat for predators.

Each animal within a non-human primate "herd" knows every other at once by its facial and bodily configuration, and is familiar with its repertoire of facial expressions, body language, vocalisations, tactile and olfactory signals, traits of personality, bond and dominance relationships, and its usual disposition within the foraging or sleeping "herd". In non-human primates the herd bond and dominance ranking produce deference towards the most dominant males, whose presence will be sought, and who will be groomed, by juniors at times of rest. This would be analogous to a human monarch holding court. As with sexual jamborees amongst chimpanzees which take place if several females simultaneously display receptivity, the whole "herd" indulges in periodic spells of social hyperactivity under herd bond influence, during which a buzz of electrified excitement spreads infectiously throughout the community, intensifying activities such as play, grooming and food sharing, all lasting half an hour or more (EEI96p291). There are obvious links here with the gregariousness, conviviality, partying and carnivals which humans enjoy so much.

In human life, cultural institutions, activities and rites play an important part in herd bonding, although some forms of association, through their exclusivity, are actually socially divisive. Many calendrical and passage rites can be shared by all, even if they have an ostensibly religious or nationalistic basis. The agenda of guilds, unions, alumnii associations, religious splinter groups and closed societies can not.

The Elaboration of Encounter Signs in Human Social Development

All primates reap the benefits of "herd" formation and integration in terms of co-ordinated defence, the most effective use of available resources, individual development and conditioning, the transmission of culture, skills and knowledge, role differentiation, discipline, mutual assistance and conviviality. But in the case of the protohuman "herd", the combined evolution of an increasingly complex social unit and an ever burgeoning brain provided the impetus for further vigorous behavioural development and the acquisition of entirely new skills.

The catalyst for the intellectual, technical and aesthetic protohuman advances which were to follow was provided by the elaboration within the "herd" of its encounter signs, and in particular that of *vocalisation.* The vocal repertoire of non-human primates is limited to 10-15 types of sound signal (BV79p52), and only human primates can vary vocal pitch and rhythm. The ability to use language is dependent upon possession of the FoxP2 gene which has also been found to have been present in Neanderthals, a closely related species to our own which became extinct 50 thousand years ago. The human child speaks at 15 months, by 3 years has learned 900 words, and by 5 years has 2,100 words in its vocabulary (MD96(a)p71). With the acquisition of language, almost the entire currency of primate social intercourse is converted into sound signals and thereafter behavioural transactions are undertaken in a symbolic code consisting of phonemes (the smallest distinctive units of diction) and intonations. The five basic emotions can be descriptively expressed; instruction, knowledge, culture and tradition can be imparted, and the fundamental behavioural traits of bonding and dominance confrontation can be acted out verbally. Whereas non-human primate communication can only transmit the crudest forms of information relating to the immediate present, human language can portray the past and future, symbolism as well as reality, metaphor and simile, and, above all, is infinitely variable in its descriptive possibilities. Even the grooming practised by non-human primates is transmuted into the small talk of human chatter. The only fundamental primate traits which retain necessarily physical expression in humans are possessiveness, coitus and offensive aggression, and even these are attended by the use of language.

Music is a further elaboration of primate vocalisation and can express the anger of a Beethoven grappling with deafness, the fear of a throbbing pulse, the joy of true harmony, the sadness of a dirge, the disgust of modern atonality, or the sexuality of a serenade. Most staged pop music resembles a cross between a war dance and a fertility rite.

Facial Recognition and Expression also became more elaborate as humans developed. Facial recognition manifests in the human infant at two days. The human facial musculature allows a much greater range of facial expression than that found in other species, and the right side of the face tends to be more emotionally expressive than the left. The smile is an uniquely human expression of joy and begins at four weeks. The Balinese file a child's front teeth at puberty to ensure a perfect smile. Cinema photography scores over live theatre in that it can portray facial expressions in "close-up", a deficiency for which the Ancient Greeks compensated by having their actors don masks with fixed expressions of joy or grief which all could recognise, and which the Victorians sought to overcome with opera glasses. One of the basic defects which autistic children suffer is that they cannot "read" human faces and, by contrast, some breeds of domestic dog learn to do so.

The range of significance of *Body Language* is far more extensive and sophisticated in humans than it is in any other animal, and it varies with gender and age group. Body language elaborated as dance shares much of its emotional expressiveness with music - anger in the fandango, joy, sadness or disgust in ballet, dominance in the tango, and sexuality in ballroom. Closed circuit television allows scrutineers to identify probable troublemakers in city streets by their body language. Interestingly, human deceit is accompanied by involuntary body language - a decrease in limb movement, frequent nose touching, and an increase in muscle stiffness. The non-human primate will steal and tease, but, deprived of language, cannot lie.

Of all the encounter signs, *Tactility* has undergone least change with human development. Tactile encounter signs in non-human primates are hand patting, touching and holding, kissing, hugging, and non sexual mounting which really ranks as another form of hugging. All these have equivalent use in human encounters, and some have been ritualised. Hand shaking as a greeting has been used by humans at least since Homeric times. Farewell rituals are only found in man (EEI96p73).

Socialisation is so essential to primate existence, and so closely linked to encounter signs that when the latter are not evident the non-human primate becomes both nonplussed and distressed. The sight of a moribund or deceased conspecific from which all encounter signs are inevitably absent, causes the chimpanzee obvious anguish, and prompts attempts to revive limb movements. High ranking bonobos have been observed to continue grooming a fresh conspecific corpse for an hour or more, presumably in the hope of eliciting the return of responses (BAMZ:02:08).

What Prompted the Emergence of Basic Human Intellectual Patterns?

Early man's primary need was to excel as a hunter gatherer in the face of competition from larger and more rapidly mobile predators. To meet this need his evolutionary progression, often more adaptable than that of other species, furnished him with a combined package of pre-eminent cognitive function and a more sophisticated, yet robust, social infrastructure - a seed bed from which further skills and faculties could later germinate. The twin influences of enhanced cognition and close knit social interdependence mediated by language have since catalysed all man's further development.

Logic, Innovation and Organisation must rank as the most important human intellectual attributes. The uniquely human skills of innovation and deductive reasoning derive from curiosity which is an attribute of all carnivores (BLGGW64p47). The rat, cat and dog are always keen to explore new territory. The monkey is repeatedly willing to expose itself to the frustrations inherent in problem solving. The chimpanzee, despite punishment, teases peers and humans in order to test their reactions. The human power of organisation finds its precursor in the leadership and decision making functions which are prominent features of primate alpha male behaviour.

Altruism is not a uniquely human quality, and is clearly identifiable in non-human primates and some other species such as the dolphin and dog. Experiments using rhesus monkeys showed that if one animal was provided with the means of stimulating an electric shock in another conspecific in an adjacent cage, it would studiously avoid doing so, even to the point of going without food (MJ99(a)p64). Chimpanzees attend to each others' pustules, wounds and splinters, and will remove grit from a neighbour's eye. A chimpanzee will hand food to a begging companion (EEI96p181), and will come to the aid of another "herd" member under attack, even though it risks its own life by doing so. Altruism is not merely motivated by herd bondage. The great apes have been found to show compassion to other species - a gorilla was seen to rescue a human child, and a bonobo cared for an injured starling (WR02p287). Humans rationalise the attribute of altruism as the humanitarian ideal, and often channel its expression through conduits such as charities, The Red Cross and Crescent, the Hippocratic Oath, Amnesty International and the Bill of Human Rights.

Like altruism, humour is a shared interactive behaviourism. Humour derives from play, but adds further encounter signs - facial expressions of pleasure and the vocalisation of laughter. The chimpanzee is one of the most playful primates and its laughter is usually associated with play and teasing. Most jokes in western culture have been about mothers in law, unpaid bills, drunks, taxes, tramps, corpses, excretory functions, politicians, vermin, bad taste, bad breaks, sexual ineptitudes, pomp, egotism, stinginess and stupidity (BV79p344) - all subjects which initially engender disgust, but which ridicule renders harmless and the play-tease of satirisation makes risible. Some races are able to laugh at, but not with, other people - a cultural defect known as shadenfreude.

The discovery of grave goods dating back as far as 75 thousand years, and beginning with pierced marine shells for personal adornment, implies, though it does not prove, a belief in the afterlife (JP99p83). On the other hand, sacrificial practices such as the premeditated submergence beneath the waters of a lake of reindeer weighted down with stones, the multiple decapitation of bears whose heads were stacked in caves fifty thousand years ago, and the widespread stencilling on cave walls thirty thousand years back of the outline of hands from which finger segments had been amputated, all provide evidence of a belief in a supernatural being who had to be propitiated (KH68). The cave art of prehistoric man, although competent, was not intended primarily to be decorative, since it was executed in the deeper recesses of the cave systems, whereas his hearths and living areas were located near the entrance. Representations of animals dating back thirty thousand years depict those used as a source of meat, and often show them being hunted - a format suggestive of telepathic magic or religious supplication (WR02p292, JP99p100). Did primitive man's aesthetic impulse develop in parallel with his spirituality or religiosity? His early prowess in graphic art took place in the most resonant chambers of the cave where the earliest bone flutes dating back forty thousand years have been found, where he sometimes depicted himself playing crude musical instruments (JP99p106), and where, as we have seen, he recorded his finger sacrifices. It is also interesting that left hand outlines predominate, showing that, as with stone knapping, the right hand was more often used in execution. Right handedness derives from the same brain area as the use of language.

Until relatively recently it was believed that only human beings knew how to use tools, but it must not be forgotten that many birds show considerable skill in manipulating twigs when nest building. Amongst primates in the wild some monkeys and chimpanzees crack nuts with stones (NGMZ:92:03), and chimpanzees use sticks to fish termites from their mounds. The orang utan uses sticks to prise seeds from fruit (NGMZ:03:10), and the gorilla uses sticks to harvest fallen fruit from ponds.

In order the better to adapt to his environment, man has always used his growing intellect to develop new technology, but in prehistoric times progress was stepwise and painfully slow. He began to sculpt stone tools 3.4 million years ago, to use fire 1.6 million years ago, he learnt to build rafts 800 thousand years ago, fashioned wooden spears 450 thousand years ago, and bone arrows and harpoons a hundred thousand years ago. Personal adornment with sea shells began 75 thousand years ago, man learned to make sewing needles from bone 61 thousand years ago, and by 35 thousand years ago was shaping pro-fertility statuettes and phallic symbols from bone, ivory and stone. Flint chippings embedded in wood were employed in sickle design 17 thousand years ago when grindstones were used to process wild cereals. Pottery began 9 thousand years ago, and the discovery of native copper 7 thousand years ago led to the manufacture of pins, awls, fish hooks and small ornaments. Five thousand years ago smelting tin and copper together brought about the production of bronze whose increased strength made it suitable for use in knife, sword, armour, axe and adze fabrication, and 3.3 thousand years ago iron began to be extracted from its ore.

The earliest artificial shelters were supported by the limbs of trees and appeared 900 thousand years ago. Timber framed shacks using wattle and daub infill became the basis of small villages 8 thousand years ago , and formal architectural development began 5 thousand years ago with the appearance of corbelled collective tombs in Western Europe and dressed stone temples in Malta (RC73). The world's first civilization emerged 5200 ~~thousand~~ years ago in Sumeria where centrally controlled redistribution of goods spawned the development of tally records in which triangular ("cuneiform") impressions made in wet clay could be rendered permanent by firing. Egyptian picture writing began almost contemporaneously. The use of symbolic characters engraved on the stone of caves in India suggest that much earlier attempts at systematised writing had been made as far back as 250 thousand years ago (HSC11). (see also timeline of refinement in human behaviour - table 6.1)

(Sources Reviewed: BAMZ02, BBCT109, BLGGW64, BV79, EEI96, HSC11, JP99, KH68, MD96(a), MJ99, NGMZ92, NGMZ03, RC73, SC:BBCR4, WR02)

CHAPTER 7

SEX AND WHY WE CAN'T DO WITHOUT IT

No subject engenders more ribaldry, titillation, misunderstanding, embarrassment, hypocrisy and duplicity than sex. The fallacies, fetishes, phobias and fixations associated with it are legion, parents and children find it difficult to communicate with each other about it, and most couples have only the vaguest idea of what is going through their partners' minds during coitus. Moreover, because the sexual act constitutes the third form of pelvic evacuation and the other two are solely concerned with sewage, it seems totally out of kilter that nature should make us so besotted about it. Where else but to behavioural science can we turn to put the record straight?

The instinctive sexual urge is second only in strength to the instinct for self preservation. It will not be denied, and it is crucial to the perpetuation, integrity and evolutionary development of the species. Everybody has a sex life, though the family doctor is one of the few people privileged to know this. Since man's evolution diverged from that of the apes, the simple act of coitus has become subject to the embroidery of an astonishingly wide range of variations, perversions and substitutions in sexual behaviour. The social, legal and religious mores introduced to contain these wayward developments have merely served to make them clandestine. Accurate statistics on sexual habits are notoriously difficult to obtain. Only when the veil of secrecy is partially lifted by criminolegal, political, media, or internet exposure do we begin to see the bigger picture.

How are we to understand this wide diversity in human sexual behaviour. The basic problem in primate terms is that man is a sociosexual mongrel, having inherited not just one, but all four, of the procreational relationships of his nearest relatives - the nuclear family pattern of the gibbon, the harem pattern of the gorilla, the orang utan's "one night stand" and the chimpanzee's sexual free-for-all. Whilst all four patterns within him compete for expression, man is genetically most closely related to the chimpanzee, which helps to explain why, for example in the mid 20th century, few American men and only around 50% of American women were virgin at the time of marriage, and 50% of married males and 26% of married females experienced extramarital sex by the age of 40. The number of partners with whom a western woman consorts during her lifetime has now reached an average of 8, nearly 50% of first babies are born outside wedlock, and half of all marriages end in divorce (DMN:03:08:02, HC03p446, MD94(a)p62, WR02p151). A UK survey of a thousand males in 2005 revealed that 9% have experienced paid sex with a prostitute (BBCR4:05:12:01). By comparison, Kinsey's figure of 70% for American males would seem unrepresentative (DMN:03:08:02). Although humans aspire to the ideal of the nuclear family and permanent pair bonding, they are distracted from it by ape-like genetic influences known as the "pan" factor.

Uniquely Human Aspects of Sexual Behaviour
Since man's evolution diverged from that of the apes, there have been uniquely human developments in his sexual behaviour patterns. Human partner selection differs from that of other primates. In gorilla harem and in orang utan "one night stand" relationships, partner selection is dictated by male physical dominance, whereas in the promiscuous chimpanzee coital partnerships are purely opportunistic. The gibbon with its nuclear family and pair bonding selects by mutual agreement. Human mate selection is also mutual, and dependent not merely upon physical attributes but those of personality, status and

possessions. The fundamental primate behavioural traits of dominance, possessiveness, sexuality and sociability are therefore all involved in the process.

We have already seen that the five basic emotions of anger, fear, joy, sorrow and disgust entail the employment of distinctive species specific encounter signs (see chapter 2). Sexuality invokes its own specific repertoire of encounter signs which have been extensively elaborated by human evolutionary development. Facial attraction is the sexual equivalent of the facial recognition stage of socialisation, with the human male drawn towards a youthful countenance which displays symmetry, prominent cheekbones and flushed cheeks, a small rosebud mouth, sparkling eyes, and a well shaped nose and ears. Fleshy ear lobes have visual and tactile importance and are spotlighted by the use of ear rings. "Come hither" facial expressions, and mannerisms involving the lips, such as licking them, constitute more direct signals.

Female body language and configuration are always interpreted sexually by males - an hour glass but slim torso, the act of crossing and uncrossing legs, a provocative stance and a "cat walk" gait which draws attention to the hips are all familiar examples. Vocalization plays its part in the sexual behaviour of both genders, and characteristically features a soothing voice which reassures, persuades, entices, flatters and is ostentatious. Tactility leads from handholding through caressing, foot fondling, hugging, nuzzling and kissing into foreplay (EEI96p162, WR02p95). Licking as a sexual preliminary is common to most mammals. The male hamadryas baboon bites its partner to cause her to follow him (EEI96p116), and both human partners may bite to cause arousal.

Whereas many other animals use olfactory signals territorially and for "herd" member identification, humans only use them for sexual purposes. Human pheromones attract the opposite sex and reinforce paid bonding. They are secreted by tiny apocrine glands within the skin, of which females possess 75% more than males, and which are situated beside the genitalia and in the armpits. Attraction towards musk develops at human puberty and is stronger in women. All female facial, bodily and olfactory characteristics which advertise sexuality are purposely emphasised by cosmetics, couture and perfume.

Non-human primate mothers usually have single pregnancies, and cannot nurture more than one infant at a time, so that they have to reject the elder in favour of a younger sibling. Because the human female has to provide for all her children concurrently during their prolonged phase of protected maturation, she has, of necessity, to rely on her consort's allegiance and assistance. In this regard she is aided by her extended span of sexual responsiveness which is not restricted to ovulation, but persists throughout the month, and also by the fact that her uniquely human female orgasm reinforces emotional bonding in both parties. The sensual reward of copulation is much stronger, and the act lasts much longer, in humans than it does in other animals, and human potency often continues into old age (EEI96p156). The strength of the coitus induced bond is well demonstrated by the fact that in some individuals further sexual activity may only prove possible with a regular partner, and that if one partner tries to break the tie, the strength of jealousy which results occasionally leads to murder or suicide. Around 13% of all UK homicides involve spouses and are the result of partner jealousy (WR02p115).

Like the gorilla and bonobo, but unlike other primates, human coitus takes place face to face, with the result that the receptor sites for erogenous arousal in both parties are mutually and simultaneously stimulated, creating a sense of partnership. With the possible exception of the bonobo however, other primate females experience neither clitoral orgasmic appetite, response nor satiation.

(Sources reviewed: EEI06, HC03, MD94(a), WF05, WR02)

Regeneration is Every Species' Cardinal Adaptive Mechanism
Regeneration is the key strategy by which a species is enabled to adapt to the surround, because it allows each generation to pass on reshuffled genes to the one which follows it. The evolutionary process is both

subtle and intriguing, and it is of fundamental relevance to an understanding of human behaviour. Let us put its salient points in a nutshell.

All life forms are built upon a genetic heritage which has been moulded over aeons by the need to adapt in order to survive against the odds in an ever changing environment. The anatomical, physiological and behavioural constructs which have emerged are seen at their most sophisticated in humans. All steps in the evolutionary process have been genetically cumulative, leaving attributes within us derived from each of our more primitive forebears.

The stringent challenges of competition, predation, a harsh environment and natural disasters require that the genetic code which constitutes the blueprint for a species' existence should itself be capable of change. The random mutations brought about by the sun's radiation and asexual cell division were too haphazard to produce adaptation in all but the most primitive life forms, and, at a time when the earth was populated entirely by unicellular organisms, evolution stumbled upon a way of amalgamating two disparate cells, then redividing them so that each possessed some of the other's genes. Whichever offspring cell then proved more adaptive would survive its changing circumstances (survival of the fittest).

A species is a population which can interbreed with the production of fertile offspring, and it constitutes a gene pool. The bigger the gene pool, the more versatile gene interplay and the production of advantaged variants is likely to be. A small human gene pool that has fewer than the global tribal average of 500 individuals causes inbreeding and the production of congenital abnormalities. Most species have behavioural taboos towards incest which prohibit procreation between near relatives. The older parents are when they conceive, the more mutations will have occurred through repeated cell division in their bodies, and the more defects will be present in their offspring. High mutation rates cause premature senility, and in humans this characteristically manifests itself as Alzheimer's and Parkinson's diseases, arthritis or cancer.

The process of culling which weeds out less fit organisms occurs at individual level (the runt of the litter has less chance of survival), at the level of the nuclear family (if parents die, offspring usually founder; if all offspring die there is no succession), at "herd" level (as when resources fail or an epidemic strikes), and at species level (extinction). Natural selection can take place gradually, when only the most disadvantaged perish or fail to procreate, or catastrophically when only the most advantaged survive.

It is of equal importance to the success and persistence of genes that they confer on their bearer both the ability to survive as an individual and the ability to raise offspring to the point of independence. Once they have raised their offspring to the point of independence parents become evolutionally redundant and, after an interval which varies between species, a pre-programmed senescence gene will bring about their death. If parents did not die they would be competing with their descendants for available resources. Many species which do not nurture their young die shortly after procreation. Death is a necessary mechanism for the further evolutionary development of a species, the third component of a life cycle whose others are regeneration and maturation.

The cyclical principle is well illustrated by the life history of the unicellular organism Paramecium. After 200 cloning subdivisions, this organism will die unless its senescence clock is reset by sexual conjugation. After conjugation the two offspring cells go through a preliminary period of maturation similar to prepubescence in animals, inasmuch as during this phase they cannot conjugate. Higher animals modified the conjugational process by evolving sexual differentiation between the conjugal cells and also between the animals producing them. Sexual genetic chromosomes are referred to as XY for male, and XX for female. Human lifespan is genetically determined. On average, randomly selected siblings die with an average 106 months of age difference, fraternal twins with 75 months average difference, and identical twins with 36 months average difference (CWR96p82). The longevity limiting chromosomal component is referred to as a telomere.

High fecundity rates (reproductive rates) enhance the chances of species survival and evolution, always provided that there are sufficient resources to support them. Species with single foetus pregnancies and infrequent sexual cycles are more prone to extinction. Biological processes tend to adjust fecundity to match the availability of resources, stimulating procreation when environmental conditions are favourable and depressing it in times of famine. Overdensity of population increases intraspecies and interspecies aggression and mortality.

The evolutionary mechanism and its outcome are influenced by mate selection. In many species the female decides who will fertilise her, and the male uses plumage, sexual dimorphism (the physical difference between the sexes) and courtship rituals to advertise. With variation between species, females will be attracted by size, power, agility, speed, versatility, intelligence, blazonry, armour, camouflage or weaponry - all attributes which will enhance species survival in a competitive world. In the human it is the female who is more likely to decorate. Unlike many other species, humans sexually pair bond, and the human female's prolonged phase of receptivity, together with the sensual rewards of human coitus which accrue to both parties, dynamize the selective process and reinforce the bond. In general, people are attracted towards those of their own socio-economic class, race and interests.

Racial Variation shows us that when subpopulations of a species become geographically segregated their subsequent evolutionary paths diverge. Basically, there are three broad racial categories of human - Caucasian, Mongoloid and Negroid. All human races have the same intellectual potential. The inherited physical differences of race are the result of environmental exposure - skin colour ultimately derives from climate, and build from nutritional status.

The genetic blueprint is not the sole determinant of eventual outcome in an individual. The 30-40 thousand protein coding genes present in man are vastly outnumbered by the 100 thousand billion cells of the adult human body and by the quadrillions of possible permutations of brain cell connections, so that whilst genes are responsible for overall structural and functional management, secondary influences must clearly be involved in the production of the final organic or behavioural entity. Anatomical and physiological biodevelopment, in which there is little room for latitude, employs the body's secretion of internal endocrine glands and contextual strophism (the developmental influence of adjacent tissues upon each other) as intermediaries between the gene and the finished product. Whereas the "housekeeping" brain's maintenance of vital functions, such as respiration and blood pressure, is genetically determined and hardwired, the "conditionable" brain's propensity is genetic but its final patterns of behaviour are moulded by environment and culture. (see also chapters 2 & 4).

The conclusion that we have a common heritage with other primates is inescapable, as demonstrated by shared anatomy, physiology and behavioural patterns, our shared embryological cadence, shared blood groups, the fossil record and, above all, the near 99% genetic correspondence which we have with the chimpanzee. Charles Darwin's penetrating insight into the evolutionary process was published in 1859 in his book "The Origin of Species by means of Natural Selection" following journeys aboard the Beagle in her voyage of exploration across the Southern seas.

Have Humans Ceased to Evolve?
With progressive refinement in investigatory techniques, it has become clear that almost no evolutionary modification has been made to man's anatomy and physiology since the stone age. We can also infer that

during this time no further behavioural evolution is likely to have occurred, since structure and function are always closely inter-related, and that such behavioural changes as have taken place are the result of cultural influence. Let us look at the evidence that evolution in man is now at a standstill, and at the ways in which man himself is now largely responsible for this state of affairs.

The first set of clues concerns adaptation to dietary change, or rather, the lack of it. Wild game and the stone age men who preyed on it were lean and physically fit, because each vied to outpace the other in the battle for survival. Our Palaeolithic ancestors are estimated to have been able to average a successful hunt, and the feast that followed it, once every two weeks, with supplementation coming from plant sources. By contrast, modern domesticated livestock share the same tendency to lay down excess fat and take too little exercise as the modern humans who feed on them. The deleterious effects of a hypersaturated fat diet (which causes cardiovascular disease and a range of cancers) and of the ingestion of red meat more frequently than twice weekly (which promotes the development of bowel cancer) show that in important respects humans have not yet evolved appropriate physiological adjustments to the introduction of agriculture which occurred 11 thousand years ago. For most of us the optimal balance of intake between fats, proteins and carbohydrates is the same today as it was then. The only race which can cope with high levels of saturated fat is that of the inuit who lives off seal blubber and fish and was bypassed by the domestication of plants and animals.

The only notable evolutionary change which has been shown to have occurred since farming began concerns the digestion of the sugar lactose. Analyses of 8 thousand year old skeletons reveal that humans of that time did not possess the enzyme lactase, without which the ingestion of cow's milk would have produced violent diarrhoea. The subsequent evolution of human lactase took place relatively rapidly, presumably spreading through families whose mothers had difficulty in breast feeding. Nowadays 90% of northern Europeans possess lactase, but 80% of southern Europeans do not (DMN:07:02:27).

What impact has civilisation had upon evolution? In highly significant ways modern man has taken control of his own destiny and, in so doing, has actively suppressed his own Darwinian progression. In the developed world medicine has already virtually eliminated most diseases of childhood and young adult life by using immunisation, antibiotics and hygienic procedures. (it is poverty which prevents these benefits from being extended world-wide). Medicine keeps alive those suffering from genetic errors which would otherwise kill them in the first decades of life. It is no longer only the fittest who survive.

Man now tampers with his own gene pool. Despite the fact that eugenic principles have temporarily fallen out of favour since they were abused by the Nazis, many married couples act responsibly by avoiding procreation if their offspring are liable to have serious heritable defects, and foetuses with recognisable genetic defects can be aborted in early pregnancy. Genetic variation is markedly limited when birth rates fall, as they do with birth control programmes. The more highly educated also tend to limit their families more than lower socio-economic groups, a policy which runs counter to evolution.

Man has homogenised his immediate environment instead of adapting to it and lives in boxes within which temperature, humidity, illumination and dust levels are strictly controlled . As he no longer exposes himself to low temperatures during childhood he loses the ability to adapt to them.

Man wages war in which the fittest do not survive. By creating a warrior class, the strongest and healthiest males are selectively destroyed. With the upgrading of weapons to those which produce mass destruction, young and old, male and female are culled indiscriminately. One in every fifty of the world's population perished during the second world war.

Will All Further Refinement Of Our Species Cease Without Evolution?

It may be argued that man's technological prowess has abolished the need for his further evolution. In any case, as a species we have already reached a developmental stage at which our anatomical and physiological equipment can, if used wisely, provide all the functions which a happy and fulfilling life requires. Given the standard of living which we in western societies now take for granted, happiness and life fulfilment are the products of the use of our own faculties and the quality of the relationships which we share with others. Only the malconditioned suffer from values and judgements which are disturbed in such a way as to make them seek deviant emotional rewards.

We now live in an era of biological engineering in which, for instance, human cell cultures can be used to regenerate defective organs, or infertile women are enabled to conceive. Genetic engineering in which eugenic embryo selection allows congenital abnormalities to be avoided, or which enables immunity against disease to be programmed in, are clearly beneficial. But further genetic manipulation which might modify the senescence gene to prolong life, or which might enhance physical, intellectual or emotional functionality, raise important and controversial ethical issues, since these changes would involve repersonalisation of the individual. The surgical procedure of brain lobotomy to treat depression rightly fell into disrepute when it was found to cause marked personality changes. The nub of the problem is to strike a balance between what technology can achieve and what else makes life worth while.

The progressive rise in living standards from which we continue to benefit is closely linked to technological advance. Other than this, improvements in human well being will depend upon our ability to solve outstanding sociological problems. It is misguided to expect science and engineering to make good the flaws in behavioural development which have plagued our species since late evolutionary and post evolutionary times.

Human behavioural dysfunction falls into two broad categories - defects which are primarily of an individual nature and those which are communal. Individual maladjustments are either due to malconditioning during immaturity, in which case they give rise to a wide range of personal delinquencies, or else are consequent upon sporadic genetic errors expressed as mental illness or the chronic malice syndrome. Communal maladjustments are also of two types - intercommunal warfare which is attributable to a genetic error endemic for the species, and vicissitudes which are the product of contentious sectarian ideology or the inept management of the industrial era. Further chapters in this book will examine all five of these issues, their root causes, manifestations and remedies.

Given enlightenment and equanimity, man could easily live in Utopia, enjoying peace, fulfilment and a happy social and family life. That he does not do so is nobody's fault but his own. All his problems, save those of disease and ecological crises, are of his own making, sins of commission and omission which can only be obviated by making changes to values, attitudes and conduct agreed as a norm by the global community. The first step is, of course, to enable Homo Sapiens Sapiens to understand himself as the product of biological and historical progression, and to recognise that he has been both led and misled by these two antecedents.

(Sources Reviewed :-BDM04, BV79, CSLL00, JS96, MD94 (a), NGMZ:03:10, NGMZ:04:02, WMLMAE78,)

CHAPTER 8

CONTROVERSY

BELLICOSITY, MASCULINITY AND THE POPULATION SQUEEZE

Antagonism and controversy are by definition repellent, but at no time throughout human history and prehistory have they been absent from our behavioural repertoire. Beginning as a dominance confrontation in a simian progenitor where they were attenuated by the herd bond, they became more fulminating and lethal during our Darwinian chimpanzee-like phase, setting the pattern for the vendettas and wars which still plague us. It is only during the last few centuries that attitudes of more rational proclivity have allowed controversy to be acted out verbally in such settings as Parliaments, law courts and television interviews. Language can even go the extra mile needed to resolve antagonism through compromise, a mutually beneficial end result denied to the simian dominance confrontation in which you either win or lose.

Aggressiveness is the inherent trait which catalyses controversy, and its barbs run throughout the human and pre-human story like a stretch of razor wire, but confrontation and conflict are much more likely to follow if this trait has been disinhibited by adverse nurture during immaturity, high testosterone levels or overcrowding.

Aggression

Because all forms of aggression are species specific and have an instinctive, evolutionary basis, the apparent paradox that Darwinism might produce a behavioural feature which most people would consider to be counter-productive posed a considerable problem for evolutionists. Philosophers, such as Friedrich Nietsche, suggested that the blood letting of combat was needed to refine the species and produce supermen, notwithstanding the fact that the net effect of most wars is to devastate, to impoverish and to increase the burden of human misery. The riddle was not made any easier to solve by the fact that for many years aggression was regarded as a single behavioural entity, which it is not. It can best be understood if we explore it in greater detail.

There are four quite distinct forms of aggression, and confusion between them arose because all four are accompanied by the adrenaline mediated response which is triggered by anger and antipathy, and which, as we saw in chapter 3, manifests as physiological changes designed to prepare the animal for conflict - hair erection, increased awareness and reactivity, increased blood flow to brain and skeletal muscle, sweating and panting. What distinguishes the four forms of aggression, however, is the context within which the adrenergic response is generated, the focus of its application, and the subsequent behavioural response.

Defensive Aggression is a manifestation of the first of the primate fundamental behavioural traits - the response to danger - in which, primed with both options, the urge to fight has eclipsed the urge to take flight. The "fight or flight" reflex is an automated survival mechanism common to all vertebrates (animals with backbones).

Dominance Aggression is a manifestation of the third of the primate fundamental traits. Here again the urge to fight has eclipsed the urge to take flight or to submit, but confrontation employs a form of aggression which is attenuated, and sometimes even ritualised, under the influence of the herd bond so as to avoid conspecific destruction. Confrontations have the purpose of creating a hierarchical command and control structure which defines the social and sexual status of the individual within the "herd". This is the adult form of the rebuff which the primate first learnt from its mother in infancy, and later from its fellow peer group members. Challenging encounters between two individuals, which specifically avoid the use of lethal weapons, lead to sparring for supremacy and the formation of a dominance-submission bond. Often a mere threat is sufficient to cause submission in the non-human primate, just as war dances, mass protests and solicitors' letters may do in human affairs. Dominance contests in human society may be overt as in social climbing, competitive career structures and marital disputes involving third parties. Alternatively, they may be ritualised as they are in sport, and most obviously so within the martial context of boxing, wrestling, fencing or jousting.

Just as the use of weaponry in a dominance challenge is attenuated, so also is the response to it. A subjugated chimpanzee may take to its heels, or may in turn project its difficulties by attacking a third animal which it knows it can dominate. Alternatively, it may hold its hand out in supplication to the more dominant animal in the hope of being patted or stroked in return, a gesture of compassionate reassurance which is often given, which reduces stress and which reinforces bonding between the two animals. Whipping boys and whipping posts were used as scapegoats in the middle ages upon which anger could thereby be vented and dissipated. Dominance ranking provides the underlying structure of the societal unit, thereby enhancing its survival and those of its members.

Offensive Aggression. Herbivores have no need to kill other species, and their aggression is limited to defence and dominance contests. Carnivores must kill other species to eat, and have modified their essentially subjective defensive aggression to reconfigure and remotivate it as an objective, provocative and premeditated attack strategy, necessarily accompanied by stereoscopic colour vision, pronged front teeth and fast mobility. The hunter's aggression is accentuated by hunger and must originally have developed as a natural progression from the consumption of insects common to early primates, probably doing so at a time when the energy requirements of some emergent species could not be obtained solely from vegetation.

The herd bond prevents overt offensive aggression between "herd" members because this would run counter to the evolution of the "herd", but if overall food supplies dwindle below subsistence levels, disputes arise between rival "herds" which may boil over as violent confrontation. Here the behaviour patterns normally seen in predation are refocused to target competitors, as the whole "herd", or a subset of it, is swept by a wave of anger triggered by contested resources. . In general, non-human primate "herds", whilst on trek for forage and other foods, sound each other out and avoid confrontation, but in lemurs and some monkeys, "herds" will engage in pitched battles if food is in critically short supply. In doing so, they demonstrate that the herd bond has much more powerful influence than the species bond.

Chimpanzees have many endearing qualities, but skinning and eating members of a rival "herd" cannot be said to be one of them. Groups of chimpanzee males do not wait for inter-herd disputes to arise over resources, but attack other chimpanzee groups for the pure thrill of risk taking and the prospect of the cannibalistic feast which will result. This is taking offensive aggression to its gratuitous and wanton extreme. Estimates put the overall mortality rate for male chimpanzees killed in battle at 30% and it may be even higher, since "herd" females often outnumber males by two to one, despite gender parity birth rates. Such carnage could hardly be described as having "herd" evolutionary survival value, nor could its selectivity be described as natural. The adrenaline rush of risk taking is what turns gamblers into addicts, and the counter-productive but instinct driven aggression of the chimpanzee foray appears to be an evolutionary blunder brought about by endocrinal chemical addiction acting on the brain's reward centre. It is interesting to speculate on the magnitude of male attrition rates which could realistically be sustained by a "herd" before the latter's functional integrity crumbles. Similar male attrition rates in human societies, such as the sicilian town of Corleone in the grip of the Mafioso vendetta, deplete the community of its breadwinners to such an extent that productivity and prosperity wither, children grow up fatherless and prejudiced, nobody feels safe to leave his house during daylight hours and social intercourse is paralysed.

Studies of human twins show that the willingness and desire to take risks is, to a large extent, genetically determined (BBCT1:09:10:03). The propensity for wanton conspecific destruction, which chimpanzees and humans share, point to its inheritance from a common ancestor. It was at this juncture in our evolution that paradise was lost, and the curse of war became embedded in our genes, a festering sore which will not heal until rationality and conditioning are used prophylactically to reorientate the race. Such a metamorphosis can only be brought about by totally impartial and pragmatic educational policies. When evolution falls short, man must take full responsibility for his own further development.

Chronic Malice. Whereas all chimpanzees and men are in thrall to the species specific endemic gene which prompts them to indulge in adrenaline fuelled war, there are a number of species in which the spasmodic occurrence of a rogue genetic anomaly in an individual may manifest as episodes of unpredictable, illogical, and gratuitous violence. This syndrome is only found in a small minority of animals. In chimpanzee communities it may be present in members of either sex, but in humans it is an almost entirely male phenomenon (BLGGW64p47), and amongst other bizarre atrocities accounts for the single killer's spree of irrational mass carnage. Chronic malice may be associated with other genetic defects such as general mental subnormality, epilepsy, and anatomical abnormalities in parts of the unconditionable brain (EEI96p81: see also chapter 15). There is a correlation between high levels of the hormone vasopressin and lifelong malicious aggression (RJJ01p334).

Why does aggressiveness in all its forms vary so much in intensity from one animal to another? Since the underlying propensity for aggression is highly species specific and genetically determined, the answer to this question must at least in part be an evolutionary one. The most obvious disparity is that which exists between the sexes of nearly all species, with the creation of contrasting roles which must clearly be of importance to survival. In defensive aggression it is more often the male who acts out in hostile self defence, whilst the female stands guard over the young. Dominance aggression promotes the perpetuation of the genes of stronger males. The offensive aggression characterised by hunting is predominantly a male pursuit whereby the female can be fed without distracting her from caring for the young. The offensive aggression of inter-herd warfare is, of course, only selectively advantageous for the evolution of the "herd" if the strongest males and their genes survive the onslaught in adequate numbers.

Offensive aggression has strong genetic links with predation, from which it derives. In common with other forms of aggression it is considerably influenced by testosterone secretion (see below), but not exclusively so. Spayed cats still hunt, lionesses do most of the killing, and rogue female chimpanzees have been observed to prey upon infants of other mothers.

Aggressiveness also varies with the individual and with age. In chimpanzees, whilst males are always much more aggressive than females, some animals of the same gender are by nature more aggressive than others, and adult males exhibit aggressiveness four and a half times as frequently as male adolescents. Male chimpanzees show a sharp rise in testosterone levels between the ages of 7 and 9 years, when they become more provocative and bellicose and acquire a taste for flinging stones around, and slapping, punching, scratching, biting, kicking and wrestling with other herd members. This change to a more aggressive form of behaviour prepares them for their adult roles in hunting and venturing into new territory for forage, where they will encounter competition and danger (GJ90p95).

In lower mammals, aggression is almost entirely hardwired. Differing strains of mice are either inherently peaceful or aggressive, and offspring of aggressive mothers who are given to peaceful mothers for rearing still grow up to be aggressive (EEI96p66). By contrast, primate offensive aggression is open to considerable cultural influence and conditioning. If a monkey from an aggressive species is fostered by a "herd" of a tranquil species it will adapt to the latter's style of behaviour (WR02p240)). It is possible to trigger offensive aggression by implanting an electrode in a monkey's brain (DP72p282). In humans the offensive aggression trait is, to a large extent, culturally conditionable (EEI96p71). Freud observed that conditioning during immaturity played an important part in the development of aggression, and that children who had been persistently thwarted during their development became aggressive adults (FS91p7). On the other hand, children who are overindulged by their parents become aggressively antisocial in later life (see also conditioning, chapter 4).

Although there is no human need or motive that cannot be gratified by means other than violence (BLGGW64p406), warfare has been reported for societies at all levels of man's cultural evolution. Two in seven adult male hunter-gatherers in Australia, and one in four adult male horticulturalists of New Guinea and Venezuela die in warfare (BV79p313). Nomads frequently tend to be warlike. In unstructured societies without law enforcement Mosaic revenge is the only form of redress, and it doubles the death rate. Pueblo Indians only fight in defence, the Lepehas of Sikkim always submit to invaders, but the Sioux and Maori view warfare as desirable and fulfilling. (BLGGW64p261). The Balinese register their quarrel with the gods and place offerings in the temple to dissipate their antagonism. Among the Arapesh of New Guinea the aggressor is taken away, held fast, but allowed to stamp, scream, throw stones, and roll in the dust until his anger passes (EEI96p77).

In tribal and hunter-gatherer societies the most successful group members in terms of wealth, status and number of children are often those who engage in most violence against others within and without the group (WR02p223).Peer group "yob" culture, racial prejudice, warped values in the entertainment industry, jingoism and the inflammatory preaching of theocratic or nationalistic leaders exert a profound effect upon the intellectually immature mind and have a great deal to answer for. Humans alone are able to overcome, by conscious choice, the dictates of their biological natures, yet only humans inflict suffering for its own sake, and enjoy doing do (GJ90p180). The way in which adverse nurture during immaturity influences aggressiveness can be clearly identified by examining the life histories of those who exhibited it to an extreme degree. One of the clearest examples was Genghis Kahn.

The Triumphant Desperado
In 2003, a Ph.D. student working on the distribution of DNA components throughout Eurasia made the surprising discovery that a distinctive form of the Y male chromosome was carried by one in every 200 men on earth. Tracing this back through time and space it was possible to pinpoint the common ancestor as having been a 12th century Mongolian (ZT03). It seemed that the originator of this gene must not only have been unusually virile, but able to disseminate it over a vast expanse of territory. The dating corresponded with the expansionist incursions of the Mongols under Genghis Khan (1162-1228) whose extraordinary successes on the battlefield were duly matched by a ravenous sexual appetite.

Despite their measured political correctness, the chronicles of near contemporaries tell us enough of Genghis to understand his character and background. The grass and scrub of the raised steppe plateau and mountains of Mongolia could not support agriculture, and were inhabited by nomadic tribes whose dependence on sheep, goats, horses, yak and camel forced them to itinerate in a constant search for fodder. Seasonal weather variations were extreme, and unless animals had been sufficiently fattened during summer they would not live through the winter snows. Humans had to augment their own diet of milk and butchered domestic meat by hunting, which meant that accurate archery was critical to survival. Hides and furs were traded beyond the steppe for the iron required to make weapons.

The constant battle for existence against the forces of nature was compounded by interminable inter-tribal warfare and banditry. Trust was a very rare commodity, vested solely, if at all, in those of immediate kinship. Tribes preyed upon each other with relentless savagery and treachery. Allegiances shifted like weather vanes in the direction which appeared to serve the tribal leader's immediate best interest, and predatory alliances were built on the basis that coveted pickings looked rich enough, measured in terms of horses, herds, flocks, and women and children whose men folk had first to be annihilated. Captive boys were beheaded if they were taller than the linchpin of a wagon wheel.

The knife edge upon which life was lived inevitably moulded Genghis' character. When he was nine his father was poisoned by Tatar enemies, and at eleven he murdered his half brother during a petty quarrel. Under the harshest conditions of deprivation and humiliation which his father's death brought upon the family, he developed a fierce sense of self reliance, becoming an unerring judge of his fellow men, able to recognise at once those upon whom he could rely, those he should distrust, and those he needed to destroy. Tribesmen who threw in their lot with him saw in him an iron will, a ruthless determination and a flair for leadership.

Having proved that he could succeed in mounted skirmishes against other tribes on the steppe, Genghis incited them all to unite and plunder further afield under his leadership. Gradually he turned nomadic rabble into disciplined cavalry units whose phenomenal accuracy in using short bows from the saddle, whilst themselves posing a moving target, made them invincible. Many submitted to him without a fight, but those who did not could expect to be obliterated. In dealing with a revolt in China's West Hsia province he established the precedent of genocide, leaving none alive, a fate shared by the inhabitants of any walled city who had the temerity to shut their gates on him. In his own words he defined happiness as being vested in "the conquest of one's enemies, in driving them in front of oneself, in taking their property, in savouring their despair, in outraging their wives and daughters" (JAAM97). His "Golden Hordes" swept across China, Tibet, Russia, the Middle East, and much of India and Eastern Europe, only turning back from the gates of Vienna in 1242 when disputes over the succession forced leading contenders to return to their homeland after the deaths of Genghis and his son.

The dog eat dog philosophy which Genghis had learnt as a child was directed against whole nations as he attempted to slake his unquenchable thirst for domination, possession and sexuality. Always he had the pick of the hundreds of captive women brought to his tent for their beauty. He had a predilection for virgins, and having verified the status of one, ravished her on a tiger skin in his tent to the acclaim of his assembled retinue. The Novgorodians paid him an annual tithe in young girls in order to avoid the sacking of their city. His blood brother, with whom he had once shared a bed for thirteen months, reproached him for being too fond of the fair sex.

It may well be Genghis' gene that so many men now share, but what else has he left us? The era of Mongol rule in China was entitled "Yuan", a name still given to the Chinese currency unit. Other than this, his net achievement was to refine and exploit the skills of the mounted archer, and these vanished with the demise of his dynasty. A huge Mongolian armada intended for Japan was sunk by a typhoon which subsequently became dubbed the "divine wind", the original meaning of the word Kamikaze. Mongolian hegemony lasted less than a century, and has been described as a disastrous, unmitigated and retrogressive curse (BP76).

With hindsight we now know that the 12th century Mongolian Y chromosome mutation produced no evolutionary advancement whatsoever. In stark contrast with Genghis' failure to contribute to civilisation, empires such as those of ancient Egypt, Greece and Rome were all at the forefront of man's post evolutionary development. By ironic coincidence, a totally unrelated form of genetic accident affecting chromosome 21 produces mentally subnormal children who have a distinctive Mongol-like appearance, those suffering from Down's syndrome.

Had the Mongolian regime not imploded politically, it might well have completed its conquest of Eurasia, with dire consequences for civilised humanity. Genghis' taste for dominance, barbarity and rapine was clearly the result of his desperado upbringing. Any behavioural trait which has the potential to wreak havoc on this scale needs to be more fully understood than it usually is.

What Else Makes Aggression Boil Over?

The prevalence and outcome of offensive aggression in humans has always been influenced by the availability of weapons. Hunter-gatherer mortality must have increased significantly with the advent of the arrow, the spear and the slingshot. In Britain during the middle ages violent crime plummeted when short swords were banned (JS96p213). Britain nowadays convicts about 500 perpetrators of homicide per annum, but, until recently, deaths from gun crime in the USA per head of population were ten times as high as they were in Europe as a direct result of more liberal gun laws. In the UK, during the early years of the 21st century, there was an increase in the carriage of knives and consequent knife attacks which also spread to school children. Whereas most civilisations have iconified the warrior, his accoutrements and emblems, his traditions, ethos, and triumphalism, Switzerland has invested in neutrality for centuries, although it has to be said that during Hitler's rampages throughout Europe the fact that most Swiss spoke German and that the Swiss army adopted the German uniform did not go unnoticed.

Human aggression is always aggravated by intoxicants. In the 20th century 67% of cases of violent crime in America, and 33% of cases in Europe were associated with drunkenness. The action of recreational drugs on the brain seldom provokes violence in itself, but the addictive craving for these substances is now the predominant cause of crime in the developed world (see also chapter 15).

Testosterone
Testosterone's primary role is to induce masculinity and its secondary role is to accentuate aggression in all its forms. We need to look at these two roles in order to understand the relationship between them. Testosterone is the principal male hormone and is secreted by the testis under the control of the pituitary gland. Human male hormones, identifiable in boys from the age of 6 years onwards, rise to adult levels by puberty, peak between the ages of 18 and 25, and then diminish slowly with age (HAMZ02:09, STN:06:04:02). Testosterone increases bone and muscle mass, vitality, optimism, and physical and mental stamina, it promotes libido, erection, and ejaculation, it is the determinant for penile size, and it is responsible for the appearance of the secondary sexual characteristics - facial and body hair, vocal pitch, and bodily size and shape. Sexual dimorphism - the marked difference in bodily configuration between the two genders - is greatest in harem-organised species in which it is an adjuvant to dominant male sexual supremacy, singling out the best physical genes in the "herd" for evolutionary advantage.

The link between testosterone and aggression is easily proven in all its forms and in most species. Juvenile primate and rat males show more overall aggression than females - a finding which can be corroborated by administering testosterone to the latter (DV97p256, DP72p282) ; in many male vertebrates aggressive readiness fluctuates with the level of testosterone in the yearly breeding cycle - for example tame male squirrels become aggressive in the spring (EEI96p70) ; data taken from 101 different types of human society found that boys were invariably more aggressive than girls, although the levels varied with the influence of socio-cultural conditions (RRP76p457).

With regard to defensive aggression, some fish are aggressively territorial during the breeding season, but shoal at other times (LK66p126). When testosterone is administered to male voles it makes them aggressive towards outsiders, but friendly and nurturing towards their own pups (RJJ01p334). Bulls and domestic pets which have been castrated lose most of their defensive ferocity, though carnivores continue to hunt.

Dominance aggression, which is unnatural in young turkeys can be artificially stimulated by injecting them with testosterone (EEI96p70). Higher dominance monkeys have higher testosterone levels than lower ranking animals (EEI96p164), and ground living monkey males have higher testosterone levels when they have been fighting (DV97p256). In Hamadryas baboons aggression between adult males is only seen in relation to the sex drive. If a sufficient number of receptive females is available, then fighting does not occur (HKRC63p4).

The human emotional brain matures at puberty, but the intellectual brain does not do so until the later age of 25. Between these milestones the level of testosterone has reached its apogee, but its action on the emotional brain is as yet unrestrained by a mature intellect, and both waywardness and offensive aggression peak. Petty crime, joyriding, vandalism, graffiti, football hooliganism, rioting and irresponsible sexuality result. As puberty starts at a progressively earlier age in developed societies, so does violent crime (HC03p436), the latter being perpetrated almost exclusively by males. Body builders who take anabolic steroids may be subject to fits of "steroid rage". Recruitment for the armed forces always targets the 18-20 year age group, and women are seldom sent to the front line. Testosterone is an important determinant of hunting behaviour in most, but not all species. In hunter-gatherer communities men do the hunting and women the gathering. Game shooting, angling, bullfighting and poaching are primarily and predominantly male prerogatives.

By now, our review of the evidence has shown us that defensive, dominance and offensive aggression all have survival value, and that non-human primate males are more aggressive than females because this disparity supports a differentiation of respective roles in offspring protection, genetic selection and hunting. On the other hand, the cannibalistic forays of the chimpanzee would appear to buck the evolutionary trend by offering no selective advantage, and even, very possibly, proving counter-productive as is the human male Mafia vendetta. War as we understand it took over from chimpanzee-like forays of our precursors with the introduction of weapons.

Population Density, Resources and Aggression

Whereas many animal species occupy and defend home territories with fixed boundaries, most primates forage in transit across a fairly wide home range which may overlap with the ranges of other conspecific "herds". Because they are foraging for the same diet, clashes between conspecific "herds" are always possible, but are usually avoided by a system of vocalisations which warn one "herd" of the other's presence in the vicinity. Where foraging areas are shared with other species foraging different diets there is, of course, no conflict of interest, and peaceful co-existence is the rule.

Within the typical foraging primate "herd", members spread themselves out to make optimal use of the vegetation which is available. Each animal is defensively possessive of an immediate space around itself, the size of which is dictated by what it can reach and consume on the spot, whilst still keeping close contact with its neighbours for conjoined security, and this personal space is the determinant of overall population density. (Humans boarding a half empty train, or using a multi-male urinal allocate themselves space in much the same way). Personal space apportionment in animals incorporates another factor. Social encounters between individuals are either synergistic or agonistic, and personal space allows time for encounter signs to be read before a possible physical dominance challenge is launched.

The balance between overall population density and available resources is so critical to "herd" and species survival that drastic hardwired mechanisms are embedded in the animal brain to prevent overpopulation. These mechanisms act both by intensifying aggression, with consequent destruction of individuals, or even whole "herds", and by depressing reproduction. In laboratory mice, overcrowding delays or inhibits sexual maturation, even when food, water and shelter are adequate, it reduces sperm formation, produces smaller testes, retards ovulation, prolongs the reproductive cycle, and depresses lactation. Overcrowded offspring are stunted despite adequate maternal food supplies, adult aggression is increased, cannibalisation of young occurs, and mothers desert (WMLMAE78p458). In most experimental animals, when overcrowding reaches a critical point at which social architecture disintegrates, animals fight viciously, kill their young, mutilate themselves, become infertile and develop disease. After many deaths the overpopulation is reduced and normality slowly resumes (MD94(a)p67).

If the population density of tree shrews in the wild exceeds an optimum, the animals become irritable towards each other and hormonal changes occur which cause the animals' demise. The scent glands of females, normally used to mark their young and which prevents them from being eaten by conspecifics, cease to function, as do the mammary glands and gonads (HDV69p1). Rat reproduction stops automatically when a certain state of overcrowding is reached (LK66p204). Rhesus monkeys confined in close quarters become aggressive (RT72p82), even in the presence of adequate food supplies.

In human child institutions an increase in population density increases aggression. The human "herd" architecture and bonding -

seen typically in village life with the use of forenames, mutual support and communal conviviality - is revoked in urban communities where personal tactile and verbal contact is usually studiously avoided, and each individual strives to preserve as much surrounding space as the situation allows. The impersonality and anonymity of urban life disinhibit possessiveness and offensive aggression, which are further fuelled by boredom and the abuse of drugs.

Just as overpopulation and contraction of personal space cause antagonism, so does competition for scarce resources. Both contingencies act independently as disinhibitors for the attenuation normally applied to offensive aggression within the "herd" by herd bondage. The lower primates only fight over food supplies when these are in critically short supply, which for them is seldom the case. Man, by contrast, competes for, and frequently contests, all his natural resources - land, water and food supplies, and oil.

What is to be the effect of ever increasing global population density on human aggression? Some cultures cope with overpopulation better than others. The Japanese have twice the population density of the UK, yet their crime rate is amongst the lowest in the world. The global population has increased tenfold since the mid 18th century and is projected to reach 9.2 billion by the year 2050 (SJ07RL3). Inevitably we are moving towards a situation in which the demand for living space, coupled with rising sea levels and desertification if these are brought about by global warming, threaten to leave us with insufficient arable land upon which to grow the cereal foods on which life depends. Pressures on food, water and health care provision, all of which are interdependent, will then become uncontainable (CSVL00p93, BV79p427). Already over one billion people in the world suffer from extreme malnutrition. As Thomas Malthus suggested two centuries ago, the justification for birth control is incontrovertible. It is no longer acceptable to rely on wars, epidemics, and famines to control the size of human populations.

(Sources reviewed: BBCT1:09, BLGGW64, BP76, BV79, CSVL00, DP72, EEI96, FS91, GJ90, HC03, HDV69, HKRC63, JAAM97, LK66, MD94(a), RJJ01, RT72, SJ07, WMLMAE78, WR02, ZT03)

CHAPTER 9

ONE MAN'S MEAT

DIETARY BEHAVIOUR AND THE CARNIVOROUS INSTINCT

When production companies or farmers find that the markets for their goods are shrinking, they diversify in order to stay in business. Throughout his Darwinian development it has been the adaptability and versatility of man's behavioural patterns which have enabled his species to survive against all odds, and eventually to dominate the planet. The evolutionary pathway of his diet illustrates one aspect of this adaptability, his remote prehistoric ancestors having at different times consumed insects, plants, other animals, and their fellow beings, or a combination of all of these.

Vegetation in the wild provides low energy food, and herbivores must compensate for this by finding bulk sources and spending most of their time feeding. The bigger the animal, the more the waking hours which must be devoted to grazing. The extinct woolly mammoth is estimated to have spent 16 hours a day filling its belly, and the giant panda spends 14 hours of the 24 chewing bamboo shoots (BBCT1:04:11:30). By contrast, lions can subsist on one kill every 8 days. By eating herbivores, carnivores hijack the energy rich substances which their prey have assiduously accumulated in their tissues over time. Of course, an animal that can eat any and every type of food inevitably has a better chance of survival. Bears, badgers, some baboons, chimpanzees and humans are all omnivorous.

There is a close association between the anatomy of an animal and its diet, because the evolution of its body must respond to the manner in which it obtains its food. The gastronomic repertoire of primates, like the evolution of their bodies, has been summative. As they added new categories of food to their diet, so digestive, metabolic and anatomical changes developed, with particular emphasis on the functionality of locomotion. The early primates, which first appeared 80-50 million years ago, were insectivores, obtaining their prey from the ground or low bushes. The earliest monkeys added fruit and nuts to their staple 35-25 million years ago and developed both brachiating arms to swing from the branches and tails to help them balance. 5 million years ago apes added roots, bulbs, ground based nestlings and eggs, then, later, small animals to their diet. Some, such as the chimpanzee, formed small hunting groups and were not averse to cannibalising other groups of the same species. The ape's need to retain brachiation for arborealism, but also to adapt to a partially terrestrial existence, led to the development of walking on two legs with balance and weight bearing being augmented by knuckles and disproportionately long arms.

Two and a half million years ago, with forestation decreasing, protohuman existence dispensed with tree living and knuckle support altogether (NGMZ:92:03), standing, walking, and running with increased speed to catch small animals, and scavenging on what was left of the kill of big cats (JP99p29). Bones of animals eaten by early man sometimes show the gouge marks made by big cat teeth overscored with the human butchery marks etched by sharp stones (WR02p43). It was at this time that the hunter-gatherer dietary intake ratios, based on contemporary availability, of one third vegetable and fruit, one third starch, and one third protein and fat, became established as a norm to which protoman's metabolism adjusted by evolutionary processes. With the exception of lactose digestion, there would seem to have been no further evolutionary modification of man's metabolism since those early days, a fact which explains why this balance of dietary ingredients still proves optimal today.

The great apes spend their waking hours foraging for food, and early hunter-gathering protoman must also have done so. If he was to make time for other activities he needed to find ever more energy rich sources of food in the form of larger animals. Even with better organisation and the use of bone and stone weapons rather than mere wood, a kill could only be expected approximately twice a month, and meat had to be partially augmented by food from vegetarian sources. Animal long bones were smashed so that marrow could be extracted, and decapitation allowed brain extraction from the underside of the skull. Meat was preserved either by drying it in the sun or, if the latitude permitted, by freezing. The complex team work involved in scouting out prey, developing strategies of attack, moving in for the kill, and butchering, preserving, storing, and rationing meat called for the formation of larger, better disciplined and expertly led social units. As we have already seen, this societal upgrade was the principal determinant which led to the development of a larger brain. No longer shackled by the need for day long foraging, and with greatly increased thought processing capacity, this larger brain could now turn its attention to intellectual activities such as the development of rationality, organisational expertise, and innovation.

Protoman evolved in East Africa, but between 1.5 millions and 300 thousand years ago spread across Africa, Asia and Europe. Mass slaughter of migrating herds of mammoth and giant baboons took place. Kitchen middens dated to 500 thousand years ago show bones from a diet which included horse, bison, rhinoceros, deer, bear, sheep, mammoth, camel, ostrich, antelope and hyena (MD94(a)p4).As did his ape like forbears, protoman killed and ate his conspecifics to augment his diet. Discoveries of protohuman skulls in association with food debris have been found in very early sites in China and South Africa (BV79p247 and EEI96p98) which show clear evidence of damage to their thinner under surface, damage which could only have been inflicted after decapitation, and which allowed cannibalisation of brain matter. Protoman's earliest stone weapon was the shaftless hand axe, a piece of rock knapped into the shape of an axe head whose utility was such that its design persisted unchanged for many thousands of years. With it, its owner could chop wood, hunt or murder. From then on, and with the further development of weaponry, interherd warfare, and the cannibalisation which followed and which often prompted it, became institutionalised.

Our brief review of our prehistoric timeline has shown us that we have been carnivorous predators since our earliest primate days, and our DNA shows that our more definitive dietary instincts must have been laid down during our ape-like phase of evolution. We did not follow a similar developmental line to that of the gorilla who is a vegetarian, but that of the chimpanzee who eats both animals and vegetation. When as hunter gatherers we could not obtain enough calories from seasonal fruits, berries, and wild grass seed, meat eating was not only an option but became an evolutionary, and thereby instinctual, necessity. Isotope analysis carried out on a 30 thousand year old human jawbone showed that its owner had been just as carnivorous as contemporary wolves and bears (WR02p49).

Man Starts To Take Charge Of His Environment
Eleven thousand years ago, as the subzero rigours of the last ice age receded polewards leaving the planet more temperate and hospitable, man began to take over active management of his immediate environment. Agriculture and animal domestication now not only provided him with dependable and continuous supplies of food, but brought about fundamental changes in his dietary patterns. The ability to cultivate cereals with much improved yields meant that he could, from now on, use them as the paramount source of staple which they remain today, with the most suitable crops proving to be barley, oats, rye and wheat in Europe and North Asia, rice in Southern Asia, and maize in Mesoamerica. These cereals were augmented by fruit,

102

vegetables, cheese and fish according to availability, but the premium now placed on red meat effectively put it beyond reach of most commoners. As slave based civilisations emerged, wide social disparities enabled the privileged few to indulge in ostentatious dietary diversification which reached its apogee in Ancient Rome. Columbus' discovery of the New World set in train an exchange of plants, animals, culture, slavery and communicable disease between America and Europe which disseminated the potato, tomato, maize and tobacco eastwards, and the chicken, goose, cow, pig, sheep, many fruits and cereals, rice and coffee westwards. In the modern era dietary diversification has continued, with culinary cultures being shared worldwide.

No less than 80% of global calorific requirements are provided for by grain, yet its levels of cultivation are never constant, and its supply is now coming under increasing pressure. The availability of fertile agricultural land is being reduced by factors such as soil degradation from over use and desertification caused by climate change, whilst demand for cereals burgeons because of their use in bio fuel production and the need to feed an ever increasing world population. Soil degradation is worst in Africa where, in 2007, 40% of the continent's agricultural land had become barren and where, by 2025 if trends continue, a mere 25% of Africans will be able to subsist on regional produce (UNU07). The impending crisis will be exacerbated by any further fall in water tables which are already known to be taking place in China, India, the USA, Mexico, Iran and Pakistan, and by the disproportionate increase in population which is forecast for several of these countries. Until now, human fecundity has always burgeoned in response to more prolific production of food. In the year 500 CE the world population is estimated to have been 200 million, rising to one billion by the early 1800's, and six billion by 1990. Clearly we are approaching a point at which our successors would suffer escalating levels of starvation if they did not implement effective methods of birth control.

The failure of our stone age bodies to adapt to the agricultural revolution has left us with health problems. Dental caries, which had only occurred briefly in protoman 200 thousand years ago, returned with a vengeance when agriculture arrived (JP99p59), possibly aggravated by the rock dust created by milling. Whereas wild game has only a 4% adipose content, the relative physical inactivity of domestic cattle means that they have a 25-30% fat bulk, consisting largely of saturates (WR02p52), and this fatty overload is passed on in his diet to the modern consumer who is usually equally inactive. Human fat storage, originally intended to tide the hunter over between kills, is now laid down as excess deposits, not only in the internal tissues and beneath the skin, but also in the lining of the arteries, contributing to their blockage. Between a quarter and a third of US citizens are clinically obese, and a further fifth are overweight. 70% of modern cardiovascular disease is directly related to obesity, as is much diabetes and several forms of cancer.

The damaging effects of a high animal fat diet and inadequate physical exercise (the average westerner watches television for 14-28 hours per week) are compounded by modern man's encapsulation in a thermally homogenised environment in which his metabolism no longer has to increase in response to a fall in ambient temperature. Brown fat cells, located at the back of the neck and chest, whose function is to create extra heat in response to chilling, atrophy in adolescence if not stimulated. Hunter-gathering involved everyone in taking exercise and, in the case of men, vigorous exercise. Nowadays, since industrialisation and mechanisation have enabled food to be mass produced, a mere 5% of the population is engaged in supplying it, and the remainder access it by travelling in their car to the supermarket.

We can assume that since there have been no evolutionary changes to man's anatomy nor physiology since the introduction of agriculture, then likewise there has been no fundamental modification of his carnivorous and hunting instincts. These can, of course, be culturally suppressed as cannibalism has, but are, like cannibalism, capable of being disinhibited by hunger. The adjustment man required to switch his predominant staple from meat to cereal 11 thousand years ago was therefore made possible by his versatility as an omnivore, and not by an instinctual expunction.

Our metabolism as omnivores does not oblige us to partake of all the foods the supermarket has to offer, even though evolution has put us in a position to do so, but this versatility comes at a price which animals that have a much narrower dietary spectrum do not have to pay. Preservation of good health requires that we should always retain sufficient variety in our intake of food to guarantee that a number of vital constituents are included. Although cultivated grain provides most of the world's calorific intake, our tissue construction and our biochemistry require proteins, eight components of which are amino acids that cannot be synthesized by the body, and will always have to be obtained from our diet. Some fat must also be eaten in order to provide critical fatty acids, and although a few fats and proteins are present in plants, meat provides a very much richer source of both (WMLMAE78p342). Vitamin and trace element deprivation manifest as conditions such as scurvy, rickets, pellagra, beri-beri, anaemia, goitre and eye degeneration, all now rarities in the developed world thanks to improved education, but still, like general malnourishment, observable elsewhere. Vegans have to take great care in planning their diets, and are advised to use supplemental vitamins, minerals and protein in order to meet the demands of a metabolism inherited from prehistory. Many more women than men become vegetarians and vegans, a preponderance which may be due either to a strong element of protective maternalism, to a low level of hunt motivating testosterone, or both.

Hunting
Baboons hunt singly, and hunting is both instinctive and cooperative in chimpanzees, so that given our evolutionary pathway and our omnivorousness, hunting must be presumed to have an instinctive basis

in humans. Bipedality, which freed the use of man's hands in the hunt, allowed him to use weapons more effectively. Initially short jabbing spears were used, and groups of as many as forty or fifty could be assembled for the attack, but when projectile weaponry was subsequently developed by emergent Homo Sapiens it proved to be much more effective, and gave the new species a competitive edge over its rivals the Neanderthals - a factor which may have contributed to the latter's demise. All human races hunt, shoot and fish, and they have trained dogs, ferrets, hawks and cormorants to assist them. The bow and arrow, firearm, trap, snare, net and line are all integral features of a developing culture. Until the introduction of agriculture, hunting was an inevitably necessary occupation for protoman as carnivore. Nowadays his latent flair for predation is more often expressed through the pleasure he derives from sports and pastimes involving pursuit and the use of projectiles.

Modern Regional Variations in Diet

A few isolated communities have been bypassed by the agricultural revolution as we know it, and continue to subsist on food intake which predated it, and to which their metabolism must, presumably, already have adapted. Eskimos live entirely on seal and fish, and have evolved a cold adaptive metabolism boosted by the supplemental heat production of brown fat cells in their bodies, which enables them to cope with an almost 90% fat intake. Desert nomads exist almost entirely on sheep, goat, and camel milk and flesh. By contrast the Maya have, for many centuries until very recently, subsisted on a diet confined almost entirely to beans, maize, squashes, chillies and the occasional small wild animal. The most significant regional variation in diet is, of course, the disparity which exists between rich and poor countries. Westerners tend to overeat, sourcing their food from the four corners of the earth and throwing away one third of it, whilst one billion of the global population struggles to exist, at or below starvation level.

(Sources Reviewed: BBCT1:07:11:04, BV79, DJ98, EEI96, JP99, MD94(a), NGMZ:09:02, UNU07, WMLMAE78, WR02)

CHAPTER 10

"LIKE A WOMAN WHO CARESSES AND DECEIVES"
(Charles Baudelaire, Describing The Effects Of Opium)

DISRUPTION OF BONDING WITH REFOCUS ONTO "RECREATIONAL" DRUGS

The enigma of human evil has always been at the hub of dramatic tragedy. The ancient Greeks staged lengthy, gut wrenching plays, attracting huge audiences who knew they were about to be shocked into moral rectitude by the cathartic effects of the scenes displayed before them. Shakespeare plumbed the depths of every form of human depravity in order to galvanise his audience, from the blood dripping murders of his greatest tragedies and the invidious tyranny of Richard the Third to Shylock's unspeakable avarice, whilst King Lear's two eldest daughters callously drove him mad by rejecting the bond of affection they owed him. Falstaff's delinquency was merely derided, but the full horror of the sexual atrocity meted out to Titus Andronicus' daughter leaves nothing to the imagination when we are told that she is first raped, and then has her tongue and both hands cut away. It is no coincidence that the bard pinpointed the main distortions of personality which we now recognise as having resulted from malconditioning of any of the seven fundamental primate patterns, or from the genetic fault which codes for gratuitous aggression..

Since the dawn of self consciousness, Homo Sapiens Sapiens has struggled to come to terms with the curse of his own evil streak. In order to maintain order and harmony within communities, enlightened rulers have always tried to stamp out human depravity in all its many forms, initially engraving codes of laws on tablets of stone which were displayed in temples so that all might see them and know that they disobeyed them at their peril. The earliest of these inscribed protocols seems to have been one drafted in the Sumerian cuneiform language by Lipit Ishtar, the autarch of Isin, seventy six years before the better known diorite inscriptions of the Babylonian potentate Hammurabi. Owing to its biblical references, the most renowned ancient code it that of Moses, known as the ten commandments and dated to 1300 BCE, although in reality a total of 613 rules for Hebrew conduct is known to have existed. The notorious Athenian lawgiver Draco drew up his codes in 621 BCE, in default of which any transgressor paid with his life. An excellent example of a Dorian law code is still to be seen at Gortyn in Crete, dated to the fifth century BCE.

Whilst perpetrators of acts of delinquency and depravity can be punished in the hope that this will discourage further offence on the part of the culprit or others, it frequently fails to do so. These problems can only be prevented by fully understanding and expunging their root causes, a challenge to which we must all respond in our roles as parents, educators, local authorities, politicians or global citizens. As a preliminary step in analysis it is useful to break down the causes of all human behavioural aberration into five broad but discrete categories - early phase nurtural malconditioning which may distort any of the fundamental primate behavioural traits; late phase nurtural malconditioning which creates compulsive prejudice; the endemic genetic defect which we share with the chimpanzee and which prompts interherd war; the sporadic genetic defects which cause mental illness and chronic malice; and naked human ineptitude (see also chapter 5). This chapter and the nine which follow will examine the problems derived from the first of these categories, supported as necessary by their underlying historical evidence, and later chapters will explore all other causalities and their outcomes.

The seven fundamental behavioural traits of primates are each inherited as a propensity which has to be elaborated and refined by interaction with the environment during the first and second phases of human nurture. Malconditioning during these critical periods results in permanent deformation of the persona. As an overview, these detrimental effects can be summarised as follows:-

Lack of security during early immaturity leads to subsequent over reaction, such as panic or rampage, in response to potential danger.

Thwarted or dislocated bonding leads to substance or gambling addiction, over eating, fetishism or overdependence.

Compulsively aggravated possessiveness results in extreme avarice, hoarding and repetitive theft.

Tyranny and slavery are opposite sides of the same coin of distorted dominance ranking which, in its less extreme form manifests as bullying and self effacing inhibition.

Dislocated socialisation results in delinquency and other forms of antisocial behaviour.

Unhinged sexuality manifests as a wide variety of perversions and sexual atrocities or, conversely as frigidity.

The hunter-carnivore instinct is susceptible to considerable positive or negative cultural influences during immaturity.

The damaging impact of malconditioning on human post-Darwinian development has been profoundly counter-productive. It can be followed throughout the historical record and is strictly relevant to behavioural study. Let us begin by examining an aberration which has brought degradation to countless individuals, which causes so much heartache to their loved ones, and which is highly corrosive in terms of the damage it inflicts on society at large.

Distortion of the Bonding Cadence and the use of Artificial Bond Substitutes

Long term memory, automated behaviour patterns and bonding are all functions of the conditionable brain. Bonding is a fundamental instinct which has evolved to structure and integrate interpersonal relationships within the context of the family group, the peer group and the "herd". Its propensity is hardwired, and its normal development depends upon an emotional rapport which links, first, infant to parent, then playpeer to playpeer, and subsequently "herd" member to "herd" member during adulthood. If this cadence of sequential bond development is balked or dislocated, the individual feels rejected, undervalued and isolated, and substitution usually fills the emotional void. Pets, deities, dummies, dildos, drugs and a host of other artifices become bond substitute icons upon which the conditionable brain fetishtically refocuses, but since these substitutes cannot reciprocate the relationship as another human being would, the response is a contrived one.

Because of their direct molecular action on the brain, the use of addictive chemicals as bond substitutes is particularly invidious. The enslavement they produce is akin to that of the bonding which exists between human lovers who crave each others' company, are fulfilled by it, are habituated by it, and suffer psychologically if deprived of it. But the chemical psychotrophic bond is much stronger than any human bond. Tempting its user with promises of narcosis, hallucination or hyper excitation as substitutes for reality, the drug habituates, often with the first dose, and, like the cuckoo, displaces other bond linkages in favour of its own. Drugs are highly dangerous when used in excess or in the long term, they often have to be taken in steadily increasing dosage in order to replicate the initial effect, and their withdrawal after habituation precipitates a psychological crisis, sometimes accompanied by serious physical illness.

Psychotrophic drugs are inhaled, sniffed, ingested, rubbed into the skin, or injected, and thence carried through the bloodstream to the brain, where they act upon all its component modules. There are three basic pharmacological types of action - narcosis (opium, heroin, methadone, alcohol, cannabis and benzodiazepines), hallucination (LSD and ecstasy), and hyper excitation (cocaine and amphetamines). The unconditionable brain's thought processing is retarded by narcotics and accelerated by hyper excitants, and, correspondingly, the emotional brain registers mood changes of depression, anxiety, euphoria or excitement, the sensory brain mediates visual, auditory or tactile hallucinations, the conditionable brain habituates, providing the urge for further intoxication, and the housekeeping brain is either depressed with reduction in respiration and cardiovascular activity, or over stimulated with the production of high blood pressure and pulse rate. In the long term, all psychotrophic drugs cause deterioration of brain structure and function, and each causes its own specific forms of somatic damage. "Hard" drugs and excessive alcohol intake lead to social, occupational, financial, marital, physical and mental disintegration. The social consequences of addictive substance use in terms of lifestyle disruption, accidents, family suffering, crime and health care costs are monstrous, destructive and degrading.

Realistic figures for illicit drug taking are limited to the developed countries and, of these, Britain may be cited as a microcosm. 20% of the adult UK population will have taken some form of illicit drug at least once in their lives, 8% will be habitual takers of illegal substances of one category or another, and around one and a half thousand will die annually as a result of taking them. With regard to class A drugs (opiates, cocaine, crack, LSD, ecstasy and "magic mushrooms"), 6% of the UK adult population will have tried them at some time, 2% will be addicted to them, and each year there will be a thousand fatalities attributable to them. Cannabis will have been tried by 20% of adults, 4.8% will be regular users, but although dose related brain damage may ensue, deaths from this drug are unusual. Between the ages of 11 and 16 years, 25% now try illicit drugs - predominantly cannabis, although 1% try heroin and 1% try cocaine. Up to 10% of teenagers use cannabis regularly. (CMON03, CMNMZ:05:02, DTN:04:04:01, DMN:01:07:27).

Most crime in developed countries is now fuelled by addictive drug taking. In 2003, 133,470 drug-related offences were committed collectively in England and Wales by 110,400 offenders (TTN:05:03:02). Around 1 in 7 of the UK population is at undue genetic risk of drug and alcohol tolerance and addiction, and the use of cannabis predisposes towards later "hard" drug habituation.

The Historical Perspective. Why, And By Whom, Were Narcotics First Extracted?

Drugs which suppress the brain have a long history, used on the one hand as analgesics, anaesthetics and patent medicines, and on the other by the dilettante and the harrowed as a temporary escape from reality. Opium, obtained from the poppy Papaverum Somniferum, can be traced back to 3400 BCE when it was cultivated in Lower Mesopotamia. Subsequently, the Sumerians, Assyrians, Babylonians and Egyptians all used it, and the Minoans and the Phoenicians spread knowledge of it throughout the Mediterranean. The classical writers Ovid, Homer and Virgil all refer to it, and in 460BCE Hippocrates, the father of medicine, advocated that it should be employed to treat a number of specified disorders. Its use spread to Persia and India with the conquests of Alexander the Great, and to China with Arabic mercantile expansion.

In the 8th century CE, the Chinese Tang dynasty harvested opium to treat dysentery, and subsequently developed the drug as a marketable commodity, both at home, and as an export through wide ranging Muslim trade channels which extended as far as mediaeval Europe. Smoked in combination with tobacco from 1500 onwards, its use became so extensive throughout China during the ensuing three centuries as to warp that country's national consciousness and subvert its economy. Opportunistic European trading nations exacerbated matters by flooding the Chinese domestic market with supplies from

India, which they exchanged for much prized tea and silk. The word "Yen", still used in English to denote an especial preference, originally meant a craving for opium (HB99p34).

In 1799, the Chinese Emperor resolved to stem the tide of ever increasing national addiction by destroying all domestic crops and blockading imports. By way of retaliation, the British and their European allies took to force of arms, waging two opium wars which proved so damaging to the Chinese that they had to buy off their adversaries by ceding Hong Kong and re-opening all other ports. Inevitably, Chinese national humiliation was now compounded by further escalation in drug dependence, not only within the homeland, but among Chinese diaspora abroad. Chinatown communities in London and the major US cities became renowned, not only for their gambling emporia and brothels, but for their several hundreds of opium dens, in whose neighbouring streets small groups of torpid, dishevelled and disorientated habitués could be seen staggering around. It was not until 1895, after more than two centuries of his country's moral and physical degradation, that the Emperor finally managed to extract from Britain a treaty which outlawed further trafficking.

By the end of the 19th century the refined opioid heroin had become the addict's first preference. For several decades heroin production was a monopoly of French Indochina, but sourcing later spread to Burma, Bengal, Turkey and Mexico. Currently, 95% of the world supply is provided by Afghanistan. In 1970 there were an estimated 750 thousand regular users in the United States (BM96).

Those who sought refuge in opium have included the Emperor Marcus Aurelius, the poets Keats, Elizabeth Barret Browning, Andre Malraux and Charles Baudelaire, the novelist Wilkie Collins, the composer Hector Berlioz, Robert Clive of India, and the explorer Richard Burton. In 1821, Thomas de Quincey published his contrite autobiographical treatise on opium addiction.

Hemp was cultivated in China during the first millennium BCE for the manufacture of ropes, netting, bowstrings, textiles and paper, and the Aryan invasions of 1500 BCE were instrumental in spreading this application of the plant throughout the Middle East, Europe and Egypt. It was used extensively in the fabrication of sails and cordage by the Roman navy. Narcotic extracts of hemp first appeared in the second century CE when the Romans used it mixed with aconite as an anaesthetic, and Hindus and Buddhists induced religious euphoria with it. Arabic communities took it up, and during the Islamic conquests of the 7th century propagated its use throughout Europe and North Africa as a nostrum, analgesic and anaesthetic. The drug was given cult status by Sufi Muslims as a means of inducing religious ecstasy, and in the mid 16th century the Hashashin Islamic subsect used hemp extract to dupe their footpads into assassinating their political opponents, a practice from which both the words hashish and assassin derive.

In 1550 the Spanish discovered that much stronger psychotrophic derivatives of hemp could be obtained by cultivating the plant in the climatic conditions of Mexico, which offered higher temperatures and more prolonged sunlight (BM03p38). The medical use of hashish in Europe went into abeyance with the invention of aspirin in 1890, but has been revived in recent years as an adjunct to the treatment of multiple sclerosis. Its employment as a euphoric has made it by far the most popular recreational drug, but as an undoubted cause of schizophrenia, it should be distrusted.

Coca was the exclusive prerogative of the Peruvian royal family and priesthood until the Spanish conquest brought Europeans into possession of it in 1531. Refinement and concentration of the cocaine in coca as "crack" has turned it into a formidable toxin.

Are Drugs The Refuge Of An Inadequate Persona?
How can we get to grips with the scourge of drug enslavement? In the first place we must understand the type of personality we are dealing with. Most initial dalliance with illicit drugs occurs between puberty,

when the emotional brain matures, and the age of 25, when the intellectual brain attains full adult competence, and with it the potential for greater rationality. In addition to his immaturity, the drug taker's persona is usually inadequate and often incompetent, he is overly and morbidly curious, he is prepared to take risks despite the lessons learnt by his elders, partly as a matter of teen age rebellion and partly in response to peer pressure, and he may be suffering from a feeling of low self esteem, depression or anxiety.

All forms of addiction are emotional substitutes for the robust support the addict should have received from his nurtural bond cadence, especially the maternal-infant and then peer to peer bonding of the first and second phases. A US study of five thousand youngsters published in 2010 showed that parental policies are all important in determining the level of alcohol consumption and, by implication, of drug use, which followed in later life. The combination of parental supportive affection, and reasoned and reasonable supervisory control led to the development of offspring who, although they experimented with chemicals, did not subsequently become addicts or heavy drinkers. By contrast, those children denied this combination of critical parental influences were two or three times more likely to intoxicate to excess (BE10). Other determinants of character formation must also play their part, in particular the inculcation of self confidence and the provision of environmental security

In his attempt to escape reality, the drug taker involutes - he turns in upon himself, entering his own private world from which everyone and everything else is excluded. In return for the transitory euphoria, visual, auditory and tactile hallucinations, or pseudo-orgasmic hyper excitation he receives from the drug, he plays a sinister game of Russian roulette with his health and even his life, risking acute overdosage, chronic poisoning, increasing dependence and insidious brain damage with disintegration of his personality, mind and body. He is at the mercy, not only of his own fecklessness, but also of the lack of any competent method of purification or standardisation of the drug which has been supplied to him by the street trader.

Whereas the delinquent's malconditioning antagonises him towards society and makes him aggressive, the addict's malconditioning makes him a docile social isolate. It is only the latter's desperation to find the wherewithal to pay for his next "fix" which propels him into crime. The addict's malconditioning is primarily one of bonding, whereas the delinquent's malconditioning is primarily one of socialisation, but since bonding and socialisation are interdependent there is no clear dividing line between the two aberrants. The addict's crimes are usually against property, but the delinquent's crimes may be either against property or persons.

Are Some People More Vulnerable to Bond Malconditioning and Bond Substitution?

The propensity for bonding is genetic. Unlike other non-human primates, bonobos share with humans a specific gene which facilitates bonding, but some humans are more susceptible to bond malconditioning than others. 10-15% of the human population carry a gene which makes them vulnerable to addiction. Many Chinese, Koreans, Japanese, Amerindians and Russians also possess a gene which accelerates the absorption, and delays the metabolism of alcohol, making them unduly prone to drunkenness. As many as 50% of Muscovites carry this gene, Russians drink an average of 15 litres of pure alcohol a year, one in seven Russians is an alcoholic, and life expectancy throughout their country has recently been reduced to 59 years (TTN:04:01:19). The long nights and low temperatures of northern winters also exacerbate addiction.

A disproportionate number of addicted gamblers have underlying depression, a condition for which there is a genetic predisposition. Children of parents taking "hard" drugs or overeating tend to follow suit. It has been estimated that 50% of women suffering from addiction were abused as children (TGN:04:05:19).

117

Vervet monkeys pillage Caribbean beach resorts for the unfinished drinks they find at tourist venues. Observers found that some monkeys were always teetotal, some varied in their tastes, 12% were steady alcohol drinkers, and 5% drank alcohol to excess, which suggests a genetic spread similar to that found in humans.

There is no such thing as a safe recreational drug, and the manner in which we are poisoned by them will be determined by whether the substance used was sedative, hyper-excitatory, or hallucinogenic. Let us learn from other people's mistakes by seeing what hospital Accident and Emergency departments and Detoxification Centres have to cope with when drug abusers are brought to them.

Acute Intoxication by Addictive Chemicals

Central Nervous System
Large doses of sedative drugs depress the brain, as would an anaesthetic, producing at first stupor with flaccid limbs, then coma.

Opiates have a selective effect on the control of respiration and cause death from respiratory failure.

Stimulant overdosage causes convulsions and strokes.

Cardiovascular System
Overdosage with sedative drugs depresses the heart rate and blood pressure, leading to circulatory collapse. Cannabis users have a fourfold higher risk of myocardial infarction, and risk sudden death from cardiac arrhythmia.

With cocaine, crack, amphetamines, ecstasy and kat, a racing pulse, high blood pressure and heart arrhythmias may lead to angina, heart attack, sudden heart failure, or bursting of the body's main artery.

Glue and solvents can cause rhythmic heart disturbance with sudden death, and nitrites ("poppers") may cause sudden reduction in blood pressure with unconsciousness.

Other Dangerous Sequelae

All injected drugs such as heroin can contaminate with viruses, causing AIDS, and Hepatitis B and C, or cause blood poisoning with septic organisms.

All smoked drugs such as cannabis and crack have similar, but more pronounced, risks to tobacco - lung cancer, heart attack, respiratory disease, and cancer of the mouth, throat and windpipe. All forms of cocaine can cause gangrene of the bowel. Sniffed cocaine leads to destruction of the nose.

Chronic Poisoning and Problems Caused by Withdrawal

All inveterate drug and alcohol users suffer long term brain damage, premature ageing, and physical and mental disintegration. Chronic opiate users experience anorexia, nausea, constipation, dry skin, nails and hair, restlessness, impotence, and a poor resistance to infection.

The effect of a single dose of cannabis lasts up to a week, during which motor control, co-ordination, reaction time and physical strength may be impaired, with implications for drivers, pilots and machinery operators. Small doses of cannabis are sometimes used to prolong coitus, but larger doses diminish libido. Long term teenage cannabis use is now known to carry a tenfold increase in the liability to develop schizophrenia, and offspring of mothers who used the drug during pregnancy carry the same risk. Anxiety, depression, paranoia, depersonalisation and persistent tremor are recognised complications of long term cannabis use (DMN:05:06:20). Rats exposed for a long time to the active chemical in cannabis develop demonstrable brain decay, as do human addicts.

If hallucinogenics are used over a prolonged period they cause mood changes, anxiety, disturbances of vision, and distortions of the perception of time and space. When stimulants are taken in the long term, they cause delusions, hallucinations, anorexia, nausea, insomnia, tremor, convulsions, violent behaviour and emaciation. Psychological changes resulting from recurrent over stimulation are restlessness, irritability, aggressiveness, anxiety, paranoia, disorientation and impotence.

The phenomenon of tolerance, in which steadily increasing doses of a drug are required to replicate the same level of response, is an inevitable concomitant of taking sedative drugs. It is most pronounced in the 10-15% of the general population who share a genetic predisposition towards it. Although users of all illicit drugs become psychologically dependent upon them as an escape from reality, habitues of sedative drugs suffer actual physical illness on withdrawal, the severity of which may be incapacitating, or life threatening. Opiates, and in particular heroin, cause the most severe dependence problems. After 24-48 hours' deprivation the habitual user may well develop anxiety, depression, tremors, cramps, vomiting, diarrhoea, cold sweats, insomnia, hallucinations, circulatory collapse and convulsions. Cannabis withdrawal induces anxiety, depression, paranoia, and other psychotic manifestations.

The effect of a dose of the pseudo-orgasmic crack cocaine only lasts 10 minutes, but its effect is so overstimulating that sedation may be required to calm the user and allay his compelling craving for immediate redosage as the drug wears off.

(Sources reviewed: BHF06, BM03, BM96, BT00, CMHMZ05, CMON03, DMN, DTN, HB99, :MD07, PNMZ:05:04:02, TMOSN:10:10:03, TTN, QD21)

CHAPTER 11

DUTCH COURAGE AND THE DEVIL'S WEED

BONDING SUBSTITUTION WITH ALCOHOL AND TOBACCO

Bemused by the way wine connoisseurs tended to defend their reputations by using ostentatious and outspoken descriptions of vintages, the French scientist Louis Pasteur resolved to put their palates to the test. Having introduced a new method of fermentation, he invited a group of eminent cognoscenti to compare and rate the contents of two wine glasses with which he presented them. There resulted, of course, a difference of opinion as to which of the two was superior in terms of bouquet, colour, flavour and aftertaste, but when all disputation was at an end, Pasteur pointed out that the two wines were in fact identical. As most of us would acknowledge, alcohol occupies a very special place in our affections and affectations, an affinity which for some develops into an irresistible bond.

In the previous chapter we saw that recreational drugs are used as substitutes for interpersonal bonds and as an escape from reality into an "Alice in Wonderland" environment. The illegality of these drugs is a measure of the explicit dangers they pose. By contrast, alcohol and tobacco habits have for long, and by most people, been regarded as socially acceptable, and it is only relatively recently that the public has been made aware of the full extent to which they endanger health. That some late 20th century governments were remarkably slow to increase downward pressure on the consumption of alcohol and tobacco, even when the need to do so became obvious, was a reflection of the fact that a high proportion of the decision makers involved, and the electorate to whom they were beholden, were themselves habitués.

At Once The Capricious Plaything, Lubricant, Soporiphic And Firewater, How Did Alcohol Become Inextricably Woven Into Our Cultural Fabric?

The position of alcohol in the human behavioural repertoire is unique. Whereas all psychotrophic drugs, of which alcohol is of course one, offer the individual a temporary escape from reality, produce euphoria and disinhibition, and like all forms of addiction provide him with a bondage substitute, alcohol also oils the wheels of conviviality and socialisation. Although the drinker can shut himself away in a private world as the drug addict does, he far more commonly imbibes in like-minded company where camaraderie reinforces the herd bond instinct. Undesirable side effects are shrugged off with amused and image enhancing banter.

Alcohol has other redeeming features. Moderate doses are eliminated from the system within 24 hours (cannabis may take up to a week), dosage can be accurately measured and impurities avoided by quality control, and licensing laws and taxation can exert an element of control over supply. There is also some evidence that a daily unit of alcohol reduces cardiovascular morbidity and increases longevity, although this may only apply to those persons already suffering from arteriosclerosis (GMMZ:04:06). It is sad, then, to have to acknowledge that in medical, social and behavioural terms the overall disadvantages of drinking far outweigh the advantages. As students of behaviour, we need to examine the impact of alcohol on humanity in greater detail.

Alcohol, the intoxicating product of starch and sugar fermentation, is consumed as wine, beer or spirits. Grape wine production around the Mediterranean, and rice wine manufacture in the far east, feature in the earliest records of all major civilisations except Islam. Alcohol has been as much an integral part of human cultural development as domestic animals, sculpture or folk music, being used, for example, to endorse special occasions such as rites of passage or calendar, to prime warriors before battle or, in a medical context, to resuscitate, relieve pain, sedate, or anaesthetize.

In ancient times, the rite with which wine was most closely associated was the celebration of death and regeneration as a life cycle, whose patron deities were Osiris in Egypt, Dionysos in Greece, and Bacchus in Rome. In the original Greek version, a handsome youth representing the incarnation of the god was ceremonially immolated and cannibalised, but later protocols moderated the sacrifice to that of an animal. At the end of the ceremony, the victim's flesh was eaten and his blood drunk to symbolise rebirth within the bodies of the worshippers, whilst by the same token the respiritualised god resumed his rightful place in heaven. Vestiges of this ancient rite are still to be found in the Christian mass (FJG22p511). Over time, the Bacchanalia became progressively more bucolic, with depictions of the god portraying him as clad in a bull's hide, horns atop his head and a garland of grapes and vine leaves gracing his brow, whilst audience participation degenerated into a drunken sexual orgy. Pan with his pipes and cloven hooves is a sanitised transfiguration of Bacchus.

In more northerly latitudes, until very recently, wine was regarded as a luxury commodity because of the cost of its transportation from the point of production. Instead, all classes drank locally brewed beer in quantities which we would now find astonishing. The beverage was usually safer to drink than local sources of water and added important nutrients to a predominantly bread-based diet.

Although sixteenth century alchemists knew how to distil alcohol from grape wine, the distillate was expensive and was originally used exclusively for the production of medicines. During the seventeenth century it became realised that any form of grain, fruit or vegetable could be fermented and distilled to form a spirit, which was not only cheaper to produce than beer, but significantly stronger. When Marlborough's troops returned to England in 1713 with a taste for

Holland's gin which they had acquired in the low countries, and which later became referred to as "Dutch Courage", the craze for the new tipple soon spread nationwide, uninhibited by the British Government's attempts to skew taxes against spirits and in favour of beer. Flavoured with juniper berries ("genever" in Dutch), the alluring firewater was a recipe for rapid inebriation, and both commercial production and homestead stilling burgeoned eagerly to meet a meteoric demand. The result was disastrous.

The apogee of subsequent gin consumption was reached between 1721 and 1751. The fashionable new intoxicant was indulged in by folk of all classes and ages, being sold in liquor shops, tobacconists, chandlers, barber's shops, factories, brothels, prisons and workhouses. Barrow boys and pannier traders peddled it in the streets, and private householders opened up businesses on their own doorsteps. But tasting turned to habituation and habituation turned to excess. Everywhere men, women and children were to be seen lying semicomatose and incontinent in streets and alleyways. By 1793, in London alone, 8 million gallons of gin were drunk annually (HC03p43).

Contemporary accounts show that urban development and the employment opportunities of the time led to migration from rural areas to the towns, where swollen populations could only be contained by accommodating them in overcrowded, insanitary and disreputable boarding houses. Strangers of both sexes and all ages were offered cheap lodgings, and gin at a penny a quartern, by unscrupulous landlords, and had to lie several to a bed with several beds to a room. The combination of overcrowding and intoxication was explosive in terms of societal disintegration. On the one hand, the cost of funding gin addiction led to starvation, beggary and destitution, and on the other, it spurred men to rob and murder, women to prostitute themselves, and children to pick pockets. Venereal disease became pandemic (WJ02, WJ76). Attempts to suppress alcohol-driven crime by raising spirit tax merely provoked riots, to which Parliament responded by drafting the Licensing Act of 1751 that regulated the type of establishment which could sell spirits, and the amount permitted to be sold.

Because alcohol can be produced so readily, complete control of its abuse is unattainable. Instead, an uneasy compromise is reached between government and toper through the use of health education, taxation and licensing. The dilemma with which regulating authority has to grapple was never more clearly highlighted than it was in America during attempts to abolish alcohol altogether. Ever since the early days of white settlement in America, the drinking saloon had been a focal and traditional community institution. When, during the first half of the 19th century, these establishments became hotbeds of local political and commercial corruption, the temperance lobby seized its opportunity to press for a national ban on alcohol consumption as a means of eliminating the twin societal evils of sleaze and drunkenness.

At first, only a few states voted for prohibition, beginning with Maine in 1851, but the movement slowly spread, and in 1920 the 18th Amendment to the US Constitution was enacted, banning all alcoholic liquor nationally, save for that used in medicines or the sacrament. As a result, alcoholic beverages became a black market commodity, with supplies being controlled by rival gangs on the high street. The drinking saloon was replaced by the drug store, a refreshment parlour which not only sold ice cream soda, but offered thinly disguised patent medicines for their high alcohol content. When the authorities clamped down on drug stores, the "speakeasy " emporium appeared, run by rum barons, in which customers had to make covert requests for bootleg spirits, heroin or cocaine, which would be served to them under camouflage. Thereafter, addiction to all three substances fulminated, with one in every 400 Americans becoming a hard drug addict. At last, in 1933, murderous gang warfare and general lawlessness reached such a pitch that the government was forced to repeal prohibition, and the equilibrium between supply and demand for alcohol slowly returned (CFFBM00, LWL87).

Just Buying Alcohol Over The Counter Doesn't Mean That We Have Finished Paying For It

If fermentation can be carried out in everyone's kitchen, if everyone has the right to drink alcohol, and if most choose to do so, then why should the state intervene at all? The answer is, of course, that government has an inherent responsibility to minimise the damage done to its citizens, their families and the community at large by immoderate alcohol intake, damage which is measured in terms of accidents, health care, crime and societal corrosion. The statistics which we have for these parameters in the UK provide a useful illustration of the size of the problem.

80% of the population uses alcohol each year, and 7.5% of all consumer expenditure is on alcoholic drinks. Since 1951 there has been a 121% increase in alcohol consumption. Six million people are binge drinkers, and one in three young women are now binge drinkers. Three million citizens are chronically addicted to alcohol.

40 thousand die annually from alcohol related disease, 4 thousand dying from acute intoxication, and the remainder from chronic poisoning, of whom 4 thousand are victims of liver failure. 15% of subjects with serious withdrawal symptoms die despite treatment. (By comparison, a fatal casualty figure of 25 thousand would be regarded as a major disaster on the battlefield).

Alcohol and Violence. In England and Wales in 2005 there were 1,184,700 recorded violent crimes, of which 50% were caused by drunkards. 45% of arrests for assault test positive for alcohol. Suicide is significantly more common in drunkards.

Accidents. Three thousand are killed or seriously injured annually in drink driving related road accidents. 25% of all road accident fatalities have blood alcohol levels above 80mgm/100ml. 100 thousand drink drivers are convicted annually. Alcohol is a salient factor in 60% of fatal accidents at work, 40% of deaths from fires, 33% of home accidents and 25% of drownings. Half of all accidents occurring at weekends are caused by binge drinking.

The Social Costs. Drink related crime costs £12 Bn annually (2002 figures). 4% of all illness is alcohol related, so are 40% of all A and E admissions (70% at peak times), 126 thousand annual mental illness admissions, 35 thousand annual admissions for liver disease, and 21 thousand annual admissions for acute intoxication. Alcohol misuse costs the NHS £3 Bn annually. Because of regional variations, UK statistics can only be taken as a general measure of the use of alcohol across the developed western world.

What Are The Precise Effects Of Alcohol Poisoning On The Human Body?

There are five main categories of adverse effect.

Acute Intoxication: Here the initial effects are slurred speech, incoordination, double vision, imbalance, disinhibition, flushing, sweating, loss of memory and vomiting. More serious effects which may follow are mania, violent antisocial behaviour, blackouts, accidents, fits, paralyses, anaesthesia, depression of respiration and blood pressure, coma, acute brain failure and death. (17% of men and 7% of women drink beyond sensible limits).

Chronic Poisoning produces a wide range of destructive diseases. In the cardiovascular system, arteriosclerosis, coronary thrombosis, stroke, kidney failure, heart muscle poisoning and heart failure occur. In the digestive tract, liver cirrhosis and failure, gastritis and pancreatitis may ensue. Brain degeneration may produce eye movement paralysis, severe incoordination, confusion and drowsiness, sometimes leading to sudden death. Characteristically there is gross impairment of judgement, intelligence and memory recall, for which the subject attempts to compensate by confabulating. Dementia or epilepsy may supervene. Peripherally there is often destruction of the nerves to the arms and legs, blindness for central vision, osteoporosis with undue liability to bone fracture, and severe malnutrition accompanied by dangerous vitamin deficiencies. Alcoholics are at significantly increased risk of developing cancer of the mouth, gullet, throat, liver, breast, or colorectum.

Expectant mothers who drink during early pregnancy risk vesting growth and mental retardation, severe behavioural problems, facial deformities and language impairment upon their unborn child, who is also likely to become an addict in later life.

Generalised Deterioration leads to disintegration of personality, mind and physique, with consequent social, relational, occupational, and financial catastrophe. Ineptitude, crudeness, impotence, fluctuating moods, delusions, irritability, pot belly, a florid complexion, red watery eyes, and tremor are all symptoms which chart this process of decay.

Withdrawal Symptoms pose a very real threat to the habitué, in whom deprivation lasting between 1 and 4 days often precipitates "delirium tremens", a condition characterised by severe restlessness, confusion, sleeplessness, disorientation for time and place, flushing, sweating, severe tremor, terror, screaming, and hallucinations affecting vision, hearing and skin sensation. In the worst cases these symptoms are followed by delirium, convulsions, and circulatory collapse with death.

Harrowing Family Penalties are exacted from their relatives by alcoholics in pursuit of their habit, and these include partner abuse, child abuse, divorce, separation, stress disorders, and precipitation of mental illness.

(Sources Reviewed:- BBCR2: 03:11:29, BBCT1: 04:03:16, CFF00, CMHMZ05v2 No.3, CMOU:03:01, CMOU: 05:04, DMN: 05:04:05, DMN: 06:07:01, EHM89, FJG22, GMCMZ: 05:03, GMMZ: 06:04, HC03, JS96, LWL87, PMMZ: 06:06:19, WGB40, WJ76, WR02 WRJ02).

"A Fire At One End And A Fool At The Other" The
Extraordinary Social History Of Tobacco

We have seen that "recreational" drugs, despite their illegality, have become entrenched within the psychologically inadequate subset of the population of the developed world, and that the addictive properties of these chemicals are so compelling that their extirpation from society is unlikely to occur. Alcohol is so widely used and accepted throughout all non-Muslim societies that it, too, will retain its position in society, despite its disadvantages. Tobacco differs from these other two toxins inasmuch as the penalties which it exacts are disproportionately severe in relation to the comparatively mild psychotrophic effect which it exerts. The risk / benefit ratio is skewed so heavily against the user that concerted governmental efforts are made in the western world to discourage habituation through the use of strident public propaganda, high taxation of the product and embargos on advertising.

Like syphilis, tobacco was unknown outside America until Columbus' crew brought the twin scourges back to their home port of Seville. The tribes of Pre-Columbian North and South America looked upon tobacco as sacred, smoked it as cigars and in pipes, and used juice made from it in drinks. They chewed the leaves and applied them to wounds, and they ground them into paste for use as a cure-all ointment. Communal smoking pow-wows were held to cement alliances and contracts. Above all, the high nicotine content of Amerindian tobacco rendered it psychotrophic, and whilst under its influence the shaman could communicate with the spirit world to invoke healing, rain making, fertility or divination.

But once Spanish sailors had unwittingly provided tobacco and syphilis with a toehold in Europe, both these seeds of destruction spread inexorably along trade routes, and by the year 1570 the "devil's weed" was being grown and used throughout the length and breadth of the continent. By 1600, cultivation had extended to Africa, India and the far east. By 1614, the fledgling Virginia settlement was not only planting, but exporting tobacco, and this now flourishing trade vitalised its struggling economy - a crucial factor in the successful colonisation of North America by the British. By 1750 the use of tobacco had become a global habit, and all social classes were enthusiastically chewing or smoking it.

Methods of administration diversified with tobacco's world-wide spread. It was smoked as cigars, and in clay pipes and hookahs. It was chewed, sniffed as powdered snuff, quaffed as potions, and administered as enemas. During the 18th century it was used extensively as a component of patent medicines. As it diminished libido, a learned article published in 1669 recommended it for use by priests, monks and friars (GJ93p78), and the papacy opened its own tobacco factory in 1779.

Tobacco provides a much less striking distortion of cognition than alcohol or recreational drugs and therefore acts as a much less convincing escape from reality. In mild doses it promotes relaxation and allays hunger, thirst and weariness, and only high dosage can result in inebriation, disorientation and hallucination. But its strongly bonding, addictive properties are notorious and were realised from the moment it first reached the old world. Full knowledge of its highly damaging effects on the human cardiovascular, respiratory and nervous systems only emerged during the second half of the 20th century, when a habit, which had hitherto been viewed very largely as a social grace, suddenly became anathematised.

Until the mid 19th century, state monopolies controlled the lion's share of the lucrative tobacco trade, and even today the exchequers of state governments continue to demand a slice of tobacco's profits by levying taxes on its use. The first half of the 20th century witnessed the eclipse of other forms of intake by that of the cigarette, and this was accompanied by an increase in US and European average annual personal consumption from 1-2 pounds to 5-7.5 pounds (GJ93p93). The second world war fuelled tobacco uptake, with many countries plying their combatants with free issue. China is now the world's largest tobacco producer and consumer, with a tally of 350 million smokers in 2008 (BBCR4: 08: 05:10)

What Is The Prevalence Of Smoking, And What Are The Mortality Rates Associated With It?

In 1900 the global population consumed 8% of its tobacco as cigarettes, but by 1990 this proportion had risen to 80%. In the USA during this time, average annual personal cigarette consumption had reached 3552, and concomitantly in that country deaths from all cancers increased tenfold, with a disproportionately high rise in lung cancer (GJ93p124). In developed countries during the decade 1990-1999 there were 21 million deaths from smoking. Among richer countries, improved education as to the dangers of smoking is achieving a slow reduction in consumption, but the use of tobacco is increasing in the third world, and it is estimated that, globally, 20% of those presently alive will be killed by tobacco. In particular, cigarettes kill 25% of their users (GRE89p574). In the UK during the year 2004, 25% of the population smoked, 40% of young women smoked and 20% of women continued to smoke during pregnancy (TTN:04:02:12). During the early years of the 21st. century, 114 thousand British smokers were killed annually by their habit, of whom 29 thousand died of cardiovascular disease (CMOU04), and 34 thousand died from lung cancer (BBCT1:04:11:09). These totals are very slowly declining as more smokers quit.

Lung cancer was rare before the 20th century, but now accounts for more deaths in the industrialised world than occur from any other malignancy. In 90% of cases, lung cancer is due to smoking. The 5 year survival rate for the disease is a bare 5% (GPMMZ:04:05:17). Non smokers regularly exposed to the smoking of others have a 25% greater risk of coronary heart disease than normal (CMOU04) and, prior to the UK government's moves to ban the habit from public places, two citizens died every day as the result of passive smoking (GPMMZ:05:03:04). Babies born to smokers are at greater risk of heart disease, diabetes and asthma in later life, and they are also three times more likely to be born prematurely, they are smaller at birth, they have a poorer chance of survival, and have greater risks of cot death, respiratory disease and ear disease (JTN:04:02:12). A child whose grandmother smokes is twice as likely to develop asthma (GPMMZ:05:04: 15).

The true cash bill paid by society for the tobacco habit is difficult to assess. Calculations must take into account the fact that one in four smokers dies before the usual retirement age of 65, and allowance has to be made for the costs of sickness or welfare benefits before or after this age milestone, for loss of productivity, for the cost of health promotion campaigns, and for the revenue derived from tobacco taxation. Although in 2010 the US Government Website quoted overall national annual smoking costs as being a staggering $167 Bn, even this may be an underestimate. Research studies undertaken at the Netherlands Erasmus University suggest that the state has to spend more on maintaining the three of every four smokers who survive past sixty-five than it saves from the 25% early death rate.

How Does Smoking Kill?
When tobacco burns it creates fumes containing nicotine, tar and carbon monoxide. All three are toxic, and nicotine, which is the component creating euphoria and addiction, is so poisonous that derivatives of it have been used as pesticides. Tar causes lung and other cancers throughout the body, and the three toxins combined also attack all bodily systems in many other ways. Cardiovascular Degeneration takes the form of angina, coronary thrombosis, hypertension, stroke, kidney failure, and degeneration of the arteries and of small blood vessels (Buerger's disease). The Respiratory System diseases asthma, chronic bronchitis and emphysema are all very much more common in smokers. 80% of cases of chronic obstructive pulmonary disease are due to smoking, and in the UK 30 thousand die annually from this condition. Damage to the Central

Nervous System manifests as a threefold increase in the risk of developing dementia of both the vascular and Alzheimer's types, and as a 3-4 fold increase in the risk of incurring age-related blindness (The commonest adult cause of blindness).

The Ability to Reproduce is adversely affected. Smoking damages male fecundity by reducing sperm counts, and it also causes DNA damage which predisposes to congenital abnormalities in offspring. In 2010 it was estimated that 3 million UK males had become impotent as the result of their tobacco habit. In Females, fertility is reduced by 40%, and the risk of miscarriage is increased (every year 5 thousand UK miscarriages are caused by smoking). Periods become more painful and irregular, the menopause occurs earlier, and lactation is less likely to succeed. There is a threefold increase in the risk of cervical cancer, and for those taking the contraceptive pill whilst smoking there is a 20 fold increased risk of heart attack.

Five years after smoking has been discontinued, the increased risk of heart attack reduces to a half. After smoking has been discontinued for ten years, the increased risk of lung cancer reduces to a half and an increased risk of heart attack no longer obtains.

(Sources Reviewed :- BBCT1:04:11:29, BBCT1:05:09:22, BAM90, CMOU04, GPMMZ:04:03:15 and 04:05:17 and 05:03:04, GRE89, PMZ03, TTN:04:02:12, WKP08).

CHAPTER 12

"WHEN ITS A QUESTION OF MONEY EVERYONE IS OF THE SAME RELIGION"
(Voltaire)

THE TRAIT OF POSSESSIVENESS AND ITS HUMAN DISTORTIONS

Detailed analysis of human behaviour may be said to have originated in ancient Athens, where one of the first paradoxes the Greek philosophers set themselves to resolve was that posed by possessiveness, since this could be dubbed as either beneficial or amoral. Early records from the fifth century BCE relate that the cryptic wit and renowned crackpot Diogenes of Sinopeus so reviled avarice as being the root of all evil that he renounced consumerism, took up residence in an empty barrel, and stalked the streets every day carrying a lantern, in what he described as an increasingly fruitless search to find an honest man. In subsequent centuries, rival philosophical attitudes towards possessiveness hardened, with the Epicurean school preaching uninhibited self indulgence in all things worldly, whilst the Stoic school advocated frugality because it considered self discipline to be the only key to true happiness.

The inbuilt fundamental trait of possessiveness has clear survival value since it prompts for the acquisition and retention of resources which are essential for animal existence. But whereas in most other species possessiveness is satiable, given adequate provision of food, water and shelter, in humans it may be insatiable and obsessive.

Exaggerative and distorted human possessiveness manifests as hoarding, kleptomania, premeditated theft, gross avarice and gambling.

Whilst it is normal for people to share their homes with collectables which have a special interest for them, 2% of the population are compulsive hoarders, accumulating consumables far beyond the point of need or utility. In such cases, refrigerators often overflow with outdated food, living spaces become choked and almost impenetrable, and pets may become so numerous as to be unmanageable. Although many hoarders come from obsessive families, the degree to which the condition is determined by genes or by parental conditioning varies with the individual. Kleptomania - compulsive possessiveness characterised by the repetitive, unpremeditated misappropriation of items which have little value - is now considered to be a mental illness of the obsessive compulsive type. In a small number of cases both hoarding and kleptomania may be caused by brain damage from trauma, addictive drugs or senility.

Premeditated theft is a very different matter, for here the monetary value of the stolen objects is the overriding consideration. There is a clear distinction to be made between thefts undertaken for reasons of destitution or drug dependence and those for which no such rationale exists. Gratuitous premeditated theft is a distortion of the trait of possessiveness which results from malconditioning during immaturity, when childhood deprivation, bond rupture, insecurity, or inappropriate parental indoctrination act as goads to later overcompensation (see also the causes of delinquency in chapter 15). Once an individual has been malconditioned, this form of hyper-acquisitiveness is addictively self perpetuating, and maybe cyclical in its expression. For instance shoplifting, which has a strong compulsive element, is more common in women, and is more likely to occur at the time of menstruation (SMGSEH28p252). The wife of a professional burglar was able to predict the latter's periodic predatory forays by noticing the irritability and restlessness which he displayed for several days beforehand (PC).

The episode of theft may also be pseudo-orgasmic, as was well illustrated by the case of an intelligent black American Harvard student who began to feel giddy and restless in the lead up to his crime. These feelings intensified over several days, until the compulsion to break and enter became irresistible. Whilst stealing, he became hyperexcited, and found himself panting and sweating. At the culmination of the burglary he experienced a precipitate bowel action, after which a feeling of exhaustion and tranquil relief surged over him (BPG27, 1,case 9). Diarrhoea is not uncommon following the commission of felony.

Gross avarice is a chronic, less episodic form of excessive possessiveness, which has more in common with gluttony than sexuality. Examples of all forms of compulsive cupidity abound throughout the archaeological and historical records - from the caches of thousands of ancient coins which metal detectors sometimes locate to the corrupt grandees of black Africa with their Swiss bank accounts, from Emelda Marcos with her three thousand pairs of shoes to the Nazi supremos who pillaged pan-European artworks, and from the vast treasure trove of the Apollonian priesthood at Delphi to that of the Vatican city, all are tarred with the same brush.

Gambling

In our saner moments we all know that gambling is a mug's game, because the odds are stacked against the punter who is bound to lose overall. It is intriguing, therefore, to wonder why anyone could get a kick out of committing slow financial suicide.

All carnivores have to seek out their prey, they are mentally excited by the sight of it, and secrete endogenous adrenaline to sustain the offensive aggression necessary to pursue and catch it. A gambler experiences the same sequence of reactions, tempted by the jackpot, and becomes addicted to his own adrenaline release, which raises his blood pressure, his pulse and his respiration rates, and galvanizes him mentally in a manner similar to other stimulant drugs. As with the phenomenon of tolerance to other chemicals, increasingly large amounts of money may have to be risked in order to replicate the same level of excitement. The addiction is constantly reinforced by the outcome of the bet. If the gambler wins, he is impelled to try and repeat his success. If he loses, he feels the urgent need to make good his losses. In the end, a crisis point is reached when, after being thwarted by repeated losses, he becomes desperate and will resort to extraordinary measures in order to obtain the money needed to keep betting. Faced with impending disaster, he cannot pull back as logic demands but must continue to be frogmarched by the distorted behavioural patterns within his conditionable brain.

Failure to react logically, and cut one's losses prior to the critical point of impending disaster, marks out the addicted gambler from other punters. As with other forms of substitution for reality and bondage, the habitual gambler uses his addiction to relieve feelings of helplessness, inadequacy, guilt or anxiety, feelings which were engendered within him by malconditioning during the first and second nurtural phases of his childhood. Many addicted gamblers are also depressives who use the frisson of risk taking to relieve melancholy (Journal of Addiction 2001:96p1629). Addiction to gambling is associated with an increased risk of substance abuse, and this would suggest that some vulnerable individuals have a similarly genetic predisposition towards it. As shown by identical and non identical twin studies, genes also play a part in the level of risk a person is prepared to take. Like the alcoholic, the gambler fabricates to conceal his habit, and family, social and occupational mores are abandoned. He relies increasingly on others to subsidise him, and he resorts to fraud, forgery, embezzlement and theft. There is a high risk of suicide when circumstances become out of control, destitution looms, his personal life disintegrates and a major depressive illness is precipitated (GPMMZ:03:09:09).

Most addicted gamblers are males in the age group 21-55 years on low incomes, but all socio-economic classes and both genders are represented within the gambling fraternity. Addicts are systematically exploited by commercial organisations, using vehicles which vary between countries. Australia has the biggest proportion of problem gamblers per head of population, most of whom access the 185 thousand poker machines offering large jackpots. In the year 2000-01 this trade was worth 8.7 Bn. Australian dollars, and fuelled 11.7 Bn. dollars costs in crime (WR02p199). Casinos relieve Americans of 60 Bn. US dollars annually, but the US government prohibits on-line gambling. UK citizens squander £10 Bn. a year on web betting and, of those who do so, 300 thousand are classed as addicts. Web betting has led to such financial hardship that the web centre Gamcare, set up to help those in crisis, counsels 14 thousand every month, of whom one thousand are women (BBCT1:06:09:12).

Avarice, Gold and the Birth of Inflation
So far we have been considering manifestations of distorted possessiveness as they affect the individual aberrant. When the ability of a whole community to acquire resources far exceeds the needs for its survival, a false market place develops, driven by possessiveness, in which some superfluous commodities become perceived as desirable, and are accorded values which are determined by their scarcity. Modern examples of grossly overheated market valuation are seen in the field of fine art and antiques. The apogee of absurdity is reached in the fine wine trade where the cost of a bottle of prestigious and revered vintage can rise to the point at which drinking from it would constitute an act of gross pecuniary impropriety. Historically, the first frippery to be subjected to this form of illogical, upspiralling demand was gold, and its story has been both the epitome and the barometer of human overpossessiveness over the ages. As an innovative lubricant of trade, gold has served humanity well, but in the process it has laid bare some of humanity's weaknesses - the cupidity, artificiality, narcissism, venality and gullibility to which the flesh is prone. Let us dig a little deeper.

Except for a miniscule role in modern electronics, gold is totally useless. It has always proved too soft to be used in tools, weapons or armour. Its principal attraction has always been its untarnishable glint, an attribute which inevitably stimulated curiosity and suggested an association with the heavenly bodies. By using it as an adornment, it not only attracted immediate attention but implied status and the gift of paranormal influence.

Gold has some exceptional physical properties. A cubic foot weighs half a ton, and one ounce can be beaten into a sheet that would cover one hundred square feet (MJ78p8). Whether as dust or nugget, gold is extracted as an uncompounded metal. All the gold mined to date would scarcely fill a modern aircraft hangar, and because it is virtually indestructible, its total volume never diminishes, despite the fact that it may be repeatedly refashioned. It resists chemical attack from all except the very strongest reagents.

Before adequate supplies permitted its general use as money or for widespread personal adornment, gold was the exclusive preserve of gods and potentates, a symbol of supreme divinity and power used in crowns, haloes, palaces and temples to dazzle and impress. Successive ancient civilisations strove to exhibit the precious metal to its most flamboyant advantage. The Parthenon sported a statue of Athena clad in pure gold. A statue of Apollo sculpted out of gold dominated the temple at Delphi, where also a vast wealth in gold and other precious objects were lodged in the treasury (CM04p19 and HDSp165). A golden statuette of Dionysos still guards the entrance to his miniature temple in the Athens National Museum (KS00p169). Mycenaean Kings were buried with masks of pure gold. King Darius of Persia took his ablutions in a golden bath, and Pharaoh Amasis of Egypt used a large golden bowl as a footbath and urinal. To repay a service rendered, King Croesus offered Alcmaeon as much gold dust as he could secrete about his person and the latter staggered home having filled his top boots and baggy trousers (HDSp165).

Much of Rome's gold came from Spanish open cast mines, and reserves were stored in the temple of Jupiter, guarded by geese who cackled in the presence of an intruder. The Roman general Crassus' lust for gold was so notorious that when the Parthians defeated him in battle they poured molten gold down his throat. The Byzantine emperor Justinian bedecked the mother church of St. Sophia with vast amounts of gold (MJ78p241). Kublai Khan lavishly decorated his enormous palace with gold extracted from his subjects at the point of a sword in return for paper money, and the Inca temple of the Sun in Cuzco was clad with 400 plates of gold, each weighing four and a half pounds (BPL00). Mediaeval Venice used gold ostentatiously in its municipal decoration (e.g. Ca d' Oro and St. Mark's Cathedral). The 16th century theocratic ruler of Benin, the Oda, who claimed descent from deity, was so heavily bedecked with polished gold that he had to be supported by two slaves who likewise manipulated his arms for him when he wanted to gesticulate (PHJ67). Even today, Bangkok still has one of the temples in its Royal complex sheathed entirely in gold leaf, and a shrine further down river houses a giant statue of the Buddha wrought from five and a half tons of solid gold.

Gold's power to embellish, its talismanic associations, its scarcity and its indestructibility have always triggered the possessiveness of potentates and high priests in all cultures, who inevitably reserved it for themselves whilst they could, turning it into a symbol of power and divinity. Once its meretricious use in regalia had been satisfied, they hoarded it in vaults. In 4,000 BCE the pharaohs had already established gold reserves in the form of bars upon which their insignia were stamped, and thenceforth gold became the price tagged precious metal which it still is. At first, only the officials of the state treasury were able to make payments in gold, but as mining progressively increased its available supply, its use as an intermediary of communal trade began to take the place of barter. A thirst for the acquisition and possession of goods was now rivalled by men's appetites for the ownership of money, not merely as a means to an end, but as a repository of security against hard times. Whilst goods provided for comfort and necessity, gold became the supreme hedge, nest egg and collateral, and was intensely desirable in its own right. Now, not only did gold have its own intrinsic value, but it became the standard against which the value of everything else was calibrated. A material which would have been useless to someone shipwrecked on a desert island was now a critically important perquisite.

Gold as Currency
Throughout history, conquest has conferred the ability to dominate world trade, to control gold excavation, and to bring about the adoption of the victor's gold coin as international currency. The use of an impressed cipher of authenticity began in ancient Egypt, where nubian gold bars were stamped. The Lydians of Asia Minor minted the first gold coins in 585 BCE using metal panned from the river that ran through Sardis, their capital city, but Lydia was overrun by the Persians who superimposed the Daric, the first coin to bear a monarch's image, namely that of King Darius. The later Roman emperors of Byzantium dominated international currency with the golden Bezant until Muslim conquests replaced it with the Dinar. In early mediaeval times Venice, Florence and Genoa straddled the east-west trade routes, becoming correspondingly wealthy, and minted their own gold coins, respectively the Ducat, Florin and Genovin. After Columbus' voyages led to the exploitation of central and south America, world stocks of gold and silver expanded five fold, and the Spanish Peso D' Oro became international tender. England's later exploitation of west Africa and dominance of maritime trade gave rise to the Guinea (named from the metal's source territory) and the Sovereign. When the USA emerged as a supreme superpower, the supply of gold became insufficient to meet demands for coinage and the dollar bill was accepted globally.

Gold Fever

Although gold is present in all continents, its deposits have been discovered piecemeal, and the variability of its natural state determines the method needed for its extraction. Panning, shallow cast pressure washing and deep excavation are all used. Some South African mines are a mile deep, and from them one ton of matrix, which demands 38 man hours of effort, renders a mere one ounce of metal (MJ78).

The pursuit of what little gold is obtainable has always been frenetic. Alchemists throughout Europe spent their lives attempting to turn base metal into gold, and this quest can be traced back as far as ancient Egypt, following which Arabic schools of the 8th century CE, Isaac Newton, Thomas Aquinas, and the psychoanalyst Jung, amongst many others, all tried their hand at it. All the great explorations of the second millennium CE were motivated by greed for the metal, such as those of Marco Polo, the Portuguese under the direction of King Henry "the Navigator", and the Spanish conquistadors Cortes in Mexico and Pizarro in Peru. King Ferdinand of Spain's instructions to the embarking Columbus were specific: "Get gold, humanely if possible, but at all regards get gold" (GT93p11).

Criminals are particularly attracted towards gold because of its value and the ease with which it can be melted down for resale. Whilst kings could and did debase gold coins at a profit, anyone else doing so was severely punished. In 1124 Henry the First of England discovered that his 200 mint masters were guilty of the fraud and chopped the right hands off half of them. Other punishments for this offence were blinding and castration (DG95p139). Coining, which shaved off the rim of a gold coin, was punished under early English kings by castration, amputation or hanging.

Tsar Alexander the First developed Urals gold, and by 1847 Russia was providing 60% of the world's production. Enormous gold strikes followed in Hungary, South Africa, North America and Australia. The Californian gold rush of 1849 involved a hundred thousand prospectors. The Australian gold rush of 1851 took fifty thousand to

142

New South Wales (HR87p561). In 1886 two thousand a week joined the stampede for South African gold, and in 1897 a hundred thousand set out for Dawson City, Alaska. Inevitably only a handful of all these hopefuls ever "struck it rich".

Possessiveness and Global Citizenship

The dilemma posed by possessiveness is that because it motivates trade, civilized society cannot function without it, but that when it is distorted and exaggerated it fuels war, crime and corruption.

Given adequate supplies of food and water, non-human primates have no need of possessiveness other than to define the personal foraging space around them. Our hunter gathering forebears formed subgroups within which resources were shared. But the advent of agriculture introduced possessive territorialism, and differentiation of labour put a calculable value on every man's contribution to the social unit, thereby incentivising his efforts, creating the profit motive, and so exacerbating possessiveness.

The communist experiment which sought to provide for all basic human needs and do away with possessiveness failed, because by removing incentivisation state economies were bankrupted. Communism's collapse underlined the fact that the profit motive is the engine which drives up living standards in the developed world. As a consequence possessiveness has come to be seen as a virtue, and success in life is largely measured in terms of personal assets.

Possessiveness and consumerism in developed countries have resulted in a gross imbalance of global resources between these countries and the rest of the world. In poorer countries one billion people live at or below starvation level, whilst many residents in the northern hemisphere overeat. Equilibrium can only be restored by pegging the size of the global population, whilst at the same time producing enough food to sustain it and ensuring that resources are distributed equitably.

Exaggerated and distorted possessiveness can only be curbed by eliminating the malconditioning in childhood which predisposes to it - deprivation, bond rupture, insecurity and malindoctrination. Given that all underdeveloped countries must be helped to lay foundations for basic economic development, the global marketplace will eventually divide equitably amongst us those resources which the planet can provide, by determining what each of us can earn and can afford.

(Sources reviewed: BBCT1:06:09:12, BPL00, CM04, DG95, GP02, GPMMZ03, GT93, HR87, KS00, MJ78, PHJ67, SMGSEH28, WR02)

CHAPTER 13

AUTOCRATS AND ARMAGEDDONS

HUMAN DISTORTION OF DOMINANCE RANKING - TYRANNY

Caligula, Nero, Attila the Hun, Genghis Khan, Ivan the Terrible, Vlad the Impaler, Hitler, Stalin, Pol Pot, and Idi Amin, are some of the many names which haunt us from our history, names of rulers who were the very embodiment and epitome of man's inhumanity to man. Impassioned by the licence for sadistic misuse which absolute authority provides, these autarchs all exploited it to the full. What is it that turns a man into a monster who relishes the thraldom and suffering he imposes upon other mortals? When Lord Acton, himself a devout catholic, remonstrated against Pope Pius the Tenth's assumption of infallibility in 1887, he coined the much quoted maxim that "power tends to corrupt, and absolute power corrupts absolutely", but his dictum does not tell us why. As detailed biographical analysis shows us all too clearly, adverse environmental pressures during immaturity have already deformed the tyrant's persona long before he assumes power, and the gross distortion of the primate trait of dominance, already festering within him, has become obsessional.

Of all the scourges man has unleashed on himself through his mismanagement of nurture, none has had a more profoundly adverse effect on society at large, nor on the course of human history, than that of unrestrained despotism. The power which a tyrant arrogates to himself is such that he can warp the behaviour of his subjects en masse, and when his power is embedded in an ideology he can warp both their behaviour and their thoughts. As global citizens with the responsibility for shaping the next generation it is imperative that we understand the pathogenesis and operative mechanisms of this invidious form of societal maldevelopment.

The Alpha males of non-human primate "herds" rise to their positions of authority through maturation, experience and a process of confrontational challenges whose resolution determines their position in the social hierarchy. These challenges have been moderated by evolution so as not to kill. To retain their position, dominants must not only demonstrate their physical superiority, but also their abilities as leader, decision maker and "herd" protector, and must cultivate the respect of other "herd" members. If we substitute political superiority for physical superiority, similar attributes are expected of human leaders. The tyrant's malicious abuse of power, which frequently involves him in killing other members of his own community, is therefore biologically abnormal, and it results from the deformation of personality attributable to malconditioning during immaturity. Virtually all nation states have suffered tyranny's dire consequences at one time or another, and some continue to do so. The larger the state, the more extreme are the measures imposed upon it in order that overall control be maintained, but the way in which despotic power is unscrupulously acquired and retained is otherwise broadly similar.

The three most profligate mass murderers of the 20th century were Hitler, Stalin and Mao Tse-tung, exceptional both for the scale of their atrocities and their impact on human history. Each rose to power by exploiting an ideology, and abused that power with utter ruthlessness when his position had become impregnable. In each case, an outstanding talent for organisation was combined with remorseless ambition and tenacity of purpose.

The tyrant's sadistically cruel streak which makes him impervious to, or even enjoy, the suffering he inflicts is all too often a form of revenge which he takes on society for the protracted suffering he himself endured as a child. Hitler, Stalin, Mao Tse-tung and Saddam Hussein all spent their childhoods being repeatedly and mercilessly thrashed by overbearing, intolerant, and paranoid fathers (BA91, DI66p23, SA75p185, www.kirtasto.sci.fl/mao.htm.). Unlike sovereign rulers who achieve supremacy by inheritance or other fortuitous circumstances, these four had to use exquisite cunning, unscrupulousness, perfidy, cruelty and bloodletting in order to rise above and dominate their compatriots. The grim, fearful determination with which they had faced parental onslaught in order to survive their childhood became translated into a blind resolve never again to be at anyone else's mercy, whatever the circumstances. Over reaction exaggerated their response to any opposition, whether real or illusory, so as to eliminate it. When paramount status was finally attained, it did not lessen the urge to tyrannise, but led to a heady sense of triumph against all the odds, to an aura of unique self importance and of predestined infallibility, all attributes which characterise megalomania.

Mao's maverick policies, designed to scapegoat the professional and managerial classes, led to famine and state bankruptcy, and are estimated to have caused the death of 40-70 million of his own countrymen. Hitler's genocide of Jews and gypsies, his extermination of the mentally handicapped, and his ravages of the occupied territories led to the deaths of 10-15 million (BA91p1055 and appendix 2). Stalin's victimisation of the peasantry, his massive purges of the managerial, party and officer classes as well as the common citizenry, cost the Russians 20 million deaths. Saddam Hussein is estimated to have massacred a million of his own countrymen (TISN:06:12:31). These losses far exceeded those incurred in armed combat by their respective nations.

Mao, Hitler and Stalin were all confronted by political and military challenges whose extremities reinforced the need for strong leadership, turned them into cult heroes and enabled them to dispense with democracy. Mao led the Chinese communist party in a bitter civil war against the initially superior forces of Chiang Kai Chek's nationalists, and eventually won. Hitler had to build his National Socialist Party virtually from scratch and win over the electorate, using charismatic oratory and theatrical ostentation to convey to the German public what they themselves wanted to believe. Stalin inherited a ready-made revolution from Lenin, and despite disgracing himself by errors made during a civil war against counter-revolutionary White Russian forces, took over core administrative tasks within the Communist Party, eventually becoming supreme puppet master within the oligarchic leadership (the Politburo), the rank and file communist party and the political police. Mao's rampant megalomania brought China to its knees, Hitler's wrecked Germany, but Stalin's, however despicable, was tempered with pragmatism, which is why he achieved a pyrrhic victory where the other two had failed. Although we have at our disposal a very considerable amount of detail as to the backgrounds and later behavioural patterns of all three despots, it is Stalin who furnishes historians and behaviourists alike with the most intriguing character study of tyranny. The Stalinist years were instrumental in shaping the modern world, because they balked the threat of global subordination by Hitler and his associates, they ushered in the use of "cold" war as a more pragmatic alternative to large scale conflict, they clearly demonstrated that totalitarianism was fiscally and sociologically bankrupt, and their sadistic extremism generated a revulsion which helped to set in train many international humanitarian initiatives. Because they have been extensively documented, we are able to see the way that sequential malconditioning of dominance during the early and later phases of a single individual's nurture can prove to be a virus which ultimately deforms, within a surprisingly short span, the cognition and behaviour of an entire nation state. The lessons we should learn from them demand that we give them individual and detailed attention. In order to assess both Stalin's crimes against, and his contribution to humanity, we need to weigh prosecutory and defensive evidence on the scales of historical justice.

Stalin: The Case for the Prosecution

The word for "why" in Russian is Zachto, a word which during the 1930's was on everyone's lips, whispered in trepidation by common citizens, communist party functionaries and professional soldiers alike, all of whom went to bed at night dreading that they might be woken by the political police in the small hours, arrested on trumped up charges, and summarily consigned to the death cell or deportation camp. The same word was also scrawled across the walls of countless prison cells and carved into the walls of timber hutments of thousands of labour camps. It was, too, the ultimate question put to Stalin by several of those senior enough to be able to communicate with him shortly before their execution. It was a question which always went unanswered.

What no one at home or abroad could understand was the motive which lay behind the apocalyptic domestic policies which Stalin instituted, and which were ultimately to cost the lives of one in every twenty Russian citizens. He persecuted and liquidated his compatriots on such a prodigious scale, and with such ruthlessness, that his actions precipitated manpower crises which dangerously imperilled the military capability, the infrastructure and the productivity of his country, whilst at the same time undermining its morale and social fabric.

In order to retrace Stalin's political career, we must begin with the so called bloodless revolution in 1917 through which the Bolsheviks seized power from the old Tsarist regime after Russia's humiliating defeat on the German front at the end of the first world war. This coup precipitated a civil war between Bolsheviks and the remnants of the White Russian Imperial Army which led to the latter's defeat, and cost nine million lives. The Bolshevik leader Lenin suffered a stroke illness in 1922 which incapacitated him, and, in consequence, the other members of the Politburo which he had set up to govern the country vied with each other for ultimate supremacy. Stalin outmanoeuvred his arch rival Trotsky and engineered his own advancement to the post of General Secretary by assuming control of all appointments to the

Communist Party hierarchy and the political police. At first, other Politburo members were able to limit his powers in conclave, but during subsequent years Stalin's subterfuge brought about the piecemeal assassination of all twelve of the other prominent contenders for the party leadership. By 1938, Stalin was in such an impregnable position that he could order the unchallenged extermination of anyone he chose. He consolidated his position by constructing a rigid framework of control throughout Russia, whereby political commissars were appointed to supervise communist indoctrination at all levels of society, and the political police with their informers were tasked with ensuring that party dogma was put into practice on pain of arrest. These measures proved so effective that all opposition and deviation was obliterated.

Looking back on Stalin's reign of terror, it still seems astonishing that he decided to cull his own people on such a massive scale and at such a hazardous time in their history. A glimpse into the workings of his mind emerged at the 18th Party Congress when he stated that "the purge of 1933-1936 was unavoidable and the results, on the whole, beneficial" (CR90p440). Yet it was during the two years following 1936 that the numbers of purge victims increased tenfold. Did Stalin really believe that the more you bled a patient, the more likely he was to recover? By 1938, the machinery for processing purgees was so grossly overstretched that it could no longer function with any semblance of efficiency, and this consideration, together with the threat of German and Japanese militarism, must to some extent have stayed his hand. At last the furore of blood letting began to subside, although it was far from over. Only Stalin's death in 1953 could bring that about. Then, in an unprecedented rapprochement with the Russian people and international community, his successor Khrushchev at last laid bare the enormity of Stalin's crimes against humanity by exposing KGB files to scrutiny.

The Political Police

The modus operandi of all tyrants is similar. In order to stay in power they must control the armed forces, deny their compatriots legal and electoral rights, and enforce obedience to their oppression though a network of loyalists given special powers. The mechanisms Stalin assembled were particularly effective in this respect. There have always been political police in Russia, and they have always exerted an all powerful, all pervasive control over the population. In Ivan the Terrible's time they were called the Oprichnina, under the Tsars they were the Okrana, the Bolsheviks reformed them as the Cheka, and they have since been successively rebranded as the NKVD, the KGB, and are now the FSB. Russian political police in Stalin's era were only secret in the sense that their operations were not open to public scrutiny or accountability. They were very much in evidence, wearing army style uniforms with magenta hatbands and epaulets, they enjoyed preferential status, living quarters and social amenities, and their powers of arbitrary arrest, deportation and execution made them reviled and feared. The political police controlled the civic police, frontier guards, the fire service, labour camps, espionage and terrorism abroad, and counter-espionage and counter-terrorism at home. They were responsible for the personal safety of Stalin and other key personnel, and for security within industrial, agricultural and transport organisations. They also infiltrated the armed forces to ensure political conformity.

As a young revolutionary Stalin had fallen foul of the political police on a number of occasions and so was well aware of their sinister potential and methodology. When he became a Politburo member he took on administrative tasks which others spurned, but which gradually enabled him to assert his authority over his erstwhile tormentors. Once in control, he restructured the organisation to suit his own purpose, and used it as the cudgel with which he bludgeoned his way towards outright dominance within the party, whilst at the same time battering the entire citizenry into canine and grovelling submission. It was a contract with the devil - Stalin needed the political police as his power base and as the instrument which implemented his purges, and reciprocally, the political police drew their authority solely from him, their perks, their status and their very existence being dependent upon their unquestionable loyalty and efficacy. Ineffectual NKVD operatives were soon immolated, and when Stalin judged that a senior police official had served his purpose, he and as many as 20 thousand of his subordinates were liquidated (CR90p177). Yagoda, the evil police supremo of Stalin's early days was thus replaced in 1936 by the slimy, sadistic runt Yezhov, who in turn was supplanted in 1938 by the heinous Beria, a man who so disgusted other members of the Politburo that they ordered he be shot when Stalin died.

Arrests could be triggered in several ways. The victims of purges might be those who were personally selected by Stalin, or who had been brought to his attention by the political police. They might be those denounced by their neighbours as having been the instigators of subversive acts or statements, or they might quite simply be those unfortunate enough to have been drafted in response to purge quotas set by central authority. An enthusiastic party member in Odessa denounced 230 of his colleagues, one labour camp commandant was ordered to shoot 1300 inmates, but in the biggest single mass cull, 26 thousand perished (CR90o326). Yezhov set regional purge quotas in terms of four or five figures, and during his tenure of office supplied Stalin with 383 lists detailing thousands of nominees of sufficient eminence to require the dictator's personal scrutiny. The political police accumulated enormous quantities of data from their network of informers, and when KGB files ultimately became available for scrutiny it emerged that no less than half the nation had been blacklisted.

Arrests were usually made at home between 2 and 4 in the morning when the victim's living quarters were scrupulously searched before he was abducted. At the police headquarters it was standard procedure for the accused to be forced to stand on tiptoe with his back to the wall, and interrogated without food or sleep for as long as it took for relays of investigators to extract a fabricated confession from him. Those who failed to incriminate themselves during this preliminary ordeal were then subjected to torture until they submitted. Battered with chair legs or heavy bags of sand, ribs and vertebrae were broken, joints dislocated and internal organs ruptured. Fingers were slammed in doors, toenails torn out, and the "hoist" so favoured by the Spanish Inquisition came into its own again, whereby the victim was wrenched off the ground by a rope which tied his hands behind his back. Stalin endorsed the use of torture, openly exhorting interrogators to "beat, beat and beat again". Estimates suggest that only 1% of purgees could withstand such measures. One army marshal's signed confession was later found to have his forensically identifiable blood stains upon it.

Sentence was then passed, either by a "Troika" of three appointees headed by an NKVD official, by a full military tribunal, or, if the accused was of prominent rank, by a "show" trial in court. A signed confession was taken as absolute proof of guilt. The show trial not only had political propaganda value since it received media publicity, but it also lent weight to the incrimination by asserting that the confession had been spontaneous, by showing that the due process of law had been followed, and by demonstrating that the accused had met his just deserts as a traitor, spy, conspirator, saboteur, or assassin. The accused was also warned that if he retracted his confession in court his family would be tortured, deported or shot. The outcome of a show trial was never in doubt, since it was scarcely possible for any defence lawyer to prevail against Vishinsky, the Procurator General whom Stalin had himself appointed in 1933.

Execution was by shooting in the back of the head. A TT 8 round automatic pistol was used from which as many as four bullets might be required. Victims were dressed in white underclothes, standing on a tarpaulin to catch spilt blood, and a doctor was present to sign the death certificate. Mass executions were usually performed in ravines or quarries. In recent years, gruesome mass graves, each containing around 50 thousand corpses have been excavated at Vladivostok, Minsk and Kiev, whilst many others still await investigation. It has always been considered the prerogative of the political police to assassinate both defectors and political opponents living in other countries. Although Trotsky was shot in Mexico, other Russian expatriates have frequently been poisoned. Yagoda himself had been a pharmacist, and took a special interest in developing this more subtle form of assassination. It was he who was believed to have set up a special poison department in the Lubyanka, and it is conceivable that Litvinenko's death in the UK in 2006 was attributable to the work of this laboratory. The political police frequently executed or deported relatives, associates and acquaintances of those they had convicted, but as a rule did not victimise children under 12 years of age. As a consequence, one million children orphaned by the state, or born in labour camps, had to be accommodated, and this was done by establishing a network of NKVD orphanages across the country.

Stalin believed that the Russian psyche could only be made to respond if was brutalised, a precedent set by his predecessors Peter the Great and Ivan the Terrible, and by generations of land owners who traditionally used the rod (Vlast) or scourge to goad the chattel peasantry into compliance. Stalin deliberately uprated and refined the political police so that under his direction it imposed a vice like rule of terror, eradicated all opposition, and forced the population to accept those agricultural, industrial and military changes which he believed to be urgently necessary if Russia was to modernise, and withstand invasion from west or east. The price the Russian people paid for these vulturine policies was psychologically crippling. Societal cohesion disintegrated as the pernicious cancer of fear, distrust, suspicion, spite and chronic insecurity slowly destroyed all interpersonal relationships, including sometimes even those of immediate family members.

The Forced Labour Camps

Those purgees who were not executed at the time of their sentence were deported to forced labour camps. Whereas Hitler's concentration camp inmates were either starved to death or gassed, in Stalin's they met their end either from overwork or from hypothermia, dysentery, scurvy, the brutality of their guards, or victimisation at the hands of the common criminals impounded with them. Periodically, mass culls were also used to fulfil quotas or stifle epidemics.

Initially set up in 1918, the number of these camps mushroomed until by 1937 there were 35 clusters of them, each cluster consisting of 200 camps, and each camp housing an average of 1200 souls (CR90p309). Situated in those bleak, scantily populated near-wildernesses of the north and far northeast of the country, the camps were organised and staffed by the political police, acting under the direction of a central administrative body, the Gulag. In 1932 there were 2 million detainees, in 1938 there were 7 million, and in the late 1940's 12 million (BA91p1056 and CR90p309). Since the latter figure represented 10% of the country's work force, and since a quarter of a million guards were needed to control the camps, the labour camp project represented a very poor utilisation of manpower in time of war. Because half the inmates died in the first nine months of detention, and most died within two years, the wastage in human life was enormous.

Transportation to the camps was by unheated cattle wagon in which, as in the case of the country's prisons, the overcrowding was so severe that it was impossible to lie down, and those who died remained upright and supported by the crush of those around until the guards' next intervention. Many failed to survive the rail journey which might last between one and two months, during which rations and drinking water were inadequate. Set to work felling trees, mining or navvying for construction projects such as the three transnational canals, the arctic railway, and the Moscow metro, it was deemed to be essential for the prisoner's punishment that he be forced to work manually and under the most arduous and inhumane conditions. Temperatures could fall to minus 70 degrees centigrade on occasions, clothing and footwear were frequently inadequate, and food consisted of rye bread and soup in quantities which were entirely dependent upon productivity, so that those who fell ill inevitably starved to death.

Reveille was at 5 a.m., and was followed by a twelve hour working day. In northern camps, where most died within two years, winter brought nights which lasted almost 24 hours, and frostbite which led to gangrene, whereas summer turned topsoil into swamps where mosquitoes bred in their billions. The gold mines of the far east were manned by prisoners whose rations could not support life for more than three or four years at most, and here the annual death rate was 30%. Escape from all camps was virtually impossible, and a guard knew only too well that should it succeed, he would take the place of the absentee. Those who managed to survive the term of their sentence usually found it arbitrarily extended by the camp commandant. The total death toll for the labour camps was eight million (CR90p326).

The Purges
When the interests of the nation were at stake, both Hitler and Stalin considered human life to be unreservedly expendable. But whereas both were prepared to pay heavy prices in terms of human sacrifice on the battlefield and when persecuting ethnic minorities, only Stalin deliberately instigated mass slaughter of his own nationals, a slaughter which was as irrational in real terms as it was extreme. Like his political assassinations, though on a much larges scale, Stalin's mass purges were used to pre-empt opposition, or else to punish whole communities or selected echelons within the various hierarchies which he considered to have failed him, and which he pilloried as an example to others. At one time or another, Stalin purged the Politburo, the communist party officialdom, the administration, the peasants, the industrialists, the armed forces, the secret police, Eastern European communist leaders, the Jews, the church, the medical profession and returning Russian prisoners of war. Between 1930 and 1939 there were

18-20 million deaths in purges (CR68 and Soviet sources). The paranoid carnage reached a peak between the years 1936-8, a period in Soviet history now referred to as the Great Terror (ACGO90 p152).

Before 1927, 80% of the Russian population were peasants, most of whom farmed between 5 and 25 acres, using primitive methods. Within six subsequent years Stalin evicted, and deported or shot, 15 million incumbents from the more profitable farms, whilst nationalising and re-allocating all land as huge collective combines, and setting fixed price production quotas which were implemented by force. 120 million people were deprived of their land, livestock and equipment, and reassembled in small communities as state vassals. The term "Kulak" (originally denoting a profitable farmer) was now used in a derogatory sense to demonise those who resisted, and against whom accusations of grain hoarding were levelled (ACGO90p140). Peasant uprisings, especially in the Ukraine and Caucasus, were ruthlessly suppressed with mass arrests, execution and deportation. In retaliation, peasants slaughtered their livestock, causing an economic disaster from which Russia took 25 years to recover (BA91p280).

In the early 1930's, in Russia's grain belt, Stalin set unrealistically high quotas for corn production, robbing farmers of both their means of sustenance and their seed corn, so that famine ensued, particularly in the Ukraine, a normally bountiful region of food production. In a paranoidal reaction to imaginary corn hoarding, Stalin convicted and executed 55 thousand peasants. The persecution was totally unjustifiable, because at that time Russia as a whole had accumulated adequate corn reserves and was actually exporting large quantities by way of overseas trade. All told, by 1938, 13.5 million souls had perished as a result of Stalin's anti-kulak dispossession policies (CR68).

The most damaging of Stalin's catharses were those which imperilled state security. In 1937, purges of almost the entire general staff and high command of the Red Army, Navy and Air Force, together with swathes of prominent industrialists, meant that both the

Russian economy and its armed forces were dangerously disorganised, weakened, and therefore vulnerable to attack by Hitler. Evidence has now become available which shows that Stalin was deceived by, and grossly overreacted to, a ruse prepared for him by the German Security Service to which Hitler, Himmler and Heydrich were all party, and which purported to show that Russian armed forces were planning a military coup against their soviet leader. In the savage response which followed, the flower of the Russian high command was tried for treason and executed. Three of the five Army Marshals, thirteen of the fifteen Army Commanders, and eight of the nine Fleet Admirals were liquidated. All told, 40 thousand officers were dismissed, and 43 thousand were shot or deported. The Air Force, and tank and mechanised units fared particularly badly (ACGO()p154, BA91p528, CR68, DI66p417, KP40, SB43, TM02p138). During the war, 5.7 million Russian soldiers were channelled through German prison camps, of whom 4 million perished of starvation, exhaustion, disease and exposure (TN77p409). When those POW's who had survived were repatriated, Stalin sent 80% of them to forced labour camps, together with the hundreds of thousands of Russians from German concentration and labour camps, and also Russian civilians overrun during the German advance, branding them all as traitors. Stalin even refused to ransom his son Yakov who died in German captivity.

The total Russian death toll for the second world war was 21 million, of whom 13.6 million were troops (BA91p844). To this dreadful tally must be added those 20 million who perished in Stalin's purges before 1940. By the end of 1946, one in eight of Russia's pre-war population had succumbed (TM02p161).

The Case for the Defence

Whilst we cannot deny Stalin's unmitigated, and totally unjustifiable cruelty towards his compatriots in the pursuit of his lust for unfettered power and control, we must also consider the grounds for a plea of mitigation. The world in which Stalin operated was politically unstable and volatile. Although Russia had twice defeated Japan in Manchuria, Stalin recognised the threat from both Germany and Japan, notwithstanding peace agreements he had contracted with each. The nightmare prospect of a war on two fronts, which was to prove so disastrous for Hitler, was ever present in Stalin's own mind. Stalin's joint annexation of Eastern Europe with Hitler, prior to war with him, was intended to provide Russia with a buffer zone against German aggression.

In 1917, four fifths of Russians were peasants, predominantly tenant smallholders, and Stalin recognised the need for agricultural reform, rapid industrialisation and armamentation to build a strong Russia which could protect itself against a repetition of its humiliating 1917 defeat at the hands of Germany. In the space of 30 years, Stalin took his country from the age of the wooden plough to that of nuclear technology (TM02p142). Stalin had to meet the challenge of building the world's first communist state, given foundations already laid by Marx, Engels, Lenin and the virtually bloodless revolution of 1917 in Russia. The only real precedent for doing so had been the Paris Commune of 1871, and world powers viewed communism as a subversive threat to their hegemony. To make matters worse, Russia lacked the level of prosperity and resources of wealth which Marx had pointed out would be required to fund a successful proletariat takeover.

By annexing adjacent territories and converting them into Soviet republics, Stalin restored around one eighth of the world's surface to Russian dominance, the extent of territory over which the Tsars had formerly held sway. Stalin was, above all, a patriot who considered himself a successor to Peter the Great and Ivan the Terrible, but his policies, unlike Hitler's or Napoleon's, were always directed towards the defence of Russia, and although he was a committed proselyte of world communism, there is no convincing evidence to suggest that he ever harboured aspirations to conquer the Eurasian continent.

Stalin's most enduring legacy to the rest of the world is that he absorbed the aggressive impact of the most efficient army in modern history. Without the bloodbath which parried Operation Barbarossa, Hitler would have used his success in mainland Europe to recruit additional manpower and invade Britain, thus depriving America of its most important foothold from which to launch a second front. The outcome of the second world war might then have been very different. Germany, Italy and Japan had aspirations to divide world domination three ways, once Russia had been defeated.

Behavioural Analysis

How are we to understand the behaviour of this man, the truth about whose worst excesses were only brought to light by his successor, Khrushchev after Stalin's death (TS71p550), and of whom Mikhail Gorbachov said "the mark of Stalin's evil was that he turned morality on its head : what was bad became good, what was good, bad." (TM02p132). For most Russians the scars will never heal. Yet when we compare him with Hitler, we see that Stalin's ferocious tyranny had some important redeeming features.

Joseph Stalin was born in 1879 to illiterate parents who had been chattel-slaves 20 years previously, until the introduction of the Tsar's emancipatory reforms. He was of small stature, standing only just over 5 feet, he had dark brown eyes, uneven teeth, his face was scarred and pitted from the smallpox he had suffered in childhood, and his left arm remained partially paralysed following an accident he had sustained when he was ten. As a high party official he was at the disadvantage of not having received the sophisticated, cosmopolitan education of his colleagues, and he spoke Russian with the coarse provincial accent of a Georgian. All these factors combined to give him an inferiority complex to which he overreacted by harbouring a bitter resentment of authority, landlords, royalty, and the professional and officer classes. His childhood home had been a single roomed hovel with a mud floor, his mother indulged her only surviving child, but his father was an uncouth, violent drunkard who repeatedly thrashed his wife and child with a stick (DI66p23). The physical abuse he had suffered so far exceeded that which is appropriate to primate dominance confrontations as to constitute offensive aggression. Other species do not treat their offspring in this way.

As a result, Joseph was malconditioned and grew up with a personal equation of obsessive, burning and cynical hatred, and a deep sense of injustice and resentment. He learned to be evasive, perfidious, acutely observant, suspicious, unscrupulous, unpredictable and totally self reliant. He had a paranoid distrust for everyone, an all consuming desire for vengeance, and a volcanic temper. He always played his cards close to his chest, was emotionally independent, and was unable to form either amicable or close personal relationships, viewing all human beings as pawns to be exploited or eliminated.

Stalin was intelligent, and possessed a formidable memory which enabled him at the age of 14 to win a boarding scholarship to Tiflis Theological Seminary. This sudden preferment, and the overweening encouragement he received from his mother, imbued him with a lifelong sense of near messianic self importance. At the seminary, twice daily services, which lasted 3-4 hours on Sundays, were held in the customary standing position of Russian orthodoxy. The monks spied surreptitiously and continually on their charges, punishing any deviation with solitary confinement in cells. These arcane disciplinary routines seem likely to have influenced the design of Stalin's later interrogation procedures. The repetitive brainwashing and methodology of the seminary made the exploitation of dogma and ritual second nature to him, but his cynicism took precedence over any thoughts he may have had of taking the vows of priesthood, and his mentors seem to have considered him an unsuitable ordinand, since he was expelled without graduation shortly before his 20th birthday.

After leaving the seminary, Stalin's bent for manipulative dogma and his inability to tolerate dissent were refocused from religion to left wing politics. He became a Marxist pamphleteer and a professional agitator, producing leaflets from an underground press, encouraging strikers and organising demonstrations. Viewed as a threat to public order, he was repeatedly arrested over a period of ten years prior to 1917, and either incarcerated or exiled to Siberia (BA91p34). The criminal elements with which he mingled in captivity taught him to be streetwise, to trust nobody and to be totally self reliant.

In his later career he made extensive use of the media, which he hobbled and perverted in his own image, using it to warp the public psyche and flaunt his show trials in a blaze of publicity, and he organised a government department of agitation and propaganda (Agitprop), whose task was similar to that undertaken by Goebbels in Nazi Germany. Stalin founded the communist newspaper Pravda and wrote books whose slanted political stance all Russians were duty bound to assimilate. In a grossly overblown autobiography he boasted of his political skills, looked upon himself as a military genius, and rewrote soviet history so as to credit himself with having been Lenin's right hand man in 1917.

Stalin's lifestyle reflected his peasant origins. He wore a drooping moustache, a smock, long boots, and a brown military coat, and he smoked a pipe. He lived in a small unpretentious house in the Kremlin, and both this and his summer house near Moscow remained state property during his lifetime. His only entertainments were watching films and throwing all-night parties at which he could humiliate guests by making them drunk. He did not crave other women or wealth, and had no interest in sport. He married twice, his first wife dying of typhus and his second committing suicide in despair - an act which Stalin characteristically condemned as treachery towards him. He had two children by each marriage, but the only one with whom he really bonded was his daughter Svetlana.

The surname Stalin was an adopted one meaning "man of steel". He was born Josif Vissarionovich Dzhugashvili, and died in 1953 at the age of 73 (DI66p614). Neither he nor Hitler gave any thought as to who would be their successors, concerned solely as they both were with their own charismatic immortality - the tell-tale stigma of a megalomaniac.

Stalin's character was moulded by the three phases of his early development. His father distorted his conditionable brain, the seminary's uses of dogma, rhetoric, theatricism and surreptitiousness were translated in his twisted brain into party propaganda, show trials and interrogation routines, and his sojourn in the criminal underworld schooled him in total self reliance, and honed his organisational skills. Any potential he had for exercising the unconditionable brain's traits of innovation or enlightened rationality were completely obscured by the paranoid overlay of his conditionable brain.

(Sources Reviewed: ACGO90, BA91, CR68, CR90, DI66, KP40, SA75, SB43, TISN06, TM02, TN77, TS71)

CHAPTER 14

DISTORTIONS OF SUBMISSION IN DOMINANCE RANKING

THE UNDERCLASS, THE SCAPEGOAT, SELF RENUNCIATION

As a firebrand left wing polemicist of the late 18th century, Thomas Paine was 150 years ahead of his time. Campaigning on behalf of the underdog, he advocated the abolition of inherited privilege and the House of Lords, and sought to establish family allowances, old age pensions and maternity grants. Viewed by the authorities as a dangerous iconoclast, he was charged with seditious libel in his native England, fled to France, and then found his way across the Atlantic to participate in the American Revolution. Paine coined the phrase "all men are born equal", by which of course he meant that all should have equal rights, at least at the ballot box and under the law. His doctrines, like those of the swiss antimonarchist Jean Jaques Rousseau, exerted a strong influence over the fledgling revolutions in France and America. Paine maintained that the huge discrepancy between "those who have" and "those who have not" could only be redressed by a return to those republican principles of government which had first been formulated in Ancient Greece

The non-human primate community is a cohesive integrated unit which has an overall pecking order, but is not divided against itself with the formation of underclasses such as those seen in human societies. Underprivileged subsets of humanity began with the conquests and slave based empires of antiquity, but have remained a persistent feature of societal architecture ever since. Perceived differences of race, religion, language, culture or occupation are used as pretexts to stratify a population and skew power and wealth in favour of an overclass. For example, South African Apartheid discriminated on the basis of race, religious intolerance accounted for the demeaning treatment of Jews by mediaeval Christians, and the Hindu Caste system defined its underclasses according to the type of work they did. Sometimes, underclasses are sadistically persecuted, scapegoated, or corralled into sequestrated communities such as ghettos, concentration camps or ring fenced slums. Always, a degree of social ostracization and opprobrium is applied to them which is an overt manifestation of adverse compulsive prejudice, a form of malfunction embedded within the immature mind during the third phase of human nurture. For this type of malconditioning, parents share responsibility with the peer group and any communal bigotry which prevails.

Whereas some underclasses are merely exploited, others are persecuted or exterminated. Mao Tse- tung victimised the professional classes, southern US whites hung blacks from trees, witches were burned at the stake as were heretics rooted out by the Spanish Inquisition, and the Nazis starved and gassed Jews in their millions. In terms of primate patterns, all these aberrations are biologically abnormal and are manifestations of the way in which the dominance ranking mechanism has become grossly distorted in human hands. With time, the biased mentality underlying such behaviour becomes culturally embedded and is then perpetuated by the collective malconditioning of further generations, prompting tacit acceptance of the unequal status quo, both by the underclass and the overclass.

In most cases an underclass has no choice but to accept the abject subordination and thraldom which is thrust upon it, but in a more extreme expression of exaggerated submission the individual actively engineers his own humiliation, using inversion mechanisms such as self degradation, self mutilation and suicide. Whether passive or active, all forms of distorted dominance submission override the herd bond, are biologically abnormal and uniquely human. Although some of these traits are globally in decline, others still flourish, and contribute significantly to the toll of human suffering. Whilst it is true that the third phase of human nurture is not under full parental control, parents have a significant degree of responsibility for countermanding compulsive prejudice in their offspring, and total responsibility for preventing all active forms of distorted submission. The many intriguing variants of these behaviourisms can best be understood through the use of key historical examples - slavery, the witch hunt, the Hindu Caste system, and self renunciation including suicide.

Why Does Slavery Still Exist?
Slavery is the antithesis of democracy. The slave has no right of ownership of land, is unfranchised, is forced to work unwaged and is a chattel of his master who, until recent times, exercised the power of life and death over him. Slaves are stigmatised subsets of society whose status is similar to that of a domesticated farm animal.

Interherd warfare exists amongst non-human primates, such as chimpanzees, some monkeys and lemurs, but subgroup servitude does not. Nor does slavery exist in the most primitive of all human societies, in which discriminatory containment cannot be enforced, and captives taken in war are simply butchered or assimilated into society (BLGGW64p281) The slave owner's control of his charges depends upon his ability to confine, stigmatise, and discipline them with measures such as fetters, branding iron and physical abuse.

In antiquity, differentiation of labour only became possible when food supplies increased to a level which rendered it unnecessary for the whole community to continue full time hunter gathering. Monarchical, priestly and warrior classes then emerged to dominate their fellows as dictatorships, theocracies and warlordships, examples of all of which persist to this day. When the ruler assumed the conjoined roles of king, chief priest and generalissimo, the social inequalities he could impose upon his subjects became so extreme that the most menial classes worked unwaged. If the ruler was deified, his authority was sacrosanct.

Until the 19th century, all major civilisations depended heavily upon slave labour. The classical writers Aristotle, Plato, Homer and Herodotus, and biblical sources considered its need unquestionable - 1 Tim. 6 recommends that "All who wear the yoke of slavery must count their own master worthy of all respect" (NEB61p348). As civilisations matured, so the demand for large labour forces increased to enable civil projects in construction, agriculture, manufacture and mining to be realised without draining the public purse. Slaves also manned naval galleys and were used as concubines, wet nurses and gladiators. Slavery on this scale could only be supported by the provision of a constant supply of captives taken in plundering forays or outright war.

At different points in their history the Jews were enslaved by Egypt and Babylon. The ancient Greeks made extensive use of slaves and, at its zenith, 350 thousand of the 500 thousand inhabitants of Athens were slaves, and 300 rules governing slave emancipation were engraved on a long wall at Delphi, the most revered shrine in Greece. Ancient Rome took slaves from all its conquered territories - 100 thousand Gauls were drafted to work Italian mines (BPL00p45). In ancient Britain, cattle and slaves were used in place of money. The Arabs traded luxuries, olive oil and horses with Europe in return for timber, iron and slaves, and invested heavily in East African slave trading from 650CE until at least 1900CE, during which time an estimated 11-17 million Africans crossed the Sahara, Red Sea or Indian Ocean to be sold in the slave markets of Arabia, Persia and India. In 1698, Oman's forces usurped Portugal's brutal 200 year old occupation of Zanzibar and dynamized the slave trade there until, by 1832, the 50 thousand annual turnover in Africans became so profitable that the Omani Sultan moved his state capital to that African enclave (NGMZ:01:10). The Arabs also penetrated Russia's river highways to trade for furs, amber, honey and slaves (from which territory the term "Slav" derived). Piratical forays from the Muslim coasts of North Africa harassed European coastlines for centuries in order to kidnap Christians for the galleys. Even as recently as 1950, one fifth of the population of Saudi Arabia remained enslaved.

The best documented era in slaving history is that in which Europeans, and in particular the English, shipped West Africans to the new world. 400 miles of the West African littoral were guarded by the white man's trading posts and castles, the entire coastline being divided into sections, each of which was named after its principal export - grain, gold, ivory and slaves. Following Columbus' discovery of America, Caribbean Amerindians were co-opted as a slave labour force for Spain's exploitation of agriculture and mining, but they succumbed to European borne infections and overwork, and the resulting deficit was made good by importing West Africans. Over a period of the next 350 years, an estimated 15 million Africans were forcibly transported, of whom at least 20% died on board ship under atrocious conditions. Of those who reached the Americas, most were destined for the Caribbean islands, around 5 million reached Brazil and the remainder settled in the USA, Mexico and Peru. The products of their labours were tobacco, sugar, rice, cotton and gold. Their descendants still constitute the predominant population of the Caribbean, 50% of the Brazilian population and 12.1% of the US population.

The practice of enslavement had been endemic in Africa since the days of ancient Egypt. In the 16th century CE, black on black warfare provided tribal chiefs with a ready supply of slaves, 80% of whom were captives, the remainder being felons guilty under tribal law of debt, theft or adultery. When the Arabs and Europeans began to take an interest in the African slave markets they had no need to kidnap their commodity but traded textiles, guns, powder, alcohol, mirrors, knives, beads, pots and pans, and iron or copper bars with the local chiefs who amassed vast wealth in kind. The latter were not alone in benefiting from the misery they caused: ship owners could net £25,000 yearly

(PHJ00p198), planters could make an annual profit of 50% on their investments, and European sovereign authorities levied a 10% tax on the legal right to trade in slaves (NGMZ:02:08).

Native African trading agents brought their captives to the coast secured by the neck in chain gangs ("coffles"), where they were incarcerated in the dungeons of the trading forts to await the arrival of European ships. To maximize capacity on board, intermediate decks were added whose restricted dimensions forced the slaves, chained in pairs, to lie flat on their backs and wallow in their own excreta for the duration of the voyage. Typically, ships plied from Europe to Africa, then to America before reloading with sugar or molasses for the return voyage. An alternative route supplied Africans direct to Brazil.

When the survivors reached their port of destination in the new world, the ship's crew prepared them for sale by swilling them down, shaving their heads, polishing their teeth and anointing them with oil to make the skin glisten. They were then rowed ashore to be exhibited naked in the slave market. Both males and females bore the monogram of their trader and purchaser branded on their cheek, shoulder or buttock. The driver's whip kept order; manacles, fetters, chains and padlocks were used for restraint, and the six days of weekly work extended from dawn to dusk. Punishments for non compliance were severe: tied to a triangular upright framework "a cool hundred" lashes would strip all the flesh from a man's back, and not infrequently noses, ears, fingers and genitalia were cut off. A slave who escaped had a limb amputated, and one who assaulted or stole from a white man received the death penalty. For more flagrant crimes, a negro was nailed to the ground and slowly burned alive (PHJ00p137). Most slaves became physical wrecks after 7 or 8 years of gruelling forced labour, and like the old and sick were turned out to die so as to make room for new blood.

Slave revolts were rare but notorious. In 73 BCE, Spartacus' rebel horde defeated the Roman armies sent against them on no less than nine occasions before 6 thousand of them were eventually overpowered and crucified with their leader. In 1804 a successful slave revolt in Haiti led to the establishment of an autonomous state.

In 1807, Britain, which until then had been the most active of slave trading nations, banned enslavement, largely thanks to the efforts of Wilberforce and Clarkson. Many other countries followed suit in subsequent decades. Twentieth century totalitarianism brought back mass slavery in the form of the Stalinist gulag and the Nazi labour camps. Men of military age in German occupied Europe were given the choice of enlisting in the German armed forces, or being drafted into enslavement. Those who resisted went to concentration camps and the protracted starvation which that involved.

Slavery persists today. Human bondage is still used in India, Pakistan, Bangladesh, Nepal and Africa as debt collateral, a practice which may entrap whole families. Globally, an estimated 27 million continue to suffer the indignity and misery of thraldom, two thirds of whom are located on the Indian subcontinent. Large numbers of Eastern European women are still kidnapped and smuggled into the bordellos of Western Europe, particularly those of Italy and Greece. It has been estimated that in the latter country at the beginning of the new millennium, revenue from involuntary prostitution exceeded fourfold that accruing from its voluntary equivalent (NGMZ:03:11).

(Sources Reviewed: BLGGW64, BPL00, NGMZ:01:10 and 02:08, PHJ67, PJM73, www.history online, WKP/slavery)

The Scapegoat. The Witch Hunts of Western Christendom
Unlike other species, humans persecute and kill other members of their own immediate community in two types of situation, each of which entails suppression of the herd bond. In the first, an event giving rise to communal misfortune may be superstitiously misinterpreted so that the blame for it becomes redirected onto individuals who are perceived to be someway different, and who are then treated as alien. The spontaneity of this process contrasts with the politically authorised and organised persecution of minorities driven by perversion of the

dominance ranking process. From the victim's point of view the difference is immaterial.

Most cultures have persecuted their endogenous minorities at some point in their history. Since late Roman times, the long list of scapegoats in the context of Europe alone has included Jews, gypsies, prostitutes, homosexuals, lepers, witches and heretics. The most paradoxical and bizarre of these catharses was the witch hunt in which supposedly sane Christian communities executed their own grandmothers. Although a few men perished as sorcerers, victims were predominantly female and usually elderly. To justify the staging of these grotesquely irrational theatricals, the church supplied deluded dogma which it was required that the secular authorities should implement. Denunciation was by neighbour against neighbour. Inevitably sadism and misogyny crept into the equation.

Witches, wizards, seers and soothsayers feature in the folk lore of virtually all world cultures, representing one facet of man's efforts to ascribe natural events to supernatural forces. Western witch lore originally derived from the Graeco-Roman cult of Hecate, goddess of the black arts, death, the after life and the pitch darkness of night. During the nine centuries prior to 1324, the church had tolerated the presence of witches within society, believing them to be for the most part non malignant. But in the 14th and 15th centuries, during the years in which the Papacy sojourned in Avignon, successive popes changed their ecclesiastical attitude towards sorcery, declaring it to be demonic and heretical. In future the church was to be the sole arbiter of all supernatural affairs (TRW01p71).

Official unease towards witches had been demonstrated in 906 CE in an order to bishops and churches issued under Charlemagne, entitled The Canon Episcopi, which proclaimed that "some wicked women perverted by the devil, seduced by illusions and phantasms of demons, believe and profess themselves, in the hours of the night to ride upon certain beasts with Diana, the goddess of the pagans, and an innumerable multitude of women, ... to traverse great spaces of earth...." However, outright physical persecution did not begin until four centuries later.

Pope John the Twelfth lived in constant fear of witchcraft. His talisman against it was a magic snake skin which he supposed would alert him to the presence of poison in his victuals. Racked with phobias, he prosecuted several members of his Papal court on grounds of sorcery and issued an urgent Papal caveat, warning that "many Christians make a covenant with hell". The outburst detonated a spate of witch hunts and trials from 1335 CE onwards. A later pope, Innocent the Eighth, took an even graver view of the machinations of the sinister spiritual underworld and served Christianity with an outspoken ultimatum in the form of a Papal Bull, in which the faithful were ordered to close ranks and extirpate sorcery wherever they found it. The text of this strident document was used in its entirety as the core of a book entitled Malleus Maleficum ("the hammer with which to crush those practising evil magic"), published in 1484 which became the standard reference for all churches and secular authorities confronted by the growing menace. This vade mecum spelt out in intricate detail the methodology which was to be employed in the interrogation, torture and trial of witches (TRW01p51). In deference to the powerful authority of the church, secular leaders usually colluded with it. Mediaeval monarchs had to tread warily - they only ruled their subjects under papal sufferance, could only marry with papal approval, swathes of the territory over which they held sway were owned by the church, creativity in music and art was mostly dependent upon ecclesiastical patronage, and the church had a stranglehold on literacy and the administration of education and justice. Moreover, all clerics preached obedience and subservience, which kept commoners in their place.

The conceptual image of a typical witch was that of a repulsively ugly hag whose sallow, hirsute and grotesquely wrinkled face sported a beak like nose, who had too few if any teeth, and whose scalding tongue and squeaking voice emitted malevolent portents. She was usually aided and abetted by the mangy black cat which kept her company in the hovel in which she lived. Given the repugnance that these physical attributes conjured up, it was all too easy to ascribe to their owner the accompanying demerits of sorcery, soul-selling to the devil, submitting to degrading sexual acts with him and ritually kissing his anus, inflicting barrenness or impotence on fellow humans, practising infanticide, making evil potions from corpses, and causing all manner of natural disasters. That the coven met at black of night matched its association with black magic and explained the fact that nobody had actually witnessed the broomstick flights of its attendees (TR76p135).

Women suspected of witchcraft were thrown into ponds, cross bound between toes and thumbs, and if they floated they were deemed to be guilty (HC03p29). Following denunciation, the accused was apprehended, tried in an Inquisitorial Court under the auspices of church or secular authority, or both, tortured into confession if she did not confess spontaneously, and, in 25-70% of cases, was then executed. In England and America, death was by hanging. On the continent the witch was burned, with or without preliminary strangling. The catholic dictum of the time assured everyone involved that God would not allow an innocent person to be punished.

The first real witch trial in Europe was at Kilkenny in Ireland in 1324, brought by the Franciscan Bishop of Ossory. The accused was the widow Alice Kyteler who had outlived three wealthy husbands and married a fourth, a circumstance sufficient in itself to suggest the use of black arts. Alleged to have carried out dastardly rituals undertaken at crossroads involving dismembered animals, to have cast spells, to have concocted magic potions and to have fornicated with the devil, Alice wisely fled the scene. Not to be denied, the bishop extracted a false confession from Alice's servant girl under torture and executed her instead by way of expiation (TRW01p73).

When the cardinals elected John the Twenty-second as pope he determined to put an end to all witchcraft and turned his particular attention to the area of south west France known as the Languedoc, a territory that had already borne the brunt of papal fury when Innocent the Third exterminated the Cathars there during the ninth crusade of 1208. Several of Pope John's witchcraft prosecutors were acknowledged misogynists, and, as usual, nearly all the victims were women. Thence the fanatical purges spread to other areas of France, Switzerland, Germany and Northern Italy, with the Dominican Friars again as prominently aggressive in their attack on their prey as they had been against the Cathars, and also were during the Spanish Inquisition (MHEE81). Witch trials reached England and Scotland in the late 16th century. The peak of all European persecutions was reached between the years 1580 and 1630. By far the greatest number took place in German speaking territories, and more than 50% occurred within a 300 mile radius of the city of Strasbourg (TRW01p4), whence the bulk of published authoritarian directives and much firebrand preaching against witchcraft had emanated. Witch hunting was common to both catholic and protestant communities, but did not occur in countries under the influence of orthodox Christianity.

The death toll for witch persecutions has been overestimated by feminists and underestimated by apologists. Levack's painstaking research for Europe as a whole suggests an all time total of 110 thousand witches tried. The proportion executed varied with locality, so that a figure of 50 thousand deaths is probably realistic, at least 75% of whom were women (LBP95). Thirty six persons perished in the tiny outbreak of witch hunting at Salem, Massachusetts in 1692, after a group of young girls manifesting hysterical behaviour were thought to have been possessed by the devil (FJB08). The undue significance given by their seniors to these juvenile fantasies is reminiscent of later reactions to supposed apparitions at Lourdes, Fatima, Knock and elsewhere - apparitions which Canadian researchers have been able to replicate by electrical stimulation of the brain in the laboratory, and which occur in some forms of epilepsy. Even in the twenty first century those denounced as witches are still liable to be executed in some parts of Africa, in India and in Saudi Arabia, a practice which suggests that the aberration is a characteristic of an intermediate stage of human cultural development.

(Sources Reviewed: FLB08, HC03, HJP52, LBP95, MHEE81, TR76, TRW01)

The Hindu Caste System
Distorted overplay of dominance ranking is well exemplified by the Hindu caste system, which developed as a result of the social stratification imposed upon the peoples of northern India by their conquerors, the Aryans, in 1500 BCE.

The caste system derives its religious precedent from the Hindu Rig Veda, a sacred text written in sanskrit which expounds the myth of the sacrificial dismemberment of Purusha, an all important deity from whose body parts the castes were supposedly derived. His head formed the priestly Brahmin caste, his arms the warrior and ruler caste, his thighs the merchants and farmers, and his feet the servants. Members of one caste were forbidden to eat with, or marry into, another, and penalties for doing so were severe. Each caste occupied its own area within the village, worshipped its own deities and was originally subject to its own laws.

The castes were ranked in the order of their perceived purity and their top-down derivation from the god - the priests being the most revered. At the lowest end of the social spectrum the most polluted were reviled as untouchable and casteless, were forced to live in hovels outside the village perimeter and were engaged in occupations which sullied them - the butchery of animal carcasses, leatherwork, fishing, brewing, sewage disposal, sweeping and cleaning. Religious reform in the shape of Buddhism was in part motivated by a rejection of the caste system, British colonialism moderated caste discrimination, Ghandi spoke out against it, and it has now been outlawed.

(Sources Reviewed: GR92, LCS89, SN89).

Self Renunciation, Including Suicide

Renunciation of self is the most extreme distortion of submission to societal dominance ranking and takes the form of self degradation, self punishment and suicide. Self renunciation is a strictly human phenomenon which deliberately and actively contravenes the most basic of animal instincts, that of self preservation and reaction to danger.

Self Degradation and Self Punishment are bizarre traits which can be traced in most cultures. The obsessive driving forces which lie behind them, as revealed by their context, will be those of religion, sexuality, custom, mental illness or extreme malconditioning. The weird varieties of self punitive procedures adopted by religious ascetics are intended either as acts of penance, to solicit divine indulgence, or to acquire spiritual enlightenment. For example, every three years in the month of May, seven day long Voodoo ceremonies take place in which devotees induce trances in themselves, and during their transcendent state they throw sand in their own eyes, place red hot metal on their tongues, and cut themselves with broken glass as a means of communicating with their deities (NGMZ:95:09). In southern India, finger sacrifice carried out by a carpenter in the local temple was expected of the wife of a man's eldest son as a way of supplicating the gods to increase fecundity in the family (LBR01p125). As a disciplinary ritual, Japanese Tendai monks were required to trek 40 thousand kilometres through mountainous terrain over a seven year period, on pain of ritual suicide (DJR01p502). The Maya pierced their tongues with sting ray barbs to appease the gods when danger threatened (NGMZ:08:10). The penances of sleeping on a bed of nails, of submitting to a two year stint of beggary, of holding one arm above the head until it fuses at the shoulder joint in that position, self flagellation, prolonged fasting, self imposed social isolation, and the drudgery of rising at all hours of the night to pray, all exemplify the compulsive nature of religious fanaticism.

The perverted fetishism of Masochism involves inversion of the dominance mechanism as a precondition for orgasm (see chapter 18).

Physical deformation is a requirement of some freakish cultural customs. Exaggerative submission involving mutilation is imposed upon female children in parts of Africa and India as circumcision, in which the clitoris and labia minora are cut away to prevent eroticism in later life. The scarring may subsequently lead to difficulty in childbirth. In Japan the criminal faction known as the Yakuza have a disciplinary code which forces them to amputate one or more finger segments if they have incurred the wrath of their leaders (TCGN81p111).If female beautification can be ranked as submissive, then a wide range of mutilations come into this category, from the neck stretching hoops worn by some tribal Africans, and the embellishing anatomical adjustments of noses, tongues and ear lobes of many primitive peoples, to the cosmetic surgery of the western world. Even children are not exempt, as is witnessed by the foot binding of far eastern girls, the head binding of Mayan babies, and the adolescent tooth filing ceremony of Indonesia.

In adults, mental illnesses such as hysteria or obsessive compulsive disorder may manifest as self harm. In Hysteria the patient tries to run away from reality by hiding behind a screen of fabricated physical symptoms, and tries to exploit these as a play for attention or sympathy, or as a strategy to obtain opiates. Cuts, sores and burns are the lesions most often seen, and these are usually linear, being transverse on the non-dominant arm and vertical on the legs. Skin damage may also be present on the face and neck. Lesions characteristically fail to heal. More serious injuries are rare, but have included eye evisceration (See also chapter 20). Most adult hysterics lack insight into the nature of their problem, though during wartime small numbers of men knowingly injure themselves to avoid active service.

By contrast, self harm in childhood is seldom due to mental illness, but is the direct result of malconditioning, a cry for help triggered by environmental adversity from which there is no escape, and over which the child has no control. Investigation of home conditions invariably reveals lack of supportive relationships, physical or sexual abuse, or alcohol or substance misuse by family members. An exacerbative emotional crisis usually precipitates the physical damage (GPMMZ:04:09:20).

Suicide

In children suicide rates are very low, at 5 per million, rising in 15-19 year olds to 30 per million, among the latter of whom girls predominate by a factor of five to one. Adult men commit suicide three times as often as adult women. Mens' suicide rates increase continuously with age after 30, rising 3-4 fold by the age of 70-80. Womens' rates rise between the ages of 20-25, fall between the ages of 30-40, thereafter increasing with age. Managerial, professional and artisan classes are most likely to kill themselves, and suicide rates rise during times of economic depression. Suicide in developed countries is more frequent than homicide by a factor of 10-100, the exact ratio varying with locality (HM78p35).

Both the rate and the means of committing suicide have varied considerably with nationality and era. For many years Switzerland recorded the highest rate, in Germany hanging was the most prevalent method used, and Italians most frequently resorted to poison. In all cultures, firearms, cutting and piercing, drowning, asphyxiation, crushing and exposure have played their part. Modern existence has increased the options by providing ready access to carbon monoxide inhalation and therapeutic drug overdosage. In 2006 the most frequently used venue for free fall was the Golden Gate bridge which claimed 34 lives during that year (BBCT1:07:01:30), and where a string of telephone points offering connection to counselling has now been installed.

There are four causes of suicide, and these may act independently or compound each other. *Mental Illness*, most of which has a hereditary basis, accounts for a third of all suicides. We have already noted suicide rates of 10% for schizophrenics, bipolar psychotics, and seriously depressed patients. To these may be added cases of severe paranoia, and patients suffering brain damage from trauma, tumours, toxins, infections or epilepsy.

Another clinically distinct group is comprised of those persons of previously stable personality and sound mind who find themselves confronted by circumstances which would inevitably prove more taxing or distressing than a voluntary controlled death, and who make a *calculated choice of the lesser evil.* Patients facing a painful terminal illness or progressive dementia are obvious examples, and some individuals facing crippling gambling debts, commercial ruin or life imprisonment kill themselves. Well known historical examples have been Cleopatra's use of the asp, the mass suicide of the remnants of the Jewish revolt at Masada when faced with inevitable capture by the Roman army, and the suicide pact of a group Rome's captives forced to train as gladiators. Altruistic suicide is a conscious decision made by those who do not wish to impede their fellows with their disabilities - Titus Oates of Scott's fateful polar expedition took his own life rather than allow his frostbitten body to be a burden to his colleagues. Frail elderly Lapps allow themselves to die of hypothermia when they can no longer trek with their tribe.

Extreme Social Malconditioning can lead to self immolation. The age-old warrior ethic that it is noble to die for one's country acknowledges that death may occur in battle, but not that it will inevitably do so. The mental state needed to impel an individual to commit an act involving his own certain death is altogether different, and depends upon the compulsive and obsessive induction of his conditionable brain. The socio-cultural pressure needed to produce this state of near automatism has to be applied to the mind during immaturity and exerted over a period of several years. Prior to its abolition under colonial rule, the protocol of suttee required an Indian widow to throw herself upon her late husband's funeral pyre. Because of the dictates of tribal custom in some backward cultures, undergrown or sickly children submit to asphyxia by being buried alive (HM30p270). Japanese kamikaze pilots flew their bomb laden planes into the ships of the American battle fleet in the second world war, mollified by the encouragement and sake of their emperor. Tamil Tiger terrorists and Islamic extremists surrounded themselves with explosive charges which they detonated in the midst of their adversaries, believing that they will thus enter paradise.

In some societies suicide is imposed as a way of atoning for an individual's failure or error. In ancient Rome, a legion judged to have been cowardly in battle was subsequently arrayed on the parade ground with the purpose of making every tenth man fall on his sword (decimation). Significant failure in Japanese military, and sometimes in civilian, circles customarily calls for the self impaling ritual of Hara Kiri or Sappuku. Until relatively recently, the captain of a ship was expected to drown with it if it sank, and acts of dishonour on the part of European army officers led to the culprit being presented with a loaded revolver.

The converse of social conditioning is passive, knowing, and resolute resistance to it, but this can effectively lead to suicide. Early Christians refused to worship the Roman state pantheon and were thrown to the lions in the arena. Heresy in 11th -15th century christendom was met with torture and death at the pyre. Islamic sharia law prescribes execution for apostasy. Under most dictatorships sedition has proved suicidal.

Bond Deprivation may prove so traumatic that it precipitates suicide. We have seen that sexual mate bonding is present in humans but absent in most other primates, and that it proves strong enough to cause jealousy which in extreme cases leads to homicide. Unrequited love and bereavement, which balk the bond unilaterally, may precipitate suicide by their disruptive effect upon the emotional and conditionable brain modules. Suicide is more common among widows and widowers than in unmarried persons, and more common among the latter than among those who are married. Within the family, the greater the number of children, the lower the incidence of parental suicide, because of the greater chance that care in old age will be forthcoming.

Herd bonding also plays an important part in the prevention of suicide by promoting mutual support, cohesion and conviviality. Urban suicide rates can exceed 400 per million inhabitants per annum, and the larger the city the greater the rate, whereas rural districts do not exceed 200, and may show rates significantly less than this. Early investigators such as Durckheim and Halbwachs observed a 78% increase in suicide in 11 of the most industrially developed countries during the course of the 19th century. Urbanisation increases population density and produces communities which, because of their size, lack the sense of local identity, self containment and self sufficiency of the rural social unit. As a result, stress is not dissipated by conviviality, cohesion is undermined by impersonality, and mutual support and conformity are sacrificed to indifference.

(Sources Reviewed: CNNT:05:06:08, GPMMZ:04:09:24, HM78, TTN:05:04:27).

CHAPTER 15

FOOTPADS, HOUSEBREAKERS AND OTHER FELONS

HUMAN DISTORTION OF PRIMATE SOCIALISATION - DELINQUENCY

During the years which followed the publication of Darwin's "Origin of Species" in 1859, a young Italian psychiatrist by the name of Cesare Lombroso convinced himself and a great many of his professional colleagues that criminals were, in essence, primitive throwbacks to an earlier stage in human evolution. The criminal's atavistic crude savagery was linked, so the theory went, to outward physical appearances which included those same prominent cheek bones, supraorbital ridges, large teeth and jaws, outsize ears, abundant hair and continuous eyebrows found in apes and early man. The clear implications were that criminality was a genetic fault, and that tracing the perpetrators of crimes would henceforth be facilitated by a search for the stereotypical physical stigmata.

It was to be three quarters of a century before more critical methodology finally laid Lombroso's theory of "the born criminal" to rest. There is now abundant evidence to show that nearly all delinquents are the product of malconditioning during immaturity. Lack of maternal affection or reasonable rebuff in the first nurtural phase thwarts the development of a moral compass, failure to learn to reciprocate with peers during the second phase prevents the development of an equitable social contract, and malconditioning during the third phase fosters and aggravates compulsive prejudice.

Institutional incarceration of a child which exceeds six months produces a strong tendency towards criminality in later life (EEI96p221), and all children taken into care homes have high risks of later conviction and of engaging in prostitution. In recognition of the strong correlation which exists between persistent school truancy and impending delinquency, a team of US investigators carried out a survey of 1452 middle and high school youths from Urban Mandatory Early Warning Truancy programmes with a view to providing preventive intervention. Two thirds of all interviewees reported emotional, physical or sexual abuse, or neglect at the hands of their parents, and this was associated with subsequent depression, suicidal tendencies, hostility, delinquent behaviour, promiscuity, or substance abuse (ACM07). Children from broken homes have significantly increased risks of later societal failure - there is a 44% greater risk of intractable debt, a 70% greater risk of drug addiction, and a 75% greater risk of failure at school. 70% of serving prisoners are from broken homes (BBCT1: 06:12:11).

The need to be able to forge an emotional bond with another individual is so fundamental to human existence that when it is thwarted, as when sexuality is thwarted, substitutes are employed for its gratification. Children who are denied parental affection feel undervalued, and are likely to seek the solace of narcotics during their teens. Drugs fuel theft by creating addiction and the need to fund further supplies, and alcohol fuels violence by suppressing inhibition. Disconcertingly, but perhaps unsurprisingly, the second UN Congress on the Prevention of Crime and the Treatment of Offenders (1960, para.72) found that an increase in delinquency was greatest in those countries in which the standard of life had risen most, an outcome which belies the theory that there is a straightforward relationship between poverty and theft, and which may to a large extent be explained by shifts in the availability of addictive substances. During the past 150 years, changing patterns of intoxicant use have led to changes in the patterns and incidence of committed crime. At the beginning of the 20th century, 67% of serious crimes of violence in America, and 33% in Europe, were attributed to drunkenness (BWA16p639). Everywhere crimes were most frequent on the days and in the months when most alcohol was drunk (HC03p231). In the 1980's, of those convicts entering San Quentin jail, 49% were alcoholics and 44% were opium addicts. In 2002, there were 250 thousand drug addicts in the UK, 75% of crimes were drug related, and 80% of new prison inmates tested positive for drugs (BBCT1:03:11:18 and BBCT1: 06:06:22). By this time, 40% of US arrestees and 10% of UK arrestees were testing positive for cocaine (BT98). Of the 80 thousand prostitutes in the UK, 95% are drug addicts (BBCT1: 06:12:13).

Those relatively few crimes which are neither overtly attributable to malconditioning, nor to the intoxicant use it may later engender, are due to heritable brain defects or, very rarely to other brain pathology. As underlying determinants of antisocial behaviour these four factors are not, of course, mutually exclusive, because any two or more may act concurrently. The seat of the social conscience that motivates unselfishness, co-operation and honesty is situated in an area of the unconditionable brain known as the dorsolateral prefrontal cortex which is among the last of the brain areas to fully mature. Experimentally, this area can be temporarily disabled if it is subjected to weak magnetic impulses (SMZ:06:10:06). Aggressive individuals often have under active areas in the anterior part of the unconditionable brain (RJJ01p237), and convicted murderers frequently have abnormalities in this area (WR02p214). Sometimes congenital cerebral malfunction is associated with other identifiable genetic defects. For instance, abnormalities in chromosome number 6 are associated with antisocial behaviour of a violent nature and a tendency towards alcoholism (WR02p229). Amongst tall adult males in US institutions for the criminally insane, one in every 11 has an XYY chromosomal defect (WMLMAY78p301). A monoamine oxidase defect is an inherited male affliction predisposing to criminality and other personality disorders (JS90p219). Sufferers from schizophrenia (a heritable disorder) have a liability to kill without warning (JS96p334). In the UK, approximately one murder per week is committed by a mentally ill person (BBCT1: 06:12:08). Congenital chronic malice is caused by a genetic error occurring almost exclusively in males, which may be associated with mental subnormality and epilepsy. and which prompts its host to commit recurrent provocative and malevolent acts.

A degree of mental subnormality may also contribute to delinquency, but in this regard we must remember that intelligence is determined both by genes and environment (WMLMAE78p431). Although home circumstances will always be the prime determinant of immature conditioning, the influence of culture mediated through school, neighbourhood, peer group, social class, religious cult and the media, becomes more noticeable during adolescence. All races are considered to have similar intellectual potential, their behavioural differences being culturally conditioned. The arrest rate for violent crime in America is six times greater for young blacks than young whites, and in the modern post industrial West the most likely person to commit a violent crime is the inner city poor black youth (WR02p212-223). The American black has a lower IQ, and higher delinquency, crime and divorce rates, but these could all be accounted for by the adverse living conditions and lower social status which blight many black communities (BV79p109). There is no IQ difference between literate American blacks and literate American whites, and degrees of admixture of coloured blood in Americans have no effect on IQ.

The younger the malconditioned offender, the more likely he is to be able to reform, since it may still be possible to influence his conditionable phase of development. Below the age of 18, incentivisation, as opposed to incarceration, has been shown to reduce recidivism by up to 50%(EHM89p365).

Between the ages of 18 and 20 in the UK, 70% of those convicted subsequently reoffend (BBCR4:06:05:08). After the age of 22, convicted criminals seldom reform. Four out of five convicts in UK jails are recidivists. 80-90% of habitual criminals sentenced to preventive detention under the Prevention of Crime Act 1908 reverted to crime on discharge (HC03p253). Overall recidivism in US Reformatories in the early 20th century was 70-80% (EHM89p365). The length of imprisonment has little effect on subsequent behaviour (HC03p253).

Why Does Delinquency Express Itself In So Many Different Ways?
We saw in chapters 3 and 6 that "herd" integration and cohesion depends upon a counterbalanced relationship of repulsion and attraction between "herd" members. Possessiveness, offensive and dominance linked aggression, and unbridled libido all have to be attenuated by societal forces of attraction in the form of herd bonding and interactive socialisation, two traits whose mature expression requires focused preconditioning throughout immaturity. If the propensity for bonding and socialisation is disrupted during immature life, then the herd bond is rejected, the animal becomes asocial, and possessiveness, aggression and sexual behaviour are no longer subjected to conditioned moderation or control. This disinhibition of agonistic traits results in delinquency.

Although there are many different classifications of acts of delinquency and criminality, from the behavioural standpoint it is appropriate to consider antisocial offences under three main headings:-

Offences against property, such as burglary and shoplifting. These occur when possessiveness is disinhibited, and are perpetrated by either sex.

Violent non-sexual offences against the person, such as assault, battery and non-sexually motivated murder. These result from the disinhibition of offensive aggression, and, because all forms of aggression have a strong correlation with testosterone levels, are predominantly committed by males.

Violent sexual offences against the person, such as rape and sexually motivated murder. These offences result from the disinhibition of sexuality to the point of sadistic libidinous frenzy, and are always perpetrated by males.

How Many Delinquents Are There Out There, And How Many Crimes Do They Perpetrate?

Of the world's prison population of nine million, half reside in US, Chinese and Russian jails. The US has the highest incarceration rate of 737 per one hundred thousand head of population and has locked away 2.2 million, whilst China's lesser rate of 118 has put 1.5 million behind bars. The UK prison population totals approximately 80 thousand and, since most inmates are recitative, the number of habitual UK criminals, whether in custody or at large, must be of the order of a quarter of a million. Figures for crimes known to the police are usually accurate for the most serious offences, but very much less so for minor incidents, because many of the latter go unreported. Moreover, the criteria upon which police classify offences vary between countries, making like for like comparisons difficult. Proportionately balanced statistics are better obtained by conducting surveys in which householders are contacted directly and randomly to ascertain their experience of victimisation.

US Reported Serious Crime

There are 2.5 million cases of serious crime known to the US police annually, which during the 20th. century included 10-12 thousand homicides (HC03p460). In 1984 the homicide rate in the US was ten times higher than it was in Western Europe (WHO84), but the ratio has now fallen to around 3:1.

The British Crime Survey (BCS)

The BCS uses random interviews with adult householders in England and Wales to determine victimisation rates for high volume crimes and reconciles these with rates for crimes reported to the police. Results for 2005-6, for example, revealed a total incidence of 10.9 million for all crime, of which three quarters were crimes against property. There were 765 homicides. Rates for victimisation from violent crimes against the person varied with region between 17 and 34 per thousand, and peaked between the ages of 16 and 20, when the incidence rose to 126. 24% of women stated that they had been victims of sexual assault by partners, and 10% stated that they had been stalked (BCS website and BBCT1:07:01:23).

Multinational Victimisation Surveys
A comprehensive victimisation survey was conducted in 1988 in which random samples of the communities of Europe, North America and Australia were contacted. This showed that annual victimisation rates for all crimes was greatest in the USA and Canada (30%), and least in Switzerland, Norway and Northern Ireland. Violence rates were highest in the USA and Australia. Multinationally the rate for property crimes was 25.2% per annum, for assault against the person or threat of assault 2.9%, and sexual attack 2.5% (DVJJM90). Multinational surveys have now become permanent features of criminological research (DVJJM90 and FDP04).

The burden of losses and expenses inflicted upon society at large by delinquent behaviour is huge. In England and Wales alone, direct annual costs are estimated at £60 billion, a figure which does not include incidentals such as insurance. Of this massive sum, 28% are consequent upon acts of violence, 23% follow fraud or forgery, 15% are attributable to offences committed within the context of commerce or public service, and vehicle crime costs the country 5%. The remaining categories each present the nation with a bill of between 2 and 4% of the total (burglary, robbery, sexual offences, criminal damage, and other forms of theft SBRP00). Drug related crime absorbs 5% of criminal justice resources, and annual losses imposed upon their victims by heroin users alone can reach £864 million (BSPR00).

A Compulsive Dereliction

The stereotypical recidivist criminal has a warped personality. His malconditioning has left him maladjusted, malcontent and malignant. He is an aggressive, insensitive, egocentric and extroverted individual who is hell bent on self gratification, and who is easily provoked to anger, indignation and retaliation. In pursuit of theft, the delinquent is also committed to, and exhilarated by, risk taking, and is always spurred on by the thought that the returns of his exploits far outweigh those obtainable from more legitimate occupations. Moreover, since less than one in ten thefts is traced to the culprit, the odds are stacked heavily in his favour. The state of excitation engendered by burgling gives rise to sweating, trembling, a racing pulse, light headedness and an urge to defaecate, a more intense physiological reaction than that produced by other forms of gambling, but correspondingly addictive. The robber convinces himself that, like Robin Hood, he takes property from those who own more than they should, that the victim's insurance companies will make good all losses, that because he had a deprived childhood society must redress the balance, and that in the final analysis everyone runs his own racket, with aristocrats, politicians, financiers and lawyers proving far more culpable than he.

If a subject's ability to carry out mental arithmetic is limited to that found in the average seven year old, that subject is judged to be subnormal. By this yardstick the prevalence of mental subnormality is 2% in the general population. 6% among those committed for violence against the person, 10% in the general prison population and those incarcerated for burglary, 13% among convicted sex offenders, and 40% among those committed for malicious damage to property (GCB13p180). Yet thieves believe they have to be, and are, more astute than others (MN51p369). Characteristically, thieves tend to squander their ill gotten gains on gambling, fast cars, drugs, drink, clothes and women. Over time, there is a strong tendency for the adult delinquent to become dissolute and degenerate.

Because the predominant cause of delinquency is early malconditioning and not heritable psychosis, psychotherapy and medication have little or no place in treating criminality. Case studies of 50 thousand violent criminals at Bellevue Psychiatric Hospital in the USA over 25 years could identify only 5% suffering from a mental illness which might benefit from medical treatment (HC03p218). By comparison, the equivalent proportion in England in 1959 was only 1%. It has always been difficult to prove that imprisonment acts as a deterrent, and a commonly held view is that it has three primary functions - to offer first time offenders the prospect of a better way of life by providing them with literacy, numeracy and vocational training, to provide drug addicts with supervised detoxification, and to protect the public from career criminals.

Juvenile Delinquency
Delinquent adults have nearly always been juvenile delinquents as teenagers, were truant and maladjusted as schoolchildren, and were the progeny of dysfunctional families. The cultural ichabod which hangs over such families often blights several successive generations. A New York survey in 1957 showed that 75% of juvenile delinquents came from 1% of families in the community, and that these were typically located in areas of high poor relief, dependency and broken homes (HC03p422). A UK study conducted in Camberwell over 30 years, involving 400 delinquent children from the age of 8 years onwards whose offences ranged from shoplifting to assault, showed correlation with a parent who had either previously been guilty of an offence, or had broken the parental partnership. These children proved disruptive in class, they failed at school, abused alcohol and drugs, and later were promiscuous and so had marriages which also failed (JS96p209). In Britain 25% of juvenile crime is committed by 3% of children (JS96p238), and a 1950 study showed that a delinquent juvenile was 31 times more likely to come from a dysfunctional family than a normal one (GC50p107). A survey conducted before the second world

war, which investigated a thousand young offenders, found that one third had a sibling who was mentally disabled, from one third to one half had illiterate parents, the majority were themselves of subnormal intelligence, most had homes which were broken by desertion, separation or divorce, and most had drunken, criminal or sexually promiscuous relatives (GSET34).

The malconditioning which an adolescent received during the first and second phases of nurture will almost inevitably be compounded by any adverse influences to which he his exposed during the third nurtural phase. Peer group and media influence has a marked effect on the immature mind. 70-90 % of young criminals act in gangs which provide the cameraderie of shared daredevilry and iconoclasm. The prior investment and training required for other risk-taking pursuits is not needed in crime (HC03p436). The gang becomes a substitute for the family which failed its offspring, and the challenge and pursuit of crime brings gang esteem. Unless it is entirely instinctive, all primates learn behaviour by imitation, instruction or personal experience, and since imitative learning is often intuitive and involuntary, all media have the potential to influence behaviour (EHM89p90). Exposure to films, television plays or computer games which portray violence for violence's sake, pornographic and sadistic literature, and sports which rely on violence and pain for their appeal, act as role models for impressionable young minds. Multiple studies on juvenile delinquency meta-analysed by Birmingham University's Forensic and Family Psychology Unit showed that watching screen violence caused chronic stimulation of the "fight or flight" response in young people, making those under the age of 11 years aggressive or fearful. Boys were more influenced than girls, and those under 5 years, particularly so. Play and spontaneous behaviour were both affected. One study claimed that 25% of juvenile offenders had committed their crimes in an attempt to imitate what they had viewed on film, television or computer games (DMN:05:02:18, quoting Lancet). The American Psychological

Association estimated that the average American child sees more than 100,000 acts of violence and 8000 murders on television (WR02p242).

Whilst the principal factors responsible for delinquency are parental dereliction during the first and second nurtural phases, and malconditioning by peers and other agencies during the third phase, there are other contributory determinants. From the wealth of research projects which have been dedicated to this subject we learn that a low IQ, emotional instability, stress, local levels of substance misuse and unemployment, lack of parental supervision, and residence in an industrial suburb are all deleterious. In keeping with the skewed four fold male predominance of juvenile delinquency is the finding that early puberty in boys is correlative (LSL03 and HJP01).

Juvenile delinquency is the retribution vented upon society by its youth for the way in which its nurture has been miss-handled. In England and Wales in 2005, young persons between the ages of 10 and 17 committed 277,986 recorded crimes, of which 41,2% involved property, 19.4% violence against the person, 9.4 % involved motoring, and 4.8% involved drugs (CISCS10).

The third nurtural phase offers the last window of opportunity to reprogramme the juvenile delinquent's mind whilst a degree of plasticity still remains, and a wide range of alternative remedies has been tried which have included police warnings and fines, tagged curfew and telephone monitoring, community service under probation, and custody. Successful rehabilitation only proves possible in around 30% of youths, and is heavily dependent upon the use of incentivised vocational training (EHM89p365). The deployment of military style boot camps in the USA attempted to recondition inmates by subjecting them to extreme physical discomfort. It caused 31 known deaths and 13 thousand claims of abuse during a three year period, but was no more successful in reducing recidivism than a prison sentence (NYTN08). Large scale trials of psychotherapy on maladjusted youths in both the US and UK showed that it had no effect in preventing initial or recitative crime (EHM89p359).

Delinquency and Crime Are Carbuncles Upon The Face Of Society: Can They Be Prevented?

In most people's minds, delinquency takes second place only to warfare in the order of humanity's self induced scourges. Although it has invariably proved intractable, this need not always be so. Let us summarise the present position.

Miscreants commit crimes against property, violence against the person, and sexual offences, but are impelled to do so either by direct malconditioning ingrained during immaturity, by chronic intoxication or, more rarely, genetically. If only one of these motivating influences exist in an offender, then we can identify it by taking tests which determine whether chronic intoxication or chromosomal abnormalities are present. If they are not, then we can infer that criminality has been due to direct malconditioning.

The wheels of the criminal justice system only begin to turn when a first offence has been committed, and the prospect of preventing subsequent offences is bleak in individuals once they have attained intellectual maturity at 25 years of age. But below that age, as the data on recidivism have shown, reoffending can be prevented in a percentage of cases whose magnitude is in inverse proportion to the age of the offender. Rehabilitation of juveniles requires a process of reconditioning which is much more effective if incentivised vocational training is used (EHM89p365). Prevention of malconditioning, which would in turn prevent a first offence, can only be addressed by social engineering which is based on an accurate use of behavioural science, and which specifically targets older schoolchildren and young adults who will be tomorrow's parents (see also further elaboration in chapter 28). Prevention of malconditioning would also have beneficial effects on the problem of chronic intoxication due to addictive chemicals - other measures required here are, of course, suppression of drug trafficking, the use of detoxification facilities, and effective public health policies.

All this still leaves us with a hard core of genetically abnormal, predominantly male, miscreants, whose crimes require a different approach, because they are in fact suffering from a heritable mental disease which cannot be reorientated. In the past, grappling with the problems of the criminally insane has always had to await the commission of a first offence, the application of McNaghten tests for behavioural responsibility, and incarceration in a secure unit. The potential for prospective genetic "fingerprinting" and long acting drug implants now offers hope of a more radical preventive approach. As always, heritable mental disorders are compounded by the fact that parents suffering from them often malcondition their children. A similar self perpetuating cycle is seen in families where genetically normal, but malconditioned, parents pass on their own disturbed cultural legacy.

The prevention of delinquency is, above all, one of the prime functions of responsible parenthood, but the intricacies and implications involved are not generally well understood. Although public opinion rightly castigates parents of delinquents where the aberration was the direct result of malnurture, it wrongly condemns them when genetic deformities are to blame, and commiserates with them when addiction, for which malconditioning has actually been circuitously responsible, is at the heart of the problem. As we have seen, the disinhibition of possessiveness, aggression and sexuality results from the dislocation of the other fundamental primate traits of bonding and socialisation during immaturity. Bonding failure is usually a consequence of malconditioning during the first phase of nurture, and socialisation failure that of second and third phase malnurture, but although the former is more likely to result in intoxicant delinquency and the latter in compulsive antipathy it is often impossible to disentangle the two forms of malconditioning for which, in any case, parents must bear overall responsibility.

Whilst society at large pays a heavy price for the nurtural incompetence which leads to so much delinquency within its ranks, it is, of course, the child who is the sacrificial victim. Through no choice of its own it has had foisted upon it a defective persona whose loss of potential brings with it a lifetime of unhappiness, unfulfilment and opprobrium. As an ill starred misfit and reject who cannot forge meaningful relationships, it continually teeters of the edge of society, and often resorts to depravity as an escape mechanism. If ever there was a cast iron case to be made out for parental training this is it.

Attention Deficit Hyperactivity Disorder (ADHD)
Although ADHD is not caused by malconditioning, it needs mention here because it is widely regarded by the general public as a cause of delinquency. ADHD is, in fact, a hereditary brain disorder characterised by inattention, hyperactivity, impulsiveness and impatience, but not by malevolence. If delinquency does ensue, it will probably have developed in response to inappropriate management from those in immediate contact who lack insight into the true nature of the problem.

ADHD occurs in 3-5% of the world's population, it affects boys three times as often as girls, and it manifests before the age of seven years. Damage to the ADHD-prone foetal brain can be increased by exposure to a pregnant mother's absorption of alcohol, tobacco smoke or lead. An afflicted child's symptoms are exacerbated by certain food preservatives and colorants, whilst they are ameliorated if these chemicals are withdrawn or stimulant drugs are administered. In ADHD there is an imbalance in brain development in which accelerated growth in the motor brain turns the child into a restless, fidgeting, impatient and interruptive chatterbox, and a concomitant three year growth delay in the unconditionable brain makes the child forgetful, inattentive, distractible, disorganised and careless. The language delay, dyslexia, failure to achieve, and insomnia which may result are compensated for emotionally by non-compliance, and deceit. Whilst the majority of cases can be helped to learn coping strategies by the time adulthood is reached, there is an above average risk of subsequent involvement in crime, road accidents and substance misuse. ADHD is present in a small number of adults (PCMZ:06:11:23, and WKP08).

(Sources reviewed in chapter 15: ACM07, BCM07, BCS06, BLGGW64, BSPR00, BT00(a), BT98, CISCS, DVJJM90, DVJJM08, FDP02, FDP04, FGL11, GCB13, GJBR95, GS50, GSET34, HJP01, HO06, HWH98, JS96, LRLRWH85, LSL03, MN51, NDTRF03, NUTN08, PCMZ:06:09:14, TDR56, WHO84

CHAPTER 16

TWISTERS, LIARS AND CONMEN

HUMAN DISTORTION OF PRIMATE SOCIALISATION - CORRUPTION

Honesty is the best policy, or is it? A class of Italian undergraduates learning English in 2005 didn't think so. When answering a multichoice exam question on English proverbs, without hesitation they all put a tick against the dishonesty option (PC05).

In the previous chapter we saw that malconditioning, particularly during the first phase of human nurture, can dislocate the primate trait of bonding and make the individual antisocial. Malconditioning due to marked deprivation or peer group antipathy acting upon the juvenile mind during the subsequent second and third phases of nurture may also warp the development of the socialisation trait, even when the first nurtural phase has already laid the foundation stones of integrity. The forms of misconduct which then ensue are not expressed physically as burglary, assault or sexual atrocity as might have followed first phase malnurture, but are more subtly crafted through the medium of verbal interchange. Non-human primates cannot deceive because they cannot falsify their encounter signs and signals, but the acquisition of language allowed humans to distort and misrepresent the verbal, printed or electronic data which they transmit to each other. Fraud, corruption and propaganda are thus added to the list of human woes, all incentivised by their profitability.

Corruption has been endemic throughout human history, and its prevalence is routinely surveyed by the watchdog organisation Transparency International. In 2005 the nations least affected by it were Iceland, New Zealand, Finland, Denmark, Singapore, Sweden and Switzerland in that order. Norway, Australia, Austria, Canada, The Netherlands, France, Iberia, The United Kingdom, Germany and Japan were rated marginally less well, but most corruption was present in Africa, Asia, The Middle East, India, and Central and South America (TTN:05:10:19). Those who attempt to stamp out corruption often pay with their lives, as in Sicily or Russia. Corruption is at its worst when it promises the greatest profits, such as in drug dealing, gambling, football promotion, election rigging and high finance. The damage which it can inflict upon the fabric of society can be apocalyptic, as two key examples, taken from the very many which could be cited, show all too clearly.

Company Fraud The Enron Scam
The most expensive US corporate debacle by that date was the collapse of Enron in 2001, the erstwhile financial empire which had been assembled by one Kenneth Lay. Lay's story is intriguing, not only because of the disastrous effects his machinations had on the lives and fortunes of those who trusted him, but because, like the sorcerer's apprentice, he unleashed havoc by taking over-simplistic short cuts which he must have known were ill advised. Lay's premature death saved him from the punishment that the US hands down to big time fraudsters.

Kenneth Lay was born in 1942, the only son of a father whose beneficent religious convictions set the pattern for his children's early nurture, but whose ill judged retail business ventures led to his family's bankruptcy and dispossession. Given shelter in farm buildings by compassionate relatives, the Lay family had to subsist without indoor plumbing and in penury. By the age of nine Lay had, of necessity, to augment the family income by delivering papers, mowing lawns, and subsequently by driving tractors and ploughing fields. When his father secured a position as a part time Baptist minister, family circumstances slowly improved, but Lay's early deprivation left him with a burning desire for wealthy self aggrandisement and the resolve not to use his father as a business model. In his teens the family moved house to be nearer to the University of Missouri so that he and his two sisters would be able to study for degrees. Ken Lay was industrious and musical, and with the help of scholarship money, loans and part time employment was able to graduate with honours in economics in 1967. His studies had acquainted him with the way market forces operate, and he had acquired basic accounting skills. When he subsequently progressed to a master's qualification he found employment, initially in an oil company and then at the Pentagon, where he was able to complete a Ph.D. thesis under the aegis of the University of Houston. Further preferment saw him appointed as the Deputy Undersecretary for Energy at the US Department of the Interior, and to an Assistant Professorship at George Washington University.

Lay joined Transco, a company piping natural gas to New York, in 1951 and rose to become its chairman. He then moved to a Texas company, Houston Natural Gas, and initiated a series of mergers which in 1985 poised him to become chief executive officer of the conglomerate, now renamed Enron. Within the succeeding fifteen years, Lay's dynamic policies of expansion and diversification so transformed Enron that it was able to dominate the US energy market. Clients, shareholders, politicians and associate companies were all anxious to be seen as an integral part of Enron's outstanding success. The company was by now handling a quarter of all US energy trading, and was dealing in gas, oil, electricity, telecommunications, metals, paper, financial consultancy services and merchant banking. It had become the seventh largest US company, and developed strong ties with the Republican Party to which it was a major contributor. It had interests in 40 countries and a global workforce of 20 thousand. Its revenue rose from $4.6 Bn. in 1990 to $101 Bn. in 2000. In August

2000, its stock value reached an all time high of $90 per share (FL03, timeline 9).

Undeniably, Enron's initial success was spectacular by any measure. It had used innovative business policies to enable it to rationalise the US natural gas industry, hitherto a hotchpotch of scattered drillfields and piecemeal distribution networks, by establishing an amalgamated nationwide pipework coverage of which it owned a substantial share. Local hubs diverted supplies as and when they were needed. Enron tailored contracts to producers and to end users, 60 % of the latter of whom were industrial, incorporating clauses to help them hedge against risks and price fluctuations. The company also provided small prospectors with loans to initiate production, for which interest was paid in kind. All deals were handled electronically and efficiently through Enron's Internet trading system.

Enron's Achilles heel was its short-sighted incentivisation policy, in pursuit of which increasing autonomy and preferment were granted to those managerial employees whose quarterly results showed rising profits. Inevitably, such a scheme leads to distortion of accounting procedures whereby, in the short term, debts and losses are concealed and profits inflated. One method by which losses escaped official notice involved the establishment of subsidiary operations in which Enron purported to hold only a part interest, and which could therefore construct autonomous sets of accounts (FL03p2). As newly assimilated companies matured, their profit margins inevitably fell, and to offset the loss in shareholder value which this represented, further acquisitions were made in the headlong rush to innovate and crank up revenue. Some acquisitions proved ill founded, which merely exacerbated Enron's problems.

The overheated growth with fraudulently represented earnings and debt levels could not last indefinitely. In late 2001, Sherron Watkins, one of the company's accounting employees, wrote to Lay to draw his attention to irregularities, and the Wall Street Journal criticised Enron's role in the conduct of partnered subsidiary operations. When the

Securities and Exchange Commission (SEC), which oversees US stock markets, scheduled an enquiry, Enron's trading partners began to withdraw, and the company's share value fell from $90 to 36 cents, wiping off more than $60 Bn of shareholder value. The company's official accountants, Arthur Andersen, panicked and shredded their Enron related records, an act for which they were later indicted by jury (JP03p13).

On 2nd December 2001, Enron filed for bankruptcy and laid off 4 thousand US employees. Lay resigned, but when he was subpoenaed to appear before a Senate Committee on 12th February 2002 he invoked the Constitution's Fifth Amendment and remained defensively silent. Subsequently, 34 Enron executives were indicted, of whom five were found guilty by jury and fifteen pleaded guilty. Lay died of a heart attack two months later. Sadly, the lessons of the Enron fiasco were not well learnt. When the developed world's banking system began to melt down in the fall of 2008, misguided short term incentivisation once again lay at the root of the problem.

(Sources:BR02, FL03, JP03, SS04, TTN:08:12:18, www.chrono.com /news/specials/enron/)

State Fraud on a Massive Scale. Joseph Goebbels the Propagandist
On 30th January 1933 the German public voted the Nazi regime into power, with Hitler as Chancellor enjoying a 52% majority in the Reichstag. The democracy embodied in the post first world war fledgeling Weimar Republic was thereby hoisted by its own petard, and Germany returned to political totalitarianism under a warlord who brooked no opposition. The event was a cultural throwback which was ultimately to propel the German people into a second global conflict in which, all told, 50 million lives were sacrificed.

Nazi rise to power was the culmination of a supremely well organised and accurately focused campaign, aided and abetted by coercion and intimidation, during which the fertile soil of nationwide post-war discontent was assiduously sown with the conceptual seed of

German racial supremacy. From 1918 onwards the essentially militaristic German psyche had been smarting from the stinging ignominy of defeat, the avaricious reparations imposed by victorious enemies, mass unemployment, and national economic failure. The earliest recruits to the lower echelons of the Nazi Party were drawn from embittered and disillusioned demobilised soldiery whose homeland could no longer provide them with employment, motivation or status. Wandering aimlessly through the streets in their thousands, Nazism offered these men back their self respect, and rekindled in them the camaraderie and sense of commitment which had been the mainstay of their morale during the war. National rallies and parades were organised in order to mould a new politico-military task force which would form the party's power base, and because formal uniforms and conventional weapons had been banned by law, the new brigades adopted the convention of wearing brown shirts. The competitive threat of a similar campaign organised by the Communist Party had to be contested, and made violent clashes between the two rival movements inevitable, until the latter was outmanoeuvred and overpowered.

As with nearly all successful political movements, Nazism's initial strategy was to tell the people what they wanted to hear and, in tandem with Hitler's iconic and mesmeric oratory, the propagandist primarily responsible for doing so was Joseph Goebbels. Having obtained the popular mandate with flattery and promises, the Nazis then set about reconditioning German cerebration in their own image, and within the surprisingly short time of a few years, its leaders succeeded in dragooning rank and file Germans into accepting dictatorial National Socialism. When the new ideology ultimately failed, and did so disastrously, Goebbels had no compunction whatever in blaming the German electorate for the nation's ill fortune. In a display of cynical, turncoat venality when the Third Reich was in its death throes, he used public pronouncements to shrug off all responsibility, telling Germans that in voting for Nazism, they had knowingly chosen a policy of political and military adventure, and that by displaying incompetence and cowardice they had betrayed the best efforts of their leaders.

In behavioural terms propaganda misuses the procedures of social intercourse - facial recognition and expression, body language, vocalisation and physical contact - to suborn the recipients' conditionable brain. As with all forms of conditioning, the process is more effective if constantly repeated, ritualised, and reinforced by incentive, coercion and intimidation. The word propaganda originated as the Catholic Missions' remit to propagate their faith ("sacra congregatio de propaganda de fide"), but the term became debased when it was used politically in the first world war to describe strategies involving subterfuge, subversion and misinformation. The process reached its zenith of sophistication and effectiveness at the hands of Joseph Goebbels who echoed, elaborated, orchestrated and choreographed Hitler's doctrines in order to engrave them on the collective German mind.

Most would regard Goebbels as having been a genius in his formulation and use of propaganda, and this indeed was how he saw himself. His cunningly twisted diatribes were so compelling that he became convinced of their veracity as soon as he had uttered them. For him, there was no such thing as objectivity. Bias, slant and prejudice were common to all human interaction, and the only acid test of propaganda was whether it succeeded. Transparency, impartiality and morality all had to be flouted when the overriding interest of the Nazi state was at stake. Hitler's three predominant goals were German national supremacy, European conquest and Aryan racial purity, and Goebbels' canine sycophancy towards his supremo rendered him so subservient, that Hitler's every word was taken as messianic. The gospel of National Socialism, as relayed by Goebbels, proved to be so effective that even during Nazism's cataclysmic death throes, the German people remained loyal to their Fuhrer (HH72p132).

Although Hitler always saw to it that his immediate subordinates had to compete with each other (SA75p363), Goebbels' control over the manipulation of information for public consumption was paramount at home and highly influential abroad. It involved censorship, falsification, repetitive brain washing, communal ritual, sanctions, enforcement and intimidation. Goebbels' output was both positive, glorifying Nazism in all its manifestations, and negative, demonising all who opposed it. Relentless use of mantras ensured that if he threw enough mud, some would be bound to stick.

Goebbels had always been the Nazi party's director of propaganda, for twelve years he was Reich propaganda minister, he was appointed Gauleiter of Berlin, he became Vice Chancellor after helping to expose the conspirators of the 20th July 1944 attempt on Hitler's life (SA75p532), and, ultimately, he was himself Reich Chancellor for a brief five hours between the time of Hitler's suicide and his own. By 1937 his ministry employed one thousand staff at the Wilhelmplatz palace in Berlin and he was effectively minister of culture, controlling all who produced or distributed any material which might conceivably influence the public.

Goebbels, under Hitler's tutelage, conditioned the Germans as to how to think, what to believe and how to act. By appropriate suppression or promotion of individuals and organisations he controlled the press, radio, film, theatre, advertising, tourism, state holidays, national and local festivals, fairs, exhibitions and state funerals. The siting and significance of banners, flags, bunting, posters and pamphlets were all carefully stage managed. During the war Germany broadcast abroad in 57 languages, including those of countries with whom Germany was in conflict, it employed "war of nerves" campaigns to misinform and cow enemy troops, it counterfeited letters and falsified documents, messages and statements of all kinds, and it set up rumour cells to promulgate whispering offensives. But Goebbels' most influential forms of communication were his well prepared speeches and the politically scintillating articles he contributed weekly to widely read party publications, such as Der Angriff, Das Reich and Volkischer Beobachter. With the approach of war, Goebbels output increased to 50 thousand words per day, and the number of directives he had issued passed the 75 thousand mark.

Goebbels had been a prize essayist at school, and a successful Ph. D. student at Heidelberg University. He took infinite pains over the construction of his speeches and articles, using evocative words and phrases, a sharp, penetrating, but fluent style, and polished grammar. His output was eagerly awaited and enthusiastically received throughout Germany. He delivered his speeches with hands on hips, displaying his preferred right profile, his sleek dark hair brushed back and his solemn dark eyes intently fixed on his audience. He had a resonant baritone voice which secured magnetic attention. Starting his line of argument with carefully selected and incontrovertible evidence, interspersed with studied pauses, he progressed to a highly charged, emotional crescendo which swept his listeners along with his fantasies and fabrications in a tidal wave of nationalistic ecstasy. The orgasmic climax left both the speaker and many of his audience quivering, and dripping with sweat. Those who attended Hitler's or Goebbels' speeches variously described their exceptionally powerful impact as electrifying, mesmerising, religious, intoxicating, pseudosexual or cathartic. Goebbels saw to it that every household could afford a cheaply, mass produced radio receiver, and outdoors he placed six thousand public address systems in streets, squares and factories throughout the land. Phonograph recordings for home use, and cinema newsreels added to the comprehensive coverage.

A New Religion, New Icons and New Rituals
Born in 1897, Goebbels was brought up in a devout Rhineland Catholic family which guaranteed that the first phase of his nurture followed traditional lines of maternal affection and reasoned rebuff. He was the youngest of three brothers, and had two younger sisters, one of whom died prematurely. As a boy, the power of the church to condition minds by its use of repetitive mantras and theatrical rituals made a deep impression upon him, and he aspired to take holy orders.

But as an adult he was easily swayed by the infectious political jingoism of his associates and, dispensing with moral principles and ideals, he totally rejected his original loyalty towards Christianity in favour of the more virile and virulent dogmas of National Socialism. Indeed he went further, and was instrumental in creating an entirely new schedule of calendrical rites which, with the exception of Christmas, usurped those of the church. The festival of January 30th commemorated Nazi seizure of power, and February 24th the founding of the party. On "Hero's Day" in March the country honoured its fallen warriors; April 20th celebrated the Fuhrer's birthday; May Day was stolen from the communists; September brought an eight day extravaganza at which the Fuhrer reviewed a march past of the massed ranks of his followers. In October, from a huge natural amphitheatre which could encompass over a million of his devotees, the Fuhrer climbed a nearby mountain to be crowned in a ceremony of harvest thanksgiving by his grateful subjects. November 9th marked the anniversary of an early party reverse when an attempted revolutionary putsch had failed.

Apart from the summer recess, therefore, each month invoked a massed national rally attended by regimented throngs of supporters, who might number up to a million or more. These undisguisedly militaristic pageants were theatricised in unsparing detail and splendour. Huge blood red banners bearing a black swastika on a white roundel usually led the procession, followed by massed troops, the SA (later displaced by the SS), the Hitler youth movement, German maiden organisations, party members and, following up the rear, packed ranks of enthusiastic commoners - all joined each other in a show of disciplined and ostentatious bravado. Brass bands, fanfares, drum rolls, multi-gun salutes, diverse uniforms, blazing torches and braziers, fireworks, mass flag waving, all presaged the tirades of exhortation from the party headmen which were about to commence. The religious fervour which such elaborate nationalistic rallies engendered cemented the population together in a common purpose, and endorsed still further its commitment to its Fuhrer.

Whilst Goebbels and his grossly over-iconified leader were offering the Germans the carrot of nationalistic supremacy, the Brownshirt Brigades, with activist cells in every street, factory and office, wielded the stick of terrorisation and subversion. Starting as a fringe element, these thugs systematically bludgeoned their way into German social consciousness, confronting and subduing all who stood in their way, to which end they used knuckle dusters, cudgels, or anything else that came to hand. Early victims to be rough handled were the Weimar bureaucrats, members of other nationalistic political parties, communists, Jews and church officials. Fatalities were often inevitable, and, as the police were impotent in dealing with these assaults, it soon became clear that one simply did not tangle with the party and its henchmen. A culture of vilification and hatred towards opponents fostered by Hitler and Goebbels had the effect of consolidating popular support and enabling the man in the street to blame the loss of his liberty on the need to protect the state against conspiratorial minorities. As in Stalinist Russia, neighbours denounced, and spies sought out, dissidents who were either deprived of their livelihood or sent to concentration camps. In response to adverse criticism abroad, Germany withdrew from the League of Nations in 1933, and during the following years, with customary mendacity, Hitler and Goebbels took the propagandist stance that Germany did not want war, but needed to expand its borders in order to accommodate its population and culture. In effect, the stage was now being set for European conquest.

Malconditioning in Mid Childhood and Later Insecurity of Personality

Goebbels was a sly, twisted, hypocritical, ambitious, treacherous, intelligent and highly articulate sycophant whose avowed aim in life was to make his mark on history in whatever measure. The thorns in the side of his ego were his small stature, his left club foot, and the sustained victimisation which his school peers had meted out to him because of these disadvantages. Thereafter, an ingrained sense of inadequacy, for which he compulsively overcompensated, dogged him throughout life, contributing significantly to the deformation of his personality. He became a cynical, overly suspicious, chain smoking, insomniac, and perpetually promiscuous adult who was subject to violent changes of mood and threats of suicide. His insecure, vapid, fickle and protean nature made him totally reliant upon Hitler, whose acceptance and approbation he craved with the emotional intensity of an addiction (SA75p61). Conversely, Hitler needed Goebbels' adulation, the society of beautiful women which Goebbels could arrange for him, and the family environment which Goebbels, his wife, and his six children could extend to Hitler whenever he wished to visit their home. Hitler had been witness to Goebbels' wedding to the latter's wife Magda, and Goebbels returned the compliment by witnessing Hitler's marriage to Eva Braun in the final hours which these two and the whole Goebbels family spent in their subterranean bunker as Berlin was being overwhelmed by the Russians. The intense symbiosis between Hitler and Goebbels ensured that their decision to commit suicide was a joint one. So as to avoid being captured alive, first Hitler, and five hours later Goebbels, shot themselves, having arranged for the poisoning of their immediate families. Attendants were on hand to incinerate their bodies. Their demise finally expunged the overburden of megalomaniacal fantasies, fixations and phobias to which the German psyche had been subjected for two decades, and which had proved so catastrophic.

Adler's psychoanalytical postulate that human interrelationships are primarily determined by social status, perceived superiority, and perceived inferiority, was the result of observations made on the German population at a time when the Junkers military tradition was all pervasive. Hitler's overdominance and Goebbels oversubmissiveness to him are clear examples of these skewed behavioural patterns at work. Hitler and Goebbels were both malconditioned during childhood, but in contrasting ways.

(Sources: BA91, BED65, GJ38, GJ62, GJ82, HH72, MGL66, NJPG83, PWAP74, SA75, SW58, www.psywarrior.com/goebbelshtml www.spartacus.schoolnet.co.uk/GERgoebbels.htm, WKP08, ZZAB64)

CHAPTER 17

"YOUNG CUPID'S FIERY SHAFT"
(William Shakespeare, In "The Merry Wives Of Windsor")

HUMAN DISTORTIONS OF SEXUALITY - HYPERSEXUALITY

As with other forms of compulsive pelvic evacuation, the frequency of coitus is open to considerable variation between individuals and with age. But unlike urination, defecation and childbirth, orgasm is addictive, and control of that addiction is strongly influenced by conditioning in immaturity and by culture. Lack of affection during the first phase of childhood nurture may result in overcompensation in later life, expressed as hypersexuality. Parental guidance needs to be transmitted, both as a moral code for which relatives should themselves act as examples, and by well considered dictum - mothers who tell their daughters that sex is dirty may make them frigid and cause them subsequent marital failure. Peer group sexual mores are intuitively absorbed, and the pendulum of national attitudes towards coitus tends to swing from Puritanism to Libertinism between generations, considerably influenced by role models such as France's Louis X1V and England's Prince Regent and Queen Victoria. The types of malconditioning from which sexual hyperactivity ensues are more benign than, and should be distinguished from, those which result in biologically abnormal sexual practices, or those in which active physical or sexual abuse experienced during childhood leads to violent perversion in later life in the form of battery, rape or serial murder (see chapters 19 & 20).

Social attitudes towards hypersexuality vary considerably. As it is a symptom which so rarely presents for treatment, standard medical textbooks wash their hands of it unless it leads to criminality or, as is occasionally the case, it is a manifestation of endocrine tumours or mental illness such as schizophrenia, bipolar disorder or paranoia (see chapter 21). Conversely, the paparazzi bay like bloodhounds when their prey unwittingly allows them to get wind of it. Society as a whole looks upon it in a more balanced way, with a lenity bordering on approval, or even envy. Clearly it is an aberration, but one which needs to be much better understood.

At the outset it is necessary to differentiate between two distinct forms of hypersexuality, each of which can affect either gender. Craved bondage is an intense, obsessive, but unrequited desire for sexual union with a specific individual who is often a well known public figure. Here the hunger to create a highly focused sexual bond is the all important factor. An afflicted woman will harass her parish priest or GP, whereas a man may stalk a film star. The attempt on Ronald Reagan's life was sparked by a delusion that his demise would cause Jodie Foster to declare love for the assassin.

By contrast, libidinous excess centres on orgasm, however obtained, and typically involves serial seduction of many different partners. Here, although both early malconditioning and raised male hormone levels are causative factors, it is the latter which exerts the stronger influence in both genders. If we consider first the human male, the average adult attains three orgasms per week, with a mere 7% of men experiencing once daily ejaculation. Rates in excess of this are regarded as indicating hypersexuality. Orgasmic frequency slowly diminishes from the age of 30 onwards, but even at the age of 70 around 70% of men are still sexually active (MD94(a)p42). Under the influence of the pituitary gland the testis secretes testosterone, the hormone needed to maintain male physique, sexual differentiation and sexual function. Not only may high levels of the hormone be associated with hypersexuality, but they are an important indicator of early death from cardiovascular disease in humans, an effect which may be likened to the arterial degeneration which attends the use of anabolic steroids.

What can history tell us about this eccentric and overindulgent form of behaviour? The record for male orgasmic hyperactivity is held by Moulay Ismail the Bloodthirsty (1672-1727), the emperor of Morocco who fathered 888 children. Given that the human male averages 3 thousand ejaculations in a sexual lifetime, the emperor achieved a fertilisation rate of 30% (GBR04). Surprisingly, organised religion has voiced its support for unrestrained male sexual activity within marriage. In the 13th century an ecclesiastical Spanish court ruled that a man was entitled to demand his conjugal rights 27 times in any given 24 hours, and Napoleon is alleged to have extended this privilege to French manhood (GP02p164). The Qur'an advises a man that "Your wives are as a tilth unto you, so approach your tilth how and when you will" (Su2,s24,v223), sometimes translated as "Your wives are as furrows, plough them how or when you will"). Islam authorises quadruple polygyny. The Prophet himself had nine wives. (CM96p23 and 43). Brigham Young, one of the originators of Mormonism, is reputed to have sired 200 children so as to increase following in the new religion.

Hypersexuality in women is also associated with either, or both, the production of raised male hormone levels and malconditioning during juvenility. Male hormone is normally present in insignificant amounts in females, but may be increased by mild over activity of the adrenal endocrine glands, and will then increase libido and produce some degree of virilism, such as facial hair growth. More marked rises in male hormone levels in women are excessively rare, but may be caused by endocrinal tumours. Hyperthyroidism increases libido by dynamizing the metabolism.

Until modern times, women's libido like their anatomy has been kept strictly under wraps, thanks to the proprietary controlling interests of male dominance. Inevitably theories as to its nature, and even its very existence, abounded. In the 2nd century CE, the Greek physician Galen believed that women who did not experience periodic orgasms became hysterical, and his Victorian English counterparts solemnly opined that excessive female sexual activity led to insanity and disease (BGE02). More recently, we have come to understand that some women are as promiscuous as some men. Sarah Bernhardt is reputed to have had a prestigious three thousand different consorts during her life (PC).

How does human sexual prowess compare with that of other primates? At an average of 5-6 inches when erect, the human penis is both the longest and the thickest in the ape world. However, the ratio of testicular size to overall body size correlates more accurately with sexual potency, and here the chimpanzee outperforms all other primates. The female chimpanzee is only receptive for a few days each month, but when she is, she becomes the centre of attention of all the males in the "herd", and may copulate as many as 50 times a day. When several females are coincidentally sexually receptive, a state of heightened excitement spreads throughout the whole "herd", and communal displays involving thumping, slapping, screaming, hooting and branch rustling indicate the mass arousal of all adults. An orgy of coitus follows (MD94(a)p92), which outstrips, but sets the genetic precedent for, the Bacchanalia of ancient Rome, or the cocaine fuelled rave of modern times.

(Sources Reviewed: BGE02, EEI96, HC03, MD94(a), WF05, WR02)

A Key Thumb Nail Biography. Giacomo Casanova (1725-1798).
The Archetype
Hypersexuality has always made good box office. Wikipedia lists no fewer than 77 major works - plays, operas, novels, films or poems whose subject is the legendary but fictitious libertine Dom Juan, of

which Mozart's Don Giovanni is justifiably the best known. In real life, the most notorious contender for eponymity in the role of womaniser extraordinary has always been Casanova. His several biographies, including one he wrote himself, help us to understand what lay behind his sexual excesses and his quite extraordinary lifestyle.

The popular image of Casanova is of a profligate serial seducer, blessed with suave and irresistible good looks, whose hypnotic heterosexuality caused him to run the libidinous gauntlet of countless society beauties, rich widows and coveted heiresses, all pestering him for his sexual attention. In reality, portrait painters had to exceed the bounds of normal artistic licence to be able to claim their fees, for he was no oil painting. He was cursed with a huge hook nose, a chin of punchinello prominence, and a complexion whose cafe au lait tint was corrugated by the cicatrisation of bygone smallpox. He had a towering and ungainly frame, and a temperament whose frenetic and overriding obsession to bend others to his will turned him into an oversexed bore and buffoon. Nearly all his conquests were individuals who were prepared to trade their bodies in return for the companionship, interest and flattery they lacked and craved. His blatant and notorious bisexuality held no appeal for the discriminating socialite who only tolerated him, if at all, as a bizarre curiosity.

Casanova was born illegitimately in Venice in the year 1725 as the result of a brief dalliance between his actress mother and her theatre manager. The moral laxity for which actresses of the time were renowned bordered on prostitution, and one of Casanova's siblings was rumoured to have been sired by the then Prince of Wales who later became George the Second of England. The grievance Casanova felt towards life as a result of his inauspicious origins was compounded by the lack of any parental warmth or love which his mother might have shown him had she not always been on tour. Attentional deprivation took its toll, and Casanova spent the rest of his life overcompensating for the emotional rapport which his parents had failed to provide by wresting it from others at the point of his penis. His massive, bull like body, his tetchy, restless and cynical intolerance, and his ruthless self will were all instrumental when it came to overmastering his sexual prey.

Casanova was utterly undiscriminating in his relentless and feckless pursuit of conquest. Partners of either gender, children, women in their seventies, lesbians, transvestites, prostitutes, actresses, nuns, his godfather's daughter, one of his nieces, and his own progeny were all grist to the genital mill. After the barren marriage of one of his daughters to a septuagenarian marquis, Casanova stepped in to ensure that an heir to the title would be forthcoming. Boasting that he had seduced women in their hundreds, he discarded nearly all as soon as he had had his way. Anxious that his lascivious powers should be acclaimed by posterity, Casanova was as prolix in his writings as he was profligate in his sexual adventures. Penning a profusion of letters and at least 20 books, his autobiography entitled "The Story of my Life" is still being published and is eminently readable (CG98). Albeit that his output exudes exaggeration and embellishment, and that he often quotes conversations which were clearly fabricated, some of the episodes he describes can be correlated with official records as a result of the many confrontations he had with authority.

It seems that his sexual apprenticeship began when, at the age of 11 he was seduced by a girl three years older than himself. His first homosexual encounter took place when he was training to be a junior priest at the seminary on the island of Murano in Venice's lagoon, a peccadillo for which he was expelled. His first multiple sexual escapade occurred at the age of 17 in a ménage a trios with a pair of sisters, and at the age of 21 he participated in a gang rape at a Venetian inn. During his early manhood, three ageing homosexuals gave him avuncular protection in return for what we can presume were sexual services, and baled him out many times when he needed influential or financial assistance. Other homosexual forays took place in Amsterdam, Constantinople and St. Petersburg, during the latter of

215

which he swore a pact of eternal fidelity with a superbly endowed Prussian army officer.

Promiscuity was not Casanova's only vice. As a young teenager he showed an addictive flair for gambling himself into debt. Whilst he was at Padua University, his grandmother had to step in with surety and bring him back to Venice, the better to curb his waywardness. It was in the latter city that as an Abbe he had originally taken the first steps towards priesthood, and his powers of oratory in delivering sermons were such as to make him realise that he had a special gift for persuasion. When he ultimately returned to Padua to complete his studies at the Department of Law and was awarded a doctorate, he recognised that providence had finally equipped him with the talents and status he would need to overawe and exploit his fellow creatures. It was at this point in his career that the four defining components of his character crystallized. He was not only an inveterate and egocentric lecher, but a gambling addict, a swindler and a manipulative propagandist. With a frisson of excitement he turned over in his mind the different ways in which he could exact revenge from society for the ignominy and deprivation vested upon him as a child.

As a young man, Casanova was at various times a junior priest, an army officer, and a violinist in a theatre orchestra. Later he spent most of his time travelling round Europe in the insatiable quest for novel sexual opportunities and speculative business enterprises in which fraud was a preferred option. He set up bogus schemes to persuade elderly widows to part with their life savings, and hawked the concept of state lotteries around the mandarins of Europe in the hope of being able to extract commission from them. Debts, denouements and cuckolded husbands often dictated the need for precipitate relocation. He became a freemason in order to infiltrate and exploit its brotherhood, and became skilled in the use of the spurious mathematical formulae of Cabalism which he propounded and promoted in order to worm his way into the presence of heads of state. The monarchs of Russia, Prussia, Scotland, England and Poland all gave him audience, as did the Pope. He even managed to persuade the Venetian Ambassador to the Holy See to employ him as a supernumerary. Like a rat in a sewer he felt completely at home amid the stench of corruption, intrigue, hypocrasy and sexual depravity which characterised the behaviour of the church hierarchy of the time.

As an inveterate traveller with a long police record, who had the uncanny ability to infiltrate all levels of society, it is not surprising to find that the Venetian authorities were able to coerce him to act both as a spy in alien countries and as a copper's nark in his own. Owing no sense of loyalty to anyone except himself, he had no compunction in at first spying for Venice on French troop and naval dispositions, and in a later assignment in acting so successfully as a secret agent for the French that they conferred the honour of French nationality upon him for his pains (CG98p282)

As a fraudster he sold spurious alchemical recipes, bogus cabalistic magical methodology and quack remedies. He issued false bills of exchange, and promissory notes that he had no intention whatever of honouring. He was repeatedly guilty of assault causing grievous bodily harm, may well have been a murderer, and inevitably had to contest duels. Arrested several times, he usually found ways of contriving to escape from prison or other places of confinement. Never out of trouble for long, he was at various times banished from Poland, Austria, France, Catalonia, Venice, and several other Italian cities. As a rake, he overindulged in food and alcohol. He was repeatedly bankrupt, either as the result of gambling or of failed business ventures. He caught gonorrhoea at least four times, soft chancre five times, genital herpes once and syphilis once. Before the advent of antibiotics, the latter disease had to be treated with the salts of heavy metals, prompting the aphorism that five minutes with Venus led to a lifetime with Mercury. His later years were plagued by the chronic prostatitis which complicated his venereal disease.

His dotage was disillusioned, embittered, querulous, and frustrated by the loss of his sexual potency. A benefactor mercifully provided him with board and lodging in Bohemia until his death. A cross of filigree ironwork marked his grave in the local cemetery. As its barbed edges rusted, they were known to snag the sweeping skirts of passing bauds and serving wenches.

(Sources Reviewed: CG01, ME04, MJ69, WKP08)

CHAPTER 18

OTHER HUMAN DISTORTIONS OF SEXUALITY

SEXUAL PERVERSIONS, FETISHES AND SUBSTITUTIONS

As it is natural for those who have children to also want to have grandchildren, parents have a vested interest in the development of their children's sexual behaviour and in knowing what influence conditioning has upon its outcome. The moulding of definitive sexual behaviour patterns takes place as the juvenile approaches sexual maturity at puberty, and is often heralded by a transitory emotional attachment to another person of the same sex. When this attachment is formed between individuals of a similar age the relationship is usually limited to one of close affection, but when one of the parties is post pubertal, orgasmic experience may follow, and same sex orientation will then be reinforced for both. Parents have more influence on this transitory phase than they usually recognise. They should prepare the child's mind for the anatomical, physiological and emotional changes which are about to take place, and discretely monitor company which is kept. After puberty, whilst sexual behaviour patterns are partly shaped by peer pressure and cultural attitudes, particularly those portrayed in the media, the predominant determinants will still be the ability to bond derived from parental-offspring relationships, the tenets of morality imbued in the earliest years, and the influence which family members have as role models. We have already considered hypersexuality as a relatively benign form of sexual maladjustment. In this and the following chapter we must see what history can reveal about other outcomes of sexual malconditioning, some of which have a much more malign impact upon society.

Why do so many human beings strive to gild the coital lily, employing art, artefact, aphrodisiac, erectile drug, and even athleticism to add bells and whistles to what, for every other primate, is a straightforward act of obedience to the call of nature? In simple terms, the human sexual act consists of foreplay, genital congress and post orgasmic bonding. Foreplay is the preliminary excitatory phase of the sexual act which arouses the individual to a state of preparedness for genital congress. Foreplay and genital congress are more protracted, sensuous and elaborate in humans than they are in other primates, and, as we have already seen, humans are one of the very few primate species to experience post coital partner bonding. The greatly increased emphasis which human development has placed upon these three phases has been arrived at by imbuing all of them with strong emotional and aesthetic overtones, thus turning copulation into an art form which inevitably prompts the search for further novelty and variety, and for exaggerated stimulus. Such a quest may lead to quixotic and idiosyncratic behaviour that has little or no bearing upon the enhanced protection of offspring which the heightened emotional rapport was originally evolved to promote.

Substitutions for normal heterosexual genital congress occur in masturbation, homosexuality, paedophilia, bestiality, and when artifices such as dildos or inflatable dolls are used. All substitutions contravene the biological purpose of the sexual act and are thereby perverse. Substitution either results from malconditioning in juvenility, or is employed when normal heterosexual partnership is unavailable.

An element of fetishism is integral to normal heterosexual activity, but when it becomes distorted or dislocated this, too, is classified as perverse. Fetishism demonstrates that both physical and psychological factors are involved in orgasmogenesis. For most people, the sight, sound, smell, and feel of any sexual partner are sufficient to complement genital stimulation and thereby prompt orgasm. For some individuals, orgasm is dependent upon coitus with a specific partner. Sometimes the fetish is purely imaginary, involving a sexual fantasy which the subject relives, either during partnered orgasm or during masturbation. Distorted fetishism, which does not occur in other species, results from malconditioning during immaturity, and imposes a perverse constraint upon the individual which only allows orgasm to be triggered if its precise requirements are met. On each occasion, a set of physical parameters must be refulfilled, circumstances which may seem ludicrous or grotesque to all but the person involved. Two of the commonest forms of malconditioned fetishism are sadism and masochism, grossly aberrant traits which are best understood by singling out brief life histories of the two eponymous perverts from whom these terms were derived.

The Marquis de Sade (1740-1814)

The correct use of parental restraint is critical to the development of normal behaviour patterns in a child. We noted in chapter 13 that many tyrants for whom biographies exist had themselves been mercilessly and repeatedly thrashed in childhood by their fathers. At the other extreme, overindulgence and the lack of parental discipline leads to the development of an intensely selfish, obstreperous, perpetually dissatisfied and antisocial individual. Whereas the former was traumatised by rebuff and reproof, the latter, for the lack of it, never learned to adjust to, or integrate with, society.

It would be difficult to find a better example of the feral deformity of personality produced by a totally undisciplined childhood than that of Donatien Alphonse Francois, the Marquis de Sade. Born the son of a count to the cousin and lady in waiting of the Duchess of Bourbon, the young Marquis' lineage made him a distant relative of the King of France. With fair hair and a cherubic face, the juvenile adonis was the darling of courtiers and servants alike. Even as a nurseling he threw tantrums, and as an uninhibited toddler he became the ultimate enfant terrible whom nobody dared gainsay. Doted on throughout his childhood, he was quick to appreciate the power that his privileged position enabled him to exert, and he relished abusing it by dominating, harassing, tormenting and manipulating all those around him. He found the temptation to shock and offend irresistible, and became conceited, sly and vindictive to boot.

Later development proved that his rebelliousness was underpinned by an above average intelligence, and coupled with an insatiable curiosity. As a teenager he was to show himself adept at dancing, fencing and horsemanship, to have a penchant for public performance both on the harpsichord and on the stage, and to have a gift for creative writing, all talents which might well have enabled him to earn his own living, had his status not cushioned him from the need to do so. As it was, the unlimited time he had on his hands, the libidinous frenzy which adolescence thrust upon him, his craving for domination and cruelty, and the moral laxity of the environment in which he grew up, all conspired against him. He found the unlimited opportunities for natural and unnatural sex which court life offered to be irresistible, and he exploited them to the full, becoming actively deviant in the process.

The malconditioned young Marquis had good reason to expect that early adult life would enable him to spread his wings ever further afield until they were peremptorily clipped by the prospect of an arranged marriage. Matrimony amongst members of the French nobility of the time had more in common with the bloodstock cattle market than it had with cupid, and Alphonse was aghast to learn that his spouse to be was the eldest daughter of the wealthy President of the Chamber of Deputies, a social climber who aspired to put his own family's foot on the aristocratic ladder in return for a liberal endowment which would solve the Marquis' family's crippling insolvency. At first Aphonse rebelled, since he was already acquainted with the girl in question whom he found both unbecoming and as dull as ditchwater. What made matters even worse was the fact that he already had designs upon her younger and considerably more attractive sister, a girl he later managed to seduce.

In the end his father's attitude became so intransigent that the Marquis realised he had no option but to comply, and he embarked upon a union which could never have been anything but a disaster. The hapless bride was totally unequal to the demands of her husband's extravagant and deviant sexual appetite, and without hesitation or compunction the reprobate now resumed what had become a ceaseless quest for profligate and perverted orgasmus wherever it could be found. In doing so, however, he had reckoned without the retaliatory venom of which his formidable mother in law was to prove capable. Stung to the quick by the realisation that her plans for her daughter's future were now in total disarray, and apprehensive of the ignominy in which her own family might be held as a result of the Marquis' activities, the redoubtable matriarch embarked upon a war of attrition against him. Using all the power and influence which she and her husband could muster, she was able to enlist the co-operation of the police and judiciary in order to hamstring and confine the reprobate. By way of riposte, Alphonse was sometimes able to use his royal connections to shield himself against conviction. The battle was unremitting and interminable, fought out with invective, insinuation, intrigue and bribery, until at last death assuaged the desire for further acrimony.

What was the true nature of his depravity? Impelled by sexual overdrive, perverted curiosity, an obsession to dominate, and a satanic craving to inflict pain, Alphonse was determined to find out how far erotic foreplay could be distorted and exaggerated in order to heighten orgasm. The funds which his marriage had put at his disposal enabled him to conduct many hundreds of real time experiments in human potency and sexual appetite, both at a property he owned in Paris and at another belonging to his family in Provence. At each of these venues, it was the remit of a madame he had engaged for the purpose to comb the gutters, brothels, and doss houses for riff-raff, street children, the destitute, and prostitutes of both sexes, who were to be the guinea pigs in his set piece debaucheries. Every possible means of achieving orgasm was explored. After aphrodisiacs had been administered, pain was routinely inflicted, typically in the form of flagellation or multiple skin lacerations. Subjects were required to undertake any revolting and degrading erotic acts which the Marquis' fevered imagination could devise. Participants copulated in pairs or multiples, some contorting their bodies, others being bound hand and foot. Whilst the Marquis was a committed participant in most of his orgiastic extravaganzas, he also played the voyeur by building an annexe to the salon des obscenitees from which he could observe, and make voluminous notes upon, the depraved sexual athleticism of others. In his annotation entitled "The 120 Days of Sodom" he detailed 600 different perversions, most of which required a measure of overt cruelty for their execution. The Marquis' debauched ethos was not altogether out of step with the times, for he lived in an age when the pillars of French society flouted marital loyalty as of right, pursuing sexual careers of the utmost licentiousness behind a facade of stilted ostentation and hypocritical court protocol. Royalty made no secret of it, the Fourteenth King Louis installing mistresses in his palaces, whilst the Fifteenth Louis ran an enormous brothel of his own in Paris. Where the monarchs led, the nobility had no compunction in following, and neither church nor police had the power to make them do otherwise, unless their excesses spilled over into criminality.

The Marquis' nemesis began when accusations of physical assault, poisoning with Spanish Fly, and the indictable offence of sodomy surfaced, and were accompanied by attempts to blackmail him. Forced to run the gauntlet of one scandalous accusation heaped upon another, he found himself repeatedly arrested, then conditionally reprieved, until in the end the authorities were no longer able to brush aside the mounting tally of charges brought against him, several of which could clearly be substantiated. From then on, he was committed to spend the rest of his life in close confinement for the better protection of the public, either in a prison such as the Bastille, or in a lunatic asylum. Although the battle with his mother in law still raged, and would do so as long as they both drew breath, she now knew that he was at her mercy, and she had no intention of letting him regain his liberty. He gave vent to his seething frustration by attacking all forms of authority, whether political, legal or ecclesiastical, through the medium of scathing invective penned with white hot emotional intensity.

De Sade wrote prolifically and habitually throughout his life, using many different genres. By the age of 48, he had already completed several novels, many short stories, a book of poems, 35 plays, and had launched a journal. His writings always used scurrilous, sexually perverted plot construction and phraseology to drive home their cruel impact. It was his bitter, salacious parody of Napoleon in 1801 which led to his permanent incarceration as a public enemy, and it was the incoherence of some of his scribblings and vocal outbursts, suggestive of insanity, which had led to his subsequent transfer to a lunatic asylum at Charenton near Paris, where he was befriended by the establishment's director and was encouraged to set up a live theatre in-house. Relishing his new role as playwright in residence and theatre manager, he used various more or less disturbed fellow inmates as most of the cast, and hired fashionable Parisian actresses for the leading roles. For two years, the venture was so successful that the cream of Paris society patronised its performances.

The marquis had always been a dapper, five foot two inch tall, agile man with delicate features and sensuous curling lips. In his 60's, the fires of indignation and spite faded within him, and he drifted into befuddled senility, wandering about the asylum, muttering to himself and acting with docile inconsequence. He died of pneumonia, which probably complicated earlier tubercular damage, and was buried in the asylum cemetery. His lasting legacy is the concept of sadism which he exemplified and to which he gave his name. Freud later developed the theory that cruelty was closely linked with libido, and pain with foreplay.

(Sources Reviewed: BJ06, CJ51, GJ06, HR03, PGF99, RGF99, SR86, TDS92, WAH64, WKP08)

Leopold von Sacher Masoch (1836-1905)

In the ape world, although some females are relatively more dominant than others, female adults are always subservient to adult males. Among humans, there are wives that "wear the trousers", displaying greater aggressiveness, and sometimes more redoubtable physique, than their husbands. Although such women have functioning ovaries and may bear children, an increased level of male type hormones, originating elsewhere in the endocrine system, frequently accounts for their more dominant behaviour.

Overly dominant mothers tend to stunt the behavioural masculinity of their sons, who then have a greater tendency than normal to become homosexual. Alternatively, these sons may, as a result of their childhood conditioning, develop an overawed attitude towards females and may acquire a compulsion to appease them. In the most extreme cases, the desire to express submissiveness and sue for appeasement becomes so intense that it impels a male suitor to beg for punishment and forgiveness before intercourse can be satisfactorily consummated. In these cases the fetish of received punishment takes the place of sexual foreplay as a phase of preliminary excitation, just as a fetish of inflicting punishment does for sadism.

Because Masoch was an eminent literary figure in his day, making no secret of his fetish, and because his estranged first wife wrote memoirs of her own, his sexual eccentricity became notorious, giving rise to the term masochism by which it is still known. Having been exposed to the influence of a succession of dominant viragos during childhood and adolescence, Masoch found that he was only able to sexually fulfil himself and his consort if he had first been humiliated by her and had suffered physical violence at her hands. Severe beatings, flagellation administered with nail studded whips, the application of red hot needles or searing poultices, and incisions from razors were all used as necessary precursors to coitus, the excitatory stimuli needed to prime the pump of his ensuing orgasm. Masoch also found that his intellectual inspiration as a writer of German plays, novels and short stories was dependent upon the frisson of perverted sexual excitement he derived from his dominatrice's torments.

Masoch was born and nurtured in an area of Eastern Europe known as Galicia, where it seems that many young girls are overly indulged and poorly disciplined in childhood, later displaying an unfortunate tendency to develop into outspoken, provocative, egocentric and overbearing martinets. We cannot be sure that Masoch's female relatives were built in this image, but it was one with which he was all too familiar, and which influenced his immature conditioning. In his novels and stories the heroines are almost invariably tyrannical dominatrices, frequently bisexual and with a herculean physique, who typically wear luxurious furs, astrakhan hats and men's cavalry boots, and who are equipped with an armoury of instruments with which to inflict pain. Masoch's two wives, each of whom bore him three children, and all his many mistresses, were only able to catalyse his sexual response by conforming to this fantasised stereotype, dressing for the part and acting out his persecutory pantomime. His work obliged him to travel throughout Europe, and his search for new sexual partners who could fulfil his fetishes was always uppermost in his mind. In time, his aberrations became so notorious that most women shunned him.

When the self degradation required by Masoch's perversion became extreme, he deliberately contrived that his consorts should be unfaithful to him as a way of demeaning himself still further in his relationship towards them. On several occasions he organised assignations for them with other men, and, like Sade, played the voyeur by peeping through the door at the ensuing proceedings. His first wife had the gross ill fortune to catch syphilis doing her husband's such extraordinary bidding and was promptly evicted for her pains.

Masoch was a tall man who had dark hair, a large mouth and a pale thin face. He exuded sensuality and was highly excitable, nervous and restless. Ten years before he died, he began to deteriorate mentally, a change in him which could very well have been caused by quarternary syphilis. As lunacy overtook him, he strangled his favourite pet kitten and attempted to throttle his second wife, as the result of which he was committed to a lunatic asylum for the rest of his days.

Brothels run by dominatrices can charge high fees for administering torture and humiliation, but when the methods used are too extreme the punter may not survive. To the horror of his family, in 2010 a well known 58 year old man was found dead in a Belgian bordello "dungeon", trussed, gagged and with a ball and chain around his neck (DMN:10:06:26).

Both Sade's and Masoch's fetishes distorted the foreplay phase of human sexual behaviour and were engendered as a result of childhood malconditioning. Although normal coitus in primates invokes an element of dominance-submission interplay, Sade's perversion grossly exaggerated the role of dominance, and Masoch's perversion grossly exaggerated and inverted that of submission.

(Sources Reviewed: BRHR07, CJ51, DG71, HR00, KER86, KM79, SR86, VSMW91, WTS09)

Substitutions for Adult Heterosexual Congress

Masturbation is practised by nearly all human males and over 50% of females at some time in their lives. Some apes, monkeys and lions are all recorded as occasionally masturbating.

Homosexuality has given rise to more controversy than any other sexually substitutive practice. There is no convincing evidence that orgasmic homosexuality exists in any other than the human species (MD94(a)p63). Although other primate males may mount males, and females females, the act is an expression of either dominance or greeting, and no eroticism nor orgasm is involved - it is in fact the

228

direct equivalent of a human non-sexual hug. Interestingly, it has now become common practice for football players to mount a goal-scoring colleague in order to reinforce herd bonding.

We are never likely to learn when it was that male homosexuality was first practised by our forbears, but historical records show that it was accepted as a social norm in all ancient civilisations until such time as religion, and in particular the biblical authorities, took issue against it. Following this, it was outlawed, at least throughout Christian Europe, since when allegations of sodomy have often been used as a means of discrediting and vilifying political opponents, as when King Philip the Fair of France successfully slandered the Knights Templar in order to avoid repaying them crippling debts.

The Wolfenden Committee, whose investigations led the British Government to decriminalise homosexuality in 1954, estimated the number of exclusively male homosexuals in the community as being between 4% and 5%. Investigations carried out by the American sociologist Alfred Kinsey after the second world war suggested a 37% incidence for males who at some time in their lives had had a homosexual experience, but as the interviewees for this research had not been randomly selected, and as Kinsey was himself an avowed bisexual, these findings fell into disrepute (KAC48, CWG53).

Because male human homosexuality substitutes the rectum for the vagina, it is an infertile act which cannot therefore persist genetically, and can only be the result of inappropriate conditioning. Being orgasmic it is bond forming, and because emotional maturity precedes intellectual maturity by ten years, early homosexual experiences in either sex tend to be uncritically self perpetuating. What began as mutual masturbation leads to further experimentation under the bond's influence.

Because bonding experiences in the earliest years of life become the template for more mature relationships, both a dominant mother and an effeminate father tend to produce homosexual children (MD94(a)p64, HC03p445). As with all sexual substitutions, homosexuality is more likely to occur when the normal dictates of biology are denied, and closed same sex communities such as boarding schools, prisons, navies, monasteries and convents inevitably promote the practice by default. Noteworthy homosexual communities throughout history have been ancient Greek and Roman army units, the Buccaneers, the Japanese army, and the upper echelons of the Nazi Brownshirts.

The psychoanalyst Irving Beiber found that a significant proportion of completely homosexual males are capable of reorientation to complete heterosexuality by psychotherapeutic reconditioning techniques, given the will to do so (HC03p445).

Sexual role reversal may occur in either men or women, the cause in both cases being malconditioning during immaturity. Male role reversal takes the form of transvestism, and in more extreme cases requires palliation with hormone substitution and emasculative surgery. Female role reversal notably occurs in families in which parental desire to have a son is so intense that female offspring are only acceptable if they are raised as boys, following which the reorientation often remains permanent.

Paedophilia, the term used to describe the sexual abuse of juniors by adults, is a uniquely human perversion. It is fetishistically abnormal inasmuch as a biologically inappropriate sex object - the immature body - is required to produce and satiate arousal, and it is also abnormal in that it is not reciprocally orgasmic. Fetishes are usually conditioned at or around puberty and many paedophiles were themselves abused as children. The female face does not undergo a fundamental change with puberty as does the male, and the freshness of complexion, suggestive of immature innocence, proves attractive to the heterosexual male. In paedophiles these prepubescent factors in their victim are important in the extreme and confer a sense of power which proves sexually stimulating.

The paedophile is compulsive, devious, deceitful, manipulative, and seeks out positions of authority over children, such as those offered by nurseries, boys' boarding schools, scout troops and hierarchical religious organisations. Where their occupations do not offer a ready supply of victims, paedophiles often operate in organised procurement rings. Paedophilia is predominantly a male perversion, although it has been estimated that female deviants account for up to 20% of known cases (TTN:09:10:17). The paedophile's offences are recurrent and prolific, and their perpetrators cannot be reorientated by psychotherapy.

The UK police operation Ore, set up in 2005, investigated the 7200 subjects from all walks of life who were known to have paid to download images from a child pornography web site - an illegal act in this country. It is estimated that the number of active UK paedophiles, which will include many of these viewers, must be significantly higher (TTN:03:08:31).

Institutional Paedophilia has a marked tendency to develop in establishments where heterosexual activity is barred, and mature and immature males live under the same roof. Paedophilia amongst Catholic clergy is an age old phenomenon. In 1600 a Spanish cleric Jose de Calasanz initiated a network of Catholic schools across Europe run by the Pietist (Pious) order for the free education of poor children. Because of the endemic paedophilia within them, these schools were abruptly shut down 46 years later by the Pope, amidst a furore of scandal. Despite the fact that he knew very well that these abuses were taking place and that he tried to cover them up, three centuries after his death the Vatican elected to raise Calasanz to the status of Patron Saint of all Catholic schools (LK04p256). Martin Luther cited unnatural sexual practice in the church as one of the reasons for his break with Rome, describing sodomy as "a sexual behaviour characteristic of bishops, cardinals and, most of all, of Popes" (PH03p143).

For centuries the malpractice of clerical paedophilia has been concealed by moving offending priests to alternative parishes when scandal became imminent, by the complicity of colleagues vowed to the secrecy of the confessional, and by the unwillingness of the faithful to undermine clerical authority. The silence of victims was sometimes bought with payoffs. Brazen threats that victims would not be believed, or that they would be punished if they divulged, were all too common. By former Vatican decree, any clerical offender, victim or witness who made a public disclosure in relation to an act of paedophilia was to be summarily excommunicated (BBCT1: 06:10:01).

The protracted mental suffering, and sometimes suicide, of those who had been abused as children did not seriously touch the corporate Catholic conscience until evidence of the scale of abuse within its ranks began to emerge towards the end of the second millennium. There were warning signs of the impending denouement in 1985 when leading insurance companies decided that they would no longer provide cover for the US church where priests faced allegations of sexual abuse filed by parishioners (TFTN:02:04:20). Within the next two decades 450 lawsuits were filed in Boston on counts of former child sexual abuse, and the Boston court allowed claimant lawyers to inspect the church's files covering a 30 year period. This investigation revealed a litany of depravity, with efforts to shuffle priests between posts, and to buy the silence of victims (STELN:02:12:08). Over a billion dollars were paid in compensation, and the senior US Catholic authority resigned.

An outraged Catholic laity at last understood that it had both the right and the power to bring its offending clergy to book, and thirst for litigious vengeance spread to Portland, Santa Fe, Tucson, Dallas, Chicago, New Mexico, New York, Pennsylvania, Florida and New Hampshire (BBCT1:06:10:01). All told, at least 65 priests and one bishop in 17 dioceses were suspended in sex abuse cases in the three month period to April 2002, and within the US more than a thousand victims were believed to have been compensated (GWN:02:04:28, TTN:02:04:16). Payouts ranged from 10 thousand dollars for unwanted kisses to 600 thousand dollars for oral sex or sodomy (DTN:93:12:23).

Catholic communities worldwide now joined in the revolt, with significant payouts to victims being made in New Zealand, Australia, Austria, Italy and Hong Kong. In England and Wales, between 1995 and 1999, one in every 266 Catholic priests was convicted for offences against children and, during the year 2001, 50 priests or lay preachers were languishing in UK jails on this account (TTN:01:04:18).

Clerical paedophilia in Eire led to the formation of victims' pressure groups and the conviction of 50 priests (BBCT2:03:19:06), but overall prevalence of the vice was more difficult to assess, since it was compounded by the serious mental and physical abuse and neglect which had occurred throughout state schools and orphanages between the 1920's and 1980's. These institutions catered for children from poorer families, were administered by the Catholic orders of the Christian Brothers and the Sisters of Mercy, and became the target of mass litigation towards the end of the 20th century. Since the ranks of victimised former pupils threatened to swell to 150 thousand if all claims had been lodged, incurring compensation of 15 billion euros, and since the state authorities felt partly responsible for allowing the excesses to occur, the Eire government underwrote the lion's share of damages (DTN:03:10:02).

That the Catholic clerical educational system perpetuates paedophilia is shown by the fact that 80% of abusing priests were themselves abused at school (TON:98:07:14). The all male enclave of the seminary inevitably fosters homosexuality and accounts for the estimates of the 50% of Catholic priests in the US, and the 10-50% world wide, who share this orientation (TGN:01:04:18). That practising homosexuals are attracted towards Catholic clerical orders is illustrated by the high proportion who constitute the intake for late vocational training (PC). Practising heterosexuals are discouraged from joining the priesthood by the Catholic requirement for celibacy, an anachronism which was introduced by Pope Gregory the seventh in the 11th century to prevent priests' families from inheriting church property (TON:98:07:14). This requirement is not regarded as the underlying cause of either homosexuality or of paedophilia in the church, and there would hardly be a stampede towards matrimony were it to be rescinded.

Bestiality, the commission of sexual association with animals, is only likely to take place when heterosexual human partnership is unavailable, but, like all perversions, once initiated, it may habituate and even become fetishistic. Kinsey's figures for its incidence were 3.6% for US females and 8% for US males, rising to 17% in farm boys (DMN:03:08:02).Captive animals occasionally attempt to copulate with members of other species, but never do so if conspecifics are available.

In common with all perverts, bestialists often feel ashamed, dirty, sinful or apprehensive, but few seek treatment, regarding the perverse act as a solution to their problem rather than the cause of it (PC00p63).

There is some evidence that all perversions may be more likely to develop in an individual whose mother suffered from a personality disorder (PC00p54 and 63).

Incest taboos apply to all human cultures and are demonstrable in many other species such as the Japanese macaque, the chimpanzee and the greylag goose. With puberty, in most animals, a strongly emotional sexual barrier against sibling coitus develops (EEI96p162), and this is heavily influenced by the change in orientation required when switching social relationships away from those formed under peer-play group pressures to those required by hormonal maturity (WAP66). Kibbutz raised human children seldom intermarry (WR02p256).

Incestuous fertilisation results in a marked increase in congenital abnormality. Intermarriages between the closely related European royal families produced numerous tragic cases of porphyria and haemophilia, and Islamic first cousin marriage practices result in a 13 fold increase in birth defects (BBCT1:05:11:15).

CHAPTER 19

SADISM IN THE RAW

TORTURE, RAPE AND SERIAL KILLING

The observation that civilisation is only skin deep is nowhere better exemplified than in man's inhumanity to man. It takes little to peel back the veneer and make the school bully persecute his victim, for two drunkards to start fighting, or for the mob to be roused and have it baying for blood. Why, too, when every sane person abhors cruelty, is it possible to turn over the pages of history and discover that most cultures have sanctioned the use of it as a political weapon - ancient Rome, the Mediaeval Church, Islam, Fascism, Communism, and the South American and Sub Saharan dictatorships, to name just a few?

Animal studies show us that the trait of offensive aggression, originally evolved for carnivorous hunting, has been further developed by a few species such as the chimpanzee as an instrument of inter "herd" confrontation. Forays which may lead to the killing and cannibalism of conspecifics are carried out, not merely when resources are in short supply, but as gratuitous warfare conducted for the excitement of contention and risk taking. Interherd warfare introduces a new factor into the evolutionary equation, since with its appearance successful individuals have not only to prove their fitness to survive the adversity of nature and interspecies competition, but the additional hazard of hostility from their own kind. We have already noted that the liquidation of a critical number of adult males in a community has an adverse effect upon its evolution. Likewise, the use of increasingly powerful weaponry is counterproductive in evolutionary terms inasmuch as it kills unselectively.

If it is true to say that interherd warfare with its gratuitous offensive aggression takes humanity into a Darwinian blind alley, then so does the closely related phenomenon of sadism with its gratuitous cruelty. Sadism is a uniquely human adverse attribute which, as Freud noted, delivers pseudo-sexual gratification. Goodall observes that only humans inflict suffering for its own sake and enjoy doing so (GJ90p180). Sadism may occur in either sex, but it is rare in females, such as when Berber women emasculate male prisoners of war. Although both men and women are capable of deriving pseudo-sexual excitement either from inflicting, or from experiencing, pain (sadism and masochism respectively), whether or not they do so is almost always determined by their conditioning during immaturity. Only in its most barbaric and irrational outbursts is sadism the product of a genetic defect akin to that which causes chronic malice. That sadism is predominantly a male attribute is a consequence of the way in which testosterone fuels aggression, and especially offensive aggression. Torturers and executioners have always been men.

As a prelude to sexual congress, a fetishistic process converts perceived physical attraction into sexual desire. This psychological adjustment is normally consensual, but sadists pervert it unilaterally, deriving sexual excitement by eliciting pain, whether or not this is consummated by coitus. The propensity for fetishism is instinctive, but its mature expression can be distorted by nurtural malconditioning and, in particular by those influences which also lead to delinquency, those which deform the dominance ranking process, or those which are the legacy of the abuse that the sadist himself suffered as a child. Fetishistic patterns of motivation are laid down during adolescence, and are strongly influenced by orgasmic experience.

The relationship between sexuality and violence is readily demonstrable. Being tortured or witnessing torture may induce ejaculation (SGR95p16). Ovid observed that some Roman noblemen were in the habit of taking women acquaintances to gladiatorial games to increase their sexual arousal (SGR95p16). The association between sexuality and violence is nowhere more starkly evident than in human warfare, where, like plunder, the prospect of rape has often been used to motivate attacking troops. In the Congolese civil war which had claimed 4 million lives by the end of the second millennium, women were not only raped in their hundreds of thousands as a considered policy, but also sexually mutilated such as to require reconstructive surgery (BBCT1:06:07:27). Stalin condoned the rape of German women by his victorious armies as an act of retribution. In its most extreme form, sadism may actually substitute for coitus. The serial murderer Herr Kurten, known as the Dusseldorf monster, told his psychiatrist that "it was not his intention to get satisfaction by normal sexual intercourse, but by killing" (SGR95p16).Violence can also cause mass excitation of the sexual psyche. In 1807 two murderers were publicly hanged at Newgate in London, and the 40 thousand spectators who thronged to see this gruesome spectacle became so tightly compressed that several women and children were trampled to death, and nearly 100 were left dying in the surrounding streets (HC03p70). The same macabre magnetism, which can induce erection, still draws large crowds to attend public executions in the Middle East and China, to see bullfights, cockfights and dogfights, and to witness boxing matches and dramatised violence on television.

There are four major manifestations of overt sadism - punitive sexual fetishism (which we considered in the previous chapter), torture, rape and sexually motivated murder. A brief survey of these grisly skeletons in the cupboard of humanity serves to reinforce the paramount importance of instilling humanitarian principles alongside aversion to warfare as a component of human nurture. Since informed conditioning based on hard evidence stands a better chance of bearing fruit, let us see what history has to teach us.

Torture

Torture has been a feature of most major cultures, being perpetrated at an intermediate stage in their development. Although war and cannibalism are of great antiquity, there would have been no point in torturing an enemy destined for the cooking pot, or an adversary earmarked for death in a blood feud. Likewise, a civilisation emerging from mediaevalism into modernity has no justification for the use of torture, recognising it as the biologically abnormal and inhumane act which it is.

Torture applies sadism to the process of extorting information, false confessions, and the payment of taxes or outstanding debts, and it is used extensively by totalitarian regimes to intimidate and eradicate political opposition. Torture has also been widely employed as retributive punishment. When man first developed weaponry, the primate method of imposing top-down discipline by physical confrontation in sequential dominance contests had to be abandoned, and settled communities had to agree rules of conduct. In order to enforce these rules, the punishment of transgressors was, and always will be, necessary. Thus exile and execution were imposed for major offences, and preventive detention, fines and physical suffering were inflicted for minor ones. The ingenuity and diversity with which penalising authorities have added to their repertoire of mutilatory procedures would seem to have been unlimited.

Archaeological evidence of torture is found in the cruel methods of execution used, such as those inflicted upon the peat bog preserved bodies found in Denmark with multiple fractures and the ropes used to hang them still around their necks (GPV71p70), or the immolation of groups of young men buried alive in a seated posture. One of the earliest historical records of torture is of captives taken in battle being flayed alive by Assyrian warriors, a scene depicted in a relief stone carving which may date back to Sargon the Great's rule in the third millennium BCE. All slave owning empires enforced submission with torture. The Egyptians and Greeks flogged with the bastinado (scourging rod), and the Romans used a flagellum (a multi-stranded whip) for day to day discipline. For more forcible persuasion the Greeks enclosed the slave in a metal casket provided with inwardly pointing spikes (the "iron maiden "), and the Romans employed the stretching rack (CAM96). Neither Greece nor Rome tortured free men.

The use of torture throughout the historical period in Europe, the Middle East, India, China, Japan, and North and South America is amply documented. In England, torture to extract evidence and confession (the "quaestro") became officially illegal after 1406, but the king, the Privy Council and the Star Chamber could override the common law in serious cases and frequently did so. Torture was rife in England between the 15th and 17th centuries (HC03p8), but all forms of it, with the exception of flogging, were legally banned after 1827.

Until the modern era, punishments were always levied promptly, once the offender had been pronounced guilty. Fines had to be paid on the spot, and physical forms of punishment were carried out there and then on court premises. Preventive detention was regarded as an intolerable burden on the public purse, and was only used for those awaiting trial, or for debtors. Executions were invariably preceded by torture to ensure that remorse and atonement were elicited.

There have been five principal methods of applying torture - distraction, compression, mutilation, sequestration in a public place, and flogging. Distraction required the use of the rack or the pulley. The "rack" was a wooden platform about 12 feet long with a rotating wooden drum at each end of it. The victim lay supine on the platform with his wrists and ankles fettered by ropes which were wound around the drums, so that purchase upon these extended his arms and legs in diametrically opposite directions and dislocated the limb joints. The rack was in common use from the time of ancient Greece, Rome and India, at least until the 18th century (EAM96).

The "pulley" involved tethering the wrists together behind the victim's back with a rope, the end of which was then threaded through a pulley in the ceiling, and which could be used to lift him. Jerks applied to the rope dislocated the shoulders. The method was used throughout Europe, and in Russia and Japan. In the penal colony of Norfolk Island prisoners were suspended from the ceiling by a chain shackled to one wrist.

Compression could be applied to the whole body or selected components of it. The "scavenger's daughter " was a cage of iron hoops, the two halves of which were hinged together. When enclosed, the victim was compressed into a position similar to that adopted by praying Muslims, and breathing became difficult. The device was in frequent use in England from the 15th to the 17th centuries. "Peine dure et forte" was a method of compression used specifically to force accused persons to plead before trial. The victim was lashed to the floor, and a wooden tray was placed on top of him, upon which heavy weights were loaded. Food and drink were withheld. The practice continued in England until 1772.

The "boot" was a knee length replica of a cavalry boot, cast in iron, into which a victim's lower leg was inserted. Wooden wedges were driven into the intervening space between the cast and the flesh to constrict the circulation. The Chinese compressed the hands and feet with clamps, and the Japanese constricted the limbs with cord bindings. Europeans constricted the head and neck with iron bands (the "witch's collar"), or the wrists (the "iron gauntlet"). A vice was used by the Inquisition to crush the exquisitely tender human heel bone, and "thumbscrews" pulped thumb joints in efforts to secure confessions. The Nazis used testicular compression during interrogations.

The purpose of mutilatory punishment was not merely to inflict suffering and partial disablement on a miscreant, but to do so in such a way as to leave clear evidence of the link between a crime and the retribution meted out for it, evidence which would then act as a deterrent to others. Stigmatisation was by amputation or branding, or both.

Mutilatory punishment has been in common use at some point during the emergence of every civilisation (IG14). The Romans punished adultery by flogging and nasal amputation (GP02). In 16th - 18th century France, thieves had one or both ears amputated, and blasphemers had their tongues cut out. In Alfred's England the law prescribed hand amputation for sheep stealing, and Canute's law punished adultery in women by excising both nose and ears. Henry the First's laws punished coiners with castration and with amputation of both hands, female perjurers had their eyes torn out (HC03p9), sexual offenders were emasculated and forgers lost their right hand. Mutilatory punishment reached its apogee between the 10th and 15th centuries CE and was principally meted out to the poor who were unable to pay fines which would otherwise have been used to swell the coffers of the king, the church and the feudal landlord (HC03p9). During the 15th and 16th centuries, amputation of the ears and splitting of the nose was conducted at the pillory and imposed in cases of minor theft (SGR955p207). The response to non-capital offences in the Sandwich Islands was enucleation of both eyes. Islamic Sharia law still advocates hand amputation for theft, and the protracted suffering of stoning which attends the execution of adulterers.

Branding was extensively practised in France, Russia, India and England, being finally abolished in the latter country in 1829 (HC03p5). Alphabetic letters were seared with a red hot iron upon the cheek, the forehead, or the palm of the left hand. R stood for rogue or vagabond, T for thief, A for arsonist, P for perjurer, M for someone who had committed manslaughter, and SS for a person found guilty of sedition. Branding was usually accompanied by other forms of punishment.

Sequestration was another method of punishment which stigmatised the miscreant, and it did so by exhibiting him under constraint in a public place, exposed to the opprobrium and ridicule of passers by. The pillory was a stout pillar of wood or stone to which the offender was chained. The stocks were notched and hinged pairs of wooden planks whose apertures when the planks were brought together held the culprit fast, either by the neck and wrists in a standing position, or by the ankles if sitting on the ground. The duration of immobilisation was tailored to the gravity of the offence, and its perpetrator was at the mercy of his family for victuals and the mob for rough justice. At best, the punishment was degradation, but at worst a death sentence delivered by missile. Homosexuals were often stoned to death. Every town had a street corner reserved for the fettering of dishonest traders, rumourmongers and slanderers, and the method of detention made no demands upon public funds as imprisonment would have done. England abolished the pillory in 1837 (SGR95p44).

Historically, criminals everywhere have always been flogged. Chastisement has been meted out by cart whip, "cat-o-nine-tails", birch, bastinado, cudgel, paddle or split rattan. Moses prescribed a maximum of 40 lashes for offences against society. Ancient Egypt, China, Japan, and India used the bastinado. The Romans and ancient Greeks considered flogging degrading and restricted it to slaves - the Roman "flagellum" whip with multiple strands was the precursor of the "cat-o-nine-tails". Russia under Ivan the Fourth used the multistranded knut, whose lacerations gouged out the flesh so deeply that its use had to be discontinued in 1845.

The Anglo Saxons whipped their prisoners with knotted cords (HC03p402). In England, the Whipping Act of 1530 authorised the chastisement of all vagrants, and throughout the 16th and 17th centuries men and women were sentenced to be whipped for an immense variety of offences such as vagabondage, illegitimate motherhood, pedlary, beggary, drunkenness, fortune telling and sex offences. The flogging of lunatics was supposed to bring them to their senses (HC03p400). Criminals condemned to crew galleys were flogged at their toil as a matter of course, which is why many failed to survive the four or eight year term of their sentence. In 1812 England limited the maximum number of strokes permitted at any flogging to 300, albeit that some so punished might well expire before this total had been reached. In 1948, the use of flogging in prisons was limited to the punishment of gross violence against prison staff, and to prison mutiny or the incitement of it.

The multistranded English "cat-o-nine-tails" whip had always been used to keep discipline in civil life, prisons, the armed forces and the colonies - in particular those colonies which employed slaves. Typically the offender was bound standing against an upright triangular wooden frame with stripes delivered every half minute by a pair of flagellators. Whip thongs cut through the skin of the back to deflesh it and leave a tattered and bloody pulp into which salt and pepper were rubbed.

Prior to the modern era, execution was inevitably preceded by torture to ensure that the offender paid for his crime with agony as well as extinction. Human sacrifice sometimes required preliminary torture, as practiced by the Maya before they threw their victim into the cenote - a deep water chasm. Many forms of execution were inherently prolonged, and thereby involved intense suffering.

Rome flogged slaves before crucifying them, and used the amphitheatre to have convicts and dissenters dismembered by wild beasts (GE88). The Japanese death dance was engineered by igniting tightly fitting inflammable clothing in which the victim had been dressed. Japan used death by 21 defleshing cuts, of which the ultimate was the coup de grace. Both ancient China and the Peruvian Antis tribe employed death by a thousand cuts, and Amerindian tribes practised slow dismemberment and gradual incineration. In China and South East Asia offenders were flayed alive as they had been in ancient Carthage, and burying alive occurred in mediaeval France, Germany and Switzerland (SGR95p217). In England highwaymen and pirates were gibbeted by suspending them with chains, or in iron hooped cages, to die by starvation, a process which usually took between one and two weeks. Germany suspended malefactors just within reach of starving dogs. India bricked up brigands, leaving their heads exposed to the vultures. Execution by decapitation often required a dozen blows with the axe, and hangmen often slowly strangled their victims in error when they should have dislocated their necks. Crucifixion, with its agonisingly slow demise, was perpetrated by the Phoenicians, Scythians, Romans, Greeks and Persians.

Two methods of slow execution were particularly vile. Traitors were deemed to merit being partially hung, before being cut down, disembowelled, and then dismembered. Breaking on the wheel involved the offender being lashed akimbo to a large cartwheel turned on its side, and systematically having every bone and organ in his body smashed with a sledge hammer.

As we know from former detainees, despite signing up to the UN Convention Against Torture, and despite the fabricated responses which are often all that can be extracted from the victim, many state authorities, including those of the great powers, still employ interrogative torture. Near drowning, sleep deprivation, and enforced prolonged standing are the most frequently adopted techniques, with exposure to extremes of temperature, light or sound less often used - all procedures which purposely leave behind no tell-tale scars. Mutilation by electric shock, power drill or chain saw is usually the prerogative of the dictator or gangster.

Rape

Male sexual activity is periodic, the phase of desire alternating with satiation and quiescence after orgasm, a cycle which is governed overall by pituitary endocrine secretions. Because of this, heterosexuals, homosexuals, paedophiles, rapists and reciditive killers all exhibit serial (i.e. recurrent) activity in their fields. The heterosexual's fetish is the female body, the homosexual's fetish the male body, the paedophile's fetish the immature body, and the rapist's fetish is the sense of fear which he engenders in his victim. The reciditive killer's fetish is the sight and sensation of the death throes in the women he slays and, as with the Dusseldorf monster, this fetish may be compelling enough to displace the need for genital intercontact altogether.

A man who did not wish to engender fear in his female partner would have no need to commit rape - he could pair with a regular partner, date promiscuous women or pay prostitutes without risking prosecution. The non-homicidal rapist only displays violence towards his victim if she fails to show fear, and puts up a determined resistance. Normally, threats of the use of a weapon are sufficient to produce the level of intimidation he seeks. The psyche of a typical rapist exhibits aggressiveness, egocentricity, callousness, impulsiveness and general antisociability, and the inability to form bonds of affection (GNBHJ79). This would suggest that in a few cases, at least, the offence may be traced back to those chromosomal personality disorders producing heritable forms of delinquency which are cited in chapter 8. By analogy with the psychopathogenesis of other forms of sadism, however, we can also infer that malconditioning during juvenility plays an important part in the character formation of a rapist, and when full life histories are available they often reveal that emotional trauma was experienced in childhood. The taxi driver John Warboys, who may have drugged and raped as many as 500 victims in the back of his cab, lost his mother to cancer when he was 13 years old. The bisexual sex attacker Andrezej Kunowski had been taken into care as a toddler when both his parents were imprisoned. The bizarre Josef Fritzl had been brought up by a mother who constrained him with harsh principles and iron discipline, who frequently beat him, and who allowed him no childhood friends. Later as an adult, Fritzl incarcerated his own daughter in a cellar over a period of 24 years, repeatedly beating and raping her, and siring seven children by her.

British Crime Survey statistics taken over a six year period to 2001 showed countrywide annual incidences for male rape on females as varying between 4.9 thousand and 7.9 thousand, of male rape on males as varying between 150 and 664, and male gross indecency with a child occurring at levels of 1.2-1.3 thousand. It is acknowledged that rape is grossly underreported, owing to the diffidence victims feel towards the need to produce proof, and towards the level of support offered by authority. Allegations of coitus between cohabitees without female consent are usually impossible to substantiate and tend to distort statistics.

Serial Murder

On occasions, male chimpanzees have been observed to pound and drag unresponsive females in order to coerce them into sexual submission (GJ90p72). By contrast, reciditive libido-driven murders of other "herd" members does not occur in non-human primates and is grossly biologically abnormal. Human perpetrators of such crimes are invariably male and their victims are either female or, less often, male homosexuals, circumstances which serve to confirm the close link which this form of homicide has with sexuality (HC03p214). Whereas the sexually driven killer serially reoffends, the criminal who murders for other reasons seldom kills again.

The man hunt triggered by serial killing is so urgent and extensive that no offender would be likely to set it in motion were it not for the impelling obsession which the sexual fetish of the victim's death agony holds for him. After all, it would prove much more straightforward to pay, or default on payment to, prostitutes like any other punter, than to risk conviction by killing them. Additionally, sadistic acts of mutilation of victims, particularly involving the genitalia, often follow their murder. Surprisingly, there is sometimes no attempt to bury the victims' corpses, so the motive for killing, at least in such cases, cannot be to suppress evidence of the crime of rape.

Because of vigorous police and media reactions nowadays, serial killers' victims seldom reach double figures. Jack the Ripper (1888), Peter Sutcliffe (1977), and Dennis Nilson (1978) all raped and mutilated their prey. Other notable serial killers were Haigh (1946), Christie (1953) and Glatman (1958). The all-time record for large scale atrocity in this field is held by Baron Gilles de Rais ("Bluebeard"), a paedophile who in 1440 confessed to the murder of 800 children, as well as to acts of sodomy and witchcraft, and who was hanged over a fire for his crimes (BJ71).

It is difficult to see how malconditioning could distort the human personality in such an extreme way as to cause serial murder attended by mutilation, and it is likely that these offences, like a single episode of mass carnage for which a disturbed individual's brainstorm is responsible, are usually, or always, manifestations of chronic malice determined by chromosomally mediated brain defects. The most prolific serial killer of modern times was Harold Shipman whose case was highly unusual, not only for the number of his victims, but for the fact that his crimes were not attended by sexual congress. Shipman increased our understanding of serial killing by underlining the fact that this manifestation of sadism is usually associated with brain pathology, whether genetic or otherwise, rather than with immature malconditioning.

Key Character Study: Harold Shipman (1946-2004)
In 2003, Britain was aghast to learn that an NHS family doctor in Manchester had been found to have murdered 215 of his patients, with a further 45 almost certainly having met their death in the same way.

Shipman's victims were either middle aged or elderly, and although they were predominantly female, the total included 39 men (PC05p240). As a serial killer Shipman was altogether atypical. There was no evidence of sexual molestation nor mutilation, indeed victims were left fully and neatly dressed, looking as if they had just fallen asleep. Other than the gender bias, and the fact that Shipman had altered a few wills before death in his own favour, there seemed to be no common thread in the way he selected his victims. Some murders were actually committed in the near presence of third parties.

Shipman killed by administering morphine or heroin intravenously, intramuscularly or by mouth to patients on his list, providing a variety of excuses as to why he was doing so. To obtain the necessary supplies he overprescribed these drugs for cancer patients, stockpiling residues, and he falsified paper and computerised patient records, cremation forms, and statements to relatives and other doctors, to cover his tracks. Investigations reveal that what began as euthanasia for the terminally ill, practised in his earliest professional years, degenerated into an obsessional compulsion to exercise a godlike power of life or death, with emphasis on the latter, over those who trusted him in his later career.

Shipman's father was a lorry driver who believed in disciplining his children. His mother never concealed the ambition she harboured for her son, and thanks largely to her encouragement, he struggled through the exams needed to qualify from Leeds Medical School in 1970. If a general practitioner is to engender respect, appreciation and affection, then he must earn these attributes by dedicated hard work. Shipman's attention to his professional commitments was always conscientious and enabled him to recruit a well above average number of patients, and to acquire an enviable, albeit totally illusory, reputation.

Shipman's achilles heel was his own drug habituation which began in studenthood. Later, whilst training for a midwifery diploma, he took advantage of the access to pethidine offered by the extensive use which this drug has during childbirth. As well as relieving pain, pethidine also provides euphoria for those intent on escaping the stresses of reality and responsibility. It is, like all opiates, highly addictive. Shipman never forgot the overwhelming sense of relief which pethidine had produced in his mother when he was 17 and she was dying of cancer - an episode of emotionally charged imagery which continually played on his mind.

From the time he qualified as a doctor with the power to prescribe, Shipman was a lifelong opiate addict. In 1975, after he had begun to suffer from toxic blackouts, the Home Office Drugs Inspectorate and West Yorks Drugs Squad became aware that he was obtaining unlawful quantities of pethidine, and when his partners at his first general practice discovered that he was misappropriating controlled drugs for his own use, he admitted to it and resigned. Eighteen months later, after he had first been to an addict rehabilitation unit and then employed as a medical officer at Hatfield College where there was no access to opiates, he was readmitted to general practice on probationary sufferance.

Long term opiate use, like that of cocaine, high dosage cannabis, or high alcohol usage, causes brain damage which may be cognitive, emotional or moral in its impact. From 1971 onwards, Shipman's personality was increasingly dichotomised. The outwardly caring physician became ever more obsessed by the emotionally traumatic image of his mother's final days, and his pethidine riddled brain sought to impart the same terminal benefits which she had derived from opiate drugs to all the elderly patients for whom he had a duty of care. He saw himself as an angel of mercy, but his toxicity made him behave like the devil incarnate. Based on the evidence available, Shipman's brain is not thought to have been malconditioned during his council house or Nottingham Grammar School upbringing (he was a successful rugby player as a boy), but to have sustained damage as a result of long standing opiate addiction.

During his middle age, Shipman dissociated himself emotionally and intellectually from his fellow beings, taking refuge in an insularity which he imagined would help him continue his criminal activities unheeded. His attitude became aloof, arrogant, self centred, dictatorial and supercilious. Following the precept that attack is the best method of defence, he used assertiveness to pre-empt criticism, and guile and fabrication to sway those who might otherwise doubt him. Convinced that he was now impregnable, his risk taking became ever more profligate and audacious. The smoke screen of intrigue, bluff and bluster proved so effective that the nature and staggering scale of his crimes remained undetected for 25 years. With hindsight, it is clear that systematic cross checks on medical and pharmaceutical accountability were at that time woefully inadequate. Chemists, fellow doctors, and the Registrar of Births and Deaths must have felt increasingly suspicious, and one funeral director he knew confronted him, but was gainsaid. In 1992 he moved surgery premises and became an independent single practitioner in order, no doubt, to avoid the closer scrutiny of his immediate colleagues when they became a fund holding consortium.

When, in April 1998, a partner in a neighbouring practice responsible for countersigning his cremation certificates reported the high incidence of Shipman's patient deaths to the police, the latter's initial investigation absolved him. Eventually a solicitor, the daughter of a murdered patient whose will Shipman had falsified in his own favour, conducted her own investigations into his conduct and made sure that he was brought to book. At long last, a line was drawn under the litany of homicides. Shipman was convicted in January 2000 at Preston Crown Court, and subsequently, in 2004 whilst at Wakefield Jail, he hanged himself with his own bed linen. The enormity of his atrocities led to a public enquiry under Dame Janet Smith, and long overdue changes were made to the supervision of mortality in medical care. In 2005 a memorial garden was opened as a mark of respect for his victims.

(Chapter Sources Reviewed: BBCT1:06:07:27, BK38 , BSC71, CWM68, EAM96, FJA63, GE88, GJ90, GP02, GPV71, HC03, HJ84, http://news.bbc.co.uk/1/, IG14, LEH31, PC03, PLA33, SGR95, SJ31, WKP08, www.the-shipman-inquiry.org.uk)

CHAPTER 20

"IN 1802 EVERY HEREDITARY MONARCH WAS INSANE"
(Walter Bageholt 1826-77, Writing On The English Constitution)

SPORADIC GENETIC ERRORS INFLUENCING BEHAVIOUR - MENTAL ILLNESS

Most of us take good physical health for granted, but recognise that it may not last and so maintain an active interest in what we can learn from the maladies of others. Not so mental illness, from which we think we should be, and probably are, immune and from which we tend to distance ourselves. But mental illness cannot be ignored. In terms of health care and social support it constitutes a communal responsibility of major proportions, it is a harrowing, often lifelong and crushing, imposition upon the patient and his family, and it demands to be much better understood than it is, whether by relatives, prospective parents, the public at large, or students of human behaviour. Because mental illness causes sufferers to warp their interpretations of their surround, an insight into its thought processes helps all of us to look at life more objectively and eschew compulsive prejudice. Mental illness is also a subset of the human behavioural repertoire that helps us to understand more about brain functionality. At the outset it is important to be able to distinguish between mental illness and the long term detrimental effects of childhood malconditioning. Case studies which illustrate the difference are easy to find. Let us take a glimpse at two from American history.

In 1957, the schizophrenic George Meresky was committed to a New York psychiatric treatment centre for the criminally insane. Although there could be no prospect of curing him, he had to be incarcerated for his own protection and that of the general public. Whilst it was true that he had never actually succeeded in killing anyone, this could hardly have been for lack of trying, for over a sixteen year period he had planted 54 bombs in locations which were as varied as they were bizarre. The devices usually contained gunpowder taken from shotgun cartridges, but often had no detonator. Following the 22 explosions this mad bomber did finally manage to notch up, there were mercifully few injuries. Fulminating within his deranged brain was an obsessional grudge he held against the Consolidated Edison Corporation, a grudge as deluded as his bomb targeting was off target. He was suffering from a heritable mental defect which deprived him of the ability to think rationally.

By total contrast, six years later on the 22nd of November 1963, Americans were to learn to their horror that their president had been assassinated in a motorcade in Dallas, Texas. John F. Kennedy died within minutes after his skull had been pierced by a bullet from a 6.5mm precision Mannlicher-Carcano Italian military carbine fired from a sixth floor window by Lee Harvey Oswald. Although no evidence could be obtained from Oswald, since he was gunned down two days later in what appeared to be a vigilante act of retribution, details of his previous activities and background were already held in the files of his neighbourhood judicial authority, and by the CIA.

Coming from a broken home, with a self centred mother who married three times and proved incapable of providing him with either true affection or the basic necessities of life, he was forced to spend part of his childhood in an orphanage. Drifting into juvenile delinquency, his persistent truancy from school led to court appearances and probation. When assessing him, the psychiatrist to whom he was referred could find no evidence of psychotic change in him, such as mental illness would have caused, but noted that he was emotionally disturbed and had a "potential for explosive, aggressive and assault type acting out". IQ tests put him in the high normal range.

In early adulthood, Oswald's life continued to be turbulent. When he reached the age of 17 he was able to enlist in the Marine Corps, despite the fact that he was at that time an avowed communist, but he proved unable to cope with military discipline. Within the space of three years he was court-martialled twice and dishonourably discharged from the Marines, whereupon he renounced American citizenship, emigrated to the USSR, and found himself a Russian wife of his own age. After applying for, but being refused, soviet citizenship he attempted suicide by cutting his wrists, was treated in a Russian psychiatric unit and, disillusioned and embittered, found his way back to the USA with his tail between his legs. Seeking work, he was offered jobs by two successive employers, but both found him unsuitable and dismissed him. Goaded now by a false sense of injustice, he became restless and resorted once more to left wing politics as a means of asserting himself. The burning resentment he felt over US intervention in Cuban affairs made him cast round for ways in which he could turn his military training to account. He bought himself firearms and ammunition, honed up his skills as a sharpshooter, and in an effort to leave his mark on history attempted to kill a retired army general, whose life was only spared when the bullet was deflected as it passed through a windowpane. The thirty-fifth president of the United States was to prove less fortunate.

Although both Meresky and Oswald were impelled by an intense sense of grievance against society, the mental disturbances afflicting them differed, as their case histories show. The mad bomber's delusions were the result of a genetic error in brain development, whereas the crippling prejudices under which the assassin laboured stemmed from malconditioning during childhood.

The study of human behaviour must encompass, and distinguish between, mental illness and the results of malconditioning. Most mental illness is episodic, disrupts the life of the individual but not, as a rule, of the community at large, is usually inherited, and most frequently involves the emotional brain and the five basic emotions. By contrast, malconditioning causes a disorder of one or more of the seven fundamental primate behavioural traits whose effects are persistent, which stem from adverse environmental pressures which acted upon the conditionable brain during immaturity, and which may impact widely upon the community, particularly if the malconditioned individual is in a position of authority, or if many individuals have been similarly indoctrinated. Mental illness and malconditioning are not mutually exclusive, and both may be present in the same individual.

Mental illness is exposed when the patient or his relatives seek medical help, usually because of subjective symptoms, with or without social or occupational dysfunction. The magnitude of the mental health care problem is such that the World Health Organisation predicts that by 2020 mental and neurological disorders will account for one sixth of the world's disease burden, with depression alone becoming the second leading cause of disability (TFTN:01:04:07 and TTN:04:04:14).

Six principal conditions account for most cases of mental illness. Four of these - bipolar affective disorder, schizophrenia, paranoia and hysteria - only manifest in genetically predetermined subjects, whereas anxiety and depression do have genetic predispositions, but may also manifest in all but the most redoubtable individuals if environmental circumstances are harrowing enough. All six conditions may occasionally be mimicked by physical diseases such as tumours, infections or poisoning, but if these are present, treatment must clearly target the underlying cause, and the outcome will be determined accordingly. Let us take a brief look at the way these illnesses torment those who suffer from them.

Anxiety States

Debilitating anxiety without proportionate provocation has a lifetime prevalence of 5% in the UK population (PMMZ:02:07:05), but in the USA has been found to reach much higher levels (KRE94). Women are affected twice as often as men, and onset usually occurs between the ages of 15 and 25 years. Sufferers experience unaccountable anxiety ranging from disturbing unease to panic stricken terror, and are tormented by unwarranted fears of prospective accidents, illnesses, insanity, victimisation, rejection, unemployment or imprisonment. The overdrive of panic may cause thought distortions called delusions, or disorders of perception called hallucinations, which convince the sufferer that his worst fears are being realised.

Because of the mental overburden of fear, there is impairment of insight, and judgement, concentration and sleep are impaired. Activity may be frenetic, or in abeyance with the patient stuporose. Speech may be voluble or suppressed. Repeated mannerisms such as hand wringing or nail biting are common. Accompanying physical manifestations are sweating, trembling, mouth dryness, a fast pulse, raised blood pressure, diarrhoea, urinary incontinence and impotence. Some cases only manifest when triggered by a phobia such as the fear of spiders (arachnophobia), crowds (agoraphobia), or heights (acrophobia).

Among those who have risen to prominence, authors appear to be unduly prone to overanxiety. Gustave Flaubert, Ford Madox Ford, Auguste Strindberg, Henry James, Jane Austen, Arnold Bennett, Karl Marx, H. L. Menken and Benjamin Disraeli all suffered from it. So also did many who earned their living in the performing arts - Judy Garland, Betty Hutton, Al Jolson, Gary Cooper, Edith Piaf, Oscar Levant and George Gershwin, to mention but a few. The disorder makes some resort to alcohol or drugs, and psychotherapeutic procedures such as the Alexander Technique have been devised to help deal with it.

Depression

Debilitating depression appearing without proportionate provocation may either occur alone, or else be interspersed with episodes of mania. In the latter case it is referred to as manic depression or bipolar affective disorder (see below). There is a lifetime prevalence for all types of debilitating depression in the UK, whether unprovoked or reactive, of 6.6%. It occurs at all ages, but females suffer from it twice as often as males, and city dwellers markedly more often than country folk. 3.5 million UK citizens take SSRT drugs daily for depression (DMN:04:12:07), and more GP consultations are devoted to depression than are required for any other single complaint.

Depression may be provoked by contemporaneous physical illness, chronic pain, premenstruation, pregnancy, the menopause, marital disruption, unemployment, bereavement, social isolation, handicap or by the long nights of winter (seasonal affective disorder). The sufferer feels hopeless, helpless, worthless, useless, guilty, remorseful, miserable, and unreal, and hallucinations deceptively convince those afflicted that they are the victims of derision, insanity, physical illness or body odour. Delusions reinforce their guilt and inferiority complexes. Self criticism may be intense, and may centre upon relationships, finances, or civic or religious misdemeanours. There is retardation, apathy, indecision, brooding, poor sleep, lack of appetite and libido, weight loss, constipation and menstrual cessation. Physical activity is reduced and may reach stupor in extreme cases. Effort and responsibility are dreaded and avoided. There is a suicidal risk in severe depression of one in six.

Of those depressives who were in the public eye, Marie Curie and Charles Lamb had to be hospitalised because of the severity of their psychosis, Dante Gabriel Rossetti's depressive illness was compounded by increasing mental instability, John Ruskin's was accompanied by hallucinations and impotence which ended his marriage, Russia's monarch Rudolph the Second's black melancholy seriously impaired his ability to rule, and William Cowper, Nicholai

Gogol and Mark Twain all had to take time out to recover from bouts of severe and protracted despondency.

Bipolar Affective Disorder

When episodic disabling depression is interspersed with episodes of mania it is categorised as bipolar affective disorder (BAD) which has a lifetime prevalence of 1-1.5%, and affects men and women equally (CMHM05 vol.3 No3). For every manic episode there are, on average, three depressive episodes. BAD is a disease of adulthood and occurs more often in cities than rural communities.

In extreme contrast with the episodes of depression, the phase of mania is geared to over-excitability, gross mood elevation (as opposed to despondency), and supercharged (as opposed to diminished) levels of mental and physical activity, appetite, self esteem and sexuality. The subject is exuberant, over confident and over optimistic, whilst he is at the same time confused, irresponsible, repetitive, distractible, voluble, grandiose, liable to drink heavily, extravagant, licentious, exhibitionistic and irritable. His thoughts come so thick and fast that he loses control over them. Hallucinations and delusions occur, misjudgements and misrepresentations are common, sleep is brief but deep. At first strong and tireless, as his energy reserves are depleted the sufferer becomes exhausted. The suicide rate is 15%.

Manic depressive illness makes it difficult for sufferers to lead independent lives, but notable exceptions were the successful writer Ernest Hemingway who, like four other near relatives, eventually committed suicide, Charles Lamb's wife Mary who stabbed her own mother to death, the actress Vivien Leigh, Oliver Cromwell whose depressive phases were sometimes sufficiently debilitating to require treatment, and Terence ("Spike") Milligan who had to be restrained from shooting fellow actors on more than one occasion. A disproportionate number of European monarchs suffered from manic depression during the 15th, 16th and 17th centuries (see below).

Paranoia

Debilitating, obsessional compulsive behaviour (paranoia) has a lifetime prevalence of 2-3% in the overall adult population. In the elderly this rises to 4%. It is an interesting observation that normal children between the ages of 2 and 6 years pass through a phase of play which incorporates repetitive and ritualistic behaviour. Although paranoia is primarily a defect of the conditionable brain (the seat of the fixed idea), there is also a disturbance of the emotional brain involving an unwarranted reaction of fear or disgust to specific events or objects (referred to as a phobia). Subjects who feel unduly aggrieved may sue for redress, if querulous will become antisocial, if they feel contaminated may wash repetitively, if they feel disorderly may spend much of their time tidying, if jealous may pry and snoop, and if they feel persecuted may hallucinate and delude with falsely perceived jeers and insults. The oversensitive are plagued with doubt as to their physical, mental or moral worth. and believe that others must also be viewing them with the contempt they feel for themselves.

Sufferers become obstinate, morose, irritable, vacillatory and depressed, acting out the obsessional ideas, images, impulses and phobias which beset them, in a futile attempt to purge themselves of the devil within. Masturbatory guilt leads to repetitive hand washing, and fear of social rejection leads to repetitive visits to the mirror or frequent changes of underclothes. Though most paranoiacs have above average intelligence they have no insight into their condition, and this may make them aggressive, obscene or suicidal.

Several public figures were markedly paranoidal, for example Auguste Strindberg whose phobias included an abject fear of dogs, Howard Hughes whose terror of contamination and infection was so all embracing that he made his secretaries wear gloves when they opened his mail, and Hans Christian Anderson whose fear of open places made it difficult for him to go outdoors. The obsessional monarch Ludwig the Second of Bavaria spent most of his life commissioning the construction of fairy tale castles throughout his realm.

Hysteria

Common use of the term "hysterical" suggests ridicule and is technically incorrect. Whereas the paranoiac deals with his fears and phobias by employing senselessly repetitive rituals, the hysteric uses a difference stratagem. Faced with life's difficulties and his own inability to face up to them, he retreats from reality by erecting and hiding behind a shield of contrived physical symptoms, a device intended to attract sympathy, support, prestige, affection or sexual attention. Having constructed his fantastic scenario, he acts upon it with childish conviction and has practically no insight as to how or why he does so.

Contrived sensory symptoms include blindness, deafness, and local anaesthetic or other tactile disturbances. Contrived motor symptoms include fits, faints, tantrums, spasms, tremors, stammering, paralyses, squints, limps, hyperventilation and eroticism. Psychotic symptoms include stupor, delirium, dementia, infantilism, amnesia, self harm, and mock suicide. Flight from reality involves the blotting out of memories which it would be painful to recall, and results in a split or totally dissociated persona, together with the realignment of relationships. Hysteria is more common in women, may result from psychosexual immaturity, and may be associated with frigidity and coquetry.

Schizophrenia

Schizophrenia has a lifetime prevalence of 1%, occurs with equal frequency in men and women, and is more common in city dwellers. It is a disease of adult life, symptoms first appearing between the ages of 10 and 25 years. 10% of children born to an affected parent will inherit the disease, prolonged cannabis use causes a tenfold increase in its incidence, and babies born to mothers who contracted influenza in the early months of pregnancy are more likely to develop it (GPMZ:05:09:09).

Schizophrenia usually presents in episodes, and is disruptive of unconditionable, sensory, motor and emotional brain functionality. The effects are bizarre and debilitating, with thought, perception, activity and mood simultaneously and erratically disturbed. The subject becomes unpredictable, unsociable, inconsistent, indecisive and inconsequential. Memory is usually unimpaired, and although the subject is characteristically introspective, he has no true insight into the nature of his problems. He is lost in a mental wilderness. Hallucinations may be auditory, visual or tactile, delusions persecutive, grandiose or phobic, and mannerisms, postures, speech and behaviour totally incongruous. There may be raving, impulsive and wild excitement, or else stupor, social withdrawal, apathy, self neglect, and total detachment and depersonalisation. There is a suicide rate of 10% and a twice normal mortality rate from physical disease. There is a strong predilection for addictive substances.

Dementia
Deterioration in unconditionable brain function with advancing years is present in three quarters of a million UK citizens, of which half are suffering from Alzheimer's disease.

Sporadic Genetic Brain Defects Affecting the Frontal Lobes
These occasionally lead to persistent aggressive antisocial behaviour known as chronic malice and may affect rogue individuals in any primate species. Traumatic or toxic damage to this area of the brain may produce similar dysfunction.

Inbreeding, Monarchies and Mixed Psychoses
Intense inbreeding causes severe mental defects which may combine the symptom patterns of several different psychoses. Such combined psychoses are particularly well identifiable in the case histories of the monarchs of western Europe, rulers whose determination to confine their heritable powers to their immediate families led to incest and marriages of political convenience. Since a king or prince could only take a princess for a wife, and princesses with their territorial dowries were used as pawns by royal parents jockeying for alliances, a newly

wed couple might find that they were first cousins twice over, or that they possessed only four grandparents between them. The genetic outcome of such restrictive practices were often disastrous, producing individuals who were not only unfit to rule but who were condemned to a lifetime of suffering. Because of royalty's uniquely important status, details of its day to day life, health and genealogy are a part of recorded history and provide unparalleled insight into the problems of human inbreeding.

All European royal families were interrelated by the matrimonial merry-go-round. Genetic errors which were thrown up included gross physical deformity, bipolar psychosis, schizophrenia and a biochemical disorder called porphyria, any of which could be present in the same individual. Porphyria usually manifests in early adult life, and produces intermittent attacks of abdominal pain, vomiting, red discoloration of the urine, severe muscle cramps, and a wide range of mental and neurological disturbances including insanity, delirium and coma. An early death may ensue but is far from invariable. For three centuries beginning with the 15th, the great Habsburg and Bourbon dynasties vied with each other for the possession of continental Europe. The Habsburgs, renowned for their huge lower jaws, overlapping lower lips and short legs, openly prided themselves on the territorial gains they had been able to make through marriage, notwithstanding the fact that at least one bride they had frogmarched to the altar was already so insane that she should not have been deemed fit to take her vows.

During these three momentous centuries the type of monarchical psychosis varied from country to country. In Iberia, the 15th century Isabella of Portugal passed her schizophrenia on to her granddaughter, Joan the Mad of Castile, and the trait reappeared in the 16th century Habsburg Crown Prince Dom Carlos of Spain, a sadistic, mentally and physically retarded hunchback with a shortened right leg. A century later, Charles the Second sat on the Spanish throne, hardly able to rise from it, since his legs would scarcely support him. A near imbecile,

Charles was cursed with a huge misshapen head, a tongue which was so large that it would scarcely fit in his mouth, a Habsburg jaw which was so protuberant that his teeth would not meet, epilepsy, baldness, deafness and poor eyesight. In the 18th century, three Iberian monarchs suffered from bipolar psychosis.

The Spanish arm of the Habsburg family was not alone in spawning gross mental and physical deformities. In the 16th century, Rudolph the Second of Austria also exhibited the trademark lip, chin and stunted limbs, and was plagued by a bipolar psychosis which turned him into a deluded, bisexual, agitated and ill tempered recluse. His son inherited his malady, but exhibited mood swings which were even more extreme, ranging from paranoid melancholia to animated and uncontrollable rage, during one of which episodes he murdered his mistress with extreme savagery. The bland docility which earned the 19th century Frederick the Good Natured of Austria his epithet appears less virtuous when one learns that he was a simpleton with the usual Habsburg stigmata. His sister Marianna was an imbecile. Sweden and the German states of Saxony and Hesse each produced two schizophrenics of royal blood, and this was the form of psychosis which also afflicted the French Bourbon Kings Charles the Sixth, the Seventh and the Ninth. Some of Charles the Sixth's descendants also suffered from porphyria.

England imported monarchical madness from Germany in the 18th century in the person of George the Third, when succession to the throne had faltered. A classic case of porphyria, George shared this malady with four siblings, four nephews and six of his fifteen children. Relapses of his disease undoubtedly affected his cognition and judgement, but sanity appeared to return during remission until in his later years when, blind and deprived of reason, he was to be found wandering through the rooms of his palace, addressing imaginary parliaments, reviewing phantasmogoric troops, and holding ephemorised courts (TWM49p115). He was doomed to live on until he was 81.

Syphilis

Although it is not genetically transmitted, no account of mental illness and behaviour would be complete without a reference to the venereal disease of syphilis.

Infections, especially plague, malaria, smallpox, cholera, dysentery, typhoid, typhus and influenza have all changed the course of history. Pandemics were instrumental in causing the demise of both the ancient Greek and Roman civilisations (CFF00p5). Prior to the military campaigns of the twentieth century, more warriors were slain by epidemic disease than ever perished at the hands of the enemy, and naval operations were always restricted to the pitifully short period of time during which crews could remain active before infection and scurvy inevitably swept through the ship.

But syphilis had a more subtle and perfidious impact upon humanity. It was a sexual Trojan horse which caught both potentate and pauper with his pants down. For many years the short-lived rash which followed infection was not attributed to promiscuity. Neither were the cataclysmic complications which followed as long as 10 years later, and which rotted the brain, erupted as pus from bones and tissues, or burst the body's main artery. During its malignant and smouldering sojourn in the body, syphilis could turn a man into either a maniac or an imbecile.

A few excavated pre-Columbian skeletons have shown evidence of syphilis, but despite their relaxed sexual mores the disease was not rife amongst 15th century Amerindians who must therefore have benefitted from a degree of acquired immunity. Not so the Europeans for whom syphilis was a new disease when Columbus' returning sailors introduced it to the brothels of Seville, and it was disseminated thence throughout the trade routes of Eurasia. By the early part of the 16th century one third of Parisians had been infected, and by 1569 the sinister contagion had become a world problem. During Victorian England one third of all mental hospital beds were occupied by degenerating syphilitics. In 1996 the World Health Organisation estimated the incidence of global syphilis at 12 million per annum.

Eminent Syphilitics

The circumstantial evidence of his personal and family medical history strongly suggests that England's monarch Henry the Eighth contracted syphilis when the disease was first spreading throughout Europe, and that his daughter Mary Tudor was a congenital syphilitic. The severe personality changes which overtook Henry in his forties, the miscarriages, stillbirths and infertilities which beset his marriages, and the description of Mary's physical deformities leave little doubt that syphilis was largely responsible for the tempestuous ruler's behaviour and policy making. His only surviving child, Elizabeth the first, described herself as "barren stock" (CFF00p55).

History has been distorted by other reputed syphilitics such as France's King Francis the First whose paranoidal condemnation of Protestantism led to the persecutions which followed under his son, or the ruthless and flagrantly immoral Borgia Pope Alexander the Sixth who sired a son, Cesare, so venal and unscrupulous that he became the model for Machiavelli's "Prince". (LWL87).

The most notorious syphilitic was Russia's Ivan the Terrible, who became Tsar in 1547. A profligate womaniser, he suffered a total change of personality at the age of 30, as the result of which he metamorphosed into a drunken, debauched, irrational and paranoidal sadist. Fearing himself surrounded by conspirators, he insisted upon having a personal bodyguard of six thousand picked troops. He took refuge in a fortress just outside Moscow, within which he instituted a rigidly ascetic religious cult moulded in accordance with his own twisted fantasies, and from which he could orchestrate a rule of terror (TM02p105). Unparalleled atrocities of torture and execution were perpetrated by royal death squads operating throughout the length and breadth of Russia. Citizens perished in their thousands, and methods of execution were as varied as their tormentors could devise. Boiling, roasting, battery, drowning, suffocation and dismemberment continued throughout two decades, and the bloodletting only ceased when Ivan's hallucinations and delusions terminated in a fit of apoplexy (CFF00p52). His son Fodor's congenital syphilis rendered him unfit to rule, and Boris Godunov, immortalised in Moussorgsky's opera, became regent.

Ivan's disinterred bones have shown unmistakeable evidence of syphilis. Like Henry, Francis and Alexander he lived in the early part of the 16th century at a time when the first wave of this venereal scourge spread across Europe. The roll call of later syphilitics includes such well known names as Guy de Maupassant, Henri de Toulouse-Lautrec, Beau Brummel, Frederick Nietzsche, and the composers Schubert, Schumann, Smetana, Hugo Wolf and Scott Joplin The advent of penicillin means that syphilis will no longer be a determinant of distorted personality in high places but, like other venereal diseases, it remains both a partial measure of human promiscuity and a pillory for it. Non-human primates do not suffer from sexually transmitted diseases.

(Sources Reviewed:BJNW08, BS99, DMN: 08:03:08, ECPMJT06, ENCTA08, FAMTX08, LR74, PF78, TWM49, WE06, WKP08)

CHAPTER 21

"NATURE RED IN TOOTH AND CLAW"

ENDEMIC GENETIC ERRORS INFLUENCING BEHAVIOUR - WARFARE AND CANNIBALISM

In primitive tribal warfare you had every reason to fight to the death. If you were captured, you would be sacrificed to the victor's tribal deity and probably eaten into the bargain, your women folk would be raped, and your children taken for slaves, the most invidious combination of events which could befall a man. In the wars of later antiquity fought with sword and spear, opposing armies advanced towards each other to join battle at the cutting edge, and as the foremost combatants fell, those behind had to clamber over their bodies to continue the conflict, each man hoping he would not be hamstrung from behind by a grounded antagonist. It could take as many as twenty eight slashes with a sword to kill a man. After the battle, camp followers finished off the wounded, plundering the corpses and not infrequently dismembering them for the cooking pot. Cannibalism as an adjunct to warfare was still in evidence as recently as the second world war, being a considered policy of some Japanese armed forces units, and as a matter of dire necessity being practised by Russian prisoners of war held starving in German camps.

Warfare and cannibalism are so abhorrent to modern man that few can understand why either trait ever persisted as part of the human behavioural repertoire. The uncomfortable truth is that although neither offer any evolutionary advantage, both are deeply embedded in our instinctual heritage. War and cannibalism are not merely as old as humanity, they are much older. They were features of protoman's lifestyle handed down from an ape-like predecessor. Both can be clearly identified in the chimpanzee, with whom we share 98% of our genes, and in the archaeological and historical records of all emergent cultures. They are, in fact, widespread and endemic genetic errors to which our whole human species may be said to be prone.

War As An Error Of Human Evolution

The curse of war is ever with us. At any one time, around 40 armed conflicts of one sort or another are in progress somewhere on the planet. The second world war killed off one in fifty of the global community and, more recently, both the Congolese civil war and the Rwandan genocide destroyed one tenth of those countries' populations. Only the bloody mass battles of the brown rat approach the ferocity and scale with which humans destroy their conspecifics. During the course of the twentieth century, nuclear proliferation provided the human species with the wherewithal to procure its own extinction, thereby reducing to the point of absurdity the theory that warfare is a natural means of adjusting the birth rate/death rate equilibrium, and greatly strengthening the view that it is, instead, an instinctual error into which the human evolutionary process has blundered.

We saw in chapter 8 that there are four basic forms of aggression - defensive aggression in response to danger; the attenuated form of aggression involved in dominance confrontations; chronic malice (which occurs in a small number of individuals and is a sporadic, as opposed to an endemic, genetic fault); and offensive aggression evolved for the predatory behaviour of the hunter carnivore. In times of plenty there is a bond of affinity and empathy between all members of the same species of lower primate, which stems from the fundamental trait of socialisation and the instinctive recognition of the potential for interbreeding. But when resources upon which the species depends are in critically short supply, interherd competition results, the herd bond which is much stronger than the species bond takes precedence, and herd members close ranks in a display of defensive aggression to protect dwindling food stocks. This form of antagonism must be distinguished from those unprovoked and savage forays of the chimpanzee in which the offensive form of aggression, originally directed against prey, is gratuitously refocused onto conspecifics as splenetic outbursts, and which are motivated by the addictive, adrenaline driven excitement of confrontation and risk taking. Such self intoxicating mechanisms also exist in humans and disinhibit offensive aggression, but in human warfare other fundamental primate behavioural traits also become distorted, often with official "herd" sanction, in a manner which further incentivises aggression. Disinhibition of possessiveness prompts the seizure of territory, booty and tribute; overheated dominance leads to oppression, atrocity and slave acquisition; unbridled sexuality provokes rape and the abduction of women as concubines; and carnivorousness leads to the extortion of cattle and the committal of cannibalism. Inevitably, high testosterone levels and the intellectual immaturity of early adulthood reduce the threshold at which violence occurs. The cannibalistic feast which accompanies the chimpanzee's maverick sallies were also a common feature of man's interherd warfare until a relatively late stage in his development.

Weapons were initially developed for hunting, but as their design became more refined over time they catalysed warfare and led to increases in the size and effectiveness of the organised fighting unit. The discovery of metal smelting around six thousand years ago led to technical advances which included the manufacture of piercing and slashing weaponry, and more deadly missiles - upgrades which enabled ever richer booty to be plundered and which brought about the emergence of warlords. As the scale of conquest increased, simple cattle rustling was superseded by territorial seizure, and when occupying armies became large enough to cope with the logistics of serfdom, slaves were added to the tally of trophies. Progressively, tribal chiefs became suborned by emergent kings whose feudal systems indentured the peasantry to function as infantry on demand. Kings in turn became subservient to emperors as the aggression fuelled race for supreme power gathered momentum. When feudalism with its ready made war-prone military assemblages finally went into decline, it was replaced by new precipitants for armed conflict under the umbrella of religious, pseudo-religious and nationalistic ideologies, all of which tended to increase the motivation, fanaticism, ferocity and self justification with which wars were fought.

Nothing has changed relationships between national communities more than the atomic bomb. When the nuclear explosions of 1945 killed 140 thousand in Hiroshima and 74 thousand in Nagasaki, they not only brought the second world war to an abrupt end, but made man realise that he had stumbled upon the ready means of destroying himself as a species. An era of cold war posturing followed between the superpowers, which nearly ended in disaster during the Cuban nuclear missile crisis in 1962, but the awesome prospect of retaliation stayed every one's hand. By bitter irony it had been the Japanese who had initially developed weapons of mass destruction during the Sino-Japanese war of 1937 at their infamous Unit 731 near Harben, on the Chinese mainland. Grotesque experiments using plague, anthrax and dissection of unanaesthetised individuals were followed by the massacre of 250 thousand in major Chinese cities when aircraft released plague infected fleas over them (NGMZ:03:11). Although a more responsible attitude towards atomic warfare has now been adopted by the great powers, the threat of misuse by rogue states or terrorists remains. So called "conventional" weapons continue to be used to fight wars around the globe, and to perpetrate acts of terrorism.

A chimpanzee like phase in human evolution has left man with a self destructive tendency which leads to senseless waste of young adult lives. The incessant haemorrhage of the reciprocal blood feud seen in all early cultures, and the carnage of later full scale war, are sterile outcomes in terms of human development, sacrificing those who should be fulfilling their roles as bread winners and parents. Species self destruction, even on a limited scale, confers no benefits, and is particularly counterproductive when those immolated were in other respects the fittest to survive. Moreover, because man now culls populations almost indiscriminately and unselectively, war has become a mere process of competitive extermination with no pretence of making any change to the genetic make up, physique or mental capacity of the species. The craving for endogenous adrenaline has proved to be considerably more damaging to humanity's interests than other forms of drug habituation. We have, in fact, been betrayed by evolution.

Both self interest and global citizenship require all governments to exhibit self control in matters of nuclear technology. Although, by the year 2005, 188 countries had signed up to the Nuclear Non Proliferation Treaty and its test ban augmentation, it was recognised that 8 of them already had nuclear weapons, and that a further 40 had the capacity to manufacture them within a few months (Head of International Atomic Energy Agency quoted in TTN:03:11:01). Posturing continues between the global community at large and recalcitrant states in the grip of rule-of-thumb ideologies. Star Wars technology can intercept intercontinental rockets, but not warheads delivered by boat, truck or plane.

Humanity's parochialism narrows its viewpoint. We all live in racial, linguistic, national and religious pigeonholes usually determined by our place of birth, which determine the ambit of our social contract. But we have seen that all forms of factionalism are manifestations of herd tribalism and have the tendency to become elitist, discriminatory and xenophobic, with conflict as an option. We have to learn to recognise that there is a species bond whose expression is destined to become more important to survival than the herd bond which we inherited from our primate ancestors. If, as we now seem to agree, all men are equal in law and at the ballot box, then all men should be equally rational and pragmatic in their behaviour towards each other, balancing self interest with the general global interest, and disallowing all forms of compulsive prejudice. From now on we sink or swim together, and a policy of fully integrated global interdependence is the key to mutual self preservation and well being.

At an individual level, the taste for war is culturally conditionable, as witnessed by the jingoistic influence which compulsive ideologies and nationalism can exert. By the same token, parental, peer group and media mores acting in conjunction can produce strong aversion to murder in all its forms. In the final analysis, aversion conditioning of the immature mind is the only way war can be prevented with certainty, and this is dependent upon the provision of relevant, accurate and validated historical evidence as to the cause and effect of wars, such as this book targets in several of its chapters.

Cannibalism

The term cannibal derives from Columbus' discovery of the man eating Carib tribes of Guadelupe. Throughout his evolution man has instinctually eaten his fellow creatures in order to supplement his carnivorous diet, and in some parts of the world still did so, at least until the end of the 20th century. After a battle it was the custom to remove from the bestrewn corpses those choicest cuts which could easily be carried away - the limbs and head - and leave the much heavier and less nutritious trunk to the vultures. After the victory feast, all that was left of this primitive "take away" were the skull and limb bones, the familiar emblems on the pirate's flag. Human limbs were reportedly still on offer in some remote African, and the occasional North Korean, market places during the 1970's.

Archaeological Evidence of cannibalism is provided by the finding of human bones in association with animal bones and hearths, by the presence of scratches made by sharp stones on human bones during defleshing, by the discovery of long bones split so as to allow marrow extraction and skull bases broken open to allow brain extraction, and, in a few instances, by the detection of human DNA in cooking pots and in the stomachs of well preserved corpses. Such evidence dates back 780 thousand years in Spain and Italy (Archaeology Magazine 06 Jan-Feb), 500 thousand years in China, and to later dates in South Africa, France and Jugoslavia (TR76p6).

Most of the cannibalised bones discovered were those of young adult males of warrior age, and where disinterment reveals the remains of clusters of such individuals it is indicative of an established ritual, most probably that of *eating enemy captives*. One Chinese site exposed a group of 45 trepanned skulls (WMLMAE78p242), a finding highly suggestive of a feast celebrating conquest. We know from historical sources and from tribes which, until recently, still practised cannibalism, that ingestion was regarded as the final stage of conquest through which the spirits and strength of the vanquished were assimilated by the victor. Enemy eating was practised by pre-dynastic Egyptian soldiers (GPO2 p24), by Scythian tribes at the time of the Roman empire (HDS54,4,64), by the Q'in armies in China in 200 BCE (GTR52), by the Mongol hordes, by Australian aborigines, by primitive Indonesians and Oceanians, and the Meons, Hurons, Iroquois, Aztecs, Ashanti, Uscochi, Kalmuks and Chavantes (TR76p16). Towards the end of the second world war, the Japanese ritually executed British and US aviators who had been shot down, and ate their hearts and livers. (The downed President George Bush Senior had a lucky escape when he was rescued from the Pacific ocean by a US submarine). Hundreds of executed class enemies in Mao Tse-tung's 1960's China had their livers publicly eaten in the name of revolutionary purity (TMZ:93:01:18). During the 1950's the Mau Mau of Kenya drank assassinated Europeans' blood in the belief that its magic properties would help destroy white supremacy. The Khmer Rouge killed their prisoners and ate their livers to absorb their victims' inherent strength (STN:95:04:23). The Maoris killed Captain Grant and ate him to reduce the potency of his comrades. The Tahitians butchered the explorer James Cook and distributed his dismembered body parts for their talismanic properties amongst the tribal elders (MS99p17).

Until very recently, cannibalism persisted in remote areas of New Guinea, Borneo and Central Africa. Kuru, a disease closely similar to CJD and BSE, was endemic in New Guinea, and can only be transmitted by ingesting human brain tissue. After cannibalism was banned throughout that country in the 1950's the incidence of Kuru fell by 90% (TR76p234).

An entirely different significance was vested in cannibalism by its use as a *reverential or religious ritual*. Kinsmen of the fifth century BCE Issigones tribe of central Asia were in the habit of eating the flesh of the father of the family after death in order to perpetuate his influence amongst them (HDS54, 4, 26). Until the third century BCE, the rites of the cult of the ancient Greek deity Dionysos required that its priests should select a good looking youth, dress him in finery to simulate the god, then ritually sacrifice him, distributing his flesh for ingestion by all devotees present, who thus were enriched by the god's divine presence (BAR65p135). Strabo noted that in the first century BCE the Irish ritually cannibalised their dead (SBO,4, 201). In the 15th century CE Marco Polo observed that Tibetan families actually cut short the last days of an ailing father whom they wished to assimilate (YH21p137).

Vivid descriptions of religious cannibalism occur in the writings of Bernal Diaz, one of the Spanish conquistadors who took part in the subjugation of Aztec Mexico. "In hastily abandoned villages they found temples with the bodies of men and boys who had been sacrificed, the walls and altars all splashed with blood and the victims' hearts laid out before the idols ...... most of the bodies were without arms and legs ...... these had been carried off to be eaten ...... in the city square where some of the temples stood there were many piles of human skulls ...... more than a hundred thousand ......" (DB63p234). The sun's "rebirth" each morning was considered to depend upon a daily human sacrifice.

Religious cannibalism exists to this day as Voodoo, a ceremony emanating from West Africa but exported to the Caribbean. This cult sacrifices a child who is decapitated and flayed, and whose head is borne aloft in a procession amidst singing, dancing, drinking, debauchery, and feasting on the sacrificial flesh (SSJ86p196). The disturbing discovery of the limbless, headless torso of a young negro boy of around five years of age in the river Thames in 2001 showed that the Voodoo cult was still active, even in England. The vestige of religious cannibalism remains embedded in Christian religious ritual when the tokens of wine and bread are transmuted into Christ's blood and flesh and ceremonially consumed by the faithful (Doctrine of transubstantiation).

Cannibalism sometimes has *Sexual Connotations*. That serial killers are almost exclusively male, and that they predominantly prey on women or homosexuals and may cannibalise them, provides clear evidence of the role of testosterone in this form of depravity. The gruesome list of examples include Vincenz Verzeni, who in 1871 near Rome strangled, disembowelled, and drank the blood of 12 young women; Fritz Haarman, who in 1924 bit to death 27 young homosexual males and made sausages from them; Edward Gein, who in 1950 in Wisconsin committed murder, necrophilia and cannibalism on at least 15 victims, some of whose organs were found in his icebox; Geoffrey Dahmer, who from 1988 in Milwaukee committed murder and cannibalism on 17 young homosexuals; Andrei Chikatilo, who in 1978 in the USSR savagely tortured, mutilated, eviscerated and ate the sexual organs of 52 children and young women (TR76p252 and 263).

Perhaps the most bizarre example of sexually motivated cannibalism in recent times, was that of Arnim Meiwes who videotaped the killing, dissection and ingestion of Bernd Jurgen Brandes, whose consent to the cannibalisation he obtained after making contact through the "Gay Cannibals Internet Chat Room". The crime took place in Germany where ironically no law against cannibalism existed in 2003. Meiwes stated in court that the killing satisfied his sexual desire and his need for brotherhood. After heavy sedation, the victim's severed penis was cooked and eaten, and further dismemberment led to unconsciousness from haemorrhage. The coup de grace was a stab in the throat, after which 55 pounds of meat was stored in the freezer. Meiwes claimed to have had offers from four other willing victims.

Cannibalism has provided the basis for *Nostrums, Panaceas and Quack Remedies* throughout history. In ancient Egypt, tincture of mummy was a cure prepared by marinating flesh taken from the cadaver of a malefactor who had been executed. The meat was mixed with myrrh, aloes and spirits (FJG22). Pharaohs and French kings alike resorted to imbibing draughts of human blood in an attempt to cure leprosy. The Chinese used pith balls steeped in the blood of executed criminals as a cure for tuberculosis, and soup made from aborted human foetuses as a complexion rejuvenator (TMZ:95:05:01). In an effort to regain her youth, Countess Elizabeth de Bathory of Hungary in the early 1600's bathed in, and drank the blood of, a reputed 650 young girls slaughtered for the purpose, and as a consequence established the legend of Dracula.

Gastronomes and Gourmands can develop perverse tastes. Sometimes human flesh was devoured for no other reason than that it was regarded as a delicacy offered at feasts or sold in the marketplace. Tasting like spicy pork, the Fijians set a premium on the heart, thighs and upper arms, whereas the Nigerians preferred the palms, fingers and toes. The Nomadic Hun Chief Shihu in 334 CE in North China periodically had one of the most beautiful girls in his harem beheaded, cooked and served to guests. In 367 CE, the Argyllshire Attacotti tribe were noted for their cannibalism, and signed on as Roman legionaries for the pickings of the battlefield (TR76p144). During the first crusade, the Thafuri, a troop of barefoot cannibal camp followers of the Crusaders, spread terror among the Saracens by eating enemy corpses (JGPR30p178). On the west coast of 18th century Africa all prisoners of tribal wars who could not be used as slaves were fattened up and

275

sold to butchers (BJ71p479). The Ugandan despot Idi Amin was known to have stored some of his enemies' body parts in his freezer.

Faced with a choice between death from starvation or survival through cannibalism, human beings almost invariably opt for the latter, a practice known as *famine cannibalism*. Sometimes a group of unprovisioned isolates will wait for the first of its members to die naturally, but in other cases lots are drawn, or the weakest selected and killed, to provide sustenance for the remainder. In ancient China and ancient Egypt when the crops failed, parents ate their children (PK50p145), as did the Italians during the famine of 450 CE, and the British during the famine of 938 CE. In northern Europe there were disastrous famines during the 9th, 10th and 11th centuries when cannibalism was commonplace. During the Song dynasty, Chinese cities under siege from the Mongols sacrificed every tenth man to feed the populace.

Retreating defeated armies are often deprived of supplies and perpetrate large scale cannibalism on their casualties, as did Napoleon's Grande Armee in 1812, which lost two thirds of its complement of half a million men (TE42p282). The Japanese armies marooned in Borneo and New Guinea in 1945-6 at first ate their prisoners of war, then killed two and a half per cent of their own soldiers every day to feed the remainder. Two particular instances of famine cannibalism impacted particularly strongly on the public imagination. In 1816 the crew of the wrecked ship Medusa took to a raft, and subsequently murdered and ate several of their number before they were rescued (an episode depicted in Gericault's famous painting), and in 1972 an Uruguayan rugby team with some of their supporters crash landed in the Andes, and after 10 days elected to eat their dead colleagues before help eventually arrived.

(Sources Reviewed: BAR65, BJ44, DB63, EEI96, FJG22, GP02, GTR52, HDS54, HG66, JGPR30, KGC09, MS99, PK50, SBO, STN95, TE42, TMZ93, TMZ95, TR76, WMLMAE78, YH21)

CHAPTER 22

THE PURSUIT OF THE IDEAL THROUGH THE SURREAL

RELIGION - THE CURATES EGG

Protoman had now reached a stage in his evolution where his larger brain, developed to meet the complexities of living in a larger social unit and the need to hunt big game, had given him spare cognitive capacity, and the access to energy rich foods had given him spare time. He was no longer condemned to the daily grind of perpetual food finding. Hitherto, his brain had developed through a process of Darwinian evolution, but now he began to take charge of his own data processing upgrades. Instead of subsisting as an organism driven solely by inherited or rigidly conditioned behavioural traits, the pattern, and even the total number, of his brain cells were determined to a considerable extent by the use to which they were put. He now began to apply himself to the search for rational enlightenment, to the urge to innovate, and to the acquisition of organisational expertise, the three intellectual activities which above all distinguish man from the apes. Rational enlightenment is based on accurate observation and logic, innovation is based on pattern matching and extrapolation, and organisational expertise is based on the ability to evaluate, juggle and assemble variables.

But it was to be many millennia before man's critical faculty became sharp enough to recognise the need for scientific methodology, whereby proof can be checked and conclusions reproduced. Plagued by

277

the desire, yet denied the ability, to understand his environment and the purpose of his own existence within it, he clutched at straws in the form of belief systems based on conjecture, anecdote, and hypothesis. When ill fortune in the shape of famine, hypothermia, epidemic, accident, or attack from predators coincided with a completely unrelated circumstance, he made a false association between the two and superstition was born. His enforced submissiveness in the face of natural disasters argued for the existence of a supremely powerful force, as yet not identifiable or understood, which must be taken into account, propitiated, humoured and bought off to minimise the damage which it was clearly capable of inflicting. Even if he could not actually prove the presence of such a conjecturally supreme third party, he was in no position to ignore the possibility that it existed.

Just as his early striving for rational enlightenment went awry, so, too, did his early efforts to exercise organisational expertise. Although for the most part the fundamental primate traits of possessiveness and sexuality were counterbalanced by bonding, the dominance ranking process and socialisation within the context of the "herd", there were times when interherd discipline broke down and anarchy ruled. Then, too, there was the problem of friction between "herds", the propensity for which had been instinctually inherited from his chimpanzee-like antecedents, which manifested as warfare and cannibalism, and which was still a major cause of male mortality. Primitive religious authoritarianism attempted to confront both these problems, firstly by providing a societal protocol for controlling intraherd behaviour when the balance of instinctual traits failed to do so, and secondly by creating a vehicle for justifying interherd aggression by assuming control of interherd warfare and cannibalism, and rebranding them, respectively, as holy war and human sacrifice. All armed conflict which had a component of self interest was now deemed to be the will of God. Religious leaders exploited man's fear of a supernatural power with carrot and stick imagery of heaven and hell in order to enforce rules of social conduct within the "herd", and promised land acquisition, booty and the license to ravish enemy females as incentives to engage in battle. Martyrs to the cause could be promised immediate paradise and more heavenly virgins than they could cope with. Symbolic ritual cannibalism still exists in Christian practice, and the Jewish Herem, the Christian Crusade and the Islamic Jihad are all prominent examples of warfare fuelled and justified by religion.

Religious belief is an ephemeral concept which combines elements of ethics, folk lore and surrealism, and which is engraved on the conditionable brain in an obsessive compulsive format. Typically, indoctrination takes place during the third phase of nurture, when the juvenile is more impressionable and more easily prejudiced than he will be after the acquisition of full intellectual maturity. Intraherd pressure to conform, and habituation reinforce the process, and compliance is lubricated by the desire for group acceptance. However, the world is currently undergoing a process of unprecedented cultural metamorphosis in which the pragmatic utility of the old orders and values is increasingly called into question. As aspiring global citizens or prospective parents we have a responsibility to share in this reassessment and pass judgement on the track records of existing religious movements, using verdicts reached exclusively on the basis of candid unexpurgated historical evidence. At the outset, we must not overlook the fact that, in company with most of the world's population, it is likely that each of us will already have been subjected to religious orientation of one kind or another. This orientation will form part of our "personal equation", an attitude of mind ingrained in the conditionable brain during immaturity which skews our judgement in favour of a particular viewpoint. Just as the religious ascetic learns to suspend his desires, so we must learn to circumvent our personal equation if we are to make a full, accurate and impartial appraisal of the religious process.

Are Religions Just Transitory Phases in Human Development?
The relics of sequential belief systems embedded in the English calendar are intriguing. Of these, Sunday and Mon (moon) day are obviously the most primitive. Tiw's day, Woden's day, Thor's day and Freyr's day venerate four deities of the Norse pantheon. The months named after the Caesars Julius and Augustus revere the supposedly divine qualities of two Roman Emperors, and Christmas commemorates the founder of the most widely accepted version of western monotheism. There is a tussle between left wing politicians, pagans and churchgoers as to who owns May Day. It must be chastening to the protagonists of rule-of-thumb ideologies to see from such fossil records that a set of hypotheses which cannot be fully substantiated always proves to have a time limited tenure.

The conceptualisation of the supernatural power passed through several different phases :- The heavens gave man light, heat and rain which stimulated the earth's fertility to furnish him, directly or indirectly, with the raw materials needed for food, clothing and shelter. The analogy with parental beneficence was compelling, and it was a short step from the symbolical representation of father - sun and mother - earth to the accreditation of both with live and active personalities. When these surrogate parents failed to provide, the surrogate offspring instinctively feared that his own behaviour might have been the cause of their displeasure, and propitiation, penance and adulation were employed to rectify matters. Nearly all early cultures developed this symbolic representation of divine surrogate parenthood.

The next step in man's attempt to influence natural and supernatural outcomes was to fragment and particularise the elemental phenomena to which he was in thrall. By treating tempest, thunder and lightening, earthquake, volcano, water supply, harvest, human and animal health and fecundity, home, and hearth as discrete entities, man sought to break down the task of propitiation into bite sized pieces. The physical characteristic of each natural phenomenon was now held to portray the personality of the individual god responsible for it, and a pantheon was conceptualised, whose members variously exhibited all the strengths and weaknesses of human behaviour. Man had created his gods in his own image, albeit that they were more powerful than he.

Eventually the multiplicity of deities, each with his or her own sanctuaries, temples and cults, became so complex as to make it impossible for rulers, priests and worshippers to judge from divine responses whether the correct devotional balance had been struck, and each god adequately propitiated. A simpler, more focused, system was needed, and individual communities made a direct approach to the deity they considered to be the most influential and appropriate to their cause, conferring on him the status of tribal god. Tribal gods singled out their followers for preferential treatment and were invariably jealous, and they might well demand the extinction of all rival deities, together with their devotees.

The Babylonian, Egyptian, Greek and Pre-Constantine Roman empires were polytheistic, respecting, and often sharing in the worship of each others' gods. The ultimate accolade for a supreme ruler was that he, too, should be accorded the status of god, as were the Pharaohs, several Roman emperors, and even Japanese emperors as lately as Hirohito, until the latter was forced to renounce deity at the end of the second world war.

No emperor has ever conquered the world. Had he done so he would have been in a position to enforce global uniformity of worship of his empire's tribal god - the utopian dream of pan monotheism which has never been realised. Instead, the concept of monotheism has been riven by schisms. Contention is no longer a matter of whose tribal god is the most powerful, but who enjoys the most preferential relationship with god if he is singular.

There is good evidence that monotheism began in Persia with the Zoroastrians prior to one thousand years BCE, and that the Jews subsequently adopted the concept (KP02p183). The ancient Greek philosopher Xenophanes (570-484 BCE) opined that "there is only one god, the universe itself" (http//en.org.wiki.xenophanes). The emperor

Constantine made the Christian variety of monotheism the Empire's official religion after he found that placing the Christian Chi-Ro monogram on his battle standards gave him victory. Islam's monotheism derives in large part from Old Testament texts as reframed by Mohammed's visions. The ultimate irony of monotheism is that it aspires to produce uniformity and universality, but that it has given rise to so many cults and splinter groups that it has proved to be far more globally divisive than polytheism, with its overlaps and compromises, ever was.

Christianity claims 2.1 billion adherents, Islam 1.3 billion, and Judaism 15 million - monotheisms which together represent over half the world's population. By comparison, there are 870 million Hindus, 405 million followers of the Chinese National religion, and 379 million Buddhists (NGMZ:05:12). Antagonism and spasmodic aggression between the three monotheisms of middle eastern derivation, and between their splinter groups, has been prevalent for 14 centuries and continues today.

Ideologies have frequently acted as wet nurse to emergent civilisations, as witness the dynamism which Judaism, Hinduism, Christianity, Buddhism and Islam all brought to the sense of purpose, the social structure, and the artistic and intellectual prowess of the nations in which these religions held sway. When a cult preaches idealism through surrealistic concepts and it attains a critical mass following, it becomes the cultural bedrock of a community. But in historical perspective civilisations come and go, as do their ideologies, and only history can judge whether the rhetoric which attracts people to become part of a mass movement becomes translated into long term benefit for the world at large.

Although some form of religion has been practised by most emergent cultures, there is increasing evidence from the secularisation taking place in the western world that it represents only a transient phase, albeit a prolonged one, in human cultural development. Like Nazism and Communism, the Jewish, Christian and Islamic theocracies have been totalitarian regimes, imposing preconditioned patterns of thought and behaviour as rule of thumb ideologies, where the ultimate benefits were often outweighed by the disadvantages. Moreover, we must move with the times. Social systems and dogma which were appropriate to the middle ages cannot be expected to meet the needs of a 21st century global community. As long as cultism still exists, so will partisan attitudes and the aggressive tendencies inherent in them. Religious wars have been amongst the most barbarous in history. Battles are at their bloodiest when God fights on both sides.

What Factors Combine To Make People Religious?
With mass veneration of the conjectural supernatural power, a specialised class of intercessor emerged - the priesthood - which elaborated, formalised and disciplined the belief systems over which they had control. The consequent religious regimentation which conditions both priests and laity is characterised by sublimation, iconification, ritualisation and autocredulity.

Sublimation is a state of mental abstraction akin to day dreaming which can be brought about, either by intensive meditation and prayer, or by physico-chemical brain disturbances. Amerindians starved themselves in order to experience divine visitations, and a similar state of light headedness is induced by hyperventilation, or by the vertigo of the gyrational Dervish dance. Drugs, alcohol, tobacco, epilepsy, tumours, and artificial electrical stimulation of the brain can all produce a sense of "other worldliness", and there is evidence that a spiritual mood is more readily experienced by those possessing the VMAT2 gene (BBCT1:05:12:14). Monozygotic twin studies have shown that the degree to which a person will be attracted by and practice any form of religion ("religiosity") is a partly inherited characteristic (BBCT1:09:10:08).

Iconification exaggerates the perceived dominance ranking status of both the conjectural deity, who is exalted, and his human devotee who demeans himself. The skewing process is facilitated by the induction

283

of inferiority and guilt complexes, and the use of self debasing terms such as "unworthy " or "miserable sinner". Symbolic objects are often used to bridge the subservient relationship with the deity, and these themselves may then become objects of worship in their own right - Greek Orthodox fine art portraiture, Latin statuary and reliquary, or Muslim holy texts. Hindu iconification of the cow extends to veneration of the animal's urine (LCS99p32). Earliest known icons were podgy female statuettes fashioned in stone, bone or ivory, dating back 30 thousand years. Cave paintings also began at this time, and because they depict animals used as food, some of which are shown speared, are thought to have been examples of symbolic magic. Formal burials incorporating grave goods, which imply belief in the after life, date from 25-30 thousand years ago (NGMZ:06:01). The significance of ochre stained animal bones in human inhumations of a much earlier date is unknown (JP99p100).

Ritualisation of symbolic acts and mantras, with or without music and dance, is the overt, demonstrative and interactive form of religion, through which repetitiveness and the herd bonding reinforcement of mass action engrave dogma upon the conditionable brain.

Autocredulity, also known as faith in the religious context, is an act of belief in something which cannot be proven by any scientific, mathematical, legal or logical process. We like to escape the stress of life's reality by creating an inner fantasy world, hence the insatiable public appetite for novels, fairy tales, cinema, theatre, soap operas, the lottery, horoscopes and gutter press hyperbole. Most people believe what they want to believe most of the time, but some believe what they want to believe all the time, and "nothing is so firmly believed as what we least know" (MMSde00). Autocredulity suspends the critical faculty and the process of rational enlightenment. Like an illicit love affair or an overdraft, autocredulity, better known as wishful thinking or autosuggestion, allows humans to break the chains of unforgiving, mundane and conventional realism to enter the world of pipe dreams and paranormality. All religions are based on autocredulity, and act as a psychological refuge for those whose immature nurture has been inadequate or disrupted, for those who have been emotionally damaged as adults, and for those who are unable to recognise what modern physics teaches us (HS11). The discovery of the basic unit of creativity, the so-called "god particle", by the CERN European Nuclear Research Organisation can never substitute for the emotional bond which the religious believer craves.

Scientific tenets are constantly modified in the light of experience, but religious tenets cannot be changed, because criticism of them is regarded as blasphemy. This *immutability* is, of course, an expression of obsessive compulsive behaviour which leads to the mental fossilisation of a closed mind. Clerical resistance to change has often prompted the suppression of science. Galileo was put under house arrest by the church inquisitors when he suggested that the earth orbited around the sun (AK94). In the middle ages, the Catholic church forbade the dissection of human bodies, for fear that what was discovered might cast doubt on the Christian doctrine that God created man in his own image (WR02p213). In a joint statement with a colleague, Archbishop James Ussher, on the basis of biblical genealogy, confidently pronounced that creation occurred at 9 a.m. on 23rd October in the year 4004 BCE (WMLMAE78, and BV79p36). In 1925, the young schoolteacher John Thomas Scopes was tried and found guilty under state law in Dayton, Tennessee, of teaching Evolutionary theory, and, even today in the USA, 45% of all citizens still reject Darwinism in favour of the biblical explanation of creation (BBCT1:05:12:04).

The most damaging recent manifestation of clerical immutability was the embargo imposed, both by Catholicism and Islam on the use of condoms or any other form of contraception, in the face of the mounting AIDS epidemic and overpopulation in countries where hundreds of thousands are born to starve. A duplicitous statement made by the Pope in 2010 authorising condom use "under exceptional circumstances" marginally rescinded the ban.

A curious feature of religious and quasi-religious practices is that asceticism induces a state of *self negation* - the denial factor. Obsessions laid down within the conditionable brain frequently override and negate the cognitive functions of the higher centres and the evidence of the five senses. Denial of any of the seven fundamental primate traits may also be manifested - sexual denial as celibacy, denial of bonding and socialisation such as is exhibited by hermits, suppression of dominance challenges by self imposed humility, negation of possessiveness through self denial and abstinence, and denial of the hunter-carnivore instinct by vegetarianism, veganism and the dislocated sentimentality of animal rights activism. Even the most primitive trait of reaction to danger was denied by early Christians who were torn to pieces by lions in Roman amphitheatres rather than renounce their faith. One branch of Buddhism seeks to distance itself from all forms of human desire. Many religions advocate episodic fasting.

When organised religion preaches *impracticality,* conflict arises between religion and state, or between religion and the individual, and dogmatic slippage becomes inevitable. The Christian doctrine of unconditional forgiveness is a crook's charter, some types of work must inevitably be done on the sabbath, a number of Islamic countries are very far from being teatotal and many allow hashish despite the Qur'an's ban on intoxicants (Su5s12v90), in an Israeli restaurant turkey on the menu is frequently an euphemism for pork, Ireland and Italy have the lowest birth rates in the world, and the blaze of adverse publicity to which the Catholic clergy have been subjected in relation to heterosexual, homosexual and paedosexual misdemeanours in recent years exposes the hypocrisy of chaste celibacy.

Whilst religious law is still state law in countries such as Iran and Saudi Arabia, most nations have separated state legislation from religious edict, and where there is conflict between the two, state law now takes precedence. At the personal level, when a cultist is faced with dogmatic impracticalities, he practices those tenets with which he can conform, and ignores those which he cannot, a process referred to as cherrypicking.

The Rise and Fall of the Priesthood

Hunter-gathering was a full time occupation for our palaeolithic ancestors, but the advent of agriculture meant that food supplies became plentiful enough to allow diversification of labour within the tribe. In all early civilisations a priestly class emerged, credited with special powers and accorded special privileges. Always an intercessor between humans and the spirit world, the priest initially combined this role with the magical activities of healing, foreseeing the future, and wizardry, skills which are still claimed by shamans. Like a hawker of patent medicines, the primitive priest preyed upon the anxieties, fears and hopes of his listeners, and his success depended upon his persuasive powers and the credulity of his audience.

In more developed societies, because it clearly could not be substantiated by the outcome of events, clairvoyance and wizardry have been abandoned by the priesthood, as in most cases has healing, although claims for the latter persist in centres such as Lourdes, and in Spiritualist churches. The Catholic church also still gives credit to paranormal phenomena such as miracles and apparitions.

Because the high priest was God's mouthpiece he could not be refuted and, whenever they could, the monarchs of early empires saw to it that they kept the control of religious, as well as military and political, affairs in their own hands. When monotheism displaced polytheism there was a shift of emphasis, the high priest himself now became politically supreme and theocracy was ushered in. High priests incited and led Hebrew armies into battles in which all enemies had to be exterminated, Byzantine emperors drove their Christianising message home against Persia at the point of a sword, mediaeval European monarchs were effectively papal vassals when it came to implementing crusades or inquisitions, and Mohammed himself combined the roles of politico-religious leader and generalissimo. Some present day middle eastern clerics are still politico-military puppeteers, manipulating theocracies in which they impose draconian laws and declare jihads and fatwahs.

In the West, the priest's role is in decline. He has lost all his secular and political power, his military power has been reduced to the command of a token Vatican bodyguard, his pastoral duties towards the sick, destitute, and those needing counselling have been taken over by social welfare schemes, and in most nations he receives no state stipend. In the middle east the clerics of Islam perceive creeping secularisation to be the threat to their doctrine and hegemony which of course it is. But the scapegoating of American culture, world trade centres, night clubs and prostitution carried out in the name of Islam is futile, since the root cause of secularisation is the employment of an educational methodology which exercises and develops the unconditionable brain. By contrast, madrassas only focus on the conditionable brain. In the far east most religion is structured subjectively and not theocratically, so that here secularisation does not present the same problems.

The Arguments For and Against Organised Religion

In order to put the controversial subject of organised religion into perspective, it is useful to summarise the benefits claimed for it and the disadvantages attributed to it.

Benefits
- Organised religion has been a feature of nearly all emerging cultures, so there must have been a need for it, at least during a prolonged phase of human development
- It creates cohesion within the community of the like minded
- Within its ambit, religion replaces inter-individual dominance challenges with a three tier fixed dominance ranking - God, priests and laity.

- It ameliorates fear of harsh reality and the unknown
- By conditioning a code of personal ethics it improves social relationships and social stability
- It improves cardiovascular health and longevity (GMMZ:05:05, NSMZ:06:01:28), and helps the individual cope with depression and stress (A.J.Public Health as quoted in DMN:11:02:19). Unless these benefits are produced by the same gene complex which determines religiosity, they must be psychological or psycho-physiological.
- Religiosity has three components whose demands, if satisfied, produce a sense of equanimity and well being, thereby reducing anxiety. These are an emotional need for a beneficent overseer which harks back to childhood's first phase of nurture, an emotional need for a supportive peer group which harks back to the second phase of nurture, and a credo, however contrived, which encourages blindfold optimism, and thereby gives a positive slant to the third phase of nurture and the personal equation. All three components are addressed by most communal, repetitive religious rituals.

Disadvantages
- It suppresses the critical faculty
- It imposes cut and dried behaviour patterns regardless of the individual's responsibilities, or of the consequences of doing so.
- Because no single cult has proved universally applicable, organised religion is globally divisive
- Cults promote elitism (the "chosen" race) and xenophobia (gentile, infidel, atheist, pagan, heretic and heathen are all terms of derogation).
- Because religion is immutable it produces a fossil mentality which fails to adapt to the changing world.
- Ritualism, emotionalism, and carrot and stick incentives play on the conditionable brain to produce obsessional and prejudicial behaviour which, in its extreme form, leads to fanaticism, warfare,

witch-hunting, inquisition, ethnic cleansing, and child and adult human sacrifice. These outcomes flagrantly contradict the principles for which religion avowedly stands, and have proved so damaging to human interest than we need to learn from some of them in greater detail in the chapters which follow.

- Doctrinal impracticabilities affect humanity adversely, increasing AIDS, inappropriate overpopulation, clerical paedophilia, and the tally of children with gross genetic defects
- The perpetuation of Draconian punishment under Sharia law contravenes human rights.

If Organised Religion Becomes Obsolete, What Replaces It?
Religious following is expanding in Africa and shrinking in Europe, a reflection upon the relative state of cultural development in the two continents. Europe's increasing secularisation is concomitant with its rising educational standards and the development and refinement of critical faculties by individuals who, as a consequence, find it difficult to accept doctrines based on the paranormal. Dogmatic impracticalities, cherrypicking and doctrinal hypocrasy have taken their toll on the church's credibility, and the clergy are becoming increasingly marginalised. In 1999, Church of England attendances fell below one million for the first time ever, a trend which will accelerate as the elderly, who make up the bulk of the congregations, die. Non-conformist chapels now frequently close and are sold off. Within the Roman Catholic church apostasy is rife, rituals such as confession are in decline, and it becomes ever more difficult to attract recruits to the ministry. The mass middle eastern uprisings of 2011 exposed a groundswell of public opinion in favour of greater freedom of thought which must eventually impact on all aspects of Islamic culture.

Can a moral code be inculcated without the practice of organised religion? The critical age at which conditioning must take place for the development of a moral conscience is from 2 to 4 years, an age at which the cleric does not normally have access to the child, and at which religious comprehension could hardly be expected. The responsibility for the instillation of moral values therefore rests with the parents and nursery group. Ideally, tomorrow's parents should derive their moral principles from yesterday's parents, but whether or not they do so, it is imperative that schools should teach sixth form students the important timing, and optimal manner, of conditioning the behaviour of their future offspring. Parenting classes should also be an integral part of antenatal care. It is entirely unrealistic to expect teachers of older children to repair the damage caused by parental failure in the earliest, and most morally formative years of life. That such an abysmal failure exists was vividly illustrated by the results of a poll of the UK teaching profession in 2009 which showed that one in four teachers had sustained physical violence from a pupil, and that forty percent had been verbally abused by parents for disciplining pupils (BBCR4 09:04:06). Instillation of the qualities of personal integrity, trustworthiness, fairness and benevolence are the qualities we require in our future global citizens, and unless these are taught at the mother's knee they are never truly learnt.

Increasingly, cult religion is being viewed as the last bastion of superstition. A host of moral philosophers, which include Plato, Holyoake, Kant, Stuart Mill and J P Sartre have shown us that it is not necessary to act out rituals or subscribe to the paranormal in order to live ethically. As they point out, principles of conduct must ultimately be judged by their ability to foster individual integrity and responsibility, and to enhance humanitarian ideals and societal harmony. There is a subtle but vital distinction to be made between rationalised ethical behaviour and the mere act of adhering to codes of legal, social or religious conduct. Personal ethics should be motivated by the subjective desire to be accepted and appreciated, a desire whose seeds have to be sown in early and mid childhood, and whose gratification has to be earned by actions which are seen to be in the general interest. Unless we are lucky enough to have been born with one, the optimistic outlook we all need is probably more effectively acquired by cultivating a generous sense of humour to which we can all subscribe, rather than through an ephemeral belief in the afterlife which many find implausible.

CHAPTER 23

RITUAL EXECUTION

HUMAN SACRIFICE AND CAPITAL PUNISHMENT

For protoman, as with the chimpanzee, warfare and cannibalism went hand in hand. You couldn't eat your enemy unless you killed him first, and if you had killed him, it seemed a waste of good protein not to eat him. Of course, in the case of early man the tribal god had to be taken into the equation as well. It was he who had demanded the destruction of his rival's followers in the first place and had delivered victory, so the battlefield meat, like the booty, had to be shared with him and was consumed by the priests on his behalf, before the residue was offered for general consumption (DB63p234). It was clear that the tribal god was not only strongly polarised in favour of his followers and against those who did not worship him, but that he must possess a warlike and cannibalistic nature.

Even in times of peace, the tribal god's carnivorous and bloodthirsty appetite still had to be appeased, and human victims, who were often either criminals or captives taken by foray, were despatched by priests who butchered according to ritual. Altar sacrifice had the additional advantage that a fire could be kindled on top of the votive stone slab and the meat cooked there and then, as the smoke from it wafted godwards. Unlike battlefield cannibalism which celebrated victory, ritualised temple sacrifice to the tribal god could be used in supplication for, or as a token of gratitude for, a range of other concessions such as protection against natural disaster, famine, or pestilence. The greater the threat to his safety and survival, the greater the sacrifice early man made to his tribal god. The most desperate situations called for the surrender of the most valuable possession of all - the life of his first born child. In less pressing circumstances a slave, beggar or malefactor could be substituted.

Early religion addressed the traits of interherd aggression and cannibalism which man had inherited from his ape like forbears, but it did not proscribe them. Instead it took over control of both of them, sanctioned both of them, and rebranded them as holy war and human sacrifice. The gradual emergence of humanitarian principles has modified both these traits over the ages. Warfare persists, but its most barbarous excesses have, to some extent, been curbed in recent times by the Geneva Convention. Dating as far back as 30 thousand years BCE, burials of whole skeletons, no longer dismembered or defleshed but accompanied by grave goods, demonstrate an increasing belief in the afterlife and may suggest the beginning of a slow decline in cannibalism. It is possible to detect a common sequential pattern in the way most cultures phased out firstly battlefield cannibalism, then ritualised temple cannibalism, followed by religious human sacrifice without ingestion of the victim. When, finally, animals took the place of men and boys on the sacrificial altar, the only form of ritual human execution to persist was that reserved for malefactors - capital punishment, a practice now also in decline. This slow progression towards humanitarianism can be regarded as a norm for the post evolutionary development of the species.

We have been bequeathed five grossly repulsive primal forms of barbarity by our post simian developmental process. All are either useless or overtly counter productive in evolutionary terms. The expunction of cannibalism and ritual execution will still leave warfare, torture and sexual atrocity to be addressed by the global community as a matter of civilising and corporate responsibility. Because of their importance, all five have been given dedicated sections in this book.

Adult Human Sacrifice - A Brief History

Murder is regarded as the most heinous of crimes unless it is committed in the name of society or religion. To ritualise it is to sanitise it. All emergent cultures ritually executed members of their community as a *religious requirement*. Archaeological evidence shows the practice to have been of considerable antiquity, and historical records tell us that it continued throughout the iron age in Britain, Gaul, Celtiberia, Germany, Etruria and Phoenicia (GMA01p97). Rome, by an edict issued in 97 BCE, and Judaism by a doctrinal adjustment symbolised by the legend of Abraham and Isaac, took the lead in banishing it. In North, Central and South America, and in Asia, human sacrifice was rife for many centuries, and in Central Africa it was commonplace, and is still believed to persist under the auspices of the Voodoo cult (GMA01p1966).

Human sacrifice was primarily an act of atonement, supplication or gratitude designed to influence a god's attitude in favour of his followers (propitiation sacrifice), but it was also used in entirely different contexts either to provide a ruler with servants in the afterlife, to protect a building from evil spirits, or to assist in the process of divination. All human sacrifice was religiously orientated and the word sacrifice comes from Latin, meaning to make sacred. The method of despatch which sought divine intercession had to be tailored to the milieu over which the particular deity held sway. Gods of the sea required that the victim be drowned, of the underworld that he be buried, and of the sky that he be burnt so that the smoke created rose to heaven. When blood was sprinkled on the ground it accelerated plant growth, so its shedding became symbolically associated with the god of fertility (LBR01p83).

The ancient Greeks sometimes used propitiation sacrifice of human beings to expiate communal guilt (LBR01p123), but the cannibalistic ceremony of the Greek cult of Dionysos was banned throughout Italy by an edict passed in the third century BCE (BAR65p135) and would not have survived in Greece once that country had been occupied by the Romans. Perhaps the most poignant cameo of archaeological evidence came from Crete when the ruins of the Minoan temple of Anemospilia, standing on a hill high above the sea, were excavated. Demolished by an earthquake around 1700 BCE, the falling roof had trapped three individuals as they were in the very process of conducting a human sacrifice to avert the impending disaster. The skeletal remains of a young man of 18 lay bound on an offertory table with a bronze spearhead on top of him, his bones blanched white from a catastrophic haemorrhage. Beside the table were the bones of the sacrificing officials, one a man of 37, and the other a woman of 20 (SYSS97p269).

The Romans inherited the practice of human sacrifice from the Etruscans and used it to supplicate the gods, burying gendered pairs of Gauls or Greeks in the Forum Boarium as a means of warding off disaster. Both the requirement and the protocol for this procedure had been inscribed by the Sibylline priestesses in their religious texts prior to the third century BCE. In 97 BCE, Rome discontinued all religious forms of human immolation, although capital punishment and gladiatorial combat continued to be practised without moderation. The Roman Emperor Claudius considered the Druidic religion with its macabre rituals to be so barbaric that he abolished it (GMA01p197).

Julius Caesar in his account of the Gallic wars (De Bello Gallico) refers to the Gaullish practice of incinerating human beings on a regular basis to appease the gods. A huge wickerwork effigy of a man was filled with victims and set alight. Criminals caught red handed made especially efficacious sacrificial victims but, failing this, slaves, prisoners of war and the physically deformed were pressed into service. The Gauls also believed that religiously motivated cannibalism practised as a adjunct to execution was especially evocative.

Like the Gauls, the pre-Christian Celts, Germans, Balts, Swedes and Russians are all recorded as practising religiously motivated human sacrifice in sacred groves, often by hanging victims from trees. During the 1st and 2nd centuries CE, a method of triple execution, by which the victim was first strangled, then had his head battered in and his throat cut, was considered to have outstanding placatory significance. Bodies mutilated in this way and then pinned down by wattle hurdles in bogs have been found in Ireland and across Northern Europe. Although some of these bog bodies date back to 3500 BCE, most were immolated during the iron age.

The large scale Aztec human sacrifices were cannibalistic (see chapter 21). Believing that the sun god would not rise unless a human being was sacrificed to him each day, four priests held their victim down upon a stone slab at the top of a stepped pyramid and, slitting open his chest wall with an obsidian knife, wrenched his beating heart from its socket so as to be able to hold it aloft to the god in front of the watching crowd (DB63p234). All Central American tribes used human sacrifice in acts of devotion to each of their many gods, and the method of execution for each god differed. The Maya used slow haemorrhage, scalping and flaying alive, and disembowelling, and all cults employed decapitation, drowning, burying alive and the infliction of multiple penetrating wounds.

Japanese records show that from the 7th century CE each of their provinces not only performed its own obligatory human sacrifices, but had to send the Emperor a regular supply of suitable victims. The Vietnamese drowned men in order to placate the gods who protected fishing (LBR01p127). The peoples of Sulawese, Borneo, and the Marquesas, and the Ashanti all practised human immolation rites.

A victorious army always has to cope with prisoners of war. If they could not be assimilated as slaves, captives proved to be a hazard to security and a drain on resources. The simplest and most expeditious policy was one of radical *Prisoner Sacrifice* to the god of victory as a gesture of propitiatory thanksgiving. The ancient Chinese always executed their prisoners of war as victory offerings (LBR01p130). The Song dynasty alone sacrificed an estimated 13 thousand captives (NGMZ:03:07). After victory the ancient Hebrews slew their prisoners of war as a sacrificial thanksgiving to Yahweh, and if that god had ordained the war's necessity, every alien man, woman and child would be slain (the "herem"). The ancient Greek leader Themistocles ritually sacrificed prisoners of war in 480 BCE after the battle of Salamis in which the Persian fleet was destroyed (GMA01p139). Tacitus records the slaughter of prisoners of war in the 1st century CE by the Druids on Anglesey. The Scythians of South West Russia slaughtered one of every hundred captives to Ares, the god of war, pouring the victim's blood ceremonially over a sword (HDS54p62), and the Celtiberians also sacrificed war prisoners and horses to Ares (GMA01p172).

Retinue Immuration had a very different rationale from propitiation sacrifice. Early grave goods interred with the deceased were armaments, ornaments and victuals, all items which by analogy with this life would provide for his needs in the next. In behavioural terms, belief in the after life is a form of autocredulity derived from extrapolation of the fundamental primate instincts of self preservation and possessiveness. If the corpse was that of a potentate, and he was to retain his power in the after life, then he must needs be accompanied not only by his accoutrements, but by his wives, concubines, court retinue and army. The psychopathogenicity for this type of human sacrifice has been found to exist world wide at comparable stages of post evolutionary human development.

The ancient Egyptian belief in the after life originally derived from the concept that each Pharaoh was a further reincarnation of the deity Osiris. The first dynasty Egyptian king Wadji was buried with 335 members of his household, and his queen was buried with 119 members of hers. At a later date, small clay figurines (shabtis) were used as substitutes for human retinue immurates (LBR01p123).

A scythian burial mound of the 5th century BCE in South West Russia included 360 horses, a consort, guards, servants and concubines, all buried with their master. The historian Herodotus observed that when a scythian king died he was interred with his immediate household, but that at the year's end a second ceremony took place at which 50 of the best of his remaining servants, together with 50 of the finest horses, were strangled, disembowelled, stuffed with chaff and buried around the tomb (HDS54). The Gauls buried slaves, and dependents known to have been their master's favourites, alongside him, together with all his most prized possessions (GMA01p144).

In 612 BCE, Duke Mu of Anyang in Korea was buried with 177 human sacrifices, and the female general Fu Hao was buried with prisoners of war, servants, chariots, charioteers and horses, weapons and ornaments. China also practised human immuration, but in the 3rd century BCE, the Q'in Emperor Shinuango broke with tradition by using 7 thousand terracotta effigies of warriors as substitutes for his army.

Human immuration accompanying the burial of high ranking personages has also been archaeologically investigated in Mesopotamia, Japan, Scandinavia (viking), Germany (iron age), Sudan (2nd and 1st century BCE), England (anglo-saxon), Central America (Maya) and West Africa (LBR01p6, PHJ00, NGMZ:03:10, WD71p35). In July 1986, Duke Ephraim of Calabar was buried with 50 slaves who had been decapitated in his honour, his wives who had been ceremonially strangled with silk, and his retinue. In addition, even though there was no evidence that he had been murdered, an extensive search was made for all who might have had reason to welcome his death, and these unfortunates were immolated beside him (PHJ00p212).

Portentous or Oracular Sacrifice often required the subject to die in agony. Just as prophecy could be formulated on the basis of an inspection of a newly slaughtered animal's entrails in ancient Rome, the Druids used the dying throes of human subjects to foretell the future. The historian Strabo writing in the 1st century BCE observed that Druidic sacrificial victims were stabbed in the back, shot through with arrows, impaled through the temple, drowned or hanged, so that their death agonies could be given interpretive significance by the priests (LBR01p6). The Cimbrian tribes of North Germany and South Denmark employed elderly priestesses to visit their army camps, cut the throats of their prisoners of war, and inspect their entrails for portents (GMA01p61, and Strabo 7, 2, 3).

There have been other even more bizarre motives for sacrificing human beings. In *Talismanic Sacrifice* an adult or child could be sealed into the wall of a building during its construction to act as its guardian against evil spirits. This practice was extensive in ancient China (LBR01p120). In many Burmese cities human sacrifices were immured in the masonry surrounding the main gate. At a site on the Bosphorus the master mason's wife was said to have been so sacrificed (TR76p37). The practice occasionally occurred in Roman Britain (GMA01p28, and PC).

Other Motives For Human Sacrifice have incorporated an element of altruism. In both ancient America and Africa, ageing kings were sometimes sacrificed to make way for younger successors (LBR01p6). In southern Sudan the ageing Dinka tribal village chief ritually buries himself alive at a time of his choice in order, by so doing, to become a permanent protector of his people (GMA01p194). In ancient Greece it was considered fitting for a wife to substitute herself for her husband if he was condemned to death (GMA01p139).

Child Sacrifice

If they are perceived to pose a competitive threat to their own offspring, some carnivores such as lions, wolves and bears will kill and eat the young of other conspecific parents, but the act of deliberately killing one's own offspring is grossly biologically abnormal. It flouts the parent-offspring bond and runs counter to the evolutionary process. This anomaly occurs rarely in non-human species such as the pig. In man its psychopathogenesis is usually religious, but it may also be associated with eugenics, population control, or famine (see also chapter 21).

The perimediterranean gods Baal, Molech and Kronos-Saturn of the 8th-2nd centuries BCE were different manifestations of the same powerful deity, whose appeasement required human sacrifice and, more especially, child immolation, as a result of which the latter was prevalent throughout the region. The walls of imposing temples used for this god's worship still stand in parts of the middle east. The Carthaginians-Phoenicians, who emanated from the area of present day Lebanon, established trading posts throughout the Mediterranean taking their Baalite culture with them, and some of the memorial sanctuaries (tophets) they established have been discovered in Tunisia, Algeria, Sicily and Sardinia, all of which bear out the fact that the deity had a voracious appetite for child victims. The sanctuaries incorporated large numbers of urns, each containing charred children's bones, and votive stelae which pledged the donor's commitment to the sacrifice.

Pliny, Plutarch and other ancient writers describe the grotesque spectacle. Children aged between 6 months and 5 years, often those first born, were selected, and stabbed to death in front of their silent mothers, with musicians playing loudly to drown the shrieks of the condemned. Then each corpse was placed in the arms of a life sized metal effigy of the god, whence it fell into the fire which burned beneath the podium. When a Syracusan army threatened Carthage in 310 BCE, the Carthaginians sacrificed 500 children drawn from their noblest families. Even the Carthaginian general Hamilcar sacrificed his own son (Diodorus Siculus 8, 86, 3). At a later date in 197 CE when phoenician priests failed to comply with the injunction of their Roman conquerors to suspend further human sacrifice, they were crucified in the precinct of their temple (GMA01p74).

The Bible mentions child sacrifice several times, and illustrates both the prevalence of the practice and its progressive abolition by the Jews. Exodus 22: 29 quotes God as stipulating "the first born of your sons you shall give me, you shall do likewise with your oxen and your sheep". In Joshua 6:26 it was ordained that the successful rebuilding of Jericho was dependent upon Joshua immolating his first born. The Moab king sacrificed his eldest son, and the Israelite general Jephtha vowed to sacrifice the first person he saw on his way back from the battlefield in return for victory over the Ammonites, albeit that this proved to be his only child - a daughter. In the end, it was to be the Hebrews who introduced reforms, symbolised by the legend of Abraham and Isaac, which led them to be the first middle eastern culture to outlaw human sacrifice (Genesis 22:10).

The Swedish king Aun sacrificed his nine sons to the Nordic god Odin in an attempt to secure the prolongation of his own life, and the Norwegian king Earlhaken sacrificed his son to gain Odin's help in his war against the Jomsberg pirates (SGR95p25). The Aztec rain god Tlaloc required the sacrifice of very young children, either by drowning, or burial on mountain tops. The more tears the child shed, the greater the rainfall which could be expected (LBR01p53). The Incas sacrificed children and young virgins in the high Andes to bring an end to famine, earthquake or pestilence. Immolation was by strangling, throat cutting and evisceration of the heart. At the Sapa Inca's coronation 200 children were sacrificed, and at the festival of the sun, which lasted a month, children aged 10-12 were buried alive at the foot of the god Inti Raym's huge effigy (LBR01p57 and NGMZ:99:11).

Hawaiians sacrificed their first born children to the gods in gratitude for fertility, and Sangi islanders placated the god of volcanoes by abducting a child from a neighbouring tribe and slowly dismembering it in accordance with ritual (LBR01p102). In Rwanda-Burundi, young girls were sometimes crushed to death to ensure a good harvest. In West Africa, young persons were sacrificed to the god of the sea at the mouth of the Niger river and, during the slave trading years, if European ships failed to appear and barter for their cargo, albino children would be ritually killed to appease the white man's god (PHJ00p212). The Voodoo religious ceremony which began in mid

Africa, and was carried to Haiti with the slaves, involves child sacrifice with dismemberment, cannibalisation, and decapitation, with the head being borne aloft in procession (see chapter 21). Ritual butchery of juveniles involving decapitation and the amputation of hands and feet remained an established practice of Ugandan witch doctors as late as 2011 as a means of soliciting favours from the spirit world (BBCT1:11:10:11).

Parents sometimes cause their own children to die as a result of *Birth Control or Eugenic Policies*. Among the Boran peoples of Southern Ethiopia, all infants born within 8 years of marriage, and in rural Uganda all first born, are left to die in bush land as a sacrifice to the god Wak (FJG22p61). These are instances of thinly disguised communal policies of family limitation, and merely regularise the procedure of infanticide commonly practised by those in extreme poverty. Mediaeval Christian convents were known to practise infanticide in order to dispose of illegitimate births (PC). Even today, some young Chinese parents are known to suffocate new born females in order to ensure that the one surviving child which the state allows them will be a boy, able to provide for them in their old age.

Some adolescent bog bodies unearthed in Schleswig Holstein and the Netherlands were found bound and strangled, had the hair shaven on one side of their heads, and had significant physical deformities which suggest that their immolation was eugenic (GPV71p30). In ancient Roman law the Paterfamilias had a duty to destroy a malformed child (LBR01p71). Hitler's eugenic policies in Nazi Germany exterminated the malformed and mentally subnormal.

21st. Century Ritual Execution - Capital Punishment
So far in this chapter we have seen that ritual human sacrifice always had a religious content, albeit an illusory one, and that in the process man rendered up to his god a life which on the one hand might have been readily expendable, but on the other might have been his most prized possession.

Capital punishment is a form of ritual execution in which society believes that it expunges a life of negative value, the life of someone who has been proven to do harm to his fellow creatures and would be at significant risk of reoffending. In behavioural terms this is an example of a primate dominance confrontation, but one from which the attenuation of herd bonding has been removed, and in which offensive aggression is disinhibited. The justification for it is either overtly religious or else derives from secular laws which had their foundation in religion. In primate terms capital punishment, like human sacrifice, is biologically abnormal. Dominant apes impose top-down discipline on other "herd" members, as does the first mate of a cargo ship, but do not execute them.

Dominance sparring within non-human primate "herds" rarely results in fatality, but even when it does there is no retributive response on the part of the "herd". In human hands, and with the development of weapons, fatality became a much more common outcome of disputes, retaliation led to the blood feud whereby a man's murder could only be requited by the reciprocal death of a member of the offender's family, and an inevitable chain reaction was set up with the loss of many lives. As society became better organised, it stopped the blood feud by intervening and insisting that only the perpetrator of the original murder should die, and thus formal capital punishment took shape, later to be codified in Mosaic law as "an eye for an eye, and a tooth for a tooth".

Capital punishment has been common to all human societies during their development, but, being a cultural phenomenon, has varied between nations, both in the nature of the crimes for which it is imposed and in the method of execution adopted. Ignoring for a moment the use of execution as an instrument of political abuse, the history of capital punishment in England provides a useful illustration of the way in which this practice emerged and developed in Europe.

The legal systems of all western countries use precedent to build on the experience of the past, and incorporate features of Mosaic law,

Ancient Roman law and Canon (Ecclesiastical) law in varying proportions. In England from the 10th century and Alfred onwards, successive kings began to introduce state laws for the punishment of crime. Initially, capital punishment was only imposed for crimes against the state, the church and property as, respectively, the king, the Pope, and the barons weighed in to protect their vested interests. Murderers and fornicators were merely fined, the revenue from their fines also being divided out between the king, the church and the barons.

Authority at this time used trial by ordeal to assess the guilt of the accused as judged, for instance, by whether he could withstand plunging his hand into boiling water, or walking barefoot over red hot ploughshares. Those suspected of witchcraft had it confirmed if they floated when trussed and thrown into a pond. Such practices were abolished in 1219 CE (HC03p29). Following the Norman conquest, litigation between individuals was decided through trial by combat, a dangerous form of primate dominance sparring, which involved the use of swords, lances and spears. Courts using trial by evidence were slowly established after the 14th century.

Like mutilatory punishment, capital punishment was at its height between the 10th and 16th centuries. In 1776 there were 160 different offences punishable by death, and by 1819 a further 63 had been added, which included cutting down a planted tree, impersonating a Chelsea Pensioner or damaging Westminster bridge. At this time, England was carrying out more executions than any other country (HC03p53).

The method of execution was varied in an attempt to make the punishment fit the crime. In general, decapitation by axe was reserved for the high born. Male commoners were hanged, but female commoners were burned to protect their modesty. As Christian doctrine forbade the shedding of blood, crimes against the Church also led to death by burning, and here capital offences included denying the doctrine of transubstantiation, denying the need for clerical celibacy, eating meat on a Friday, heresy and refusal to accept the status of holy relics. Mary Queen of Scots torched more than 300 men and women under ecclesiastical pretexts.

Those guilty of defacing the coins of the realm were hanged (Edward the First despatched 280 coiners in London alone), poisoners were boiled to death, homosexuals were chained to the pillory where they were stoned to death by the mob, suspected malefactors who resisted demands that they should plead at trial were slowly pressed to death between heavy stone slabs, traitors were hung, drawn and quartered, and male and female slaves guilty of theft were respectively stoned and burned to death. Matricides were boiled in oil, those who infringed the Normans' forest rights were hacked to death, women commoners found guilty of theft were thrown from a cliff or drowned, male thieves were burned, and pirates and highwaymen were gibbeted. Other forms of execution were impaling, crucifixion, dragging apart between four horses, smothering, flaying, savaging by wild beasts, live burial, flogging to death and breaking on the wheel.

The earliest recorded suspension of capital punishment, albeit for a limited period, was in Gortyna, Crete, as evidenced by its 600BCE stone inscriptions. Tuscany and Austria in the 18th century CE were the first European states to abolish it, and by the end of the 19th century it was no longer applied in what are now the Benelux countries, nor in Portugal or Romania, except for crimes of treason and mutiny. Abolition was not found to increase the incidence of violent crime in these countries (HC03p377).

Despite the Archbishop of York's stated view in 1956 that "retribution was a moral necessity within the penal code " and the Archbishop of Canterbury's pronouncement that the death penalty was "not always unchristian and wrong", it was abolished in England in 1973. Parliament had taken into due consideration the fact that most murderers do not kill a second time, that the execution of murderers has no effect on the incidence of violent crime, and that if a miscarriage of the judicial process occurred, it led to the execution of an innocent man.

Some developed countries such as the USA retain capital punishment and seem unlikely to relinquish it, at least in the short term. In 2006 China was still punishing 68 different offences with the death penalty, and was executing thousands of miscreants, who provided a ready source of organs for transplantation (BBCT1:06:09:25). The next most prolific execution rates were possessed by Iran, Saudi Arabia, Pakistan and Iraq in that order (BBCR4:07:04:20, and NGMZ:09:08). All told, a further 51 countries, particularly totalitarian regimes, still execute.

(Sources Reviewed: BAR65, BBCR4:07:04:20, BBCT1:06:09:25, DB63, FJG22, GG56, GMA01, GPV71, HC03, HDS54, LBR01, NGMZ:99:11, 03:04 and 09:08, PHJ00, SGR95, SYSS97, TR76, WD71)

CHAPTER 24

DIVINE WARMONGERING IN ANCIENT ISRAEL

As we move slowly towards a more enlightened world order in which all will have access to the basic needs of human existence, cupidity ceases to be a cause for war. States no longer seek to acquire the territory, political control or commodity markets of others by force, and it is only the clash of ideologies which still provide man with the impetus for armed aggression. Arab fights Jew, Arab fights Christian, Muslim fights Hindu, Sunni fights Shia, Catholic fights Protestant, and Communist fights Fascist, all because the concepts imprinted in their conditionable brains admit of no compromise. They act by rule of thumb.

The principal rule of thumb ideologies of the past two millennia have been Judaism, Christianity, Islam, Fascism and Communism. The pretension of each to deliver universality, unanimity and uniformity is mocked by the intransigent differences between them. If any had been the embodiment of ultimate truth which it claimed, and which everybody could recognise, there could have been no competitor. This lack of universality has been due in large part to the underlying fusion between a particular ideology and the partisan self interest of the communal unit which founded it. Judaism centred on the acquisition of the territory of Israel, Islam on the dominance and expansion of the Arabic empire, Fascism on German and Italian expansion and supremacy, and Communism on the suzerainty of the Soviet Union. Christian partisan self interest was clearly seen in the crusading campaigns in Prussia and the Levant, and in overt Catholic support for Nationalist movements in Ireland, Rhodesia, Poland and elsewhere. This undisguised association between an ideology and the politico-militaristic bias to which it is subservient is closely similar to the contractural bond between the tribal god and his protégées. The rule of thumb of ideology is, in effect, a subsequent phase in post evolutionary human development to that of the tribal god. In their heyday, the five prominent ideologies, like the tribal god, did nothing whatever to suppress interherd warfare. On the contrary, they gave it its raison d'etre, and their enthusiastic and integral support. Warfare and the threat of it regresses as and when the ideological moral support for it ebbs.

Let us see what history tells us about such matters. Chapters 13 and 16 have already studied the impact which Communist and Fascist ideologies had on humanity. In chapters 24-26 we shall need to explore the way in which the razzmatazz and paraphernalia of ritual, iconification, sublimation, autocredulity, mass congregation, regimentation and mass indoctrination led to the development of monotheistic religious cults which were all similarly discriminatory, prejudicial and xenophobic, and which had a natural tendency to use aggression and armed conflict to make the end justify the means. Such mores are in stark contrast with any pretensions towards humanitarianism or egalitarianism to which these cults may originally have subscribed. A markedly aggressive phase has been such a prominent feature in the history of any monotheism that, as with nationalism, this must be regarded as an inevitable component of its development.

The era of tribal deities had an enormous formative impact on the behavioural patterns of man's post evolutionary development, and the rule-of-thumb ideologies which superseded them exerted an even greater influence, dominating history for two millennia. Must we wait for the creeping secularisation slowly overtaking western society to become a global phenomenon before the iron grip of such mass movements can be released, or are there cults which can fulfil man's hankering to dabble with the paranormal, but which do so without creating intolerance, bias and schism? Cults which most nearly approach this level of benignity and impartiality are to be found in the far East. Hinduism's polytheism promotes meditation and introspective self regulation in its devotees. Buddhism is a highly personalised discipline which also makes the individual responsible for his own enlightenment, but its doctrines do not presuppose the existence of a paranormal superpower. Both Hindu and Buddhist religious monuments are foci for private and independent devotional activity. Unhappily, the renunciation of both desire and reality, which the Buddhist credo requires, is at a variance with the practicalities of most peoples' everyday lives, and even Buddhism's normally unblemished reputation for pacifism was besmirched by a splinter group, the Aum Shinrikio, which released the poison gas Sarin in a terrorist attack on the Tokyo underground in 1995.

The validity of any religious movement, or, indeed of all religious movements taken as acting concurrently, must always be judged by its proven ability to bring about peaceful and harmonious co-existence between the peoples of the world. Any emotional or psycho-physiological benefits which it affords the individual, and which we discussed in chapter 22, are as nothing when they are compared with the wholesale distress and suffering involved in the interherd warfare precipitated by compulsive prejudice. In this light let us weigh the three principal monotheisms on the scales of historical justice.

Historical Abstract   The Chosen Race, The Promised Land and the Herem

How is it that the most persistently controversial race on earth manages to spawn considerably more than its fair share of genius and musical talent? Above all, how has it managed to preserve its integral identity in the face of repeated subjugation, deportation, dispersion, persecution, genocide and enforced conversion? The acquisitiveness, tenacity and shrewdness of the Jewry are as proverbial as its stereotypical dark, curly locks and nasal curvature. These traits of personality, together with an exclusive social framework of interdependence have enabled racial survival against all odds.

In spite of possessing a world population of only eleven million, the Jewish race has had a greater impact upon the world's belief systems than any other. The tenets of its ethnicity, legends and early military history were originally passed down through word of mouth, before being committed to script as the Hebrew Bible. This text is not only Judaism's doctrinal bedrock, it is the sole source of the Christian Old Testament, and the Qur'an repeatedly aligns itself with characters portrayed within it.

Jewry has always identified itself with the territory to the west of the river Jordan, whose acquisition had originally to be obtained by conquest from the Canaanites, forbears of the Phoenicians. As with other middle eastern states of the period, Israel's nationalism and religion were closely integrated. The emerging nation state believed itself to have been preferentially chosen by the all-powerful god Yahweh to be the instrument of his divine will. This special relationship allowed all who failed to worship Yahweh to be viewed as his enemies and thereby worthy of destruction. Israel's militarism, like the Jihad and the Crusade, was therefore a matter of sacred duty. Moreover, victory could be virtually assured by divine intervention, provided that God's chosen people were compliant, and human sacrifice was offered in return (NS93p148, RVG91p41, SPD91p190).

Throughout the Middle East, during much of the first millennium BCE, it was established practice to carry out human sacrifice in its various guises. Hiel, the rebuilder of Jericho, was bound by oath to make talismanic sacrifice of his eldest and youngest sons by burying them in the foundations (1Kings:16:33). Israelite captives were sometimes known to have been eaten by their enemies (Micah:3:2-3). Offspring, regardless of sex, age or status, risked being incinerated by their parents as offerings to the divinities, with the Israelite kings Ahaz

311

and Manasseh and the king of Moab setting the example by delivering up their respective sons to the fire when faced with a state crisis (2Kings:16:2-3, 2Chronicles:33:6, Moabite Stone). Child sacrifice was eventually banned in Israel by edicts of King Josiah in the 7th. century BCE (2 Kings 22:8). From then on, Yahweh's craving for blood was only to be met by the destruction of his enemies, either during the battle or after they had surrendered.

In contrast with slave holding empires, it proved impracticable for captives to be assimilated into the Israeli community, and they were butchered, both in demonstration of gratitude to Yahweh, and so that their farmlands could be commandeered. Should the priests deem it to be required as the will of God and a matter of sacred duty, a Herem would be declared, following which all opposing human beings and their livestock would be immolated, and all their towns and cities reduced to rubble. The killing spree was always accompanied by plunder of treasure and accoutrements on behalf of God as generalissimo (CJ97p121), and by the destruction of all sites where the enemy's gods were worshipped. It was seldom that the divine requirement for Herem could be rescinded, as evidenced by accounts of the massacres of Sihon, Ai, Makkeban, Libnah, Gaser, Hebron, Debir, Eglon and the kingdom of Hazor testify (Deuteronomy 5:6, Joshua 8:12, 10:28, 11:11). Rarely, women, and more especially virgins, were taken as spoil (Judges 21:14) After the fall of Jericho, one family alone was spared, the town was demolished, and all metal objects were surrendered to the Lord's treasury (Joshua 6:17). The theocrats preached that as non-Israelites were uncircumcised, and therefore unclean, they could not be assimilated within orthodox society (Deuteronomy 20:14). In any case, Yahweh had decreed that all non-believers were to be put to the sword (Jeremiah 50:14, and Exodus 22:19), just as Mohammed, St. Bernard and St. Dominic did in later centuries. Total extermination was prescribed both for those who attacked Israel and for those who merely resisted her designs. Archaeological evidence corroborates the broad outline of events described in the Hebrew scriptures, but cannot verify details such as casualty rates, as when, after the conquest of Seir by Israel's sister state Judah, the Judean army is reported to have counted 10 thousand dead enemy warriors and pushed 10 thousand captives to their death from a precipice (2 Chronicles 25:11), or the claim in 2 Kings 19:35 that God killed 185 thousand Assyrians under Sennacherib on Judah's behalf.

The priests were of unique importance to the Israeli army, playing a pivotal role in their troops' motivation before an attack and during the subsequent execution of it. Preaching God's promise of impending victory, they ritually consecrated their warriors, organised them in detail, and led them into battle. Taking up their position in the van of an assault, they ensured that their garbed presence and leadership were instantly recognisable. Strident fanfares from their ceremonial trumpets, and the prominent display of the Ark of the Covenant and the temple vessels, which they arraigned in front of the assembled ranks, all added to the flamboyant spectacle, before the conflict began in earnest. In a move calculated to demoralise the inhabitants of Jericho prior to Israel's siege of that city, the priests and their retinue repeatedly circled the curtain walls to the incantation of malevolent spells and portents. When victory followed, all treasure was impounded in the Lord's treasury.

As well as engineering the elimination of those within and without the state who opposed them, the priests of ancient Israel enforced a strict doctrine of racial purity, as many other absolutist regimes have done. Intermarriage with foreigners would have defiled Israel's bloodstock and was forbidden. A man who had not been circumcised was, by definition, an alien infidel worthy only of destruction. Obsessional doctrinal phobias decreed that warriors who had killed in battle were unclean and that both they, their garments and their captives must remain outside the confines of the camp for a week, following which they had to be ritually purified by washing before readmission (Numbers 31). All captured livestock had to be cleansed with water, and all inanimate objects cleansed with fire before assimilation by the victors. Meat had to be killed by exsanguination and pork was forbidden, traditions which both persist to this day.

The Bible's first and second books of Amos detail the wars waged against Israel's close neighbours, Philistia, Damascus, Ammon, Moab, Tyre, Edom and Gaza. These local wars were savage and frenzied conflicts, and were undertaken in order to pre-empt attack by a neighbour, or to seize his land. Even more significantly, Israel had to contend with subjugation at various times in its history by the world powers of the time - Egypt, Babylon, Persia, Assyria, Macedon and Rome. The Egyptian and Babylonian invasions of its territory were compounded by mass deportation of the Jewish population as slaves.

As so often proves to be the case, national and religious arrogance and jingoism were inextricably interwoven in ancient Israel. As Yahweh's chosen race, their divine mission to occupy the land he had promised them was always uppermost in the minds of the authors of the Hebrew bible (Deuteronomy 7:33). This self justificatory mind set made no distinction between Israel's objectives and its tribal god's objectives, and uncompromising ruthlessness in pursuit of the latter's cause was accepted as a matter of pragmatic necessity. Leaders often held the combined offices of high priest and army commander as did, subsequently, both Mohammed and the prosecutors of the ninth crusade.

It is very clear that Israel's extremist bigotries were material to its survival during the early days of statehood, and were not excessive as judged by the standards of their day. Sadly, there is also no doubt that the aggressive and violent behavioural patterns portrayed in the Hebrew Bible have had an influence far beyond their time by virtue of their incorporation within the canon of three major belief systems. As the Jewish writer Susan Niditch observes: "the particular violence of the Hebrew scriptures has inspired violence, and has served as a model for persecution, subjugation and extermination for millennia beyond its reality" (NS93p4), four barbaric consequences of paranoid xenophobia for which pseudo-religions and most religious movements still stand indicted. Such parlous outcomes are nowhere better exemplified than in the history of the Middle East, albeit with the irony that Jewry has suffered much more victimisation and persecution than any other cult. For centuries, forbidden to gain their livelihood except through usury, or else expelled from most European countries at one time or another, Jews were subjected to organised programs by successive Russian authorities, and lost 7 million of the total 18 million of their number through Hitler's holocaust. It is bitter to have to recognise that to the west of the river Jordan land hunger still exists, the Mosaic vendetta still operates, and the end still justifies the means. As things stand, Yahweh has won the war but lost the peace.

Approximate Historical Dating.

13th C BCE Agriculture, Yahweh and Canaan assimilated by early Israelites (CRB87p129)

9th C BCE Mesha Stela : Inscription detailing Moab's victory and sacrifice of the king's son

8th C BCE Books of Isiah and Micah (NS93p134)

8th C BCE Book of Amos (NS93p138)

7th C BCE Books of Deuteronomy and Kings 1 and 2 (HGC85p406)

5th C BCE Books of Esther and Chronicles 1 and 2 (NS83p126)

(Sources Reviewed: CJ97, CRB87, HBOT, HGC85, MHH63, NS93, RVG91, SPD91)

CHAPTER 25

DIVINE WARMONGERING IN CHRISTIANITY

Whilst Christianity can claim more adherents than any other belief system, the policy of mutual respect and affection on which it was founded has seldom run smoothly. Its early proselytes were persecuted with outright barbarism. For several centuries its good name was besmirched by the despotism and depravity of its senior clergy. In the middle ages it reinforced its autocracy with measures of considerable cruelty, and embarked upon a string of military adventures which were not only ignominious, but nearly always unsuccessful. Latterly its perceived doctrinal impracticabilities, improbabilities and hypocrisies have undermined its credibility. Riven by schism it continues to suffer organisational fragmentation, but the basic principle of humanitarianism for which it stands, and has always stood, opened a new chapter in human behavioural history on which the species continues to build. Let us briefly look at some of the wider implications of this patchy track record.

Christian hymn books still incorporate a certain amount of militaristic imagery in exhortations such as "onward Christian soldiers" or "turn your ploughshares into swords", and a youth movement in the early 20th century western world called itself "The Crusaders". These uncomfortable reminders of self righteous aggression hark back to an era of Christian "holy" wars which caused blood to be shed for more than five centuries. Because religion exists to promote personal and communal harmony, holy war is a contradiction in terms. The herem wars of Judaism, the Baltic crusade, and the jihads of Islamic middle eastern imperialism were undertaken for the fundamental underlying reason that they would satisfy land hunger, and the use of the term "holy" in relation to them is a self justificatory and hypocritical euphemism. The contention that western Europe had the moral right to occupy Palestine merely because Christ lived there is equally ill founded. What is more, because Christ was a quintessential pacifist who forgave his enemies, his message was the very antithesis of the wars which were being waged over his tomb. A moral authority whose actions are diametrically opposed to the principles it propounds must indeed be sick, and the moral malaise from which the mediaeval church found itself to be suffering was, in behavioural terms, the direct result of distortions of dominance and possessiveness in the psyche of its leadership. The repercussions were, however, far reaching and exemplify the way in which the conditionable brain can be programmed to eclipse rationality.

In 1059, a rift over doctrine split the eastern and western arms of the Christian church when the petulant Pope Leo the Ninth excommunicated his counterpart, the Patriarch of the Eastern Orthodox church. The political distraction which resulted was compounded by the existence of a third contender for the overall stewardship of christendom, the Holy Roman Emperor, who had no spiritual remit, but was charged with the physical protection of the Christian commune. The office of Holy Roman Emperor had originally been created in 800 CE as a mark of papal commendation for military services which Charlemagne had rendered to the church. As critics subsequently pointed out, the title was anachronistic, in that the territory over which successive incumbents presided was considerably less than that occupied by imperial Rome, often being limited to portions of Germany and Italy. Nevertheless, the appointment, which was sometimes held by the erstwhile head of one or other of the smaller German states, carried significant prestige and privilege with it, and these were jealously guarded.

Although pope, patriarch and emperor were all necessarily implicated in the crusading process, it was the pope who ultimately instigated and authorised holy war. Once the supreme pontiff had declared a crusade, church dignitaries throughout Europe preached a call to arms, in compliance with which the faithful could confidently expect remission of even the most iniquitous of their sins and be assured of everlasting life. The admonitions and oratorial zeal of St. Bernard and St. Dominic in this regard were so imperative and effective that both were later beatified for their efforts.

Because the church's doctrine forbade it to spill blood, this had to be done by proxy, and it was the implicit duty of the Emperor and all Christian monarchs to make armies and finances available to the papacy on demand. The socio-military basis of the feudalism of the age was strictly hierarchical, making knights dependent upon their monarch for their land and title, with the proviso that they raise and command armed levies in his name when called upon to do so. Leading by example, the knight had to exhibit personal qualities of discipline, chivalry and valour. When Urban the Third, the first crusading pope, summoned Europe to liberate Palestine from the Saracen yoke, many noble families, especially those of France, responded, and a new brand of combatant emerged, a cavalier who combined the enthusiasm, discipline and accoutrements of the parade ground with the asceticism and dedication of holy orders. Younger sons of the nobility saw in the crusade an exciting opportunity to prove their jousting skills against a real enemy and win their spurs, albeit that since they would be fighting in God's name these aspirations had to be tempered by the high standards of personal conduct expected of a monastery. The initiate knight had to be in good health, single and unbetrothed, and he had to equip himself with a horse, arms and armour, and a sergeant. At a formal induction ceremony he would be required to swear a solemn oath of poverty, chastity, and obedience to the Order. Henceforward, the twin disciplines of militarism and friarhood would govern his every thought and action.

The Knights Templar, named after their original headquarters in Solomon's Temple in Jerusalem, the Knights Hospitallers whose initial purpose was to care for sick pilgrims, and the Teutonic Knights drawn exclusively from Germany during their early years, were all originally founded for the purpose of protecting and assisting penitential Europeans paying homage to Christ's tomb. Following a maverick caliph's destruction of the church housing the holy sepulchre and the need to re-establish pilgrim access to it, the three orders joined forces in a campaign designed to occupy the Mediterranean's eastern littoral (the Levant).

All nine of the major crusades to appropriate levantine territory for Christianity failed in their purpose. The term crusade was also applied to campaigns launched to expel the Saracen from Spain and the Mediterranean islands, and it was used as a political expedient to sanitise invidious attacks which the pope made upon fellow Europeans in southwest France and the Baltic hinterland. It is to these last two military operations that we must now turn our attention. In studying them it becomes clear that the motives which prompted them in no way differed from those which inspired the extremism of the Israeli herem and the Islamic jihad. Although they both feature less prominently in textbooks than do the levantine incursions, the crusade in the Baltic had a greater impact than those of the middle east on later European history, and the anticathar operation in southwest France deserves prominence as being in many ways the most controversial war to be waged on behalf of the church.

Historical Brief: The Teutonic Knights
When missionary zeal and persuasion did not suffice, it was the considered view held by mediaeval popes that conversion to Christianity should be enforced at the point of a sword. Poring over his maps, Pope Alexander the Fourth saw clearly that there was outstanding business to be done in the north-eastern corner of Europe where paganism still defied him. Poland, which was then landlocked,

and Germany had already come under his sway, and much of Russian territory had converted to the Orthodox faith, but the inhabitants of lands bordering the southern shores of the Baltic sea stubbornly refused to submit. Any Christian missionaries who had the temerity to penetrate the forests and marshy wastelands which were home to these peoples fell victim to their sacrificial rites. Between Poland and the sea lay Prussia, then, further northeast, a much larger Lithuania than we know today, beyond which were lands which corresponded to modern Latvia and Estonia, all of them infidels to a man. It was time to drive home Christ's message in the only terms that these barbarians would understand, and the task force best suited to act as the pope's surrogate army was that nearest to hand, the order of Teutonic Knights, whose centres of recruitment were scattered throughout Germany, a country which at that time was a conglomerate of small states. Instated as a military order in the Levant in 1197, the Knight's original title had been The Order of the Hospital of St. Mary of the Germans in Jerusalem. Apart from their commitment to the papal cause in the Baltic, and in Palestine from which they, like other crusaders, were expelled in 1309, they also saw action at various times in Transylvania, Greece and the Balkans.

Official sanction for the invasion of the south Baltic hinterland was issued in 1226 in a papal decree known as the Golden Bull of Rimini. Pope Alexander awarded the Knights everything they could conquer in pagan lands, and the Emperor Frederick the Second lavished privileges, estates and subsidies upon them (UW03). The Order was given a jewel encrusted ring in token of the pope's authority, upon which all initiates had to swear their vows.

Land hunger was the primary motive for many, if not most, who joined the Order, that same lust for "liebensraum" which had fuelled German attempts to expand its borders ever since roman times. The lure of a chivalrous adventure in the fellowship of like-minded youths of the upper classes, coupled with the prospect of securing their own landed estates, proved magnetic to the second and subsequent sons of noble families who could not expect to inherit their ancestral titles. The fact that their exploits would be undertaken in response to God's express command seemed to clinch the argument. The firebrand preacher St. Bernard incendiarised these young knights with harangue and hyperbole, spurring them on with such trenchant epithets as "killing for Christ is malecide not homicide" and "to kill a pagan is to win glory, since it gives glory to Christ" (SD72p35). Dominican monks hastened to assure the crusading army that "once they had cut down the enemies of God, Christ himself would hurl those heathen souls into hell" (CM94). Even St. Augustine had taught that since pagans were only capable of doing evil, it was a matter of Christian duty that their lands should be occupied and ravished (UW03p157).

The campaign, which was ultimately to span three and a half centuries, began in 1229, and its first phase brought the Knights a series of hard won victories. As they overran Prussia and forced their way into the Baltic states beyond, they built fortresses and founded new towns to consolidate their gains. Each fortress was surrounded by high battlemented walls, watchtowers and moats, and incorporated a chapel, hospital, monastery, refectory, bakery, barracks, stables and prison cells. Missionaries, settlers and traders followed in the wake of the Knights to establish churches, farmsteads and businesses. The new territory was run as a military principality in which the bishops fought alongside other knight brethren, and as a condition of his tenure, each landowner was liable for service as a man at arms. The danger from attack by enemies was ever present. On the right flank of their advance the Crusaders had to contend with Poles to the south, Lithuanians to the southeast, and Russians to the east. On one occasion they even suffered defeat at the hands of the Mongols, and they repeatedly had to put down revolts instigated by indigenous tribes within the territories they had occupied.

In barracks, the Teutonic Knight's attire was clerical black. As an outer garment he wore a long white cloak emblazoned with a black cross, a sombre, austere monochrome motif replicated on his shield. At all times he carried a heavy double edged sword. In battle, a spear was added to his accoutrements, he was armoured with full body chain mail, and his head was either enclosed in a full face pot helmet with eye slits, or a plated half-helmet with chain mail neck surround which left his nose and eyes exposed. A beard was mandatory and helped to wedge the helmet in place. For every knight on campaign there would be ten times as many supporting infantry ("men at arms") who wore grey mantles. As the Order's dedicatee was the Virgin Mary, her image was prominently displayed on its battle standards. On tour of duty it was always considered essential to keep all military personnel fully occupied, with time given to exacting military and religious routines. Every man slept fully clothed with his sword beside him, there were eight spiritual observances to be made during the 24 hours, and meals were taken in silence save that the bible, and preferentially the Old Testament with its emphasis on God inspired militarism, was read out to the assembly. Discipline was severe - devotional self flagellation is reported to have taken place on Fridays, food in Lent was, for the most part, restricted to gruel, the offence of sodomy was punished by life imprisonment or execution, and on the battlefield the marshal enforced obedience with a club. During the latter decades of the crusade, in order to offset the rigours of this ascetic existence, the larger bastions arranged occasional courtly entertainment in the form of elaborate feasts with troubadours, musicians, orators, tumblers, jugglers, and fools in attendance. Hunting was so important a source of food that it was not only encouraged as a sport, but would sometimes bring hostilities to a halt when both sides agreed a truce to allow it to take place.

Teutonic battle tactics always depended upon the primary use of heavy cavalry, the mediaeval equivalent of the modern battle tank. In close formation, astride heavy horses trained to run at an armed enemy, and shouting their war cry "God is with us", the Knights' charge fell like a thunderbolt upon the weakest point of the ranks assembled against them, creating a pandemonium which could then be exploited by the infantry. After the introduction of cannon in 1391, the Teutonic heavy artillery was used for a similar purpose. The demoralisation caused by the severity of these initial hammer blows often put waverers to flight, enabling those foes who stood their ground to be outnumbered and butchered.

With the armies of Poland, Lithuania and Russia all vying with the Knights for their share of the south Baltic hinterland, it was inevitable that alliances between the various parties would be made and broken with equal ease as suited their immediate self interest. The Poles fielded secular knights who could sometimes meet the crusaders on equal terms, but the Lithuanian light cavalry was no match for the Order and was repeatedly crushed by them. The Teutonic Knights suffered five humiliating defeats - at Lake Peipus in 1240 when the Russian Prince Nevsky reputedly lured their heavy cavalry onto thin ice, in Prussia in 1242 when an indigenous insurrection took them by surprise, at Leignitz in 1297 at the hands of the Mongols, at Tannenburg in 1410 when outmanoeuvred by a joint Polish-Lithuanian force, and in the Order's northern territories in 1588 during Ivan the Terrible's incursions. No quarter was ever given, nor was it expected, in these ruthless wars, fought over terrain which became snow covered permafrost in winter, and mosquito-ridden marshland in summer. Insurrections were stamped out with unmitigated ferocity, and on one occasion when the Order assaulted a stockade occupied by four thousand Lithuanian pagans, all the men within it slaughtered their entire families rather than submit to capture, burning the bodies and all their possessions before turning their swords against themselves (UW03p133). Captured knights were almost invariably executed, some being roasted alive in their armour. Although casualty figures were usually grossly exaggerated for their propaganda value, we know that during the course of some battles, one or other side was virtually wiped out.

The turning point in Teutonic fortunes came in 1386, when the Grand Duke Jagiello of Lithuania married his way onto the polish throne, an event which united the two countries and extended polish Christianity to Lithuania in line with the new king's conversion to his wife's faith. At one stroke, Jagiello had provided himself with the manpower to build a victorious army and had expunged the raison d'etre of the Baltic crusade. Twenty-four years later at Tannenburg his combined forces killed 600 knights, including all their senior commanders, after he had parried their cavalry charge. He was then able to take control of the Order's southern territories, leaving them only a pocket in the north which was later overrun by Russia.

Tannenburg sounded the death knell of the Order, and in later years Vatican support for it cooled. As if to rub salt into the wound, Jagiello's grandson was canonised to become St. Casimir, the polish patron saint. Centuries of campaigning had left many Germans living on their newly acquired estates in Prussia, and the families they raised clung to their sense of superiority, becoming prominent members of the haughty and overbearing German Junkers overclass. Detachments of knights domiciled within Germany proper continued to defend Christianity's eastern borders when the Emperor requested their services, but these units were ultimately disbanded by Napoleon (UW03). The wraith-like vestige of the Order's former humanitarian ideals persists in Vienna to this day as a charitable body supporting hospitals, ambulances and schools.

In the Teutonic Knights' rigidly conditioned, fanatical behaviour patterns we may clearly identify the foundations of the Germanic military tradition in all its paranoid arrogance. What is more, the unity of purpose, which had been engendered throughout the German states by the crusade, sowed the seeds of later German unification. The terms "Teutonic", "Junkers" and "Prussian" with their overbearing and ruthless twentieth century connotations, and the emblem of a black cross on a white background used on German warplanes and tanks in the second world war, all hark back to the land lust turned blood lust originally sanctioned and sanitised by papal authority. Arguably, St. Bernard's bigoted and bloodthirsty diatribes helped to create a culture of regimented xenophobic aggression which ultimately played much more havoc with world peace than did those of his more modern counterpart, Osama bin Laden.

(Sources Reviewed: CE98, CEP08, CM94, RSJ90, SD72, UW03, WKP08)

Key Historical Resume: The Albigensian Crusade

The albigensian crusade, which spanned the years 1209-1243 deserves mention, not so much for its impact on later European history, as because it is an example of the way in which an obsessionally compulsive ideology will not only overrule the unconditionable brain, but may produce behaviour which entirely contradicts the premise on which that ideology was founded. We have already noted the incongruity of waging any war, and in particular "holy" war, in relation to Christ's teaching. The albigensian crusade took irrationality to its extreme by pitting one Christian sect against another, each of which believed itself invincible on the grounds that Christ Jesus was fighting on its behalf.

Like Luther and Calvin who were to introduce their radical reforms three centuries later, the Cathars (also known as Albigenses) felt both betrayed and repelled by the harm done to the good name of the established church by overt Vatican depravity. They considered that there was an urgent need to return to the basic principles of humility, unselfishness and morality propounded by Christ, and their viewpoint must have been widely shared, since similar autonomous reforms to those they formulated had already been introduced by other schismatic Christian communities in Lombardy, Croatia, Dalmatia, Thrace, Hungary and Bulgaria. By all accounts this sense of revulsion was fully justified. Repeatedly, during a 600 year period from 900-1500 CE, popes, cardinals and their acolytes had made a mockery of their office and sacred trust through their flagrant and decadent pursuit of self gratification. Venality was paramount, with positions of power and privilege within the church hierarchy being traded for money, or else passed to relatives. At one stage, even the papal succession was being sold on as if it were just another indulgence or dispensation. Sexual depravity was rife, with princes of the church keeping mistresses of both sexes and all ages, as well as raising their own families. Ostentation and extravagance were trumpeted in a blaze of finery, jewellery, palaces and possessions. The sink of iniquity was plumbed by Pope John the Twelfth who was brought to trial in the 10th century for perjury, simony, sacrilege, adultery, incest, murder, and for turning the church of St. John Lateran into a brothel (KP02p61).

The Vatican's fall from grace can be attributed to, and was commensurate with, the despotic control which the mediaeval church exercised over secular affairs throughout Europe. This unfettered papal power reached its zenith in 1215 when, through endorsement by the Fourth Lateran Council, the Pope claimed the absolute right to appoint and dismiss Christian monarchs, only allowing them to rule, or even to marry, with his express approval. As his vassals, secular heads of state had no choice but to obey any decisions he made, with especial reference to the need to stamp out heresy, in default of which a hapless sovereign would find himself summarily replaced in office by a more compliant aspirant (OZ61p177). Running what was effectively an Europe-wide theocracy, the church was all dominant in legal affairs, shaping laws in its own image and to its own advantage, and maintaining its own system of courts, prisons, informers and inquisitors, all dedicated to the suppression of any form of opposition or dissent. Teams of vigilantes were empowered to carry out systematic searches of communities in order to root out heretics from their homes, and denunciation of neighbour by neighbour led to slanted trials, often accompanied by torture, which resulted in almost inevitable conviction. Punishment was merciless, even contrite victims being flogged or imprisoned, whilst the unrepentant were burnt at the stake.

Catharism's apostasy led to the ecclesiastical secession of the Languedoc, a large area of southwest France lying between the Rhone

326

river and the Spanish border, whose inhabitants spoke their own language, the langue d'oc ("western tongue"), and whose main cities were Toulouse, Carcassonne and Narbonne. Cathars elected their own pope and bishops, and their field work was carried out by pairs of peripatetic clerics ("perfecti") who were also skilled in social welfare and medical matters. Perfecti, so called because they had renounced the carnal world to attain ultimate enlightenment, wore long hair and black robes, surrendered all their possessions to their community and devoted their lives to preaching, prayer and the relief of the destitute and sick. There were no churches, but suitable local communal houses were used for religious assemblies and as hospitals, schools and monasteries. The Lord's own was the only prayer said, and for both this and all Bible readings the local language was used. Cathars were pacifists and vegetarians, and instead of punishing sins, remitted them in assembly with subsequent re-education of the sinner.

Given the concentration of power in one man's hands, and the readiness with which that potentate was prepared to inflict the death penalty on dissidents, it is easy to see why His Holiness Pope Innocent the Third resorted to genocide in his dealings with those who defied him in southwest France. In signing a Papal Bull of Anathema, and issuing a call to arms against the Cathars, he knew that the nobles of northern France would seize the opportunity he was giving them to confiscate the estates of their southern counterparts, and that the French king would undoubtedly relish the prospect of extending his hegemony as far south as the shores of the Mediterranean. Although he would not have dared to declare a crusade against eastern orthodox Christians who had broken faith with him, the Languedoc was a softer target.

Pressure on prospective participants to join the crusade was intense. Absolution of all sins and the granting of extensive indulgences were the immediate reward for those who complied, and those who refused to do so could be punished in any one of three ways. The penalty of interdiction excluded a man from church, as a result of which he would be socially ostracised. Alternatively, he could be excommunicated which would lead to him becoming commercially ostracised and thereby destitute. The most dreaded form of papal opprobrium was, however, anathematisation which, like the Islamic fatwah, called for the condemned man's assassination by anyone of the true faith, a form of homicide both required and blessed by the Supreme Pontiff.

The tinder box was set alight when the Pope's emissary visited the schismatic and vacillatory Count Raymond the Sixth of Toulouse to excommunicate him, and was duly slain on his way back to Rome by one of Raymond's knights. The Vatican needed no further pretext, and prepared Europe for war. In the summer of 1209, massed ranks of crusading cavalry and footsoldiers drawn from many Christian countries converged on Lyons and descended the valley of the Rhone. The pope invested overall control of the campaign in Arnaud Amauric, the Cistercian Abbot of Citeaux, and under him detachments of the armies were both commanded and led by warrior clerics, who combined their ecclesiastical duties with the barbaric savagery of warfare when this was called for. At various times during the campaign, the tally of these episcopal butchers included the Archbishops of Bordeaux, Rouen, Bourges and Narbonne, and the Bishops of Limoges, Cahors, Bazas, Agen, Beauvais, Chartres, Clermont and Laon. Although the church forbade the spilling of blood, which excluded the use of the sword or lance, the knight bishop fulfilled his annihilatory duties by flourishing a mace, a heavy metal cudgel, which flattened his opponent's head instead of exsanguinating him. The French king sent his son, heir to the French throne, and later to become St. Louis for his crusading efforts, together with twelve more bishops, thirty counts, 600 knights and 10 thousand archers (OZ61p202).

At the start of hostilities, the Cathars received support from an aragonese army under their monarch Peter the Second, but when the latter was slain at the battle of Muret in 1213, Spanish involvement evaporated, leaving the Languedoc to its now inevitable fate.

Inexorably and piecemeal, catharist strongholds were surrounded and sacked, often with the extermination of all inhabitants, but at the very least with the burning at the stake of all perfecti and senior catharist ecclesiastics. The first important town to be overrun was Beziers, at the gates of which Abbot Amauric issued express orders that all within should be killed, whether or not they were Catholics, since "God would recognise his own". When the butchery was finally at an end, the Abbot was able to satisfy the Pope that the campaign had achieved its first significant victory. In his dispatch Amauric wrote: "Today, your holiness, 20 thousand heretics were put to the sword, regardless of rank, age or sex" (WKP08). The next citadel to be expunged was Carcassonne, following which Bram was stormed and taken, after putting up a strong resistance, for which the entire garrison had their eyes put out and their upper lips cut away as a deterrent to others. Mass executions followed after Minerve, the Chateau de Thermes, Lavaur, Casses, Le Bessede, Castelnaudry, Moissac and other strongpoints had been taken. Simon de Montfort, who had by now taken over leadership of the crusading army, played an active role in the mass executions, and the zealot preacher St. Dominic made inflammatory and inquisitorial contributions for which he was later canonised. It is sad to note that even St. Thomas Aquinas gave auto de fe burnings his stamp of approval.

With the loss of their lowland settlements the Cathars were forced to retreat to the fastness of the several fortresses which they had constructed on Pyrennean summits. The last of these to hold out was Montsegur, where, in 1244, 100 beleagured defenders were confronted by a host numbering many thousand. After a prolonged and desperate resistance the scales were tipped against the entrapped by the use of a seige engine constructed by the good Bishop Durand of Albi (OZ61p202). Massacre ensued, and French catharist humanitarianism was consigned to the dustbin of history. Visitors to Albi museum can still see a rack which was used to torture those accused of heresy into confession. The belligerence of mediaeval bishops is still symbolically commemorated on the chess board.

After the signal failure of the crusades, the Pope's appetite for warmongering waned, as did the willingness of European monarchs to support it, and new threats to theocratic absolutism within the church emerged which were to set the future pattern of christendom. The joint influence of John Calvin and Martin Luther, both law students turned church reformers, triggered a revulsion against the decadence of which the church hierarchy of the time was guilty, and brought about the establishment of strong reform churches in North Germany, Scandinavia, Switzerland, Holland and Scotland. Whilst Italy and Spain remained staunchly catholic, and England under Henry the Eighth dissociated itself altogether from the Papacy, the Catholics and hugenot protestants of France spent much of the 16th century slugging it out in a series of nine wars of religion to try and gain overall supremacy. In 1572, on St. Bartholomew's day, the pre-arranged assassination of three thousand protestant nobles was carried out on the occasion of their attendance at a royal wedding in Paris, and further bloodshed extended nationwide to encompass an estimated 50 thousand victims (KGC99p425). Many Hugenots took refuge abroad, but hostilities continued until the French protestant King Henry the Fourth re-embraced Catholicism so as to restore national unity. In more recent times, eighty years of Irish "troubles" have been fuelled by the catholic protestant divide, claiming three thousand lives.

(Sources Reviewed: HB72, HE89, JEF29, KGC99, KP02, OZ61, RSJ90, SAC49, SJ78)

CHAPTER 26

DIVINE WARMONGERING IN ISLAM

When compulsive prejudice reaches white heat intensity, those who harbour it give vent to their crippling emotional overburden by projecting it onto their fellow creatures. Although the outlook of a rigidly opinionated individual is characteristically the product of influences exerted during the third human nurtural phase, the emotional overdrive required to exacerbate prejudice to the point at which it is expressed as an act of violence is the result of first or second nurtural phase malconditioning. We saw in chapter 13 how true this was of dictators, but it is equally true of those who commit atrocities against the state.

The epithet "terrorist" was originally coined to fit Robespierre, whose overcompensatory use of the Guillotine to protect the ideals of the French revolution was only terminated by his own decapitation. Nowadays the term is no longer applied to leaders who use terror in order to oppress their own citizens, but is reserved for those who commit acts of violence against the state and its authorised agents. Here again, a distinction must be made between the "freedom fighter" who embodies the massed support of a downtrodden population, and the individual who antagonises both the general public and its government by committing vindictive atrocities whose only potential is to create fear, and thereby exert political pressure.

In Islamic societies the second nurtural phase is very largely the responsibility of faith schools where teachers traditionally use various forms of physical chastisement to enforce both discipline and memorisation in children from the age of six upwards. Clandestine camera footage has revealed the aura of fear and extreme religious xenophobia in which lessons are often conducted, and some childrens' textbooks have been reported to include details of brutal Shari'a punishments (TVC4:11:02:13, BBCT1:10:11:22, www.ednafernandes.com, DMN:09:07:02). Inevitably such methodology breeds emotionally charged bigotry.

It is impossible to understand the atavistic behaviour of Islamic Fundamentalism, nor what it is that this subcult attempts to recreate and why, without recourse to the essentials of Islamic history. The measure of western ignorance of this historical background was epitomised by George W Bush when he described his assault on Al Qaeda as a crusade - a ploy which was inept on two counts. In the first place, one holy war is as unholy as another. Then again, the Palestine crusades ended in ignominious failure at the hands of Saladin. The President had handed his antagonists a propaganda victory.

The atrocities committed by Al Qaeda and its affiliates are, of course, strategically futile. What purports to be a coordinated military campaign of conquest to create a global Muslim hegemony ruled by a Caliph is, in fact, a series of sporadic acts of terrorism which victimise the individual, but have no prospect of suborning the western world nor its institutions. Far from easing Islamism towards world wide acceptance, these acts cause it to be alienated and ostracised. Islamic Fundamentalism seeks to identify itself with the ethos and undoubted success of early Mohammedanism, but the time for mass conversion by means of conquest has long since passed. So too, has the barbarous phase in human history when draconian punishments were considered justifiable.

There Are Four Main Phases of Islamic History:

The 7th century CE: Unification of the peoples of the Arabian peninsula and their acceptance of Mohammed as leader, divine messenger and propounder of Islam.

The 7th - 11th centuries CE: Jihadist expansion of the Arabic empire throughout the Middle East and beyond, under the rule of Caliphs - religio-politico-military rulers in linear succession to Mohammed who were charged with perpetuating his principles. Shari'a law was imposed, but within the empire non-believers were tolerated, albeit as second class citizens (Dhimmis).

The 11th century onwards: Break up of the Arabic empire, with former provinces becoming autonomous under the secular leadership of Sultans.

The 20th -21st centuries: Whilst peaceful co-existence obtains between religion and politics in most of the Islamic world, fanatical elements view market driven modernism as a threat to the time honoured Islamic ethos, and embark on a campaign of atrocity by way of protest against change.

Mohammed was born in around 570 CE into the Qurash, one of the nomadic warlike tribes whose mobility enabled them to live very largely by plunder and cattle rustling. The Arabian peninsula was then, and still is, predominantly barren other than for the occasional oasis, fertile lands being present only at the extreme north and south. Before Mohammed, the tribes were essentially polytheistic, though Jews and Christians were to be found in more settled areas around the coasts. Trade routes between the Mediterranean and the Indian ocean crossed the peninsula, as did traffic in locally produced silver, leather and frankincense. Arabic was the peninsula's common language.

Mohammed was multitalented, with careers as an able businessman, politician, magistrate, army commander and religious leader. The best known source of his life history is that compiled by the 8th century Ibn Ishaq (CM96p12). Reportedly claiming descent from Ishmael, Abraham's illegitimate son and Isaac's half brother, Mohammed became a prophet at the age of 40 when the Angel Gabriel visited him to impart successive instalments of the Islamic scriptures, the Qur'an, together with an ordinance as God's messenger to unite and convert the Arabs. From then onwards until his death at the age of 60 in 632, he developed a straightforward system of rituals involving vows, washing, morning and evening prayers (Su11s10v114 and Su17s9v78), diet, sacrifice, charity, fasting and pilgrimage. These were combined with rules of moral conduct dealing with murder, theft, adultery, fornication, infanticide, marriage, divorce, slavery, usury, intoxicants, inheritance and women's decorum.

Mohammed referred to himself as unlettered (Su7,s20,v158). His teachings were transmitted orally until written down from memory by a plurality of followers after his death. A more tenuous supplementary collection of his reputed sayings was collated as Hadiths, whose accuracy has been disputed by some Islamic scholars (LB93p32, and CM96p23). In subsequent years a panel of Islamic jurists codified and accentuated Mohammed's principles in the form of Shari'a ethical, customary and civic law (CM96p23, HA02p114). The new juristic code introduced much more stringent provisions for conduct than had previously existed. For instance, whereas the Qur'an advocates flogging as the punishment for female adultery ("a hundred stripes" Su24,s1,v2), the juristic code specifies stoning to death. With the passage of time there has been further elaboration of the Qur'an's guiding principles, and study of ancient administrative parchments, together with non-Arabic records which predated the crystallisation of later Muslim tradition, enables us to understand the extent to which this occurred (CM96p70). Exaggerative overdevelopment of the principles reached its extreme at the hands of the Taleban regime in

Afghanistan in the late 20th century, which made the death penalty a mandatory punishment for apostasy, blasphemy, or the attempt to convert a Muslim to another faith, and which proscribed female employment, games, theatres, cinemas, bars, music, photography, kite flying, the shaving of facial hair and the wearing of short trousers - all these in addition to the usual strictures of the Shari'a (DTN:01:08:07). Madrassas - Muslim religious schools - of which 15 thousand exist in Southern Asia, teach the Qur'an by rote and forbid newspapers and television (TFTN:01:11:18).

Caravan routes crossed Arabia and linked the south of that country with the Mediterranean and the Indian Ocean, giving rise to permanent settlements in their path, such as Mecca which became one of Mohammed's bases for the development of trade. Hitherto, tariffs had been charged piecemeal for the safe passage of caravans wending their way through a multiplicity of skeikdoms, and there was a clear need to replace this practice with a pan Arabic system of coordination and control. Traditionally, tribal sheiks were each elected by a consortium of their elders. Observing the unifying influence which monotheism had on the Jewish and Christian communities, Mohammed dispensed with the partisanship of tribal deities and replaced it with Islam, acknowledging himself as God's spokesperson, and thereby supreme sheik over the Umma - the community of believers in the new doctrine (LB93p86). Mohammed's initial appeal was to the lower classes, and as his proposals proved contentious to the upper classes and Jews he turned to force of arms to impose and spread his new discipline throughout the peninsula. After a series of initial reverses his ragged army slowly began to make progress, and the negotiated conversion of the Bedouin proved a turning point. By the time of his death his organisational flair had created both a unified nation and a new religion.

Mohammed's legacy of military training and inspirational religious zeal left Arabia with a standing army whose superior mobility, armament and tactics enabled the new nation, overpopulated and land hungry as it was, to expand beyond its borders. To the north of the peninsula lay fertile territories whose defence by Persia and Byzantium had been seriously weakened by the wars between these two superpowers, the latest of which from 602-628 had brought both the Persian and Byzantine empires to their knees. Arabic armies moved in to fill the void in power, and conquest of Palestine, Syria, Iraq and Egypt was followed by the occupation of Persia itself. Ultimately, Muslim belligerence would also subdue what had been left of the Byzantine empire, North Africa and most of Spain.

At its zenith, the Arabic empire was able to dominate the Mediterranean and east-west trade. Its commercial tentacles not only crossed Europe and Africa, but reached India, China, the East Indies, Scandinavia and Russia. Its cultural impact bridged the gap between classical antiquity and the Renaissance, strongly influencing architecture, art, poetry, mathematics, astronomy, medicine, philosophy, music, agriculture and manufacture.

The Islamic empire depended heavily upon the institution of slavery. Large numbers of slaves were imported from Asia, Europe, and Africa by way of trade, or, after conquest, as captives and tribute. Children of slaves automatically inherited slave status. Slaves were used for construction and agriculture, they manned the galleys, and selected slaves were trained for military service as members of an elite caste, which at one point dominated affairs of state as the Mamluks (LB93p159).

Although the Qur'an hints that Jews and Christians would fare better than pagans on judgement day, since they believed in a single God and in the hereafter (Su2s8v62), Mohammed is supposed to have called for the expulsion of both from the Peninsula as he lay on his deathbed (CM96p23). By contrast, the Arabic Empire's newly conquered territories benefited from a more liberal attitude towards non-believers. It was no longer politic to "slay pagans wherever ye find them" if they were needed to serve their overlords, and a three tier society developed - Arabic speaking Muslims of any race who constituted the upper classes, non-believers (Dhimmis) who, although second class citizens, had property rights and religious freedom, and, at the lowest level, slaves (HA02p117, LB93p92).

Islam was, and for many still is, a religion which idealises the warrior and supports military conquest. Once the Mullahs decree that a conflict is ordained by God, a Muslim has no option but to fight, and, if necessary, die a martyr. In war those who fought Mohammed fought Allah, and initially no prisoners were taken. But when the enemy sued for peace, Mohammed negotiated. According to the Qur'an, this is what he himself had to say on the matter. "It is not fitting that a prophet......should have prisoners of war until he hath thoroughly subdued the land" (Su8,s7,v61). And, again, "The punishment of those who wage war against Allah and his Messenger ......is execution or crucifixion; or the cutting off of hands and feet from opposite sides" (Su5,s5,v32), "but if the enemy incline towards peace, do thou (also) incline towards peace" (Su8,s7,v61).

Mohammed proselytised with the sword, and his advice to his followers was unequivocal. "When ye meet the unbelievers (in fight) smite at their necks; at length when ye have thoroughly subdued them bind a bond firmly on them; thereafter (is the time for) either generosity or ransom; until the war lays down its burdens" (Su47,s1,v4). "Fight and slay the pagans wherever ye find them, seize them, beleaguer them, and lay in wait for them in every stratagem (of war), but if they repent and establish regular prayers and practise regular charity, then open the way for them: for Allah is oft forgiving, Most Merciful" (Su9,s1,v5). "Those who believe fight in the cause of Allah, and those who reject faith fight in the cause of evil: so fight ye against the friends of Satan" (Su4,s10,v76). "It is He who has sent His Messenger with guidance and the Religion of Truth, to proclaim it over all religions" (Su48,s4,v28).

Islam, its Derivation and its Legacy

Islam is by many centuries the youngest of the three principal monotheistic religions, and the Qur'an draws heavily upon Hebrew and Christian texts with which Mohammed must have been well acquainted. The Qur'an repeatedly refers to biblical luminaries such as Adam, Noah, Abraham, Moses, Solomon, Jacob, Isaac, David and Jesus, and places Mohammed as both the latest and the last of the prophets. Although Jesus is regarded as incontrovertibly human, Su3,s5,v47 makes reference to (his) immaculate conception.

Carrot and stick incentivisation, which promises paradise for good behaviour and threatens miscreants with hell, recurs throughout the Muslim text. Virtue is to be rewarded in the next life with sojourn in irrigated gardens containing luscious fruit and the provision of expensive clothing and ornaments. There are thinly veiled references to availability of youthful courtesans. Those who do not conform must expect to be consigned to the eternal fire. The Halal proscriptions in the use of meat are clearly Hebrewistic (Kosher), as are later practices, such as circumcision.

Islam, in company with most major religions, offers a system of ethics as part of a package which includes ritual, sublimation and the iconification of a supreme being. It is the world's fastest growing belief system, claiming 1.3 billion adherents. Its simple absolutism has a natural appeal to the uneducated as an anchor on the sea of life's troubles (CM96p16). It provides us with the clearest example today of the bipolarity which many religions exhibit at some phase of their development, during which the beneficial effects which they are capable of providing are counteracted, or eclipsed, by the xenophobia and license to commit certain types of atrocity which they engender.

Mohammed considered himself to be the last in line of God's prophets, and made no arrangements for his succession (LB60p45). As a consequence, Islam has always been riven by counterclaims between Sunnis and Shias. Sunnis claimed that theocratic authority had been passed down to them through Mohammed's widow, as Arabs they considered themselves socially superior, and they provided the army with cavalry. Shias claimed to have inherited theocratic authority through Mohammed's cousin, they originated from the lower classes and occupied territories, and were traditionally infantrymen. Over the centuries a number of other splinter groups have appeared. Sadly, almost without exception, schisms within Islam have fostered the bitterest and bloodiest of conflicts. Between 657 and 1200CE there were thirteen Muslim civil wars or dynastic revolts which contested the succession of absolute theocratic authority (KGC99p319).

In behavioural terms the radicalised Muslim falls into one of three categories. The footsoldiers of the regime have had their conditionable brains imprinted with the lust for Jihad, and their further commitment to the cause is incentivised by Mullah assurances that, should they die in battle, they will gain instantaneous admission to paradise, and that each heroic martyr will thereupon be able to deflower seventy two heavenly virgins of his choice. The license to commit violence and achieve sexual conquest has a natural appeal to testosterone driven young men. The clerics who malcondition these footsoldiers, and are sometimes themselves warlords, seek to enhance their power base and dominance ranking position. At the top of the organisational pyramid stands the overall strategist, the eminence grise who sacrifices his followers and their victims, but in doing so knows that there is no realistic prospect of overthrowing western civilisation or converting the world to Islamic Shari'a, and acts out of chronic malice - an aggressive trait found in the occasional rogue individual among all species of primate.

It is not possible to remove aggressive exhortations from the Qur'an, nor to expunge the militaristic tradition associated with the cult of Islam. The retrogressive dogma of religious fundamentalism can only be detoxified by far sighted secular reforms such as those which Mustafa Kemal Attaturk introduced at the end of the first world war in order to modernise the Turkish State, and for which his countrymen will always venerate him. Stripped of most of their political clout, religious leaders tend to become more benign, and the increased tolerance which Muslims showed towards non-believers in imperial times could then be replicated and bring peace to the world. It is, of course, ironic that the hammerhead methods of conditioning employed in madrassas are subsidised to a significant degree by western derived oil revenues.

The fact that love is blind is to its advantage, but the fact that faith is blind is to its detriment. Given enlightenment, the only good pagans need no longer be dead ones. In the final analysis, modernisation is irresistible and cannot be sacrificed on the altar of an outdated theocratic ideal. Islam should seek to perpetuate and enhance the enlightened and considerable cultural contribution it has made to humanity, rather than to attempt to recreate a phase in its history which was characterised by narrow, aggressive, and often barbaric self interest. Thus will it be judged by future generations.

(Sources Reviewed: BBCT1:10:11:22, CM96, DTN01:08:07, TFTN01:11:18, HA02, Humphrys J in DMN:04:07:02, The Holy Qur'an trans Ali, J, TVC4:11:02:13, KJC99, LB93, www.ednafernandes.com).

CHAPTER 27

"PATRIOTISM IS THE LAST REFUGE OF A SCOUNDREL"
(Samuel Johnson)

NATIONALISM IN THE MODERN WORLD

What is a nation state, and how have human behaviour patterns shaped it? Loose definitions abound and most are unhelpful. For instance, the suggestion that the Iroquois of North America constitute a nation is absurd, since these amerindians are co-occupants of states which are themselves subdivisions of a much larger national unit - the USA. Moreover, when a subset of the global population aspires to nationhood, it is generally understood to be striving for total autonomy and self determination, in default of which it would remain a dependent and subject province. The sovereign nation state as we know it is one which arrogates to itself the absolute control of its armed forces, its political process, laws, resources, domestic administration and foreign affairs.

Samuel Johnson's intemperate view of patriotism was very much in tune with Albert Einstein's dictum a century later which surmised that nationalism was, rather like measles, a disease of infancy against which adults should prove themselves immune. The stance taken by sages such as these two ran provocatively counter to the cultural legacies and attitudes handed down from feudal times and resonated by nearly all school history books. Nonetheless, events have proved the sages right. We have seen in preceding chapters that rule-of-thumb ideologies such as organised religious movements, and pseudo religions of which fascism and communism are well known examples, have actively promoted wars and given them their raison d'etre, but blind credo has not, by any means, been the exclusive cause of armed conflict. Men are perfectly capable of banding together in self defined units to commit aggressive acts, given a leader, a symbolic battle standard and a few slogans. They have done so persistently throughout history and no doubt did so just as often before records began.

When man begins to gain fresh insight into his behaviour he finds new words to grapple with it. "Chauvinism" is the eponymous term which was coined to describe a superiority complex that prompts discrimination and bellicosity against those of a different social grouping. Although the word was originally harnessed for use in a nationalistic setting, its connotation has since been extended to denote any form of bigoted arrogance which may be exhibited in relation to race, gender, political party or creed. Nicholas Chauvin was reputedly a soldier serving in Napoleon's Grande Armee who was renowned for his vociferous patriotism, despite the maiming and disfigurement which seventeen battle wounds had inflicted upon him. As Napoleon's popularity faded, Vaudeville made Chauvin the butt of satire, much as Cervantes had done when he used Don Quihote as a parody of elitist Spanish militarism following the reconquest. The term "Jingoism" derives from a British popular song of the first world war which included the phrase "We don't want to fight them, but by jingo if we do".

Nationalism, like other forms of partisan aggregation, differentiates and divides populations from each other, so that they become more conscious of the dissimilarities which exist between them than of the attributes which they share. As a result, the herd bond, which is always stronger than the species bond, eclipses the latter and the seeds of rivalry, antagonism and conflict are sown. The propensity for unprovoked interherd conflict was inherited from an ape-like progenitor which we share with the chimpanzee, and it is perpetuated by the adrenergic excitement of confrontation and risk taking. Because the trait is an expression of offensive aggression, which in this context is refocused onto conspecifics, it is predominantly exhibited in humans by young males between the age of puberty at 15 years, when testosterone rises to adult levels, and the age of 25 years when intellectual maturity is attained. The ensuing wastage of young male lives whether in chimpanzees or in human warfare is devitalising for both the herd and the species. Although it may be argued that in the past the grindstone of interherd attrition preferentially selected more redoubtable and resilient specimens of protoman who would make better hunters and defenders against big cats and bears, autospecific destruction is neither optimal nor necessary for the evolution of a species. We are, in effect, being confronted with a behaviour pattern analogous to the evolutionary errors which cause lemmings to commit mass suicide, or a pod of whales to beach itself.

For humanity, the net genetic outcome has been to accentuate aggressive attributes at the expense of others which would ultimately have proved more useful and beneficial to a well organised community. To use an analogy, we have produced many more yobs and football hooligans who clash with each other outside the stadium, than the handful of professional football players within it whose refined skills give the game its true value. The element of exhilaration provided by nationalistic aggression was astutely highlighted by a Northern Ireland policeman during the 2010 disturbances when he described his fellow countrymen as indulging in "recreational" rioting.

The concept of nationalism clearly derives from the herd instinct and herd bond, and manifests as a community's urge to ring fence itself, the better to parry interherd attack and to preserve within its borders all types of resource which are needed for survival. The larger a discrete politico-military community is, the less vulnerable it will be to predation, and the more likely it is to be self sufficient. Thus the creation of a nation state will always involve an expansion of territorial bounds far beyond those of a tribal area, in order that the necessary critical mass of population can be assembled. Demarcation of the boundary lines of the new larger community unit will also be influenced by other aggregative factors such as race, religion and language, or by history and geography. Within the community, bonds are formed with those perceived to share loyalty to the common interest, and dissidents are alienated. After the graeco-turkish war of 1922, the Turks expelled one million Greeks and the Greeks expelled half a million Turks (BBCT2;08:02:11), and after the partition of India following the end of British colonial rule, mass migrations of Muslims towards Pakistan and Hindus towards India took place, during which a million souls lost their lives in partisan conflict. Given the tenacity of the herd instinct and the need to be recognised as an ally, it is easy to see why nationalist jingoism and slogans embed themselves so readily in the conditionable brain, where they foster slanted judgements and compulsive behaviour patterns. The tendency that patriotism has both to inspire and justify aggression closely parallels the inspiration and justification which theocratic injunctions provide for holy war.

Typically, the nation state is the end product of three phases of interherd warfare. Prior to feudalism, the basic politico-military unit was the tribe. Rival tribal warlords fought each other for supremacy until all were eclipsed except one and a kingdom was formed. Rival kings fought each other for booty, enslavement, rapine and the occupation of each others' territory until an empire was created. Finally, imperial provinces took to arms and rebelled against their oppressors in order to achieve self determination. Much less commonly, nationhood has been attained by the consensual amalgamation of small neighbouring states (e.g. Germany). It is ironic to note that the nation state is not only the product of interherd warfare, but gives rise to it.

Unless democratisation has been unusually prompt, all aspects of public life in a fledgling nation state will be under the central control of an absolute ruler or oligarchy, but antagonism is not yet at an end. As the new communal unit struggles to attain socio-political self definition, theocratic supremacy, if it is present, must still be renounced, (as characterised by developments in Scandinavia, England and Turkey), tyrants or monarchs have to be deposed or otherwise rendered powerless (as, for instance, occurred in France, England and Russia), and civil wars will still be waged where internal differences cannot otherwise be resolved (as was seen in America, Spain, France and Russia). Ultimately, plebiscite-mediated majority rule is adopted (Ancient Greece and the modern republic), putting an end to armed factional conflict within state borders, although not, alas, beyond them.

Once a nation state has been established, it proceeds to consolidate itself by building a nationalistic ethos. National heroes are identified and iconified, legends are created, history rewritten, national rites, flags, anthems, folk music, folk dance, costumes and traditions are promoted, and national theatres, museums and educational establishments are built. Just as patriotism was employed to give birth to the new nation, so it is used to coerce the new nationals into accepting the laws, policies, policing and taxes required to run it. Excepting the parts played by language and religion, a common culture is much more the result of nationhood than the cause of it.

As we look back over the inveterate warmongering which has been such a characteristic feature of European, Asian and African history during the past three millennia, it is clear that nationalism has repeatedly served to incendiarise and aggrandise the interherd aggression whose propensity man inherited from the proto ape. But the barriers within which he defensively demarcated the boundaries of his nation state are finally beginning to crumble, as did the curtain walls of stone fortresses when technology outdated them. The inhibitory effect exerted upon nuclear aggression by the fear of retaliation has curbed interherd warfare between the larger power blocks, and has allowed the fragmentation of some nation states whose size rendered them too cumbersome, or whose disparate populations made it impracticable, for them to respond to local administrative needs (as occurred in the USSR, Jugoslavia and Czechoslovakia). Border controls are slowly being relaxed amongst the states of South America and among those of the European Union, and many nation states have introduced reforms which decentralise power, devolving it to smaller provincial political entities. Inexorably, we are moving towards the realisation that global decisions can only be made by global mandate and that, in the end, representation through the committee of a global executive will have to be made on a per head of population basis rather than one in keeping with national identity.

There is, of course, some way to go before nationalism can be dead and buried. States still exist, particularly in Africa, in which the maturation process of self definition has still to occur, with the need to abolish both tyranny and civil war high on the agenda. In essence, national prejudice is no different from racial or religious prejudice, and all are discriminatory. Is it too soon to be thinking of equal rights and fair shares for everyone living on the planet, of a politico-military superstructure which in effect would be a pan global republic within which Rousseau's Social Contract and the French revolutionary ideals of liberte, egalite and fraternite can be extended to everyone?

Three potent forms of communal bigotry have always impeded global integration - racial discrimination, religious intolerance and nationalistic xenophobia. Increasingly, democracy is understood to be the guiding principle by which we should lead our lives, and its spread confers both the freedom and the responsibility upon each citizen to reappraise the difficulties posed by the barriers which still exist between communities. As well as appointing a biracial politician of above average intelligence to the White House, the US electorate of November 2008 demonstrated its determination to expunge the last vestige of its racial discrimination. Obama's historic victory also appears to have had an exemplary effect world wide, further diminishing inter racial antagonism, save where this is perpetuated by religious difference. As long as a belief system preaches its exclusivity it will cause disruption, and the most important contribution a religious cult can make to world peace is to acknowledge all other belief systems as exact co-equals. It is only the ecclesiastic's desire to retain autocracy that prevents him from being more tolerant of competitors. Nationalism can now be seen as a lesser obstacle, since it is already being eroded by the commercial interdependence which exists between communities, and because of the uptake of the English language as a common norm. The embers of nationalism will eventually be limited to sporting contests where the opportunity to excel is open to all on strictly equal terms. Preferment will then only be given to those individuals or teams whose skills and talents earn it, regardless of their race, religion or place of birth. The arts also have a special role is fostering the concept of co-equality, since the pleasure derived from traditional costume, music, dance, fine art, architecture and film crosses all boundaries, and can be shared by everyone reciprocally. It is here that the true significance of global citizenship first takes root in the immature mind, a broadening of outlook which the wise parent would do well to facilitate both by acting as a role model and, where possible, by providing for foreign travel and cultural exchange.

(Sources Reviewed: causesofwwii.wordpress.com, CJ97, GE97, KE93, SAD10, SEP01, WKP08, www.historyonthenet.com/WW1/causes.htm)

CHAPTER 28

NOT IN UTOPIA.... BUT IN THE WORLD.... WE FIND HAPPINESS.... OR NOT AT ALL

(William Wordsworth 1770-1850 In The Prelude)

THE OPTIMISATION OF BEHAVIOUR

In our attempts to understand our existence we try to analyse its process which is biological, and its progress which is both technological and sociological. Impeded by our ignorance of the ultimate purpose and end point of our presence on the planet, we cannot calibrate our progress as a species in absolute terms, and must instead view it in terms of relative improvement directed towards securing "the greatest good for the greatest number of individuals". Using this yardstick we are forced to conclude that although advances in technology have been, and continue to be, rapid and far reaching, our post simian behavioural development has been dilatory, and blemished by the incorporation of idiosynchratically perverse and sometimes overtly counterproductive traits.

What is it then that makes us "tick"? In 2010 the results of a huge survey involving 360,000 respondents scattered across 132 different countries showed that happiness and a sense of life's fulfilment are first and foremost the products of the support of family and friends, the use of one's faculties, and the respect of the society in which one lives, all of which far outweighed income in their importance (DE10). If the secret of human happiness is predominantly a sociological one, then why have further developments and improvements in this field fallen so far behind those which have enhanced technology and science?

Happiness and life's fulfilment are impaired or annulled by all those many unsolved problems with which humanity has to contend, (these are summarised in table 28.1), and it is chastening to discover when we analyse them that, with the exception of natural disasters, disease and sporadic genetic deformities, all human tribulations are either directly or inadvertently self inflicted. Where the causes of our problems lie within us, then so must do the solutions to them, but the behavioural changes which are required can only be effectively formulated and introduced if they are based on an accurately and widely appreciated understanding of the way human motivation operates. These changes must, of course, come voluntarily from within us. Biotechnology has nothing to offer in this context - it cannot enlarge nor rewire our brain, selective human breeding policies are repugnant to us, and so are recombinant "designer baby" programmes where there is any risk of unforeseen maldevelopment or repersonalisation. Darwinian progression cannot upgrade our conduct, since human evolution has effectively ceased. All in all we will always have to make do with the number of neurones we already have as a species, but critically we must learn to deploy them to their optimal advantage.

It is particularly appropriate that we should give these enhancing sociological measures their due consideration as we approach a new age of enlightenment which will render their implementation feasible. The burgeoning influences of globalisation, democratisation and fledgling secularisation have created a milieu in which rational practicality is increasingly seen as the proven key to human concordance and contentment. But epiphany in social affairs is seldom instantaneous - only in exceptional circumstances can behavioural reform be introduced within a generation. Reorientation requires an open mind and an accurate and succinct working knowledge of the fundamentals of behavioural science such as this book provides. In this, our final chapter, we take a "bird's eye view" of the way in which behavioural data relevant to humanity's outstanding problems can be effectively organised in a way which will support their practical application.

Life-wise Logic is the Key to Responsible Global Citizenship

Logic, also known as common sense, is critically dependent upon the prior acquisition of knowledge, and our overall field of enquiry has three major components. Put in their simplest terms, these are a clear comprehension of human behaviour and its derivation, an understanding of the failings of human nurture and their remedies, and an awareness of the global problems for which we all bear joint responsibility. In order to link the first two of these prerequisites with the rationalised management of their consequences, let us briefly summarise what we have learned about them in previous chapters.

Although human nurture occurs in three sequential phases, as it does in other primates, it differs in being predominantly parent centric throughout, and in being much more prolonged. Developmental damage, which may be brought about by anachronistic parental malconditioning meted out during the first and second phases, distorts any of the seven fundamental primate traits, and subsequently manifests as addictions, compulsive possessiveness, tyranny, sexual perversions and atrocities, delinquency or corruption. The less the human child's exposure to the reciprocating influence of the peer group during the second phase, the more difficulty it will experience in socialising and integrating in later life. In the third phase of nurture, adverse influences will cause individuals to develop compulsive prejudice, and although such an obsessional state may not necessarily have resulted from parental mismanagement, it will be aggravated if previous nurtural phases have already been malconditioned. It may then be expressed as violence.

Affectionate, disciplined, secure and encouraging maternalism is crucial, and must be given predominantly by a single carer who bonds closely with the child. Total institutionalisation of very young children causes developmental problems which may be severe, and even separation of them from their parents for most of the day and night has a noticeable effect upon them. In the Israeli Kibbutz programme, localised communes were set up in which specially trained nurses and teachers raised all children, the latter only being allowed parental access for three hours in the twenty four. Because parental input was almost entirely eclipsed by peer group influence, the system tended to produce mature social integrates with a high IQ, many of whom later became professionals and intellectuals, but who found it difficult to develop any emotional bonds, and seldom married within their own community. The conformist outlook which their upbringing had stamped upon Kibbutzim later became their trademark.

How can humans get the best of both worlds and combine protracted parental affectionate nurture with exposure to the controlled communality which teaches conformity, co-operation and social skills in a way that no other form of conditioning can? Many waged young mothers, especially those from middle class backgrounds who can afford to do so, already leave their babies and toddlers at crèches during the working day, whilst for these women nursery schools plug the gap between crèche and primary education. Of the many in-care studies conducted for the purpose of establishing whether such policies are developmentally detrimental, some have shown that an element of risk to verbal and general infant progress exists if a mother returns to work shortly after giving birth. For those who resume work within a year, outcomes are better if their weekly employment is limited to 30 hours. It is becoming increasingly clear that maternity leave should never be less than twelve months in duration. For all working women the quality of an infant's development will relate to the quality of the day care attention it received (WJ10, UNICEF08). The need for better first and second phase nurture is always greatest in so called "dysfunctional" families which may be unwaged or uniparental, for it is at this social level that most antisocial behaviour is generated. The argument in favour of state provided, state regulated pre-school day care establishments and generous domiciliary health worker support for these families is unassailable, and the cost per potentially antisocial pupil is a small fraction of the comparable cost of providing for an inmate of the ever burgeoning prison population. Incentivisation for parents to engage with such a system could be linked to family allowance and unemployment benefit. In the very worst cases, where there is gross dereliction of parenthood, fostering from birth may prove to be the only way in which extreme malconditioning can be avoided (NM: BBCT1: 09:09:06).

The need for state funded nurtural training classes at secondary school level, at first pregnancy antenatal classes, at adult evening classes, and as a module at university level has already been mentioned. The propagation of this important core data as a curriculum could be expanded by the use of discussion groups based on local social clubs and societies, television programmes and internet sites. A token for attendance at a commercially run course in the subject could be used as a wedding gift. Participation in state run classes could be incentivised by linking them with maternity and child benefit payments, and, when courts become involved, attendance should be made obligatory for wayward parents. The core curriculum and the use of nurtural discussion groups also provides us with the basis for the creation of a fraternity of open minded and electronically integrated global citizens. Recognition of proficiency in the acquisition of core knowledge could take the form of a Diploma in Child Nurture, or a Certificate of Enlightened Global Citizenship.

The window of opportunity for optimal assimilation of the core curriculum opens with puberty and closes with procreation. This interval shrinks markedly as one descend the socio-economic scale, with the result that dysfunctional families who are most in need of nurtural mentoring have the least time in which to obtain it. Perhaps a booklet on the subject should be handed out with the first prescription for oral contraception.

The third nurtural phase spans adolescence and the interval between the acquisitions of emotional and intellectual maturity. Malconditioning during this phase acts strongly upon the emotional brain and distorts the "personal equation" so that compulsive prejudices are engendered, notably those which discriminate on racial, class, religious, or nationalistic grounds. Culturally, we all carry excess baggage in our conditionable brains of which we need to be acutely aware, and which we must negate, or at least allow for, if we are to make impartial judgements, and bond with other races and nationalities on strictly equal terms. The imprinting which was thus imposed upon us during juvenility skews our perception of reality in favour of what we have been taught to believe, what we would prefer to believe, and the way we react to events, both emotionally and behaviourally. This composite package of fixed preconceptions, prejudgements, predilections and prejudices not only falsifies our interpretation of what is taking place around us, but tends to make us intolerant of anyone who does not share our views. Ingrained attitudes of mind are features which we recognise all too readily in others, but seldom question in ourselves because we have already accepted them as being beyond dispute. Those who don't believe they have a personal equation need only ask their children in order to be disillusioned. Doubts can also be dispelled if one asks oneself a few simple questions such as "do I favour one particular political party or creed?", "am I strongly patriotic?", or "would I object to my daughter marrying someone of a different class, race, nationality or faith?"

Parents share the third phase influence they exert with an adolescent's peer group and the community at large, a polyglot situation which often leads to discrepancy, confusion and controversy. During this phase an adolescent will examine any detectable compulsive prejudice in a parent and react to it emotionally with imitation, rejection or indifference. All these are expressions of the emergent need for self definition and self determination, and a skewed juvenile judgement may only be preventable if parents are able to demonstrate that they themselves are unequivocally open minded. The necessary foundation for such a stance, if it is to have long lasting credibility with both adolescents and parents, is for the latter to be able to show that they have reassessed and weeded out discrimination, inconsistency and irrationality in their own personal equations. Candid and pertinent self questioning has to be employed in order to do this, a procedure which some parents will find too invasive for comfort, but which will have a beneficial effect on the parent-adolescent relationship. A morphosis will thereby be set in train, as a result of which the status of fully authoritative parenthood is exchanged for a relationship in which parent and juvenile become partners in impartiality. A comparable effect is obtained when the two generations share a sporting activity.

If we are to take the probe of intimate self interrogation to its furthest logical extreme, it must be applied to what for many will be the most difficult of all obsessions to resolve, that of religious conviction. Since the defeat of Fascism and the abolition of Apartheid, and with the slow decline of Communism, rising and impartial educational standards in the west and part of the far east have already begun to pre-empt the acquisition of racial and nationalistic compulsive prejudice. If this trend continues, the only significant sources of ideological xenophobia, discord and conflict will be the monotheisms of middle eastern origin and their myriad splinter groups. Although, in time, greater enlightenment will significantly narrow the field from which obsessional thought originates, we cannot overlook the fact that half the world's inhabitants are still ostensibly supposed to occupy the middle ground between polytheism and atheism. All self proclaimed monotheists are faced with five doctrinal dilemmas, none of which can be resolved by deductive, transparent logic, and which should therefore be confronted as an inescapable step in the self examination process.

The Progenitor Dilemma:
If God created the universe, how was he himself created? (a cyclical impasse)

The Visualisation Dilemma:
Being invisible to humans, God's image is conjectural and thereby the subject of dispute. If, as the bible avers, humankind has been created in God's image, then God is much more likely to be female, since in primate terms the maternal instinct is much stronger than its paternal counterpart which in many species does not exist at all. CERN scientists have returned to elementary principles and are using the Hadron Collider to search for "god particles" as the source of the universe. The 500 BCE Greek philosopher Xenophanes opined that there was only one god, nature itself.

The Interaction Dilemma:
Does God answer prayers? Write down a wish list, pray for its fulfilment and check results

Dilemma of the Corruption of Sacred Texts:
The core sacred texts of Buddhism, Christianity and Islam were not written down during the lifetimes of those who inspired them, but were transmitted orally as legends, whose contents sometimes developed contradictions by the time they were inscribed, thus rendering them unreliable

The Dilemma of Unipolarity:
Courts of law and Parliaments expound contrasting viewpoints in order to cancel out exaggeration and emotional bias, and arrive at a balanced judgement. Cult religion only ever presents one sided arguments, and for a cult member to challenge them is to apostatise. As a result, there is serial fragmentation between believers.

Can We Edit Out The Mischief Bequeathed To Us In Our Genes?
Genetic defects causing misconduct are either sporadic with the production of mental illness and/or chronic malice, or are endemic manifesting as a testosterone fuelled taste for the excitement which "herd" based warfare provides. Until relatively recently we should also have needed to have included cannibalism in the latter category.

We have already examined the preventive and therapeutic problems associated with mental illness in chapter 20. Does the state have a role to play in supervising the management of genetic deformities which carry a serious risk of delinquency and criminality? Once offences have been committed, the criminal justice system assumes responsibility, but, for the sake of both perpetrator and victim, it would be highly desirable to be able to assess the risk of, and thereby prevent, the commission of those antisocial acts which are in reality manifestations of heritable and incurable mental deformity. Chromosomal analysis has now become such a sophisticated science that defence counsels are justifiably able to assert that a genetically programmed malefactor cannot be held responsible for his actions - but if the latter is not responsible, who is? Must we always wait for an outrage to be committed before we act, and who has the greater human right, the assailant or the assailed? Genetic "finger printing" would now allow many of these inherited traits to be identified, following which the same probationary system which currently waits for a man to open a criminal record, could then become involved in supervision before any damage has been done. The administrative machinery could very well resemble that used for registered child protection. Like other serious genetic deformities, chronic malice features in the controversy over eugenic pre-emption.

Addiction to the adrenaline rush of interherd warfare is always markedly strengthened by any compulsive prejudices which follow third phase nurtural malconditioning, an effect clearly demonstrable in the jingoistic and hyperbolic influences exerted by rule-of-thumb ideologies and nationalism. By the same token parental, peer group, national, and media mores acting synergistically can produce a strong antipathy towards armed combat, as we know from experiences of communities such as Switzerland, the Quaker movement and the Lepehas tribes of Sikkim. In the final analysis, aversion conditioning of the immature mind is the only realistic way in which war can be expunged from the human behavioural repertoire. A knowledge of the history of human behaviour plays a crucial part in this process.

Problems For Which The Global Community Bears Joint Responsibility

So far this book has been primarily concerned with human problems caused by malconditioning and genetic deformity in the individual. We should also recognise that there are global human problems for which we all bear joint responsibility, either because they have resulted from communal human ineptitude and/or because they could not be tackled effectively without pan global co-operation. All are major long term problems whose significant impact will be shared with us by future generations, and their resolution, in as much as this is possible, will require a degree of political and economic international integration not hitherto thought practicable. Let us briefly review what has to be done.

The four prime penalties of communal ineptitude are warfare (which previous chapters have already explored), environmental degradation and strain, overpopulation, and the inequitable distribution of resources. Let us now summarise the salient features of the latter three, all of which are interrelated, in order to be able to understand the behavioural changes and remedial measures required to tackle them.

Adverse climatic changes always added to man's difficulties, but those evidenced by history may well be dwarfed by the climatic upheaval he now threatens to bring upon himself. Whereas the global warming which thawed the last ice age around 11,000 BCE enabled man to cultivate his own food, stimulating the development of civilisation as we know it, the additional rise in temperature engendered by the past

250 years of industrialisation will spell disaster for humanity if it goes on unchecked. By 2050, if corrective measures are not taken, the carbon dioxide concentration in the atmosphere will have doubled since the mid 18th century, and by 2100 it will have trebled. The consequent changes would prove catastrophic, with melting of permafrost and loss of the polar and Greenland ice caps, elimination of rain forests, droughts, desertification, the occurrence of extreme weather patterns such as hurricanes and heat waves, failure of the Asian monsoon upon which half the earth's population depends, and the acidification of oceans with the death of crustaceans. Above all, rises of up to 60 metres in sea level would inundate most major capital cities and other low lying areas such as Southern Bangladesh and Florida. Since half the world's population lives near the edge of the sea, even a few metres rise in level would call for massive resettlement. In order to be able to bring global warming under control, technology needs to provide energy from wind, tide, solar and nuclear sources. Excess carbon dioxide has to be captured and sequestrated in geological reservoirs, and increased efficiency in energy use, particularly as regards automobiles, has to be imposed. Global agreement on carbon emission quotas is imperative, and new public attitudes towards consumerism, carbon dioxide limitation and the need for responsible global citizenship will be vital.

Overpopulation and the overexploitation of resources cause global environmental strain. In nature there is a close relationship between the adequacy of food and water, the incidence of disease, and population size. Humans revoke that balance inasmuch as in the developed world birth control is practised, and in poorer countries parents deliberately overbreed in response to prevalent high infant mortality rates. In impoverished societies most families cannot afford either birth control measures or schooling, pauper girls marry early, and populations may double their size with each generation. Ultimately, overbreeding, whether as the result of religious tenet or poverty, will have to be reined in. State control as imposed in China would prove unacceptable in most countries, and the problem has to be addressed as a matter of elective personal responsibility - a choice already made despite dogma in countries such as Italy and Ireland, as shown by their low birth rates. World wide state funded birth control clinics would appear inevitable.

The world population has increased tenfold to a figure of 6.6 Bn since the mid 18th century, and the UN forecasts a total of 9.2 Bn for the year 2050, with improved life expectancy accounting for some of the increase. The deleterious effects of overpopulation are both global and local. As the per capita demands made on the environment to provide for sustenance and well-being have increased tenfold since the mid 18th century, and over the same time the population has increased tenfold, global environmental strain is now a hundred times as great (SJ07RL3). The overexploitation of fossil fuels, fish stocks, rain forests and water supplies has reached a critical point beyond which further demands will cause exponential damage. The need to farm grain for biofuels now vies with the need to feed the world's starving millions, and global warming reduces the overall land surface area upon which food crops can be cultivated. In 2008, for the first time ever, as many people resided in towns as in the countryside. Local foci of overpopulation increase societal stress and aggressivity, and place demands upon the infrastructure with which it may not be able to comply. As a result, traffic congests, power failures occur, water supplies are interrupted, sewage and trash disposal fails, and health and emergency services may be overstretched.

Although the principal milestones of development are common to all emerging cultures, the rate at which these are reached varies considerably, and this gives rise to extreme discrepancies between the living standards of different communities at any one point in time (see also table 28.2). A billion souls in underdeveloped countries exist in extreme poverty and with insufficient food. Living standards depend upon the establishment of basic agricultural methodology, the exploitation of natural resources, and the development of technology, manufacture and trade. If even the most fundamental requirements upon which to found economic growth are lacking, impoverished societies cannot begin the process of self improvement. Richer countries have a moral obligation to help the poorest, not only by providing the aid with which to avert humanitarian disasters and kick-start economies, but also by removing their own protective tariffs and domestic subsidies, so that their poorest conspecifics can trade their way out of penury. The factors which most commonly obstruct the first steps towards development in primitive societies are drought, impoverished soil, the use of seed corn with a poor yield, and inferior or absent road and rail infrastructure. All these obstacles could be overcome by adequate investment at a putative cost which equates to less than 1% of the developed world's annual income (SJ07RL5). It is sad to have to record that in the past many of the promises of aid made by western countries have not been honoured.

The disequilibrium between population size and resource apportionment will prove particularly difficult to correct, since distribution has in the past been governed by consumerism, commercialism and national interest, all of which will now have to be curtailed. Resource allocation to each according to his need is also rendered more complex by fluctuations in population size, with that of countries such as India, China and the Philippines expanding rapidly whilst others regress. Unbridled consumerism is now a global phenomenon which creates spiralling levels of overall and individual demand. Since the second world war, most westerners have not only had access to everything needed to sustain a fulfilling and happy life, but have been swamped with a plethora of scarcely relevant consumer goods. In the extravagance of our throw away society we discard a third of all the food we prepare, spend obscene sums on cosmetics, pets and addiction, and are fast running out of the land fill sites needed to accommodate our detritus. Hitherto, consumerism has provided the impulse and rationale for western economic growth and has widened the gap which exists between poorer and richer countries. But the current rate of acceleration in commodity production and sales, which has led to a degree of environmental stress one hundred fold greater than before industrialisation, cannot be sustained. Living standards double with every decade in the west, but is there really a need for them to do so? Given food, clothing, shelter, healthcare, education, a vacation and a motor car, every other acquisition seems prodigal when we compare ourselves with the one billion who starve. Despite what the advertising industry implies, supernumery possessions do not equate with happiness. King Midas was a miserable man, but the mass rejection of his ethos will be much more difficult to achieve than the acceptance by the public of those immediate measures required to curb global warming. Global citizenship calls for a new attitude towards purchase, based on whether an article is needed, not simply on whether it can be afforded. Do we really have to dynamize consumer spending in order to vitalize a country's economy, even when many of the goods involved are manufactured abroad ? Policies moulded by government and supported by the media are critical in this regard. One of the many salutary lessons which the history of Nazi Germany taught us was that it is possible to bring about a complete reorientation of public opinion in the space of a few years if central authority is sufficiently resolute, acts with unanimity, and launches a concerted campaign of re-education to promote new values, incentives and initiatives. Not since the second world war has humanity been so much in need of strong leadership.

Problems Not Attributable To Humanity

Our survey of unresolved human problems closes with a synopsis of global emergencies for which man is not causally responsible, but to which humanitarianism demands that he responds as effectively as he can. The more adaptive and co-operative his behaviour becomes, the more successful he is in doing so.

Evolving man has always had to compete with other species in order to survive, but whereas big cats and bears once hunted him, he now dominates all other predators and the pathogenic microbe has taken their place as the greatest living threat to his safety. More than half the world's population have no access to healthcare and the developed countries have a global responsibility to produce vaccines and medication to tackle the pandemics which ravage the world - most notably AIDS, Tuberculosis and Malaria. Atypically, mankind cannot be absolved from blame for the first of these, since it is spread by promiscuity. HIV AIDS was discovered in 1984, and was initially propagated by male homosexuality. During the 15 years to 2005, the global number of HIV positives had quadrupled to reach 40 million, and in that year an estimated 2 million died from the disease. In 2005 in sub-Saharan Africa, all told, 6% of the population were infected, but this figure rose to 25% in countries such as Lesotho (BBCT104:07:03, DMN:06:07:02). By 2011, 60 million people had been infected, half of whom had died (BBCR4:11:06:04).

Tuberculosis was a western European export to the rest of the world 200 years ago, and by 1980 was out of control outside the western world. In 1993 the WHO declared tuberculosis to be a world emergency. Two billion individuals, representing one third of the world's population, are currently infected, and by 2050 the annual death rate is projected to be five million. 10% of sufferers die, whilst the remainder recover spontaneously, and Africa and India are the worst affected countries (GPMMZ:06:07:14). Malaria kills 1-2 million annually, of whom more than half are children. 104 countries have some malaria risk (DMN:06:07:02, and NGMZ:02:02).

In the battle against pandemic disease, retroviral drugs can be provided to extend the life of AIDS sufferers, and the widespread provision of condoms not only retards the spread of the disease but helps to contain the population explosion. Malaria can be prevented by bed nets, and emergent vaccines and therapeutic drugs can be used to treat it. Effective vaccines and drugs also exist to deal with tuberculosis.

Is it possible to rank global problems in terms of the deaths for which they have so far been responsible? Historical sources do not always allow us to compare like for like, but those available to us suggest that during the past two millennia wars have killed 217 million of us (the numbers have increased progressively over time), and famines 158 million. These totals would undoubtedly have been outstripped by pandemic disease for which reliable figures have only relatively recently become available - for instance 145 million have died from either malaria, tuberculosis or AIDS in the past 100 years alone. Wars, famines and pandemics each dwarf all other causes of human mass morbidity. By comparison, earthquakes, floods, cyclones and tsunamis, ranked by magnitude in that approximate order, have together accounted for 19 million deaths during the past few centuries. In view of these figures it seems ironic that the latter four categories of crisis trigger a disproportionate share of international relief. There remains much to be done.

80% of seismic activity occurs around the Pacific rim. Although predictive science is capable of giving advance warning of 24 hours for hurricanes, and sufficient time for pre-flood evacuation, it provides critically little lead time when earthquakes, tsunamis or volcanoes threaten. Technology here needs to improve, as it also does in the construction of earthquake and flood resistant buildings. However, the improved co-operation and co-ordination of international rescue campaigns to deal with all these emergencies presents a new departure in which partisan interests are at last put aside and enlightened practicality tempered by humanitarian idealism finally takes international centre stage. After millennia of discord and blood shed, Homo Sapiens Sapiens is falteringly beginning to understand that the brotherhood of man is more important to the future of his species than the brotherhood of a clique cemented together by compulsive prejudice. It is the ultimate expression of the altruism and loyalty he should have learnt from his mother, the principle of reciprocation that he should have assimilated from his childhood peers, and the open mindedness and aversion to warfare that ideally he should have acquired during adolescence.

Bonding between nations must inevitably be initiated by their leaders, and when these act with overt fraternalism the individual citizen is intuitively inspired to follow suit. Further concordance will come from the use of a common language, shared cultural, sporting, trade and electronic networks, and the world wide adoption of higher but necessarily unbiased educational standards. We are, in fact, witnessing the birth of a new era in communal and interpersonal human relationships in which archaic, outmoded, and largely irrelevant rule-of-thumb ideologies are gradually displaced by rationalised entrepreneurial behaviour, based upon the knowledge of our derivations, past human experience, astute nurtural methodology, candid self assessment, altruism and pertinent foresight.

(Sources Reviewed: BBCT1:04:07:03, BBCR4:11:06:04, DMN06:07:02, GPMMZ:06:07:14, HA44, http://data.unaids.org/pub, JP99, NGMZ:02:02, NM:BBC1:09:09:06, MGMZ:03:09, SJ07, TTN03:08:18, UN Global Environmental Outlook www.unep.org, UNICEF08, WJ10)

TABLE 2.1

CHARACTERISTIC EXPRESSIONS OF EMOTION IN RESPONSE TO AN ENCOUNTER

(Hardwired Primate "Encounter Signs")

	Anger	Fear	Joy	Sorrow	Disgust
Facial Expression	Glower And Bared Teeth	Blanching and terrorized expression	Smile (Humans only)	Frown and dejected expression	Pout and wrinkled nose
Body Posture and Gesture	Tense and erect	Cower or flee from scene	Relaxed	Shoulders sag and head droops	Shiver, avert face and body
Vocalisation	Growl or Roar	Scream or whimper	Laugh or chuckle	Weep and moan	Exclamation of revulsion
Tactility	Possibility of physical attack	Vigorous avoidance of body contact, or else tactile signals registering ingratiation or supplication	Hug, stroke, or handshake	Tactile signals soliciting or entreating consolation	"Backing away" reflex to avoid all tactile contact

FUNDAMENTAL BEHAVIOURAL PATTERNS OF MONKEYS AND APES

1	Reaction to danger: Fight (Anger) or Flight (Fear)
2	Possessiveness: Food, Territory, Privileges
3	Bonding: Maternal - Infant, Sibling, Playgroup, Herd
4	Dominance Ranking: Sparring, followed by Triumph or Submission
5	Socialisation: "Herd" member recognition, Greeting Protocols, Communication by Facial Expression, Gesture and Body Language, Vocalisation, Odour and Tactile Exchange including Grooming and Play: Altruism in some species
6.	Mating: Periodically females exhibit receptivity which attracts males: Copulation: Sexual bonding only in Gibbon and Callicebus Monkey
7.	Carnivorousness and Predation

TABLE 3.1

TABLE 6.1

TIMELINE OF REFINEMENT IN HUMAN BEHAVIOUR

5-2.5 MYA	Early man switches from tree living to ground living, and uses tools.
1.9-1.6 MYA	uses fire and cooks food.
900 KYA	uses clothing and builds primitive shelters.
600-100 KYA	develops speech, a bigger brain, co-ordinated social and hunting units, and sexual pair bonding. The phase of parentally protected learning for juveniles becomes protracted.
50 KYA	Neanderthals become extinct, leaving Homo Sapiens as definitive progenitor.
30 KYA	cave art and flute accompanied ceremonial. Grave goods furnished for afterlife.
11 KYA	crop cultivation and animal domestication.
9 KYA	Pottery.
8 KYA	wattle and daub shelters.
7 KYA	Metallurgy.
5.2 KYA	Writing.
5 KYA	architecture (Malta, stone temples) .
585 BCE	uses money (Lydian gold).
510 BCE	develops humour (Athens, Dionysus celebrations, Greek satire).
508 BCE	first democratic constitution (Athens).

500 BCE	first trial by jury (Athens, dikastai).
97 BCE	first formal abolition of religious human sacrifice (Rome).
1099 CE	last organised battlefield cannibalism (Thafuri, First Crusade).
1692 CE	last witch trial (Massachusetts).
1786 CE	first permanent abolition capital punishment (Tuscany).
1807 CE	first abolition of slavery (England).
1827 CE	first ban on torture (England).
1829 CE	first abolition mutilatory punishment (England, branding).
1864 CE	First Geneva Convention (amelioration of battlefield wounded and sick).
1890 CE	last duels (Germany).
1898 CE	first women's suffrage (New Zealand).
1924 CE	League Against Cruel Sports.
1948 CE	partial banishment flogging (England).
1960 CE	last symbolic cannibalism (China and Cambodia, politically motivated).

MYA, KYA = Million, thousand years ago: BCE=Before common era, CE=Common era:

NB Although this table has been compiled using data taken from many authoritative sources, some of the older dates quoted are understandably tentative and may be subject to revision in the light of ongoing genetic, archaeological and palaeological research.

TABLE 28.1

UNRESOLVED HUMAN PROBLEMS AND THEIR ROOTS IN HUMAN NURTURE AND HUMAN NATURE

Personality defects due to malconditioning of the first and second nurtural phases	Addictions Compulsive possessiveness Aggravated dominance Sexual perversions and atrocities Delinquency Corruption
Personality defects due to malconditioning of the third nurtural phase	Compulsive prejudices: Racial discrimination Religious intolerance Nationalistic xenophobia
Personality defects due to sporadic genetic errors	Mental illnesses Chronic malice
Group malfunction due to a genetic error endemic to species	Warfare
Problems caused by human ineptitude	Environmental strain Disequilibriun of resources Global warming

TABLE 28.2

DISCREPANCIES IN LIVING STANDARDS BETWEEN THE RICHEST AND POOREST COUNTRIES

Wealthy Country	Poor Country
Overfed: one third of US and UK citizens are clinically obese. Cardiovascular disease, diabetes, cancer and arthritis result.	Underfed: one billion worldwide currently suffer from extreme malnutrition – 700 million of these live in Africa. Deficiency diseases and starvation result.
Safe water supply	One quarter of developing countries have contaminable water. 40% of world's population faces water shortage at some time of year.
Highly organised healthcare systems.	More than half the world's population has no access to healthcare.
Principal morbidity and mortality due to illnesses of late middle age and the elderly.	Principal morbidity and mortality due to illnesses of those under 40. Pandemics: AIDS, Malaria, Tuberculosis
Life expectancy above 60 years	Life expectancy below 60 years
Addictive drug and alcohol use increasing.	Addictive alcohol and tobacco use increasing
Technical proficiency.	Most Africans are unfamiliar with the plough and wheel.
High educational standards for most.	Globally, one billion are illiterate. One third of all living in developing

	countries are illiterate. Africa has no written language except for those living in S. Africa and Ethiopia
50% of population lives in cities.	> 85% of population is rural.
Wars are rare, localised and short-lived, and are usually undertaken to restore law and order.	Wars are endemic, frequent and protracted, conducted by local warlords and militias
Drug addiction, alcohol and gambling motivate theft and prostitution	Poverty motivates theft, prostitution child labour and debt slavery. Poverty, disease, malnutrition, lack of healthcare, war and illiteracy often compound each other.
Religion in decline.	Religion prevails, and is on the increase.

(Sources:-   Buerk, M.,   in DMN:05:07:02,   HA44,   JK99, NGMZ:95:10, and 98:01,   98:10,   00:01,   02:02, 02:11,   SJ07, TON:02:06:09.)

BIBLIOGRAPHY

A

AAY34 Ali, A. Y. (Trans) 1934 The Holy Qur'an. Wordsworth. Ware. UK.

ACGO91 Andrew, C. and Gordievski, C. 1991 KGB, The Inside Story of Its Foreign Operations from Lenin to Gorbachev. Hodder and Stoughton. London

ACM07 Arata, C.M. 2007 in: International J. Child Abuse and Neglect Vol. 31 No.4

AGP06 Archives Genetic Psychiatry 2006:63

AJH01 Arnold, J.H. 2001 Inquisition and Power - Catharism and the Confessing Subject in Mediaeval Languedoc. U. Pennsylvania Press

AK94 Armstrong, K. 1994 A History of God. New York

AK00(a) Ameriks, K. 2000 Kant's Theory of Mind. Oxford U.P. Oxford

AK00(b) Armstrong, K. 2000 The Battle for God. Harper Collins. London

AM01 Angold, M. 2001 Byzantium. Weidenfeld and Nicholson. London

AR66 Ardrey, R. 1966 The Territorial Imperative. New York

AS67 Alliluyeva, S. 1967 Twenty Letters to a Friend. London

AW99 Andrews, W. 1899 Bygone Punishments. London

AWH99 Atlas of World History 1999. Philips. London

AZ01 Archibald, Z. 1991 Discovering the World of the Ancient Greeks. Quarto Publishing. Oxford

B

BA73 Bandura, A. 1973 Aggression, A Social Learning Analysis. London

BAR65 Burn, A. R. 1965 The Pelican History of Greece. Penguin. Harmondsworth

BA91 Bullock, A. 1991 Hitler and Stalin. Harper Collins. London

BAM90 Brandt, A.M. 1990 The Cigarette, Risk and American Culture. in: Daedalus 119(4)

BAMZ British Archaeology Magazine

BBCR4 British Broadcasting Corporation Radio 4

BBCT1 British Broadcasting Corporation Television Channel 1

BC03 Bromhall, C. 2003 The Eternal Child. Random House. London

BCHW59 Brekelmans, C.H.W. 1959 La Harem in het Oude Testament. Nijmegen. Central Drukker-j

BCS British Crime Survey (England and Wales, annual)

BD75 Brown, D. 1975 Bury My Heart At Wounded Knee. Picador. London

BDM04 Buss, D.M. 2004 Evolutionary Psychology. The New Science of the Mind. Pearson Education. London

BEK65 Bramstead, E.K. 1965 Goebbels and National Socialist Propaganda 1929-45. L:ondon

BG94 Bell, G. 1994In Search of Tusitala. Macmillan. London

BGE02 Berrios, G.E., Kennedy, N. 2002 Erotomania: A Conceptual History. History of Psychiatry 13; 52 part 4

BHF06 British Heart Foundation Factfile 06:03:

BH90 Brogan, H. 1990 The Penguin History of the United States of America. Penguin. London

BI00 Berlin, I. 2000 The Power of Ideas. Chatto and Windus. London

BJ01 Brockman, J. (Ed) 2001 The Greatest Inventions of the Past 2000 Years. Orion. London

BJ06 Burnside, J. 2006 in: Introduction to the Translation by Brown, A. of Marquis de Sade's "Betrayal". Hesperus Press. London

BJ08 Barlow, J. 2008 BBCR4: 08:12:03 quoting Lancet

BJ44 Barbot, J. 1744 A Collection of Voyages and Travels Vol. 5. London

BJ53 Bowlby, J. 1953 Child Care and the Growth of Love. Penguin, Harmondsworth. UK

BJ69 Bowlby, J. 1969 Attachment and Loss. Vol 1 Attachment; Basic Books. New York

BJ71 Benedeti, J. 1971 Gilles de Rais, The Authentic Bluebeard. London

BJ73 Bronowski, J. 1973 The Ascent of Man. BBC Publications. London

BJD94 Barrow, J. D. 1994 The Origin of the Universe. Harper Collins. New York

BJJHJA99 Bolhuis, J. J. and Hogan, J. A. (Eds) 1999 The Development of Animal Behaviour. Blackwell. Oxford

BJNW08 Bos, J.N.W. 2008 www.madmonarchs.nl

BK38 Berg, K. 1938 The Sadist. Trans. Illner, D. & Godwin, G. London

BLDRLJ02 Barrett, L., Dunbar, R., Lycett, J. 2002 Human Evolutionary Psychology. Palgrave. Basingstoke. UK

BLGGW64 Bramson, L., Goethals, G. W. (Eds) 1964 War; Studies From Psychology, Sociology, Anthropology. Basic Books. New York

BM03 Booth, M. 2003 Cannabis, A History. Random House. London

BM96 Booth, M. 1996 Opium, a History. Simon & Schuster. NY

BM97 Brett, M. 1997 Carthage: The God of Stone. in: History Today. February

BMLR99 Baigent, M., and Leigh, R. 1999 The Inquisition. Penguin. London

BO96 Bon, O. 1996 The Sultan's Seraglio. Saqi Books. London

BP02 Bahn, P. (Ed) 2002 Written in Bones. David and Charles. Newton Abbot. UK

BP76 Brent, P. 1976 The Mongol Empire: Genghis Kahn: His Triumph and His Legacy. London

BP99 Bellringer, P. 1999 Understanding Problem Gamblers. Free Association Books. London

BPL00 Bernstein, P. L 2000 The Power of Gold: The History of an Obsession. John Wiley and Sons. New York

BRH49 Barron, R. H. 1949 The Romans. Pelican Books. Harmondsworth. UK

BRHR07 Bayron, R. & Hughes, R. 2007 True Decadence, Franz Von Sacher Masoch Leopold. Erotic Print Society

BR02 Bryce, R. 2002 Pipe Dreams, Greed, Ego and the Death of Enron. Public Affairs Pubs. New York

BRO07 Beacham, R. C. 2007 Spectacle Entertainments of Early Imperial Rome. Yale U.P. Newhaven

BS02 Barber, S. 2002 Annihilation Zones. Creation Books. www.creationbooks.com

BS99 Boteach, S. 1999 An Intelligent Person's Guide to Judaism. Gerald Duckworth London

BSA99 Berger, S.A. 1999 Natural Causes, Death and Diseases for the Serious Consumer: Amazing Facts on the Diseases and Death of Six Thousand Famous People. Gefen Publishing House, Israel

BSPR00 Brand, S. & Price, R . 2000 The Economics and Social Costs of Crime. Home Office Research study No, 217

BSRJ01 Barber, S., and Reed, J. 2001 Caligula, Divine Carnage Creation Books. www.creationbooks.com (USA)

BT00 Bennett, T. 2000 Drugs and Crime. Home Office Research Study No. 205. London

BT00(a) Bennett, T. 2000 Drugs and Crime. The Results of the Second Developmental Stage of the New Adam Programme. Home Office Research Study No. 205

BT98 Bennett, T. 1998 Drugs and Crime. The Results of Research on Drug Testing and Interviewing Arrestees. Home Office Research Study No. 183

BV67 Brome, V. 1967 Freud and His Early Circle. Heinemann. London

BV79 Barnouw, V. 1979 Anthropology. The Dorsey Press. Homewood. Illinois

BWB01 Bartlett, W. B. 2001 The Assassins. Sutton Publishing. Stroud. UK

C

CA50 Comfort, A. 1950 Sexual Behaviour in Society. Duckworth. London

CAJ74 Coale, A.J. 1974 The History of the Human Population. Scientific American 231

CAMZ10 Cambridge Alumnii Magazine 10:11

CB97 Cunliffe, B. 1997 The Ancient Celts. Oxford U.P. Oxford

CC01 Casanova, C. 2001 The Story of My Life. Trans. from French by Sartarelli, S. & Hawkes, S., selected by Azzamiglio, J. Penguin, London

CE98 Christiansen, E. 1998 The Northern Crusades: The Baltic and the Catholic Frontier 1100-1525 Cambridge London & New York

CEP08 The Catholic Encyclopaedia On-Line 2008

CFF00 Cartwright, F. F. and Biddiss, M. 2000 Disease and History. Sutton Publishing. Stroud. UK

CG46 Casanova, G. 1946 His Life and Memoirs (trans) Macuen, A. Tudor Publishing. New York

CG98 Casanova, G. 1798 The Story of My Life. (Trans. Sartorell, S. & Hawkes, S.) 2000 Marsilio Publishers, USA

CGJ58 Copley, G. J. 1958 Going Into The Past. Penguin. Harmondsworth. UK

CGN49 Clark, G. N. 1949 The Cycle of War and Peace in Modern History. Cambridge U.P. Cambridge

CHHN99 Couper, H, and Henbest, N. 1999 Universe. Macmillan. London

CISCS Civitas Institute for the Study of Civil Society, England and Wales

CJ00 Cartwright, J. 2000 Evolution and Human Behaviour. Macmillan Press. Basingstoke UK

CJ01 Carroll, J. 2001 Constantine's Sword. Houghton Mifflin. New York

CJ51 Cleugh, J. 1951 The Marquis and the Chevalier. Andrew Melrose. London

CJ60 Caesar J. 1960 (trans) Warner, R. War Commentaries of Caesar. Mentor. New York

CJ88 Carmody, J. et al. 1988 Exploring the Hebrew Bible. Prentice Hall. New Jersey

CJ97 Colvin, J. 1997 Lions of Judah. Quartet Books. London

CJ99 Cornwell, J. 1999 Hitler's Pope. Viking/Penguin. London

CJDBFS64 Carthy, J.D. and Bling, F. S. (Eds) 1964 The Natural History of Aggression. Academic Press. New York

CJH01 Cartwright, J.H. 2001 Evolutionary Explanations of Human Behaviour. Routledge NY

CK72 Chesney, K. 1972 The Victorian Underworld. Penguin. Harmondsworth. UK

CL68 Cottrell, L. 1968 The Land of Shinar. Pan Books. London

CM04 Carabatea, M. 2004 The Archaeological Museum of Delphi. Museum Publications. Delphi

CM96 Cook, M. 1996 Muhammad. Oxford U.P. Oxford

CMD97 Costen, M.D. 1997 The Cathars and the Albigensian Crusade. Manchester U. Press

CME44 Collias, M. E. 1944 Aggressive Behaviour Among Vertebrate Animals. Physio. Zoo. 17:83-123

CMHMZ Community Mental Health Magazine (UK)

CMOU Chief Medical Officer Update (UK)

CMON03 Chief Medical Officer Notes 2003 UK Department of Health

CMP51 Charlesworth, M. P. 1951 The Roman Empire. Oxford U.P. Oxford

CN71 Chadwick, N. 1971 The Celts. Pelican/Penguin. Harmondsworth. UK

CNNT CNN Television Channel

CK95 Chisholm, K. et al. 1995 Attachment, Security and Indiscriminately Friendly Behaviour in: Children Adopted from Romanian Orphanages. Development & Psychopathology 7.

COD Concise Oxford Dictionary. Fourth Edn. 1950

CP02 Cawson, P 2002 nspcc.org.uk

CPJLJ00 Cook, P. J. and Ludwig, J. 2000 Gun Violence - The Real Costs. Oxford U.P. New York

CR03 Chamberlain, R. 2003 The Bad Popes. Sutton. Stroud. UK

CR68 Conquest, R. 1968 The Great Terror. Stalin's purges of the Thirties. London

CR86 Conquest, R. 1986 The Harvest of Sorrow. New York

CR90 Conquest, R. 1990 The Great Terror: A Reassessment. Hutchinson. London

CR98 Carter, R. 1998 Mapping the Mind. Weidenfeld and Nicholson. London

CRB87 Coot, R. B. and Whitelam, K. W. 1987 The Emergence of Early Israel in Historical Perspective. Almond. Sheffield

CS00 Cavalli-Sforza, L. L. (trans) Seilstad, L. 2000 Genes, People and Languages. Penguin. Harmondsworth. UK

CWA96 Confucius (trans) Waley, A. 1996 The Analects. Wordsworth. Ware. UK

CWG53 Cochlan, W.G. et al. 1953 Sexual Behavior in the Human Female. in: J. American Statistical Association Vol. 48, No.204

CWM68 Cooper, W.M. 1968 Flagellation and the Flagellants: A History of the Rod in All Countries from the Earliest Period to the Present Time. London

CWR96 Clark, W. R. 1996 Sex and the Origins of Death. Oxford U.P. Oxford

D

DB63 Diaz, B. 1963 The Conquest of New Spain. Penguin Harmondsworth UK

DCR71 Darwin, C. 1871 The Descent of Man (Abridged 1930) Watts & Co. London

DCR72 Darwin, C. R. 1872 The Expression of The Emotions in Man and Animals. Murray. London

DCR97 Darwin, C.R. 1997 The Voyage of The Beagle. Wordsworth. London

DDH44 Demo, D.H., Acock, A.C. Family Diversity and Well Being. Thousand Oaks, CA

DE10 Deiner, E. 2010 Gallup Poll in: J.Personality and Social Psychology. 10:06

DF68 Dawtry, F. (Ed) 1968 Social Problems of Drug Abuse. Butterworth. London

DG71 Deleuze, G. 1971 Sacher Madoch: An Interpretation. (trans McNeill, J.) Faber & Faber. London

DG95 Davies, G. 1995 A History of Money from Ancient Times to The Present Day.U. Wales Press. Cardiff

DI66 Deutscher, I. 1966 Stalin. Penguin. Harmondsworth UK

DJ98 Diamond, J. 1998 Guns, Germs and Steel. Vintage. London

DJM00 Diamond, J. M. 2000 "Talk of Cannibalism" Nature No 407 September

DKC09 Diller, K.C., Cann, R.L. 2009 Evidence Against a Genetic Based Revolution in Language 50,000 Years Ago. in: The Cradle of Language, Eds. Botha, R. & Knight, C. OUP Oxford

DLFR05 Dryden, L., Forbes, R., Mukherji, P., Pound, L. 2005 Essential Early Years. Hodder and Stoughton. London

DLW36 Doob, L.W. 1936 Propaganda: its Psychology and Technique. Annals of the American Academy of Political and Social Science No. 183

DLW50 Doob, L.W. 1950 Goebbels Principles of Propaganda. in: Public Opinion Quarterly Vol.14 No.3

DM62 Djilas, M. 1962 Conversations With Stalin. London

DMN Daily Mail Newspaper

DP72 Dolhinow, P. (Ed) 1972 Primate Patterns. Holt Rinehart Winston. New York

DP94 Davies, P. 1994 The Last Three Minutes. Weidenfeld and Nicholson. London

DR76 Dawkins, R. 1976 The Selfish Gene. Oxford University Press. Oxford UK

DTN Daily Telegraph Newspaper

DVJJM08 Dijk, V. J.J.M. et al. 2008 International Crime Victims Survey: key findings from 2004-5

E

EAM96 Earle, A.M. 1896 Curious Punishments From Bygone Days. London

ECP06 Ewing, C.P & Mcann, J.T 2006 Minds on Trial. Oxford University Press Oxford UK

ED98 Erasmus, D. (trans) Hudson, H. H. 1998 Praise of Folly. Wordsworth. London

EEI96 Eibl-Eibesfeldt, I.(trans) Strachan, G. 1996 Love and Hate. Aldine de Grwyter. New York

EHM89 Eysenck, H. and M. 1989 Mindwatching. Prion. London

ENCTA08 encarta.msn.com

EP95 Elliott, P. 1995 Warrior Cults. Blandford Books. London

ER10 Epstein, R. 2010 What makes a Good Parent. in Scientific American Mind MZ 10:11:12

F

FAMT08 2008 www.famoustexans.com

FDP02 Farrington, D.P. 2002 Developmental Parenting:: Criminality and Risk Focused Prevention; in Oxford Handbook of Criminality 3rd. Edn., Ed. Baldock, J. et al. Oxford

FDP04 Farrington, D.P. et al. 2004 Cross National Comparative Studies in Criminology; in Contemporary Issues in Crime and Criminal Justice, Eds. Pinardy, G.F., Pagani, L.Upper Saddle River NJ

FGL11 Ferrero, G.L. 1911 Criminal Man According to the Classification of Cesare Lombroso. London

FJA63 Froude, J.A. 1863 History of England. London

FJB08 Fraden, J.B. & Fraden, D.B. 2008 The Salem Witch Trials. Marshall Cavendish, London

FJG22 Frazer, Sir J. G. 1922 The Golden Bough (abridged) Macmillan. London

FL03 Fox, L. 2003 Enron, The Rise and Fall. John Wiley and Sons. Hoboken, New Jersey

FLCJM59 Festinger, L. and Carlsmith, J. M. 1959 Cognitive Consequences of Forced Compliance. (in) J. Abnormal and Social Psychology

FR29 Firth, R. 1929 Primitive Economics of New Zealand Maori. Maynard, F. quoted in: Hogg, G. 1958 Cannibalism and Human Sacrifice. London

FRC99 Foltz, R. C. 1999 Religions of The Silk Road. St. Martin's Press. New York

FRN62 Frye, R. N. 1962 The Heritage of Persia. Weidenfeld and Nicholson. London

FS09 Freud, S. 1909 (Ed) Strachey, J. 1962 Five Lectures on Psycho-analysis. Penguin London

FS14 Freud, S. 1914 Psychopathology of Everyday Life. Penguin. Harmondsworth. UK

FS91 Freud, S. 1991 The Essentials of Psychoanalysis. Penguin. London

FS97 Freud, S. (trans) Brill, S. S. 1997 The Interpretation of Dreams. Wordsworth. Ware UK

G

GAJ42 Grove, A. J., Newell, G. E. 1942 Animal Biology. University Tutorial Press. London

GA06 Giddens, A. 2006 Sociology. 5th. Edn. Polity Press. Cambridge UK

GBMF95 Galdikas, B. M. F. 1995 Reflections of Eden, My Life with the Orang-utans of Borneo. Victor Gollancz

GPV71 Glob, P.V. 1971 The Bog People. London

GC50 Glueck, C. 1950 Delinquency Unravelled. New York

GCB13 Goring, C.B. 1913 The English Convict. London

GJ06 Gillette, J. 2006 The Complete Marquis de Sade. Holloway House Publications. Los Angeles

GMCMZ General Medical Council Magazine

GN97 Garnefski, N., Diekestra, R.F.W. 1997 J. Adolescence Vol. 20 No.2 April 1997

GBR04 Guinness Book of Records 2004

GDJ02 Goldhagen, D. J. 2002 Amoral Reckoning. Little Brown/Time Warner. London

GE88 Gibbon, E. 1788 History of the Decline and Fall of the Roman Empire. London

GE97 Gellner, E. 1997 Nationalism. Weidenfeld and Nicholson. London

GF59 Guirland, F. (trans) Aldington, R. 1959 Encyclopaedia of Mythology. Larousse/Batchworth Press. London

GG56 Gardiner, G. 1956 Capital Punishment as a Deterrent; and the Alternative. London

GH89 Glencoe Health, 2nd. Edn. 1989 Mission Hills Glencoe Inc.

GH93 Gardner, H. 1993 Frames of Mind: The Theory of Multiple Intelligences. Basic Books NY

GJ03 Gray, J. 2003 Al Quaeda and What It Means To Be Modern. Faber and Faber. London

GJ38 Goebbels, J. 1938 My Part in Germany's Fight 1932-3 London

GJ62 Goebbels, J. 1962 The Early Goebbels Diaries 1925-26 Ed. Heiber, H., London

GJ82 Goebbels, J. 1982 The Goebbels Diaries 1939-41 Ed. Taylor, F., London

GJ90 Goodall, J. 1990 Through a Window. Weidenfeld and Nicholson. London

GJ99 Goodman, J. 1999 Tobacco in History. Routledge. London

GJABB95 Graham, J.A., Bowling, B. 1995 The Quality of Parent-child Relationship - strength of attachment - in: Young People and Crime. Home Office Research Study No.145

GMA01 Green, M. A. 2001 Dying For The Gods. Tempus Publishing. Stroud UK

GMMZ Geriatric Medicine Magazine

GMR88 Grossarth-Miticek, R. Eysenck,, H. J., Netiek, H. 1988 The Causes and Cures of Prejudice: An Empirical Study of the Frustration Aggression Hypothesis in: Personality and Individual Differences. 9

GNBHJ79 Grothis, N. and Birnbaum, H. J. 1979 Men Who Rape. The Psychology of the Offender. Plenum Press. New York

GP02 Gigantes, P. 2002 Power and Greed. Constable and Robinson. London

GPMZ General Practitioner Magazine

GPMMZ General Practitioner Medicine Magazine

GPV71 Glob, P. V. 1971 The Bog People. Paladin. London

GRE89 Goodin, R.E. 1989 The Ethics of Smoking. Ethics. 99(3)

GR05 Gross, R. 2005 Psychology, The Science of Mind and Behaviour. 5th. Edn. Hodder Arnold London

GR95(a) Garland, R. 1995 The Eye of the Beholder: Deformity and Disability in the Graeco-Roman World.Ithaca. Cornell U.P. New York

GR95(b) Goring, R. (Ed) 1995 Dictionary of Beliefs and Religions. Wordsworth. Ware. UK

GSA00 Greenfield, S. A. 2000 The Private Life of The Brain. Allen Lane. London

GSET34 Glueck, S., Eleanor, T. 1934 One Thousand Juvenile Delinquents. Ohio State Uni.

GT93 Green, T. 1993 The World's Gold. The Inside Story of Who Mines, Who Markets, Who Buys Gold. Rosendale Press

GTR52 Grousset, T.R. 1952 The Rise and Fall of the Chinese Empire. London

GWN Guardian Weekly Newspaper

H

HA44 Holmes, A. 1944 The Principles of Physical Geology. Thomas Nelson. London

HA91 Hourani, A. 1991 A History of the Arab Peoples. Faber and Faber. London

HAMZ Healthy Ageing Magazine

HB72 Hamilton, B. 1972 The Albigensian Crusade. London

HB99 Hodgson, B. 1999 Opium. Souvenir Press London

HBOT Hebrew Bible, Old Testament

HBRT97 Hart, B. and Ridley, T. 1997 Chronicles of the Crusades. Bramley Books. Godalming. UK

HC03 Hibbert, C. 2003 The Roots of Evil. Sutton Publishing. Stroud. UK

HD05 Howe, D. 2005 Child Abuse and Neglect. Palgrave Macmillan. London

HDR00 Hofstadter, D. R. 2000 Godel. Escher. Bach. Penguin. London

HDS54 Herodotus (trans) De Selincourt, A.1954 The Histories. Norton. Penguin. London

HDS92 Herodotus (trans) Blancow, W. W. 1992 The Histories. Norton. New York

HDV69 Holst, D. V. 1969 Sozialer Stress Bei Tupajas (Tupbia Belangeri 2 Vgl. Physiol 63)

HE89 Hallam, E. (Ed.) 1989 Chronicles of the Crusades. GLB International. Godalming UK

HE94 Hobshawm, E. 1994 Age of Extremes. Michael Joseph. London

HF68 Heer, F. (trans) Sondheimer, J. 1968 The Holy Roman Empire. Weidenfeld and Nicholson. London

HFFM91 Heidensohn, F. and Farrell, M. (Eds) 1991 Crime in Europe. Routledge. London

HG66 Hogg, G. 1966 Cannibalism and Human Sacrifice New York

HGC85 Heider, G. C. 1985 The Cult of Molek. A Reassessment JSOT Press. Sheffield UK

HGN95 Hall, G.N. 1995 Department of Psychology Proceedings. Kent State Uni. USA

HH00 Hohne, H. (trans) Barry, R. 2000 The Order of the Death's Head. Penguin. London

HH72 Heiber, H. 1972 (trans) Dickinson, J. K. Goebbels, A Biography. Hawthorn Books/Robert Hale. London

HHF58 Harlow, H. F., Zimmerman, R. R. 1958 The Development of Affectional Responses in Infant Monkeys. Science 130:421-432

HHFHMK69 Harlow, H. F., Harlow, M. K. 1969 Effects of Various Infants - Mother Relationships on Rhesus Monkey Behaviour. in: Determinants of Infant Behaviour. 4 Foss, B. M. (Ed) Methuen. London

HJ80 Howard, J. 1780 The State of the Prisons. London

HJD52 Hughes, J. D. 1952 Witchcraft. London

HJP01 Hoffman, J.P. 2001 in: Social Forces, Vol. 81, No. 3

HKRC63 Hall, K. R. C., Davore, I., Kummer, H., Kurt, T. 1963 Baboon Social Behaviour. Folia Primatol. 1:4 - 19

HM30 Halbwachs, M. 1930 (trans) Goldblatt, H. 1978 The Causes of Suicide. Routledge and Kegan Paul. London

HM96 Hough, M. 1996 Drugs Misuse and the Criminal Justice System. Home Office Drugs Prevention Initiative Paper No. 15. London

HMSO19 H.M. Stationery Office. 1919 Deniken Reports on Bolshevism in Russia. London

HN00 Harrison, N. 2000 A History of Ancient Rome. Octopus. London

HO02 Hourami, A. 2002 A History of the Arab Peoples.London

HO06 Home Office Offending Crime and Justice Survey 2006

HR00 Hyams, R. 2000 Causal Connections: The Case of Sacher Masoch. in; Finke, M.C. & Niekirk, C.One Hundred Years of Masochism. Rodopi

HR03 Hayman, R. 2003 Marquis de Sade; The genius of Passion. Taurus Parke. London

HR87 Hughes, R. 1987 The Fatal Shore. Pan. London

HRWG20 Hingston, R. W. G. 1920 A Naturalist in Himalaya. Witherby. London

HSC11 history of science.com

HSPR90 Hawking, S., Penrose, R. 1990 The Nature of Space and Time. Princeton Uni. Press. Princeton. N.J.

HWH98 Hyatt-Williams, H. 1998 Cruelty, Violence and Murder. London

I

IB98 Innes, B. 1998 The History of Torture. Brown Packaging Books. Enderby. UK

ICCPR International Convention on Civil and Political Rights, 1966

IG14 Ives. G. 1914A History of Penal Methods. London

IHGSC International Human Genome Sequencing Consortium. Nature, 2001 p860

J

JA72 Jolly, A. 1965 The Evolution of Primate Behavior. New York

JAAM97 Juvayni, A.A.M. 1997 Genghis Kahn: The History of the World Conqueror. Seattle

JCG69 Jung, C. G. (trans) Hull, R. F. C. 1969 On The Nature of the Psyche. Routledge. London

JEF29 Jacob, E.F. 1929 Innocent III. Cambridge Medieval History (Eds. Tanner, J.R., Previte-Orton, E.W., and Brooke, Z.N.) Cambridge UK

JGPR30 James, G. P. R. 1930 The History of Chivalry. London

JJW17 Jeudwine, J.W. 1917 Tort, Crime and Police in Mediaeval Britain. London

JUNPOA Joint United Nations Programme on Aids

JP03 Jorion, P. 2003 Investing in a Post Enron World. New York

JP99 Jordan, P. 1999 Early Man. Sutton. London

JS96 Jones, S. 1996 In the Blood. God, Genes and Destiny. Harper Collins London

JS99 James, S. 1999 The Atlantic Celts. University of Wisconsin Press. Madison Wisconsin

JV63 Joinville and Villehardouin, (trans) Shaw, M. R. B. 1963 Chronicles of the Crusades.Penguin Harmondsworth. UK

K

KAC48 Kinsey, A.C. et al. 1948 Sexual Behavior in the Human Male. Philadelphia

KA40 Koestler, A. 1940 Darkness at Noon. London

KAT94 Kessler, A. T. 1994 Empires Beyond the Great Wall. Natural History Museum of Los Angeles County. USA

KDE81 Karpodini-Dimitriadi, E. (trans) Turner, L. 1981 The Peloponnese. Ekdotike Athenon. Athens. Greece

KDI97 Kertzer, D. I. 1997 The Kidnapping of Edgardo Mortara. Picador/Macmillan. London

KE93 Kedourie, E. 1993 Nationalism. Blackwell. Oxford

KER86 Krafft-Ebing, R Von 1886 Psychopathia Sexualis, Trans. Klaff, F.S. Stein & Day., .New York

KGC99 Kohn, G. C. 1999 Dictionary of Wars. Checkmate Books. New York

KHH85 Kelly, H.H. et al. 1986 Close Relationships. New York

KL33 Kopelev, L. 1933 The Education of a True Believer. Ukraine

KM79 Kahn, M. 1979 Fetish Negation of the Self - Alienation of Perversions. London

KM99 Kohn, M. 1999 As We Know It. Granta. London

KN70 Khrushchev, N. 1970 Khrushchev Remembers. New York

KP02 Kriwaczek, P. 2002 In Search of Zarathrustra. Weidenfeld and Nicolson. London

KRC94 Kessler, R. C., McGonagie, R. A., Zhao, S. et Al 1994 Lifetime and 12 Month Prevalence of DSM 111.R in Psychiatric Disorders in the United States. Arch. Gen. Psychiatry 51 (1) p8-19

KS00 Karouzoy, S. 2000 National Museum Illustrated Guide. Ekdotike Athenon S.A. Athens. Greece

KWG87 Kinzey, W.G. 1987 The Evolution of Human Behaviour: Primate Models (Suny Series in Primatology) State Uni. of New York Press

L

LB93 Lewis, B. 1993 The Arabs in History. Oxford U. P. Oxford

LBP95 Levack, B. P. 1995 The Witch Hunt in Early Modern Europe. Longman. New York

LBR.01 Lewis, B. R. 2001 Ritual Sacrifice. Sutton. Stroud. UK

LCS.99 Littleton, C. S. 1999 The Sacred East. Duncan Baird. London

LEH31 Lavine, E.H. 1931 The Third Degree. London

LI54 Leigh, I. 1954 In The Shadow of the Maumau. London

LK.04 Liebreich, K. 2004 Fallen Order. Atlantic Books, London

LK.66 Lorenz, K. 1966 On Aggression (trans) Latzke, M. Routledge. London

LRLRH85 Lagrange, R.L., Rankin-White, H. Age Differences in Delinquency: A Test of Theory. in: Criminology Vol. 23, Issue 1.

LMD07 Lemonic, M.D. 2007 in Time Magazine

LR74 Lockyer, R. 1974 Habsburg and Bourbon Europe 1470-1720 Longman

LR.94 Leakey, R. 1994 The Origin of Humankind. Weidenfeld and Nicolson. London

LRP14 Lister, R.P. 1914 Genghis Khan. Stein and Day New York

LS70 Legg, S. 1970 The Heartland. London

LSL0 3Leech, S.L. 2003 J. Early Adolescence Vol. 23, No. 1

LWEH.69 Lecky, W. E. H. 1869 History of European Morals. Reprinted 1946 Watts. London

LWL87 Langer, W. L. (Ed) 1987 An Encyclopaedia of World History. Harrap. London

M

MCSA01 Mee, C. and Spawforth, A. 2001 Greece. Oxford U. P. Oxford. UK

MD62 Morris, D. 1962 The Biology of Arts in the Picture-making Behaviour of the Great Apes and its Relationship to Human Art. Alfred A. Knopf. New York

MD69 Morris, D. 1969 The Human Zoo. McGraw Hill and Dell. New York

MD77 Morris, D. 1977 Manwatching. Jonathan Cape London

MD94(a) Morris, D. (a) 1994 The Naked Ape. Jonathan Cape. (used by permission of Random House Group Ltd) London

MD94(b) Morris, D.(b) 1994 Intimate Behaviour. Vintage. London

ME04 Maynial, E. 2004 (trans Mayne, E.C.) Casanova and His Time. Kessinger Publishing

MG02 Menzies, G. 2002 1421, The Year China Discovered The World. Bantam Press. London

MGE00 Markoe, G. E. 2000 Phoenicians. University of California Press. USA

MGL66 Mosse, G.L. 1966 Nazi Culture: Intellectual, Cultural and Social Life in the Third Reich London

MGS31 Miller, G. S. 1931 The Primate Basis of Human Sexual Behaviour. Quart. Review Biol. Vol 6 879

MHEE81 Midelfort, H.E.E. 1981 Heartland of the Witch Craze: Central and Northern Europe. in: History Today. 31 February 1981

MHH63 Milman, H.H. 1863 History of the Jews. Everyman. London

MHL09 MacMillan, H.L. et al. 2009. Intervention to Prevent Child Maltreatment and Associated Impairment. Lancet Child Maltreatment Series. London

MJ04 Man, J. 2004 Genghis Khan: Life, Death and Resurrection. Random House. London

MJ64 Masserman, J. 1964 in: The Chicago Psychiatrist

MJ69 Masters, J. 1969 Casanova.Michael Joseph. London

MJ78 Marx, J. 1978 The Magic of Gold. Doubleday. New York

MJ99 McCrone, J. 1999 Going Inside. Faber and Faber. London

MMG98 Magill's Medical Guide, Revised Edn. 1998 Salem Press

MN51 Morris, N. 1951 The Habitual Criminal. Longman. London

MR84 Medvedev, R. 1984 All Stalin's Men. Garden City. New York

MRI94 Moore, R. I. (Ed) 1994 Atlas of World History. Philips. London

MS73 Moscati, S. 1973 The World of the Phoenicians.Sphere. London

MS99 Marshall, S. 1999 (Introduction to) The Voyages of Captain Cook. Wordsworth. Ware. UK

MSBK89 McLanahan, S. & Booth, K. 1989 Mother-only Families. Problems, Prospects and Politics J. Marriage and the Family, 51.

MSSG94 McLanahan, S. & Sandefur, G. 1994 Growing up with a Single Parent. Cambridge MA

MT98 Malthus, T. 1798 Essay on the Principle of Population

N

ND01 Nettle, D. 2001 Strong Imagination. Oxford Uni. Press. Oxford

NDTRF03 Nagin, D., Tremblay, R.F. 2003 in: Child Development. Vol.70, issue 5. Time Publications

NEB61 New English Bible. 1961 Oxford/Cambridge Uni. Press. Oxford

NGMZ National Geographic Magazine

NH01 Nicholson, H. 2001 The Knights Templar. Sutton. Stroud. UK

NJBG83 Noakes, J.& Pridham, G., (Eds. with Commentary) 1983 Nazism 1919-45: A Documentary Reader, Vol. 2. The Rise to Power 1919-34 Exeter UK

NMZ01 Nature Magazine 2001 The Human Genome.February

NS93 Niditch, S. 1993 War in the Hebrew Bible: A Study in the Ethics of Violence Oxford Uni. Press. Oxford

NSMZ New Scientist Magazine

NYTN New York Times Newspaper

O

ODK00 O'Brien, D. K. (Ed) 2000 World History Encyclopaedia. Philip's. London

OZ61 Oldenbourg, Z. 1961 Massacre at Montsegur. Weidenfeld and Nicolson. London

P

PC Personal Communication

PC00 Pajaczkowska, C. 2000 Perversion: Ideas in Psychoanalysis. Penguin. UK

PC05 Peters, C. 2005 Harold Shipman. Carlton Books. London

PCMZ Pulse Clinical Magazine

PF78 Price, F. 1978 Textbook of Medicine (12th. Edn. Ed. Bodley-Scott, Sir R.) Oxford

PG62 Posener, G. (Ed) 1962 A Dictionary of Egyptian Civilisation. London

PGF99 Plessis, G.F. du 1999 At Home With the Marquis de Sade; A Life. Penguin, London

PH03 Puff, H. 2003 Sodomy in Reformation Germany and Switzerland 1400-1600 Chicago Uni. Press. Chicago

PHJ00 Pope-Hennessy, J. 1967 Sins of the Fathers. Weidenfeld and Nicolson. London

PJ50 Piaget, J. 1950 The Psychology of Intelligence. London

PJM73 Parry, J. M. 1973 The Spanish Sea borne Empire. Penguin. Harmondsworth. UK

PK50 Pan Ku and Swann, N. L. 1950 Food and Money in Ancient China. Princeton U. P. Princeton

PLA33 Parry, L.A. 1933 The History of Torture in England. London

PMMZ Pulse Medical Magazine

PNMZ05 Pulse News Magazine 05:04:02 Report on International Conference on Reduction of Drug Related Harm

PS00 Plant, S. 2000 Writing on Drugs. Farrar Straus Girous. New York

PS02 Pinker, S. 2002 The Blank Slate. Penguin, New York

PWAP74 Philips, W.A.P. 1974 The Tragedy of Nazi Germany.London

Q

QD21 Quincey, de. 1821 http://opioids.com/dequincey/index.htm

R

RB46 Russell, B. 1946 A History of Western Philosophy. George Allen and Unwin. London

RC01 Rohmann, C. 2001 The Dictionary of Important Ideas and Thinkers. Hutchinson/Random House. London

RC64 Roth, C. 1964 The Spanish Inquisition. W. W. Norton. New York

RG72 Ronay, G. 1972 The Dracula Myth. London

RG91 Rad, G. Von 1991 Holy War in Ancient Israel (trans. Dawn, J. and Yoder, J.H.) Eardman's, Grand Rapids

RJ01 Ronson, J. 2001 Them. Picador. London

RJJ01 Ratey, J. J. 2001 A User's Guide to the Brain. Random House. New York

RJM90 Roberts, J. M. 1990 The Penguin History of the World. Penguin. London

RM01 Ridley, M. 2001 Mendel's Demon: Gene Justice and the Complexity of Life Orion Books. London

RR99 Rudgley, R. 1999 Lost Civilisations of the Stone Age. Arrow Books. London

RRM71 Rose, R. M., Holaday, J. W., Berstein, I. S. 1971 Plasma Testosterone, Dominance Rank and Aggressive Behaviour in Male Rhesus Monkeys. Nature Vol. 231 p366

RRP76 Rohner, R. P. 1976 Sex Differences in Aggregation, Phylogenetic and Enculturation Perspectives. Ethos

RSC94 Rowell, S.C. 1994 Lithuania Ascending: A Pagan Empire Within East-Central Europe. 1294-1345. Cambridge Uni. Press. Cambridge UK

RSJ90 Riley-Smith, J. 1990 The Crusades: A Short History. Athlone Press. London

RT72 Rowell, T. 1972 Social Behaviour of Monkeys. Penguin. Harmondsworth. UK

RV96 Rogovin, V. 1996 Stalin's Great Terror? Origins and Consequences. http://www.wsws.org/exhibits/1937lecture1/htm

RW84 Rodzinski, W. 1984 The Walled Kingdom: A History of China From 2000BC to the Present. Fontana. London

S

SA75 Speer, A. 1975 Inside the Third Reich. Sohere. London

SABB99 Scientific American Book of the Brain. 1999 New York

SAC49 Shannon, A.C. 1949 The Popes and Heresy in the Thirteenth Century. Pennsylvania

SAD10 Smith, A.D. 2010 Nationalism. Polity Press. Cambridge UK

SAJ82 Spencer, A. J. 1982 Death in Ancient Egypt. Penguin Harmondsworth UK

SB49 Souvarine, B. 1949 Stalin. London

SBO.Strabo. Geography 4

SD72 Seward, D. 1972 The Monks of War. Penguin. London

SEA92 Smith, E.A. and Winterhalder, B. (Eds.) 1992 Evolutionary Ecology and Human Behaviour Aldine Transactions

SE03 Saver, E. 2003 The Archaeology of Religious Hatred. Tempus Publishing. Stroud. UK

SEP01 Stanford Encyclopaedia of Philosophy 2001. Nationalism Section. Stanford. USA

SG00 Servadio, G. 2000 Motya. Victor Gollance. London

SGR95 Scott, G. R. 1995 A History of Torture. Senate/Studio Editions London

SHR96 Schaffer, R. 1996 Social Development. Oxford

SHWF62 Saggs, H. W. F. 1962 The Greatness That Was Babylon. Sidgwick and Jackson London

SJ01 Schwartz, J. 2001 Cassandra's Daughter. Penguin. New York

SJ06 Summers, J. 2006 Casanova's Women. Bloomsbury Publishing. London

SJ07 Sachs, J. 2007 Reith Lectures. British Broadcasting Corporation Radio 4

SJ20 Stow, J. 1720 A Survey of London. London

SJ31 Swain, J. 1931 The Pleasures of the Torture Chamber. London

SJ78 Sumption, J. 1978 The Albigensian Crusade. London

SJR85 Snarey, J.R. et al. 1985 Development of Sociomoral Reasoning Among Kibbutz Adolescents. A Longitudinal Cross-cultural Study. Developmental Psychology 21(1) 3

SJSI67 Science Journal Special Issue May 1967 Reprinted as Paladin Publication 1972 The Human Brain. Granada Publishing. London

SL70 Schapiro, L. 1970 The Communist Party of the Soviet Union London

SM78 Shepherd, M.. 1978 Psychological Medicine in: Price's Textbook of the Practice of Medicine. 12th Edn. (ed) Scott, Sir R.B. Oxford Uni. Press. Oxford

SMD00 Sade, Marquis D, 2000 Letters From Prison. Harvill Press. London

SMGSEH28 Schlapp, M. G. and Smith, E. H. 1928 The New Criminology. London

SMW91 Sacher Masoch, W. Von 1991 The Confessions of Wanda Von Sacher Masoch. (trans) Phillips, M., Herbert, C., Vale, V. V. Search Publications, US

SMZ Science Magazine

SN89 Smart, N. 1989 The World's Religions. Cambridge Uni. Press. Cambridge UK

SPD91 Stern, P.D. 1991 The Biblical Herem; A Window on Israel's Religious Experience Scholar's Press. Atlanta

SR86 Stoller, R. 1986 Perversion; The Erotic Form of Hatred. Karnak, London

SRL64 Solomon, R. L. 1964 "Punishment". American Psychologist 19

SRL68 Solomon, R. L., Turner, L. H., Lessac, H. S. 1968 Some Effects of Delay Punishment on Resistance to Temptation in Dogs. J. Personality and Social Psychology 8

SS04 Shavell, S. 2004 Enron and World Finance: A Case Study. in: Ethics. Ed. Dembinski, P.H.et al. Harvard Univ. Press

STD09 Spector, T.D. 2009 St. Thomas' Hospital Twin Studies. www.twin-research.ac.uk

STN Sunday Times Newspaper

SUS57 Suetonius. 1957 The Twelve Caesars (trans) Graves, R. Penguin Harmondsworth UK

SW35 Stekel, W. 1935 Sadism and Masochism. London

SW58 Schellenberg, W. 1958 The Schellenberg Memoirs. London

SW65 Slukin, W. 1965 Imprinting and Early Learning. Aldine. Chicago

SYSS.97 Sakellarakis, Y. and Saponna-Sakellaraki, E. 1997 Archanes Minoan Crete in a New Light Vol. 1. Amos Publications. Athens. Greece

T

TAJ46 Toynbee, A. J. 1946 A Study of History. Oxford Uni. Press. London

TDR56 Taft, D.R. 1956 Criminology. New York

TDS93 Thomas, D.S. 1992 The Marquis de Sade: A New Biography. Citadel Press, New York

TE42 Tarle, E. 1942 Napoleon's Invasion of Russia, 1812. London

TEO61 Tuttle, E. O. 1961 The Crusade Against Capital Punishment in Great Britain. Stevens. Quadrangle Publications

TFTN The Financial Times Newspaper

TGN The Guardian Newspaper

TISN The Independent on Sunday Newspaper

TM02 Twiss, M. 2002 The Most Evil Men and Women in History. Michael O'Mara Books. London

TM77 Tweedie, M. 1977 Insect Life. William Collins. London

TMH48 Tacitus (trans) Mattingly, H. 1948 Tacitus on Britain and Germany. Penguin. West Drayton. UK

TMOSN The Mail On Sunday Newspaper

TMSLA87 Troy, M.S. and Roufe, L.A. 1987 Minnesota Longitudinal Study. J. American Academy of Child and Adolescent Psychiatry

TMZ Time Magazine

TN77 Tolstoy, N. 1977 Victims of Yalta. London

TON The Observer Newspaper

TR76 Tannahill, R. 1976 Flesh and Blood. Abacus. London

TRW01 Thurston, R. W. 2001 Witch, Wicce, Mother goose. Pearson Education. Harlow UK

TS71 Talbot, S. 1971 (trans and Ed) Khrushchev Remembers.London

TTN The Times Newspaper

TVC4 Television Channel Four (UK)

TWH98 Timelines of World History. 1998 Quadrillion Publishing. Godalming. UK

TWM49 Thackeray, W.M. 1849 The Four Georges. London

U

UN GOUN Environment Outlook. www.unep.org

UNICEF United Nations International Childrens' Emergency Fund

UNU07 UNU Institute for National Resources in Africa 2007 Report

UW03 Urban, W. 2003 The Teutonic KnightsGreenhill BooksLondon

V

VL62 Vygotsky, L.S. 1962 Thought and Language. Cambridge MA

VLGJ68 Van Lawick Goodall, J. 1968 The Behaviour of Free-living Chimpanzees in the Gombe Stream Reserve. Animal Behaviour Monograph No 1

W

WAH64 Walton, A. H. 1964 Introduction to Translation in: Marquis De Sade's "Justine".The Holland Press. London

WAN33 Whitehead, A. N.1933 Adventures of Ideas. Penguin Harmondsworth UK

WAN99 Wilson, A. N. 1999 God's Funeral. John Murray. London

WAP66 Wolf, A.P. 1966 Childhood Association, Sex Attraction and the Incest Taboo: A Chinese Case. American Anthropologist: Vol. 68, No. 833

WC05 Wilson, C. 2005 A Criminal History of Mankind. Mercury Books. London UK

WD71 Wilson, D. 1971 The Anglo Saxons. Pelican/Penguin Harmondsworth. UK

WE06 Wright, E. 2006 History's Greatest Scandals. Murdoch Books. Australia

WF05 Waal, F. de 2005 Our Inner Ape. Granta Publications

WGB40 Wilson, G. B. 1940 Alcohol and the Nation. Nicholson and Watson. London

WHO World Health Organisation

WJ02 Whiting, J. 1702 Truth and Innocence Defended Against Falsehood and Envy

WJ10 Waldfogel, J. 2010 Day-care Effects on Development: Study of 1000 Children From Birth to 7 Years. Columbia University

WJ76 Watney, J. 1976 Mother's Ruin: A History of Gin. London

WJG88 Wilkinson, Sir J. G. 1988 The Ancient Egyptians. Studio Editions. London

WKP09 Wikipedia validated by citation

WLL65 Whyte, L. L. 1965 Internal Factors in Evolution. Tavistock Publications. London

WMLMAE78 Weiss, M. L. and Mann, A. E. 1978 Human Biology and Behaviour. Little Brown. Toronto

WR01 Wrangham, R. 2001 Out of the Pan Into the Fire: From Ape to Human. in: Tree of Origin Ed. de Waal, F.B.M. Harvard University Press, Cambridge MA

WR02 Winston, R. 2002 Human Instinct. Random House. London

WRJ02 Warner, J. 2002 Craze, Gin and Debauchery in an Age of Reason. Toronto

WRJWMG72 Walker, R. J. and Walker, M. G. 1972 The English Legal System. 3rd Edn. Butterworth. London

WS45 Wright, S. 1945 Applied Physiology. 8th Edn. Oxford Uni. Press. London

WTS09 Weinberg, T.S. 2009 Leopold Ritter Von Sacher Masoch, (Ed.) Haeberle, E.J. Garland Publishing, Oxford

XYZ

YH21 Yules, H. 1921 The Book of Sev Marco Polo. 3rd Edn. London

ZA99 Zamoyski, A 1999 Holy Madness. Weidenfeld and Nicholson. London.

ZT03 Zenjal, T. et al. 2003 The Genetic Legacy of the Mongols. American J. of Human Genetics 72(3)

ZZAB Zeman, Z.A.B. 1964 Nazi Propaganda. London